Programming ASP.NET MVC 4

Jess Chadwick, Todd Snyder, and Hrusikesh Panda

O'REILLY®

Beijing · Cambridge · Farnham · Köln · Sebastopol · Tokyo

Programming ASP.NET MVC 4

by Jess Chadwick, Todd Snyder, and Hrusikesh Panda

Published by O'Reilly Media, Inc., 1005 Gravenstein Highway North, Sebastopol, CA 95472.

O'Reilly books may be purchased for educational, business, or sales promotional use. Online editions are also available for most titles (*http://my.safaribooksonline.com*). For more information, contact our corporate/institutional sales department: 800-998-9938 or *corporate@oreilly.com*.

Editor: Rachel Roumeliotis	**Indexer:** Lucie Haskins
Production Editor: Rachel Steely	**Cover Designer:** Karen Montgomery
Copyeditor: Rachel Head	**Interior Designer:** David Futato
Proofreader: Leslie Graham, nSight	**Illustrators:** Robert Romano and Rebecca Demarest

October 2012:   First Edition.

Revision History for the First Edition:
     2012-09-14   First release
See *http://oreilly.com/catalog/errata.csp?isbn=9781449320317* for release details.

ISBN: 978-1-449-32031-7

[LSI]

1347629446

Table of Contents

Preface xiii

Part I. Up and Running

1. Fundamentals of ASP.NET MVC 3
   Microsoft's Web Development Platforms   3
      Active Server Pages (ASP)   3
      ASP.NET Web Forms   4
      ASP.NET MVC   4
   The Model-View-Controller Architecture   4
      The Model   5
      The View   6
      The Controller   6
   What's New in ASP.NET MVC 4?   6
   Introduction to EBuy   8
   Installing ASP.NET MVC   9
   Creating an ASP.NET MVC Application   9
      Project Templates   10
      Convention over Configuration   13
      Running the Application   15
   Routing   15
      Configuring Routes   16
   Controllers   18
      Controller Actions   19
      Action Results   19
      Action Parameters   21
      Action Filters   23
   Views   24
      Locating Views   24
      Hello, Razor!   26
      Differentiating Code and Markup   27

Layouts	28
Partial Views	30
Displaying Data	31
HTML and URL Helpers	33
Models	34
Putting It All Together	35
The Route	35
The Controller	35
The View	38
Authentication	41
The AccountController	42
Summary	44

2. ASP.NET MVC for Web Forms Developers **45**

It's All Just ASP.NET	45
Tools, Languages, and APIs	46
HTTP Handlers and Modules	46
Managing State	46
Deployment and Runtime	47
More Differences than Similarities	47
Separation of Application Logic and View Logic	48
URLs and Routing	48
State Management	49
Rendering HTML	50
Authoring ASP.NET MVC Views Using Web Forms Syntax	54
A Word of Caution	55
Summary	56

3. Working with Data **57**

Building a Form	57
Handling Form Posts	59
Saving Data to a Database	59
Entity Framework Code First: Convention over Configuration	60
Creating a Data Access Layer with Entity Framework Code First	60
Validating Data	61
Specifying Business Rules with Data Annotations	63
Displaying Validation Errors	65
Summary	68

4. Client-Side Development **69**

Working with JavaScript	69
Selectors	71
Responding to Events	74

DOM Manipulation   76
AJAX   77
Client-Side Validation   79
Summary   83

Part II.   Going to the Next Level

5. Web Application Architecture **87**
The Model-View-Controller Pattern   87
Separation of Concerns   87
MVC and Web Frameworks   88
Architecting a Web Application   90
Logical Design   90
ASP.NET MVC Web Application Logical Design   90
Logical Design Best Practices   92
Physical Design   93
Project Namespace and Assembly Names   93
Deployment Options   94
Physical Design Best Practices   94
Design Principles   96
SOLID   96
Inversion of Control   102
Don't Repeat Yourself   110
Summary   110

6. Enhancing Your Site with AJAX **111**
Partial Rendering   111
Rendering Partial Views   112
JavaScript Rendering   117
Rendering JSON Data   118
Requesting JSON Data   119
Client-Side Templates   120
Reusing Logic Across AJAX and Non-AJAX Requests   123
Responding to AJAX Requests   124
Responding to JSON Requests   125
Applying the Same Logic Across Multiple Controller Actions   126
Sending Data to the Server   128
Posting Complex JSON Objects   129
Model Binder Selection   131
Sending and Receiving JSON Data Effectively   132
Cross-Domain AJAX   133
JSONP   133

      Enabling Cross-Origin Resource Sharing   137
   Summary   138

7. The ASP.NET Web API **139**
   Building a Data Service   139
      Registering Web API Routes   141
      Leaning on Convention over Configuration   142
      Overriding Conventions   143
      Hooking Up the API   143
   Paging and Querying Data   146
   Exception Handling   147
   Media Formatters   149
   Summary   152

8. Advanced Data **153**
   Data Access Patterns   153
      Plain Old CLR Objects   153
      Using the Repository Pattern   154
      Object Relational Mappers   156
   Entity Framework Overview   158
      Choosing a Data Access Approach   159
      Database Concurrency   160
   Building a Data Access Layer   161
      Using Entity Framework Code First   161
      The EBuy Business Domain Model   163
      Working with a Data Context   167
   Sorting, Filtering, and Paging Data   168
   Summary   174

9. Security **175**
   Building Secure Web Applications   175
      Defense in Depth   175
      Never Trust Input   176
      Enforce the Principle of Least Privilege   176
      Assume External Systems Are Insecure   176
      Reduce Surface Area   176
      Disable Unnecessary Features   177
   Securing an Application   177
      Securing an Intranet Application   178
      Forms Authentication   183
   Guarding Against Attacks   192
      SQL Injection   192
      Cross-Site Scripting   198

       Cross-Site Request Forgery   199
   Summary   201

10. Mobile Web Development **203**
   ASP.NET MVC 4 Mobile Features   203
   Making Your Application Mobile Friendly   205
      Creating the Auctions Mobile View   205
      Getting Started with jQuery Mobile   207
      Enhancing the View with jQuery Mobile   209
      Avoiding Desktop Views in the Mobile Site   216
   Improving Mobile Experience   216
   Adaptive Rendering   217
      The Viewport Tag   217
      Mobile Feature Detection   218
      CSS Media Queries   220
      Browser-Specific Views   221
   Creating a New Mobile Application from Scratch   224
      The jQuery Mobile Paradigm Shift   224
      The ASP.NET MVC 4 Mobile Template   224
      Using the ASP.NET MVC 4 Mobile Application Template   226
   Summary   229

Part III. Going Above and Beyond

11. Parallel, Asynchronous, and Real-Time Data Operations **233**
   Asynchronous Controllers   233
      Creating an Asynchronous Controller   234
      Choosing When to Use Asynchronous Controllers   236
   Real-Time Asynchronous Communication   236
      Comparing Application Models   237
      HTTP Polling   237
      HTTP Long Polling   238
      Server-Sent Events   239
      WebSockets   240
      Empowering Real-Time Communication   241
      Configuring and Tuning   245
   Summary   246

12. Caching **247**
   Types of Caching   247
      Server-Side Caching   248
      Client-Side Caching   248

Server-Side Caching Techniques   248
    Request-Scoped Caching   248
    User-Scoped Caching   249
    Application-Scoped Caching   250
    The ASP.NET Cache   251
    The Output Cache   252
    Donut Caching   255
    Donut Hole Caching   257
    Distributed Caching   259
Client-Side Caching Techniques   264
    Understanding the Browser Cache   264
    App Cache   265
    Local Storage   268
Summary   269

13. Client-Side Optimization Techniques **271**
Anatomy of a Page   271
    Anatomy of an HttpRequest   272
Best Practices   273
    Make Fewer HTTP Requests   274
    Use a Content Delivery Network   274
    Add an Expires or a Cache-Control Header   276
    GZip Components   278
    Put Stylesheets at the Top   279
    Put Scripts at the Bottom   279
    Make Scripts and Styles External   281
    Reduce DNS Lookups   282
    Minify JavaScript and CSS   282
    Avoid Redirects   283
    Remove Duplicate Scripts   285
    Configure ETags   285
Measuring Client-Side Performance   286
Putting ASP.NET MVC to Work   289
    Bundling and Minification   289
Summary   293

14. Advanced Routing **295**
Wayfinding   295
URLs and SEO   297
Building Routes   298
    Default and Optional Route Parameters   299
    Routing Order and Priority   301
    Routing to Existing Files   301

Ignoring Routes   302
Catch-All Routes   302
Route Constraints   303
Peering into Routes Using Glimpse   305
Attribute-Based Routing   306
Extending Routing   310
The Routing Pipeline   310
Summary   315

15. Reusable UI Components **317**
What ASP.NET MVC Offers out of the Box   317
Partial Views   317
HtmlHelper Extensions or Custom HtmlHelpers   317
Display and Editor Templates   318
Html.RenderAction()   318
Taking It a Step Further   319
The Razor Single File Generator   319
Creating Reusable ASP.NET MVC Views   321
Creating Reusable ASP.NET MVC Helpers   325
Unit Testing Razor Views   327
Summary   328

Part IV. Quality Control

16. Logging **331**
Error Handling in ASP.NET MVC   331
Enabling Custom Errors   332
Handling Errors in Controller Actions   333
Defining Global Error Handlers   334
Logging and Tracing   336
Logging Errors   336
ASP.NET Health Monitoring   338
Summary   341

17. Automated Testing **343**
The Semantics of Testing   343
Manual Testing   344
Automated Testing   345
Levels of Automated Testing   345
Unit Tests   345
Fast   347
Integration Tests   348

Acceptance Tests   349
What Is an Automated Test Project?   350
  Creating a Visual Studio Test Project   350
  Creating and Executing a Unit Test   352
Testing an ASP.NET MVC Application   354
  Testing the Model   355
  Test-Driven Development   358
  Writing Clean Automated Tests   359
  Testing Controllers   361
  Refactoring to Unit Tests   364
  Mocking Dependencies   365
  Testing Views   370
Code Coverage   372
  The Myth of 100% Code Coverage   374
Developing Testable Code   374
Summary   376

18. Build Automation **377**
Creating Build Scripts   378
  Visual Studio Projects Are Build Scripts!   378
  Adding a Simple Build Task   378
  Executing the Build   379
  The Possibilities Are Endless!   380
Automating the Build   380
  Types of Automated Builds   381
  Creating the Automated Build   383
Continuous Integration   386
  Discovering Issues   386
  The Principles of Continuous Integration   386
Summary   391

Part V. Going Live

19. Deployment **395**
What Needs to Be Deployed   395
  Core Website Files   395
  Static Content   398
  What Not to Deploy   398
  Databases and Other External Dependencies   399
  What the EBuy Application Requires   400
Deploying to Internet Information Server   401
  Prerequisites   401

Creating and Configuring an IIS Website   402
Publishing from Within Visual Studio   403
Deploying to Windows Azure   407
Creating a Windows Azure Account   408
Creating a New Windows Azure Website   408
Publishing a Windows Azure Website via Source Control   409
Summary   410

Part VI. Appendixes

A. ASP.NET MVC and Web Forms Integration 415

B. Leveraging NuGet as a Platform 423

C. Best Practices 443

D. Cross-Reference: Targeted Topics, Features, and Scenarios 455

Index 459

Preface

The web application landscape is vast and varied. Microsoft's ASP.NET Framework—built on top of the mature and robust .NET Framework—is one of the most trusted platforms in the industry. ASP.NET MVC is Microsoft's latest addition to the world of ASP.NET providing web developers with an alternative development approach that helps you build web applications with ease.

The main goal of this book is simple: to help you to build a complete understanding of the ASP.NET MVC 4 Framework from the ground up. However, it doesn't stop there—the book combines fundamental ASP.NET MVC concepts with real-world insight, modern web technologies (such as HTML 5 and the jQuery JavaScript Framework), and powerful architecture patterns so that you're ready to produce not just a website that uses the ASP.NET MVC Framework, but a stable and scalable web application that is easy to grow and maintain with your expanding needs.

Audience

This book is for people who want to learn how to leverage the Microsoft ASP.NET MVC Framework to build robust and maintainable websites. Though the book uses many code examples to describe this process in detail, it is not simply targeted at application developers. Much of the book introduces concepts and techniques that benefit both developers writing application code and the leaders driving these development projects.

Assumptions This Book Makes

While this book aims to teach you everything you need to know in order to create robust and maintainable web applications with the ASP.NET MVC Framework, it assumes that you already have some fundamental knowledge about application development with the Microsoft .NET Framework. In other words, you should already be comfortable using HTML, CSS, and JavaScript to produce a very basic website and have enough knowledge of the .NET Framework and the C# language to create a "Hello World" application.

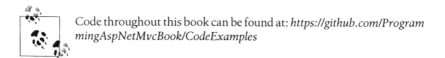 Code throughout this book can be found at: *https://github.com/Program mingAspNetMvcBook/CodeExamples*

Conventions Used in This Book

The following typographical conventions are used in this book:

Italic
> Indicates new terms, URLs, email addresses, databases and tables, filenames, and file extensions.

`Constant width`
> Used for program listings, as well as within paragraphs to refer to program elements such as variable or function names, data types, environment variables, statements, and keywords.

`Constant width bold`
> Used for emphasis in code and to show commands or other text that should be typed literally by the user.

`Constant width italic`
> Shows text that should be replaced with user-supplied values or by values determined by context.

 This icon signifies a tip, suggestion, or general note.

 This icon indicates a warning or caution.

Using Code Examples

This book is here to help you get your job done. In general, you may use the code in this book in your programs and documentation. You do not need to contact us for permission unless you're reproducing a significant portion of the code. For example, writing a program that uses several chunks of code from this book does not require permission. Selling or distributing a CD-ROM of examples from O'Reilly books does require permission. Answering a question by citing this book and quoting example code does not require permission. Incorporating a significant amount of example code from this book into your product's documentation does require permission.

We appreciate, but do not require, attribution. An attribution usually includes the title, author, publisher, and ISBN. For example: "*Programming ASP.NET MVC 4* by Jess Chadwick, Todd Synder, and Hrusikesh Panda (O'Reilly). Copyright 2012 Jess Chadwick, Todd Synder, and Hrusikesh Panda, 978-1-449-32031-7."

If you feel your use of code examples falls outside fair use or the permission given above, feel free to contact us at *permissions@oreilly.com*.

Safari® Books Online

Safari Books Online is an on-demand digital library that lets you easily search over 7,500 technology and creative reference books and videos to find the answers you need quickly.

With a subscription, you can read any page and watch any video from our library online. Read books on your cell phone and mobile devices. Access new titles before they are available for print, and get exclusive access to manuscripts in development and post feedback for the authors. Copy and paste code samples, organize your favorites, download chapters, bookmark key sections, create notes, print out pages, and benefit from lots of other time-saving features.

O'Reilly Media has uploaded this book to the Safari Books Online service. To have full digital access to this book and to other books on similar topics from O'Reilly and other publishers, sign up for free at *http://my.safaribooksonline.com*.

How to Contact Us

Please address comments and questions concerning this book to the publisher:

O'Reilly Media, Inc.
1005 Gravenstein Highway North
Sebastopol, CA 95472
800-998-9938 (in the United States or Canada)
707-829-0515 (international or local)
707-829-0104 (fax)

We have a web page for this book, where we list errata, examples, and any additional information. You can access this page at:

http://bit.ly/Programming_ASP_NET

To comment or ask technical questions about this book, send email to:

bookquestions@oreilly.com

For more information about our books, courses, conferences, and news, see our website at *http://www.oreilly.com*.

Find us on Facebook: *http://facebook.com/oreilly*

Follow us on Twitter: *http://twitter.com/oreillymedia*

Watch us on YouTube: *http://www.youtube.com/oreillymedia*

## PART I

Up and Running

## CHAPTER 1

Fundamentals of ASP.NET MVC

Microsoft ASP.NET MVC is a web application development framework built on top of Microsoft's popular and mature .NET Framework. The ASP.NET MVC Framework leans heavily on proven developmental patterns and practices that place an emphasis on a loosely coupled application architecture and highly maintainable code.

In this chapter we'll take a look at the fundamentals of what makes ASP.NET MVC tick—from its proud lineage and the architectural concepts on which it is built, to the use of Microsoft Visual Studio 2011 to create a fully functioning ASP.NET MVC web application. Then we'll dive into the ASP.NET MVC web application project and see just what ASP.NET MVC gives you right from the start, including a working web page and built-in forms authentication to allow users to register and log in to your site.

By the end of the chapter, you'll have not only a working ASP.NET MVC web application, but also enough understanding of the fundamentals of ASP.NET MVC to begin building applications with it immediately. The rest of this book simply builds on these fundamentals, showing you how to make the most of the ASP.NET MVC Framework in any web application.

Microsoft's Web Development Platforms

Understanding the past can be a big help in appreciating the present; so, before we get into what ASP.NET MVC is and how it works, let's take a minute to see just where it came from.

Long ago, Microsoft saw the need for a Windows-based web development platform, and the company worked hard to produce a solution. Over the past two decades, Microsoft has given the development community several web development platforms.

Active Server Pages (ASP)

Microsoft's first answer to web development was Active Server Pages (ASP), a scripting language in which code and markup are authored together in a single file, with each physical file corresponding to a page on the website. ASP's server-side scripting approach became widely popular and many websites grew out of it. Some of these sites continue to serve visitors today. After a while, though, developers wanted more. They asked for features such as improved code reuse, better separation of concerns, and easier application of object-oriented programming principles. In 2002, Microsoft offered ASP.NET as a solution to these concerns.

ASP.NET Web Forms

Like ASP, ASP.NET websites rely on a page-based approach where each page on the website is represented in the form of a physical file (called a Web Form) and is accessible using that file's name. Unlike a page using ASP, a Web Forms page provides some separation of code and markup by splitting the web content into two different files: one for the markup and one for the code. ASP.NET and the Web Forms approach served developers' needs for many years, and this continues to be the web development framework of choice for many .NET developers. Some .NET developers, however, consider the Web Forms approach too much of an abstraction from the underlying HTML, JavaScript, and CSS. Some developers just can't be pleased! Or can they?

ASP.NET MVC

Microsoft was quick to spot the growing need in the ASP.NET developer community for something different than the page-based Web Forms approach, and the company released the first version of ASP.NET MVC in 2008. Representing a total departure from the Web Forms approach, ASP.NET MVC abandons the page-based architecture completely, relying on the *Model-View-Controller* (MVC) architecture instead.

Unlike ASP.NET Web Forms, which was introduced as a replacement to its predecessor, ASP, ASP.NET MVC does not in any way *replace* the existing Web Forms Framework. Quite the contrary—both ASP.NET MVC and Web Forms applications are built on top of the common ASP.NET Framework, which provides a common web API that both frameworks leverage quite heavily.

The idea that ASP.NET MVC and Web Forms are just different ways of making an ASP.NET website is a common theme throughout this book; in fact, both Chapter 2 and Appendix A explore this concept in depth.

The Model-View-Controller Architecture

The Model-View-Controller pattern is an architectural pattern that encourages strict isolation between the individual parts of an application. This isolation is better known as *separation of concerns*, or, in more general terms, "loose coupling." Virtually all aspects of MVC—and, consequently, the ASP.NET MVC Framework—are driven by this goal of keeping disparate parts of an application isolated from each other.

Architecting applications in a loosely coupled manner brings a number of both short- and long-term benefits:

Development
> Individual components do not directly depend on other components, which means that they can be more easily developed in isolation. Components can also be readily replaced or substituted, preventing complications in one component from affecting the development of other components with which it may interact.

Testability
> Loose coupling of components allows test implementations to stand in for "production" components. This makes it easier to, say, avoid making calls to a database, by replacing the component that makes database calls with one that simply returns static data. The ability for components to be easily swapped with mock representations greatly facilitates the testing process, which can drastically increase the reliability of the system over time.

Maintenance
> Isolated component logic means that changes are typically isolated to a small number of components—often just one. Since the risk of change generally correlates to the scope of the change, modifying fewer components is a good thing!

The MVC pattern splits an application into three layers: the model, the view, and the controller (see Figure 1-1). Each of these layers has a very specific job that it is responsible for and—most important—is not concerned with how the other layers do their jobs.

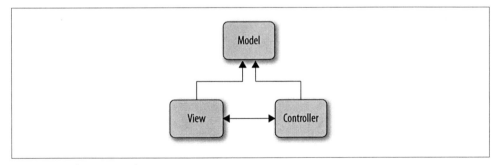

Figure 1-1. The MVC architecture

The Model

The *model* represents core business logic and data. Models encapsulate the properties and behavior of a domain entity and expose properties that describe the entity. For example, the Auction class represents the concept of an "auction" in the application and may expose properties such as `Title` and `CurrentBid`, as well as exposing behavior in the form of methods such as `Bid()`.

The View

The *view* is responsible for transforming a model or models into a visual representation. In web applications, this most often means generating HTML to be rendered in the user's browser, although views can manifest in many forms. For instance, the same model might be visualized in HTML, PDF, XML, or perhaps even in a spreadsheet.

Following separation of concerns, views should concentrate only on *displaying* data and should not contain any business logic themselves—the business logic stays in the model, which should provide the view with everything it needs.

The Controller

The *controller*, as the name implies, controls the application logic and acts as the co-ordinator between the view and the model. Controllers receive input from users via the view, then work with the model to perform specific actions, passing the results back to the view.

What's New in ASP.NET MVC 4?

This book explores the ASP.NET MVC Framework in depth, showing how to make the most of the features and functionality it offers. Since we're now up to the fourth version of the framework, however, much of what the book covers is functionality that existed prior to this latest version. If you are already familiar with previous versions of the framework, you're probably eager to skip over what you already know and begin learning all about the new additions.

The list below gives a brief description of each of the features new to version 4 of ASP.NET MVC, along with references pointing you to the sections of the book that show these features in action:

Asynchronous controllers

Internet Information Server (IIS) processes each request it receives on a new thread, so each new request ties up one of the finite number of threads available to IIS, even if that thread is sitting idle (for example, waiting for a response from a database query or web service). And, while recent updates in .NET Framework 4.0 and IIS 7 have drastically increased the default number of threads available to the IIS thread pool, it's still a good practice to avoid holding on to system resources for longer than you need to. Version 4 of the ASP.NET MVC Framework introduces *asynchronous controllers* to better handle these types of long-running requests in a more asynchronous fashion. Through the use of asynchronous controllers, you can tell the framework to free up the thread that is processing your request, letting it perform other processing tasks while it waits for the various tasks in the request to finish. Once they finish, the framework picks up where it left off, and returns the same response as if the request had gone through a normal synchronous controller —except now you can handle many more requests at once! If you're interested in learning more about asynchronous controllers, see Chapter 11, which explains them in depth.

Display modes

A growing number of devices are Internet-connected and ready to surf your site, and you need to be ready for them. Many times, the data displayed on these devices is the same as the data displayed on desktop devices, except the visual elements need to take into consideration the smaller form factor of mobile devices. ASP.NET MVC *display modes* provide an easy, convention-based approach for tailoring views and layouts to target different devices. Chapter 10 shows how to apply display modes to your site as part of a holistic approach to adding mobile device support to your sites.

Bundling and minification

Even though it may seem like the only way to get on the Internet these days is through some sort of high-speed connection, that doesn't mean you can treat the client-side resources that your site depends on in a haphazard manner. In fact, when you consider how the overall download times are increasing, wasting even fractions of a second in download times can really add up and begin to have a very negative effect on the perceived performance of your site. Concepts such as script and stylesheet combining and minification may not be anything new, but with the .NET Framework 4.5 release, they are now a fundamental part of the framework. What's more, ASP.NET MVC embraces and extends the core .NET Framework functionality to make this tooling even more usable in your ASP.NET MVC applications. Chapter 13 helps you tackle all of these concepts and also shows you how to use the new tooling offered in the core ASP.NET and ASP.NET MVC Frameworks.

Web API

Simple HTTP data services are rapidly becoming the primary way to supply data to the ever-increasing variety of applications, devices, and platforms. ASP.NET MVC has always provided the ability to return data in various formats, including JSON and XML; however, the *ASP.NET Web API* takes this interaction a step further, providing a more modern programming model that focuses on providing full-fledged data *services* rather than controller actions that happen to return data. In Chapter 6, you'll see how to really take advantage of AJAX on the client—and you'll use ASP.NET Web API services to do it!

Introduction to EBuy

This book aims to show you not only the ins and outs of the ASP.NET MVC Framework, but also how to leverage the framework in real-world applications. The problem with such applications is that the very meaning of "real-world" indicates a certain level of complexity and uniqueness that can't be adequately represented in a single demo application.

Instead of attempting to demonstrate solutions to every problem you may face, we—the authors of this book—have assembled a list of the scenarios and issues that we have most frequently encountered and that we most frequently hear of others encountering. Though this list of scenarios may not include every scenario you'll face while developing your application, we believe it represents the majority of the real-world problems that most developers face over the course of creating their ASP.NET MVC applications.

 We're not kidding, we actually wrote a list—and it's in the back of this book! Appendix D has a cross-referenced list of all the features and scenarios we cover and the chapter(s) in which we cover them.

In order to cover the scenarios on this list, we came up with a web application that combines them all into as close to a real-world application as we could get, while still limiting the scope to something everyone understands: an online auction site.

Introducing EBuy, the online auction site powered by ASP.NET MVC! From a high level, the goals of the site are pretty straightforward: allow users to list items they wish to sell, and bid on items they wish to buy. As you take a deeper look, however, you'll begin to see that the application is a bit more complex than it sounds, requiring not only everything ASP.NET MVC has to offer, but also integration with other technologies.

EBuy is not just a bunch of code that we ship along with the book, though. Each chapter of the book not only introduces more features and functionality, but uses them to build the EBuy application—from new project to deployed application, preferably while you follow along and write the code, too!

OK, we'll admit that EBuy is *also* "just a bunch of code." In fact, you can download EBuy in its entirety from the book's website: *http://www .programmingaspnetmvc.com*.

Now, let's stop talking about an application that doesn't exist yet and start building it!

Installing ASP.NET MVC

In order to begin developing ASP.NET MVC applications, you'll need to download and install the ASP.NET MVC 4 Framework. This is as easy as visiting the ASP.NET MVC website (*http://www.asp.net/mvc*) and clicking the Install button.

This launches the Web Platform Installer, a free tool that simplifies the installation of many web tools and applications. Follow the Web Platform Installer wizard to download and install ASP.NET MVC 4 and its dependencies to your machine.

Note that in order to install and use ASP.NET MVC 4, you must have at least PowerShell 2.0 and Visual Studio 2010 Service Pack 1 or Visual Web Developer Express 2010 Service Pack 1. Luckily, if you do not already have them installed, the Web Platform Installer should figure it out and proceed to download and install the latest versions of PowerShell and Visual Studio for you!

If you are currently using the previous version of ASP.NET MVC and would like to both create ASP.NET MVC 4 applications and continue working with ASP.NET MVC 3 applications, fear not—ASP.NET MVC can be installed and run side by side with ASP.NET MVC 3 installations.

Once you've gotten everything installed, it's time to proceed to the next step: creating your first ASP.NET MVC 4 application.

Creating an ASP.NET MVC Application

The ASP.NET MVC 4 installer adds a new Visual Studio project type named *ASP.NET MVC 4 Web Application*. This is your entry point to the world of ASP.NET MVC and is what you'll use to create the new EBuy web application project that you'll build on as you progress through this book.

To create a new project, select the Visual C# version of the ASP.NET MVC 4 Web Application template and enter Ebuy.Website into the Name field (see Figure 1-2).

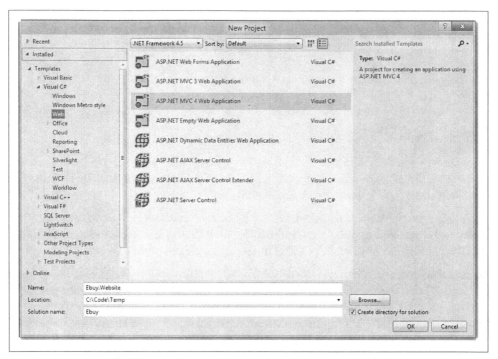

Figure 1-2. Creating the EBuy project

When you click OK to continue, you'll be presented with another dialog with more options (see Figure 1-3).

This dialog lets you customize the ASP.NET MVC 4 application that Visual Studio is going to generate for you by letting you specify what kind of ASP.NET MVC site you want to create.

Project Templates

To begin, ASP.NET MVC 4 offers several project templates, each of which targets a different scenario:

Empty

> The *Empty* template creates a bare-bones ASP.NET MVC 4 application with the appropriate folder structure that includes references to the ASP.NET MVC assemblies as well as some JavaScript libraries that you'll probably use along the way. The template also includes a default view layout and generates a *Global.asax* file that includes the standard configuration code that most ASP.NET MVC applications will need.

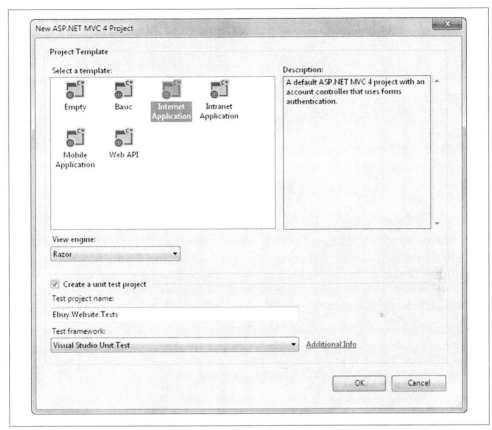

Figure 1-3. Customizing the EBuy project

Basic
> The *Basic* template creates a folder structure that follows ASP.NET MVC 4 conventions and includes references to the ASP.NET MVC assemblies. This template represents the bare minimum that you'll need to begin creating an ASP.NET MVC 4 project, but no more—you'll have to do all the work from here!

Internet Application
> The *Internet Application* template picks up where the Empty template leaves off, extending the Empty template to include a simple default controller (Home Controller), an AccountController with all the logic required for users to register and log in to the website, and default views for both of these controllers.

Intranet Application
> The *Intranet Application* template is much like the Internet Application template, except that it is preconfigured to use Windows-based authentication, which is desirable in intranet scenarios.

Mobile Application

The *Mobile Application* template is another variation of the Internet Application template. This template, however, is optimized for mobile devices and includes the jQuery Mobile JavaScript framework and views that apply the HTML that works best with jQuery Mobile.

Web API

The *Web API* template is yet another variation of the Internet Application template that includes a preconfigured Web API controller. Web API is the new lightweight, RESTful HTTP web services framework that integrates quite nicely with ASP.NET MVC. Web API is a great choice for quickly and easily creating data services that your AJAX-enabled applications can easily consume. Chapter 6 covers this new API in great detail.

The New ASP.NET MVC Project dialog also lets you select a *view engine*, or syntax that your views will be written in. We'll be using the new Razor syntax to build the EBuy reference application, so you can leave the default value ("Razor") selected. Rest assured that you can change the view engine your application uses at any time—this option exists only to inform the wizard of the kind of views it should *generate* for you, not to lock the application into a specific view engine forever.

Finally, choose whether or not you'd like the wizard to generate a unit test project for this solution. Once again, you don't have to worry about this decision too much—as with any other Visual Studio solution, you are able to add a unit test project to an ASP.NET MVC web application anytime you'd like.

When you're happy with the options you've selected, click OK to have the wizard generate your new project!

NuGet Package Management

If you pay attention to the status bar as Visual Studio creates your new web application project, you may notice messages (such as "Installing package AspNetMvc...") referring to the fact that the project template is utilizing the *NuGet Package Manager* to install and manage the assembly references in your application. The concept of using a package manager to manage application dependencies—especially as part of the new project template phase—is quite powerful, and also new to ASP.NET MVC 4 project types.

Introduced as part of the ASP.NET MVC 3 installer, NuGet offers an alternative workflow for managing application dependencies. Though it is not actually part of the ASP.NET MVC Framework, NuGet is doing much of the work behind the scenes to make your projects possible.

A NuGet package may contain a mixture of assemblies, content, and even tools to aid in development. In the course of installing a package, NuGet will add the assemblies to the target project's References list, copy any content into the application's folder structure, and register any tools in the current path so that they can be executed from the Package Manager Console.

However, the most important aspect of NuGet packages—indeed, the primary reason NuGet was created to begin with—has to do with *dependency management*. .NET applications are not monolithic, single-assembly applications—most assemblies rely on references to other assemblies in order to do their job. What's more, assemblies generally depend on specific *versions* (or, at least, a minimum version) of other assemblies.

In a nutshell, NuGet calculates the potentially complex relationships between all of the assemblies that an application depends on, then makes sure that you have all of the assemblies you need—and the correct versions of those assemblies.

Your gateway to NuGet's power is the NuGet Package Manager. You can access the NuGet Package Manager in two ways:

The graphical user interface
> The NuGet Package Manager has a graphical user interface (GUI) that makes it easy to search for, install, update, and uninstall packages for a project. You can access the graphical Package Manager interface by right-clicking the website project in the Solution Explorer and selecting the "Manage NuGet Packages..." option.

The Console mode
> The Library Package Manager Console is a Visual Studio window containing an integrated PowerShell prompt specially configured for Library Package Manager access. If you do not see the Package Manager Console window already open in Visual Studio, you can access it via the Tools > Library Package Manager > Package Manager Console menu option. To install a package from the Package Manager Console window, simply type the command `Install-Package _Package Name_`. For example, to install the Entity Framework package, execute the `Install-Package EntityFramework` command. The Package Manager Console will proceed to download the *EntityFramework* package and install it into your project. After the "Install-Package" step has completed, the Entity Framework assemblies will be visible in the project's References list.

Convention over Configuration

To make website development easier and help developers be more productive, ASP.NET MVC relies on the concept of *convention over configuration* whenever possible. This means that, instead of relying on explicit configuration settings, ASP.NET MVC simply assumes that developers will follow certain conventions as they build their applications.

The ASP.NET MVC project folder structure (Figure 1-4) is a great example of the framework's use of convention over configuration. There are three special folders in the project that correspond to the elements of the MVC pattern: the *Controllers*, *Models*, and *Views* folders. It's pretty clear at a glance what each of these folders contains.

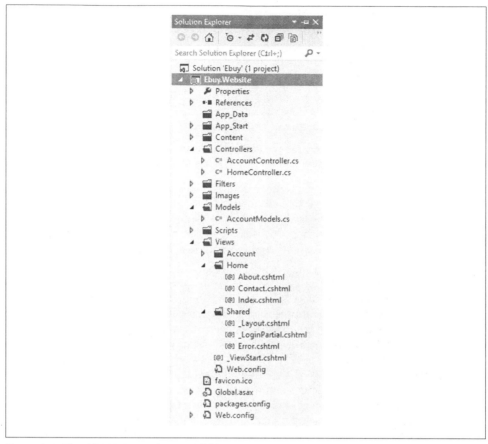

Figure 1-4. The ASP.NET MVC project folder structure

When you look at the contents of these folders, you'll find even more conventions at work. For example, not only does the *Controllers* folder contain all of the application's controller classes, but the controller classes all follow the convention of ending their names with the *Controller* suffix. The framework uses this convention to register the application's controllers when it starts up and associate controllers with their corresponding routes.

Next, take a look at the *Views* folder. Beyond the obvious convention dictating that the application's views should live under this folder, it is split into subfolders: a *Shared* folder, and an optional folder to contain the views for each controller. This convention helps save developers from providing explicit locations of the views they'd like to display to users. Instead, developers can just provide the name of a view—say, "Index"—and the framework will try its best to find the view within the *Views* folder, first in the controller-specific folder and then, failing that, in the *Shared* views folder.

At first glance, the concept of convention over configuration may seem trivial. However, these seemingly small or meaningless optimizations can really add up to significant time savings, improved code readability, and increased developer productivity.

Running the Application

Once your project is created, feel free to hit F5 to execute your ASP.NET MVC website and watch it render in your browser.

Congratulations, you've just created your first ASP.NET MVC 4 application!

After you've calmed down from the immense excitement you experience as a result of making words show up in a web browser, you might be left wondering, "What just happened? *How did it do that?*"

Figure 1-5 shows, from a high level, how ASP.NET MVC processes a request.

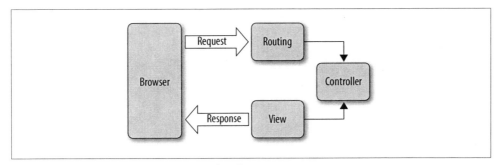

Figure 1-5. The ASP.NET MVC request lifecycle

Though we'll spend the rest of this book diving deeper and deeper into the components of that diagram, the next few sections start out by explaining those fundamental building blocks of ASP.NET MVC.

Routing

All ASP.NET MVC traffic starts out like any other website traffic: with a request to a URL. This means that, despite the fact that it is not mentioned anywhere in the name, the *ASP.NET Routing* framework is at the core of every ASP.NET MVC request.

In simple terms, ASP.NET routing is just a pattern-matching system. At startup, the application registers one or more patterns with the framework's *route table* to tell the routing system what to do with any requests that match those patterns. When the routing engine receives a request at runtime, it matches that request's URL against the URL patterns registered with it (Figure 1-6).

When the routing engine finds a matching pattern in its route table, it forwards the request to the appropriate handler for that request.

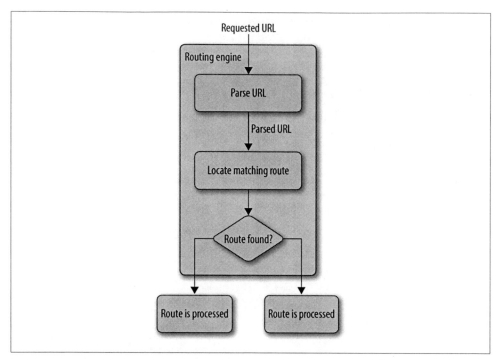

Figure 1-6. ASP.NET routing

Otherwise, when the request's URL does not match any of the registered route patterns, the routing engine indicates that it could not figure out how to handle the request by returning a 404 HTTP status code.

Configuring Routes

ASP.NET MVC routes are responsible for determining which controller method (otherwise known as a *controller action*) to execute for a given URL. They consist of the following properties:

Unique name
A name may be used as a specific reference to a given route

URL pattern
A simple pattern syntax that parses matching URLs into meaningful segments

Defaults
An optional set of default values for the segments defined in the URL pattern

Constraints
A set of constraints to apply against the URL pattern to more narrowly define the URLs that it matches

The default ASP.NET MVC project templates add a generic route that uses the following URL convention to break the URL for a given request into three named segments, wrapped with brackets ({}): "controller", "action", and "id":

```
{controller}/{action}/{id}
```

This route pattern is registered via a call to the `MapRoute()` extension method that runs during application startup (located in *App_Start/RouteConfig.cs*):

```
routes.MapRoute(
    "Default", // Route name
    "{controller}/{action}/{id}", // URL with parameters
    new { controller = "Home", action = "Index",
        id = UrlParameter.Optional } // Parameter defaults
);
```

In addition to providing a name and URL pattern, this route also defines a set of default parameters to be used in the event that the URL fits the route pattern, but doesn't actually provide values for every segment.

For instance, Table 1-1 contains a list of URLs that match this route pattern, along with corresponding values that the routing framework will provide for each of them.

Table 1-1. Values provided for URLs that match our route pattern

URL	Controller	Action	ID
/auctions/auction/1234	AuctionsController	Auction	1234
/auctions/recent	AuctionsController	Recent	
/auctions	AuctionsController	Index	
/	HomeController	Index	

The first URL (*/auctions/auction/1234*) in the table is a perfect match because it satisfies every segment of the route pattern, but as you continue down the list and remove segments from the end of the URL, you begin to see defaults filling in for values that are not provided by the URL.

This is a very important example of how ASP.NET MVC leverages the concept of convention over configuration: when the application starts up, ASP.NET MVC discovers all of the application's controllers by searching through the available assemblies for classes that implement the `System.Web.Mvc.IController` interface (or derive from a class that implements this interface, such as `System.Web.Mvc.Controller`) *and* whose class names end with the suffix *Controller*. When the routing framework uses this list to figure out which controllers it has access to, it chops off the *Controller* suffix from all of the controller class names. So, whenever you need to refer to a controller, you do so by its shortened name, e.g., `AuctionsController` is referred to as *Auctions*, and `HomeController` becomes *Home*.

What's more, the controller and action values in a route are not case-sensitive. This means that each of these requests—*/Auctions/Recent*, */auctions/Recent*, */auctions/recent*, or even */aucTionS/rEceNt*—will successfully resolve to the Recent action in the AuctionsController.

 URL route patterns are relative to the application root, so they do not need to start with a forward slash (/) or a virtual path designator (~/). Route patterns that include these characters are invalid and will cause the routing system to throw an exception.

As you may have noticed, URL routes can contain a wealth of information that the routing engine is able to extract. In order to process an ASP.NET MVC request, however, the routing engine must be able to determine two crucial pieces of information: the *controller* and the *action*. The routing engine can then pass these values to the ASP.NET MVC runtime to create and execute the specified action of the appropriate controller.

Controllers

In the context of the MVC architectural pattern, a *controller* responds to user input (e.g., a user clicking a Save button) and collaborates between the model, view, and (quite often) data access layers. In an ASP.NET MVC application, controllers are classes that contain methods that are called by the routing framework to process a request.

To see an example of an ASP.NET MVC controller, take a look at the HomeController class found in *Controllers/HomeController.cs*:

```
using System.Web.Mvc;

namespace Ebuy.Website.Controllers
{
    public class HomeController : Controller
    {
        public ActionResult Index()
        {
            ViewBag.Message = "Your app description page.";

            return View();
        }

        public ActionResult About()
        {
            ViewBag.Message = "Your quintessential app description page.";

            return View();
        }

        public ActionResult Contact()
```

```
        {
            ViewBag.Message = "Your quintessential contact page.";

            return View();
        }
    }
}
```

Controller Actions

As you can see, controller classes themselves aren't very special; that is, they don't look much different from any other .NET class. In fact, it's the *methods* in controller classes—referred to as *controller actions*—that do all the heavy lifting that's involved in processing requests.

 You'll often hear the terms *controller* and *controller action* used somewhat interchangeably, even throughout this book. This is because the MVC pattern makes no differentiation between the two. However, the ASP.NET MVC Framework is mostly concerned with controller actions since they contain the actual logic to process the request.

For instance, the HomeController class we just looked at contains three actions: Index, About, and Contact. Thus, given the default route pattern {controller}/{action}/ {id}, when a request is made to the URL */Home/About*, the routing framework determines that it is the About() method of the HomeController class that should process the request. The ASP.NET MVC Framework then creates a new instance of the Home Controller class and executes its About() method.

In this case, the About() method is pretty simple: it passes data to the view via the ViewBag property (more on that later), and then tells the ASP.NET MVC Framework to display the view named "About" by calling the View() method, which returns an ActionResult of type ViewResult.

Action Results

It is very important to note that it is the controller's job to tell the ASP.NET MVC Framework *what* it should do next, but not *how* to do it. This communication occurs through the use of +ActionResult+s, the return values which every controller action is expected to provide.

For example, when a controller decides to show a view, it tells the ASP.NET MVC Framework to show the view by returning a ViewResult. It does not render the view itself. This loose coupling is another great example of separation of concerns in action (*what* to do versus *how* it should be done).

Despite the fact that every controller action needs to return an `ActionResult`, you will rarely be creating them manually. Instead, you'll usually rely on the helper methods that the `System.Web.Mvc.Controller` base class provides, such as:

`Content()`
> Returns a `ContentResult` that renders arbitrary text, e.g., "Hello, world!"

`File()`
> Returns a `FileResult` that renders the contents of a file, e.g., a PDF.

`HttpNotFound()`
> Returns an `HttpNotFoundResult` that renders a 404 HTTP status code response.

`JavaScript():: Returns a JavaScriptResult`
> that renders JavaScript, e.g., "function hello() { alert(*Hello, World!*); }".

`Json()`
> Returns a `JsonResult` that serializes an object and renders it in JavaScript Object Notation (JSON) format, e.g., "{ "Message": *Hello, World!* }".

`PartialView()`
> Returns a `PartialViewResult` that renders only the content of a view (i.e., a view without its layout).

`Redirect()`
> Returns a `RedirectResult` that renders a 302 (temporary) status code to redirect the user to a given URL, e.g., "302 *http://www.ebuy.com/auctions/recent*". This method has a sibling, `RedirectPermanent()`, that also returns a `RedirectResult`, but uses HTTP status code 301 to indicate a permanent redirect rather than a temporary one.

`RedirectToAction()` and `RedirectToRoute()`
> Act just like the `Redirect()` helper, only the framework dynamically determines the external URL by querying the routing engine. Like the `Redirect()` helper, these two helpers also have permanent redirect variants: `RedirectToActionPermanent()` and `RedirectToRoutePermanent()`.

`View()`
> Returns a `ViewResult` that renders a view.

As you can tell from this list, the framework provides an action result for just about any situation you need to support, and, if it doesn't, you are free to create your own!

Though all controller actions are required to provide an `ActionResult` that indicates the next steps that should be taken to process the request, not all controller actions need to specify `ActionResult` as their return type. Controller actions can specify any return type that derives from `ActionResult`, or even any other type.

When the ASP.NET MVC Framework comes across a controller action that returns a non-`ActionResult` type, it automatically wraps the value in a `ContentResult` and renders the value as raw content.

Action Parameters

Controller actions are—when it comes down to it—just like any other method. In fact, a controller action can even specify parameters that ASP.NET MVC populates, using information from the request, when it executes. This functionality is called *model binding*, and it is one of ASP.NET MVC's most powerful and useful features.

Before diving into how model binding works, first take a step back and consider an example of the "traditional" way of interacting with request values:

```
public ActionResult Create()
{
    var auction = new Auction() {
        Title = Request["title"],
        CurrentPrice = Decimal.Parse(Request["currentPrice"]),
        StartTime = DateTime.Parse(Request["startTime"]),
        EndTime = DateTime.Parse(Request["endTime"]),
    };
    // ...
}
```

The controller action in this particular example creates and populates the properties of a new `Auction` object with values taken straight from the request. Since some of `Auction`'s properties are defined as various primitive, non-`string` types, the action also needs to parse each of those corresponding request values into the proper type.

This example may seem simple and straightforward, but it's actually quite frail: if any of the parsing attempts fails, the entire action will fail. Switching to the various `Try Parse()` methods may help avoid most exceptions, but applying these methods also means additional code.

The side effect of this approach is that every action is very explicit. The downside to writing such explicit code is that it puts the burden on you, the developer, to perform all the work and to remember to perform this work every time it is required. A larger amount of code also tends to obscure the real goal: in this example, adding a new `Auction` to the system.

Model binding basics

Not only does model binding avoid all of this explicit code, it is also very easy to apply. So easy, in fact, that you don't even need to think about it.

For example, here's the same controller action as before, this time using model-bound method parameters:

```
public ActionResult Create(
        string title, decimal currentPrice,
        DateTime startTime, DateTime endTime
    )
{
    var auction = new Auction() {
        Title = title,
        CurrentPrice = currentPrice,
        StartTime = startTime,
        EndTime = endTime,
    };
    // ...
}
```

Now, instead of retrieving the values from the Request explicitly, the action declares them as parameters. When the ASP.NET MVC framework executes this method, it attempts to populate the action's parameters using the same values from the request that the previous example showed. Note that—even though we're not accessing the Request dictionary directly—the parameter names are still very important, because they still correspond to values from in the Request.

The Request object isn't the only place the ASP.NET MVC model binder gets its values from, however. Out of the box, the framework looks in several places, such as route data, query string parameters, form post values, and even serialized JSON objects. For example, the following snippet retrieves the id value from the URL simply by declaring a parameter with the same name:

Example 1-1. Retrieving the id from a URL (e.g. /auctions/auction/123)

```
public ActionResult Auction(long id)
{
    var context = new EBuyContext();
    var auction = context.Auctions.FirstOrDefault(x => x.Id == id);
    return View("Auction", auction);
}
```

 Where and how the ASP.NET MVC model binder finds these values is actually quite configurable and even extensible. See Chapter 8 for an in-depth discussion of ASP.NET MVC model binding.

As these examples demonstrate, model binding lets ASP.NET MVC handle much of the mundane, boilerplate code so the logic within the action can concentrate on providing business value. The code that is left is much more meaningful, not to mention more readable.

Model binding complex objects

Applying the model binding approach even to simple, primitive types can make a pretty big impact in making your code more expressive. In the real world, though, things are much more complex—only the most basic scenarios rely on just a couple of parameters. Luckily, ASP.NET MVC supports binding to complex types as well as to primitive types.

This example takes one more pass at the `Create` action, this time skipping the middle-man primitive types and binding directly to an `Auction` instance:

```
public ActionResult Create(Auction auction)
{
    // ...
}
```

The action shown here is equivalent to what you saw in the previous example. That's right—ASP.NET MVC's complex model binding just eliminated *all* of the boilerplate code required to create and populate a new `Auction` instance! This example shows the true power of model binding.

Action Filters

Action filters provide a simple yet powerful technique to modify or enhance the ASP.NET MVC pipeline by "injecting" logic at certain points, helping to address "cross-cutting concerns" that apply to many (or all) components of an application. Application logging is a classic example of a cross-cutting concern in that it is equally applicable to any component in an application, regardless of what that component's primary responsibility may be.

Action filter logic is primarily introduced by applying an `ActionFilterAttribute` to a controller action in order to affect how that action executes, as is the case in the following example that protects a controller action from unauthorized access by applying the `AuthorizeAttribute`:

```
[Authorize]
public ActionResult Profile()
{
    // Retrieve profile information for current user
    return View();
}
```

The ASP.NET MVC Framework includes quite a few action filters that target common scenarios. You'll see these action filters in use throughout this book, helping accomplish a variety of tasks in a clean, loosely coupled way.

> Action filters are a great way to apply custom logic throughout your site. Keep in mind that you are free to create your own action filters by extending the `ActionFilterAttribute` base class or any of the ASP.NET MVC action filters.

Views

In the ASP.NET MVC Framework, controller actions that wish to display HTML to the user return an instance of `ViewResult`, a type of `ActionResult` that knows how to render content to the response. When it comes time to render the view, the ASP.NET MVC Framework will look for the view using the name provided by the controller.

Take the `Index` action in the `HomeController`:

```
public ActionResult Index()
{
    ViewBag.Message = "Your app description page.";
    return View();
}
```

This action takes advantage of the `View()` helper method to create a `ViewResult`. Calling `View()` without any parameters, as in this example, instructs ASP.NET MVC to find a view with the same name as the current controller action. In this instance, ASP.NET MVC will look for a view named "Index", but where will it look?

Locating Views

ASP.NET MVC relies on the convention that keeps all the application's views underneath the *Views* folder in the root of the website. More specifically, ASP.NET MVC expects views to live within folders named after the controller to which they relate.

Thus, when the framework wants to show the view for the `Index` action in the `HomeController`, it is going to look in the */Views/Home* folder for a file named *Index*. The screenshot in Figure 1-7 shows that the project template was nice enough to include an *Index.cshtml* view for us.

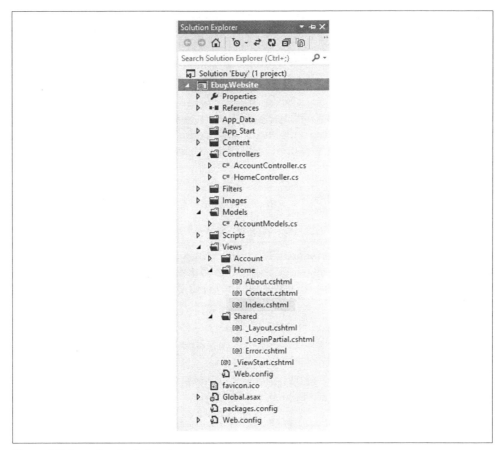

Figure 1-7. Locating the Index view

When it does not find a view that matches the name of the view it is looking for in the controller's Views folder, ASP.NET MVC continues looking in the common */Views/ Shared* folder.

 The */Views/Shared* folder is a great place to keep views that are shared across multiple controllers.

Now that you've found the view that the action requested, open it up and take a look at what's inside: HTML markup and code. But, it's not just *any* HTML markup and code—it's *Razor*!

Hello, Razor!

Razor is a syntax that allows you to combine code and content in a fluid and expressive manner. Though it introduces a few symbols and keywords, Razor is not a new language. Instead, Razor lets you write code using languages you probably already know, such as C# or Visual Basic .NET.

Razor's learning curve is very short, because it lets you work with your existing skills rather than requiring you to learn an entirely new language. Therefore, if you know how to write HTML and .NET code using C# or Visual Basic .NET, you can easily write markup such as the following:

```
<div>This page rendered at @DateTime.Now</div>
```

Which produces the following output:

```
<div>This page rendered at 12/7/1941 7:38:00 AM</div>
```

This example begins with a standard HTML tag (the `<div>` tag), followed by a bit of "hardcoded" text, then a bit of dynamic text rendered as the result of referencing a .NET property (`System.DateTime.Now`), followed by the closing (`</div>`) tag.

Razor's intelligent parser allows developers to be more expressive with their logic and make easier transitions between code and markup. Though Razor's syntax might be different from other markup syntaxes (such as the Web Forms syntax), it's ultimately working toward the same goal: rendering HTML.

To illustrate this point, take a look at the following snippets that show examples of common scenarios implemented in both Razor markup and Web Forms markup.

Here is an `if/else` statement using Web Forms syntax:

```
<% if(User.IsAuthenticated) { %>
    <span>Hello, <%: User.Username %>!</span>
<% } %>
<% else { %>
    <span>Please <%: Html.ActionLink("log in") %></span>
<% } %>
```

and using Razor syntax:

```
@if(User.IsAuthenticated) {
    <span>Hello, @User.Username!</span>
} else {
    <span>Please @Html.ActionLink("log in")</span>
}
```

And here is a `foreach` loop using Web Forms syntax:

```
<ul>
<% foreach( var auction in auctions) { %>
    <li><a href="<%: auction.Href %>"><%: auction.Title %></a></li>
<% } %>
</ul>
```

and using Razor syntax:

```
<ul>
@foreach( var auction in auctions) {
    <li><a href="@auction.Href">@auction.Title</a></li>
}
</ul>
```

Though they use a different syntax, the two snippets for each of the examples render the same HTML.

Differentiating Code and Markup

Razor provides two ways to differentiate code from markup: code nuggets and code blocks.

Code nuggets

Code nuggets are simple expressions that are evaluated and rendered inline. They can be mixed with text and look like this:

```
Not Logged In: @Html.ActionLink("Login", "Login")
```

The expression begins immediately after the @ symbol, and Razor is smart enough to know that the closing parenthesis indicates the end of this particular statement.

The previous example will render this output:

```
Not Logged In: <a href="/Login">Login</a>
```

Notice that code nuggets must always return markup for the view to render. If you write a code nugget that evaluates to a void value, you will receive an error when the view executes.

Code blocks

A *code block* is a section of the view that contains strictly code rather than a combination of markup and code. Razor defines code blocks as any section of a Razor template wrapped in @{ } characters. The @{ characters mark the beginning of the block, followed by any number of lines of fully formed code. The } character closes the code block.

Keep in mind that the code within a code block is not like code in a code nugget. It is regular code that must follow the rules of the current language. For example, each line of code written in C# must include a semicolon (;) at the end, just as if it lived within a class in a *.cs* file.

Here is an example of a typical code block:

```
@{
 LayoutPage = "~/Views/Shared/_Layout.cshtml";
 View.Title = "Auction " + Model.Title;
}
```

Code blocks do not render anything to the view. Instead, they allow you to write arbitrary code that requires no return value.

Also, variables defined within code blocks may be used by code nuggets in the same scope. That is, variables defined within the scope of a foreach loop or similar container will be accessible only within that container, while variables that are defined at the top level of a view (not in any kind of container) will be accessible to any other code blocks or code nuggets in that same view.

To better clarify this, take a look at a view with a few variables defined at different scopes:

```
@{
    // The title and bids variables are
    // available to the entire view
    var title = Model.Title;
    var bids = Model.Bids;
}

<h1>@title<h1>
<div class="items">
<!-- Loop through the objects in the bids variable -->
@foreach(var bid in bids) {
    <!-- The bid variable is only available within the foreach loop -->
    <div class="bid">
        <span class="bidder">@bid.Username</span>
        <span class="amount">@bid.Amount</span>
    </div>
}

<!-- This will throw an error: the bid variable does not exist at this scope! -->
<div>Last Bid Amount: @bid.Amount</div>
</div>
```

Code blocks are a means to execute code within a template and do not render anything to the view. In direct contrast to the way that code nuggets must provide a return value for the view to render, the view will completely ignore values that a code block returns.

Layouts

Razor offers the ability to maintain a consistent look and feel throughout your entire website through *layouts*. With layouts, a single view acts as a template for all other views to use, defining the site-wide page layout and style.

A layout template typically includes the primary markup (scripts, CSS stylesheets, and structural HTML elements such as navigation and content containers), specifying locations within the markup in which views can define content. Each view in the site then refers to this layout, including only the content within the locations the layout has indicated.

Take a look at a basic Razor layout file (_Layout.cshtml):

```
<!DOCTYPE html>

<html lang="en">
    <head>
        <meta charset="utf-8" />
        <title>@View.Title</title>
    </head>
    <body>
        <div class="header">
            @RenderSection("Header")
        </div>

        @RenderBody()

        <div class="footer">
            @RenderSection("Footer")
        </div>
    </body>
</html>
```

The layout file contains the main HTML content, defining the HTML structure for the entire site. The layout relies on variables (such as `@View.Title`) and helper functions like `@RenderSection([Section Name])` and `@RenderBody()` to interact with individual views.

Once a Razor layout is defined, views reference the layout and supply content for the sections defined within the layout.

The following is a basic content page that refers to the previously defined _Layout.cshtml_ file:

```
@{ Layout = "~/_Layout.cshtml"; }

@section Header {
    <h1>EBuy Online Auction Site<h1>
}

@section Footer {
    Copyright @DateTime.Now.Year
}

<div class="main">
    This is the main content.
</div>
```

Razor layouts and the content views that depend on them are assembled together like puzzle pieces, each one defining one or more portions of the entire page. When all the pieces get assembled, the result is a complete web page.

Partial Views

While layouts offer a helpful way to reuse portions of markup and maintain a consistent look and feel throughout multiple pages in your site, some scenarios may require a more focused approach.

The most common scenario is needing to display the same high-level information in multiple locations in a site, but only on a few specific pages and in different places on each of those pages.

For instance, the Ebuy auction site may render a list of compact auction details—showing only the auction's title, current price, and perhaps a thumbnail of the item—in multiple places in the site such as the search results page as well as a list of featured auctions on the site's homepage.

ASP.NET MVC supports these kinds of scenarios through partial views.

Partial views are views that contain targeted markup designed to be rendered as part of a larger view. The following snippet demonstrates a partial view to display the compact auction details mentioned in the scenario above:

```
@model Auction

<div class="auction">
    <a href="@Model.Url">
        <img src="@Model.ImageUrl" />
    </a>
    <h4><a href="@Model.Url">@Model.Title</a></h4>
    <p>Current Price: @Model.CurrentPrice</p>
</div>
```

To render this snippet as a partial view, simply save it as its own standalone view file (e.g. */Views/Shared/Auction.cshtml*) and use one of ASP.NET MVC's HTML Helpers —Html.Partial()—to render the view as part of another view.

To see this in action, take a look at the following snippet, which iterates over a collection of auction objects and uses the partial view above to render the HTML for each auction:

```
@model IEnumerable<Auction>

<h2>Search Results</h2>

@foreach(var auction in Model) {
    @Html.Partial("Auction", auction)
}
```

Notice that the first parameter to the Html.Partial() helper method is a string containing the name of the view without its extension.

This is because the Html.Partial() helper method is just a simple layer on top of ASP.NET MVC's powerful view engine, which renders the view very similar to what occurs after a controller action calls the View() method to return a view action result: the engine uses the view name to locate and execute the appropriate view.

In this way, partial views are developed and executed almost exactly like any other kind of view. The only difference is that they are designed to be rendered as part of a larger view.

The second parameter (`auction` in the example above) accepts the partial view's model, just like the model parameter in the `View(_View Name_, _[Model]_)` controller helper method. This second model parameter is optional; when it's not specified, it defaults to the model in the view from which the `Html.Partial()` helper was called. For instance, if the second `auction` parameter were omitted in the example above, ASP.NET MVC would pass the view's `Model` property (of type `IEnumerable<Auction>`) in its place.

> The examples above show how partial views can provide reusable sections of markup that can help reduce duplication and complexity in your views.
>
> Though useful, this is only one way to take advantage of partial views—"Partial Rendering" on page 111 shows how to take advantage of partial views to provide a simple and effective way to enhance your site with AJAX.

Displaying Data

The MVC architecture depends on the model, view, and controller all remaining separate and distinct, while still working together to accomplish a common goal. In this relationship, it is the controller's job to be the "traffic cop," coordinating various parts of the system to execute the application's logic. This processing typically results in some kind of data that needs to be relayed to the user. Alas, it is not the controller's job to display things to the user—that is what views are for! The question then becomes, how does the controller communicate this information to the view?

ASP.NET MVC offers two ways to communicate data across model-view-controller boundaries: `ViewData` and `TempData`. These objects are dictionaries available as properties in both controllers and views. Thus, passing data from a controller to a view can be as simple as setting a value in the controller, as in this snippet from *HomeController.cs*:

```
public ActionResult About()
{
    ViewData["Username"] = User.Identity.Username;

    ViewData["CompanyName"] = "EBuy: The ASP.NET MVC Demo Site";
    ViewData["CompanyDescription"] =
        "EBuy is the world leader in ASP.NET MVC demoing!";

    return View("About");
}
```

and referencing the value in the view, as in this portion of the *About.cshtml* file:

```
<h1>@ViewData["CompanyName"]</h1>
<div>@ViewData["CompanyDescription"]</div>
```

Cleaner access to ViewData values via ViewBag

ASP.NET MVC controllers and views that expose the ViewData property also expose a similar property named ViewBag. The ViewBag property is simply a wrapper around the ViewData that exposes the ViewData dictionary as a dynamic object.

For example, any references to values in the ViewData dictionary in the preceding snippets can be replaced with references to dynamic properties on the ViewBag object, as in:

```
public ActionResult About()
{
    ViewBag.Username = User.Identity.Username;

    ViewBag.CompanyName = "EBuy: The ASP.NET MVC Demo Site";
    ViewBag.CompanyDescription = "EBuy is the world leader in ASP.NET MVC demoing!";

    return View("About");
}
```

and:

```
<h1>@ViewBag.CompanyName</h1>
<div>@ViewBag.CompanyDescription</div>
```

View models

In addition to its basic dictionary behavior, the ViewData object also offers a Model property, which represents the primary object that is the target of the request. Though the ViewData.Model property is conceptually no different from ViewData["Model"], it promotes the model to a first-class citizen and recognizes it as more important than the other data that might be in the request.

For example, the previous two snippets showed that the CompanyName and CompanyDe scription dictionary values are clearly related to each other and represent a great opportunity to wrap together in a model.

Take a look at *CompanyInfo.cs*:

```
public class CompanyInfo
{
    public string Name { get; set; }
    public string Description { get; set; }
}
```

the About action in *HomeController.cs*:

```
public ActionResult About()
{
    ViewBag.Username = User.Identity.Username;

    var company = new CompanyInfo {
        Name = "EBuy: The ASP.NET MVC Demo Site",
```

```
        Description = "EBuy is the world leader in ASP.NET MVC demoing!",
    };

    return View("About", company);
}
```

and this snippet from *About.cshtml*:

```
@{ var company = (CompanyInfo)ViewData.Model; }

<h1>@company.Name</h1>
<div>@company.Description</div>
```

In these snippets, the references to the `CompanyName` and `CompanyDescription` dictionary values have been merged into an instance of a new class named `CompanyInfo` (company). The updated *HomeController.cs* snippet also shows an overload of the `View()` helper method in action. This overload continues to accept the name of the desired view as the first parameter. The second parameter, however, represents the object that will be assigned to the `ViewData.Model` property.

Now, instead of setting the dictionary values directly, `company` is passed as the `model` parameter to the `View()` helper method and the view (*About.cshtml*) can get a local reference to the `company` object and access its values.

Strongly typed views

By default, the `Model` property available within Razor views is `dynamic`, which means that you are able to access its values without needing to know its exact type.

However, given the static nature of the C# language and Visual Studio's excellent IntelliSense support for Razor views, it is often beneficial to specify the type of the page's model explicitly.

Luckily, Razor makes this pretty easy—simply use the `@model` keyword to indicate the model's type name:

```
@model Auction

<h1>@Model.Name</h1>
<div>@Model.Description</div>
```

This example modifies the previous *Auction.cshtml* example, avoiding the need to add an intermediary variable to cast the `ViewData.Model` into. Instead, the first line uses the `@model` keyword to indicate that the model's type is `CompanyInfo`, making all references to `ViewData.Model` strongly typed and directly accessible.

HTML and URL Helpers

The primary goal of most web requests is to deliver HTML to the user, and as such, ASP.NET MVC goes out of its way to help you create HTML. In addition to the Razor markup language, ASP.NET MVC also offers many helpers to generate HTML simply and effectively. The two most important of these helpers are the `HtmlHelper` and `Url Helper` classes, exposed in controllers and views as the `Html` and `Url` properties, respectively.

Here are some examples of the two helpers in action:

```
<img src='@Url.Content("~/Content/images/header.jpg")' />
@Html.ActionLink("Homepage", "Index", "Home")
```

The rendered markup looks like this:

```
<img src='/vdir/Content/images/header.jpg' />
<a href="/vdir/Home/Index">Homepage</a>
```

For the most part, the `HtmlHelper` and `UrlHelper` types don't have many methods of their own and are merely shims that the framework attaches behaviors to via extension methods. This makes them an important extensibility point, and you'll see references to the two types throughout this book.

Though there are far too many methods to list in this section, the one thing to take away at this point is: the `HtmlHelper` class helps you generate HTML markup and the `UrlHelper` class helps you generate URLs. Keep this in mind, and turn to these helpers anytime you need to generate URLs or HTML.

Models

Now that we've covered controllers and views, it's time to complete the definition of MVC by discussing *models*, which are usually considered the most important part of the MVC architecture. If they are so important, why are they the last to be explained? Well, the model layer is notoriously difficult to explain because it is the layer that contains all of the business logic for the application—and that logic is different for every application.

From a more technical standpoint, the model typically consists of normal classes that expose data in the form of properties and logic in the form of methods. These classes come in all shapes and sizes, but the most common example is the "data model" or "domain model," whose primary job is to manage data.

For example, take a look at the following snippet, which shows the `Auction` class—the model that will drive the entire EBuy reference application:

```
public class Auction
{
    public long Id { get; set; }
    public string Title { get; set; }
    public string Description { get; set; }
    public decimal StartPrice { get; set; }
    public decimal CurrentPrice { get; set; }
    public DateTime StartTime { get; set; }
    public DateTime EndTime { get; set; }
}
```

Though we will add various functionality such as validation and behavior to the Auc
tion class throughout this book, this snippet is still very representative of a model in
that it defines the data that makes up an "auction."

And, just as we will build on the Auction class throughout the book, be on the lookout
for more kinds of classes (such as services and helpers) that all work together to make
up the "Model" in "MVC."

Putting It All Together

So far we've described all the parts that make up an ASP.NET MVC application, but
the discussion has focused on the code that Visual Studio generates for us as part of
the project template. In other words, we haven't actually *made* anything yet. So let's
change that!

This section will focus on how to implement a feature from scratch, creating everything
you need to accomplish an example scenario: displaying an auction. As a recap, every
ASP.NET MVC request requires at least three things: a route, a controller action, and
a view (and, optionally, a model).

The Route

To figure out the routing pattern that you'd like to use for a given feature, you must
first determine what you'd like your URL for that feature to look like. In this example
we are going to choose a relatively standard URL of *Auctions/Details/[Auction ID]*; for
example, *http://www.ebuy.biz/Auctions/Details/1234*.

What a nice surprise—the default route configuration already supports this URL!

The Controller

Next, we'll need to create a controller to host the actions that will process the request.

Since controllers are merely classes that implement the ASP.NET MVC controller
interface, you *could* manually add a new class to the *Controllers* folder that derives
from System.Web.Mvc.Controller and begin adding controller actions to that class.
However, Visual Studio offers a bit of tooling to take most of the work out of creating
new controllers: simply right-click on the *Controllers* folder and choose the Add > Con
troller... menu option, which will pop up the Add Controller dialog shown
in Figure 1-8.

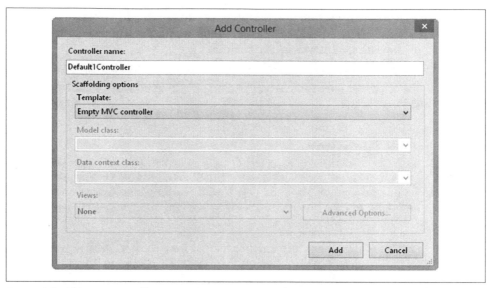

Figure 1-8. Adding a controller to an ASP.NET MVC application

The Add Controller dialog begins by asking for the name of the new controller class (in this case, we'll call it `AuctionsController`) and follows up by asking which scaffolding template you'd like to use, along with providing a set of options to give you a little bit of control over how ASP.NET MVC is going to generate the new controller class.

Controller templates

The Add Controller dialog offers several different controller templates that can help you get started developing your controllers more quickly:

Empty MVC controller
> The default template ("Empty MVC controller") is the simplest one. It doesn't offer any customization options because, well, it's too simple to have any options! It merely creates a new controller with the given name that has a single generated action named `Index`.

MVC controller with read/write actions and views, using Entity Framework
> The "MVC controller with read/write actions and views, using Entity Framework" template is just as impressive as it sounds. This template starts with the same output as the "MVC controller with empty read/write actions" template (see below) and then kicks it up a notch, generating code to help you access objects stored in an Entity Framework context and even generating *Create, Edit, Details*, and *Delete* views for those objects! This template is a great kick-start when your project uses Entity Framework to access your data, and in some cases the code it generates may be all that you need to support the Read, Edit, Update, and Delete operations for that data.

MVC controller with empty read/write actions

The next option—"MVC controller with empty read/write actions"—generates the same code as the "Empty MVC controller" template, but adds a few more actions that you'll most likely need in order to expose standard "data access" operations: `Details`, `Create`, `Edit`, and `Delete`.

API controller templates

The final three templates—"Empty API controller," "API controller with empty read/write actions," and "API controller with read/write actions and views, using Entity Framework"—are the Web API counterparts to the MVC controller templates of the same names. We will cover these templates in more detail when we discuss ASP.NET MVC's Web API functionality in Chapter 6.

An interesting thing to notice about the controller code that Visual Studio generates is that the `Index` and `Details` actions each have only one method, while the `Create`, `Edit`, and `Delete` actions each have two overloads—one decorated with an `HttpPost Attribute`, and one without.

This is because `Create`, `Edit`, and `Delete` all involve two requests in order to complete: the first request returns the view that the user can interact with to create the second request, which actually performs the desired action (creating, editing, or deleting data). This is a very common interaction on the Web, and you'll see several examples of it throughout this book.

Unfortunately, we have not yet reached the point in the book where we are able to use Entity Framework, so for now you can choose the "MVC controller with empty read/ write actions" option and click Add to have Visual Studio generate the next controller class.

After Visual Studio is done creating the `AuctionsController`, find the `Details` action and update it so it creates a new instance of the `Auction` model shown earlier and passes that instance to the view using the `View(object model)` method.

Yes, this is a silly example. Normally, you'd retrieve this information from somewhere such as a database—and we will show you how to do just that in Chapter 4—but for this example, we are using hardcoded values:

```
public ActionResult Details(long id = 0)
{
    var auction = new Ebuy.Website.Models.Auction {
            Id = id,
            Title = "Brand new Widget 2.0",
            Description = "This is a brand new version 2.0 Widget!",
            StartPrice = 1.00m,
            CurrentPrice = 13.40m,
            StartTime = DateTime.Parse("6-15-2012 12:34 PM"),
            EndTime = DateTime.Parse("6-23-2012 12:34 PM"),
        };
```

```
    return View(auction);
}
```

The View

With a `Details` controller action in place and providing data to a view, it's time to create that view.

As with the controller class in the previous section, you are free to manually add new views (and folders to store them in) directly to the *Views* folder; however, if you're the type who prefers a bit more automation, Visual Studio offers yet another wizard to do the work of creating the views—and the folders they live in—for you.

To add a view using the Visual Studio wizard, simply right-click anywhere within the code of the action in a controller and choose the Add View option, which will display the Add View wizard (Figure 1-9). This is actually quite similar to the Add Controller dialog you just used to generate the `AuctionsController`.

Figure 1-9. Adding a view to an ASP.NET MVC application

The Add View dialog starts off by asking what you'd like to call the new view, defaulting to the name of the controller action from which you triggered the dialog (e.g., *Details* when called from the `Details` action). Then, the dialog allows you to choose the syntax (aka "View Engine") that you'd like to use when authoring the view. This value defaults to the syntax you chose when you created the web project, but (as promised earlier) you are free to switch between syntaxes if it suits you, perhaps using Razor for some views and the "ASPX" Web Forms syntax for others.

As in the Add Controller dialog, the rest of the options in the Add View wizard have to do with the code and markup that Visual Studio is going to generate when it creates the new view. For example, you can choose to have a strongly typed view model (as discussed in "Strongly typed views" on page 33) by selecting the model type from the list of classes in your project, or typing the type name in yourself. If you choose a strongly typed view, the wizard also lets you choose a template (e.g., *Edit*, *Create*, *Delete*), which analyzes the model type and generates the appropriate form fields for that type.

This is a great way to get up and running quickly and can save you quite a bit of typing, so let's take advantage of it by checking the "Create a strongly typed view" checkbox, choosing our Auction model from the "Model class" drop-down list, and selecting the Details scaffold template.

 Visual Studio will only include in the "Model class" drop-down classes that it has been able to compile successfully, so if you do not see the Auction class you created earlier, try to compile the solution and then open the Add View dialog again.

Finally, you'll need to tell Visual Studio whether this view is a partial view or should refer to a layout. When you're using the ASPX Web Forms syntax to author your pages and you choose the "Create as a partial view" option, Visual Studio will create it as a User Control (*.ascx*) rather than a full page (*.aspx*). When using the Razor syntax, however, the "Create as a partial view" option has very little effect—Visual Studio creates the same type of file (*.cshtml* or *.vbhtml*) for both partial views and full pages. In the case of Razor syntax, the only effect this checkbox has is on the markup that gets generated inside of the new view.

For the purposes of this demo, you can leave the defaults alone: "Create as a partial view" should remain unchecked, while "Use a layout or master page" should be checked, with the layout text box left empty (see Figure 1-10).

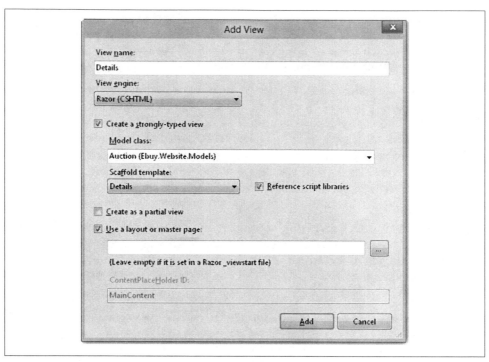

Figure 1-10. Customizing your view

When you're ready, click the Add button to have Visual Studio add the new view to your project. After it's finished, you will see that Visual Studio has analyzed the Auc tion model and generated the required HTML markup—complete with references to HTML helpers such as Html.DisplayFor—to display all of the Auction fields.

At this point, you should be able to run your site, navigate to the controller action (e.g., /auctions/details/1234), and see the details of the Auction object rendered in your browser, as shown in Figure 1-11.

It sure isn't pretty, but remember, the HTML that Visual Studio generates is just a starting point to help you save time. Once it's generated, you can feel free to change it however you like.

Congratulations—you have just created your first controller action and view from scratch!

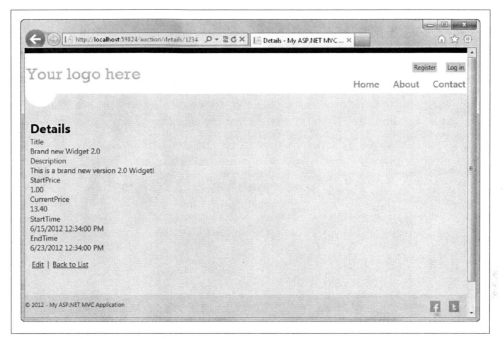

Figure 1-11. The new view rendered in a browser

Authentication

So far we've covered just about everything you need to know in order to create an ASP.NET MVC application, but there is one more very important concept that you should know about before you continue with the rest of the book: how to protect your site by requiring users to authenticate themselves before they can access certain controller actions.

You may have noticed that the Internet Application template generates an `AccountController`—along with some views to support it—which provides a full implementation of forms authentication right out of the box. This is an acknowledgment that security and authentication are crucial to just about every web application and that, at some point, you'll probably want to lock down some or all of your site to restrict access to specific users (or groups of users) and prevent unauthorized access by all other visitors. So, since you'll most likely need it anyway, why shouldn't Visual Studio generate the controller and views to get you started?

The traditional tactic used to lock down ASP.NET applications is to apply authorization settings to specific pages or directories via *web.config* configuration settings. Unfortunately, this approach does not work in ASP.NET MVC applications because ASP.NET MVC applications rely on routing to controller actions, not to physical pages.

Instead, the ASP.NET MVC Framework provides the `AuthorizeAttribute`, which can be applied to individual controller actions—or even entire controllers—to restrict access only to authenticated users or, alternatively, to specific users and user roles.

Take a look at the `Profile` action on the `UsersController` that we'll create later in the book, which displays the profile information for the current user:

```
public class UsersController
{
    public ActionResult Profile()
    {
        var user = _repository.GetUserByUsername(User.Identity.Name);
        return View("Profile", user);
    }
}
```

Clearly, this action will fail if the user is not logged in. Applying the `AuthorizeAttri bute` to this controller action causes any requests made to this action by users who are not authenticated to be rejected:

```
public class UsersController
{
    [Authorize]
    public ActionResult Profile()
    {
        var user = _repository.GetUserByUsername(User.Identity.Name);
        return View("Profile", user);
    }
}
```

If you'd like to be even more specific about the users who can access the controller action, the `AuthorizeAttribute` exposes the `Users` property, which accepts a comma-delimited whitelist of acceptable usernames, as well as the `Roles` property, which accepts a list of allowed roles.

Now, when nonauthenticated users attempt to access this URL, they will instead be redirected to the login URL: the `Login` action on the `AccountController`.

The AccountController

In order to help you get a jump-start on your application, the ASP.NET MVC Internet Application project template includes the `AccountController`, which contains controller actions that leverage the ASP.NET Membership Providers.

The `AccountController` provides quite a bit of functionality out of the box, along with the views to support each controller action. This means that your brand new ASP.NET

MVC application already contains the following fully implemented features, without any coding on your part:

- Login
- Logoff
- New user registration
- Change password

Thus, when you apply the `AuthorizeAttribute` to any of your controller actions, users are redirected to the existing login page that the project template creates for you (see Figure 1-12).

Figure 1-12. The default login page

And, when users need to create a new account in order to log in, they can click the Register link to view the prebuilt Registration page (Figure 1-13).

Plus, if you don't like the out-of-the-box views, they are easily customizable to meet your needs.

As this section shows, not only does the ASP.NET MVC Framework make it very easy to protect controller actions, but the default project template implements just about everything users will need to authenticate themselves on your site!

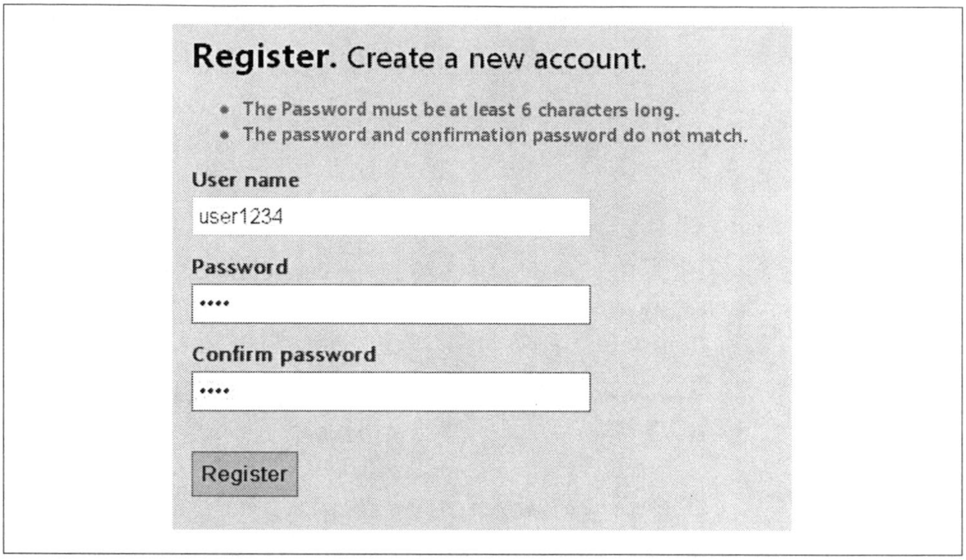

Figure 1-13. The default registration page

Summary

ASP.NET MVC leverages the time-tested Model-View-Controller architecture pattern to provide a website development framework that encourages loosely coupled architecture and many other popular object-oriented programming patterns and practices.

The ASP.NET MVC Framework gets you on the ground running right from the start with helpful project templates and a "convention over configuration" approach that cuts down on the amount of configuration required to create and maintain your application, freeing up more of your time so you can be more productive in getting your application completed and out the door.

This chapter introduced you to the fundamental concepts and basic skills that you need in order to get up and running building ASP.NET MVC 4 applications. The rest of this book will expand on this foundation, showing more features that the ASP.NET MVC Framework has to offer to help you build robust, maintainable web applications using the MVC architectural pattern.

So, what are you waiting for? Keep reading and learn everything you need to know to build the greatest web applications you've ever written!

## CHAPTER 2

ASP.NET MVC for Web Forms Developers

Even though their architectural approaches are quite different, ASP.NET MVC and Web Forms actually have a lot in common. After all, they are both built on top of the core ASP.NET APIs and the .NET Framework. So, if you are a Web Forms developer looking to learn the ASP.NET MVC Framework, you're already further ahead than you may think!

In this chapter, we'll compare and contrast the ASP.NET MVC and Web Forms Frameworks to show how many of the concepts you use to build Web Forms applications relate to the ASP.NET MVC way of doing things. Note that this chapter is geared toward helping developers who are very familiar with the Web Forms Framework and want to translate that knowledge over to ASP.NET MVC to get up and running more quickly. If you are not very familiar with the Web Forms Framework, you may consider skipping this chapter and moving along to the rest of the book.

It's All Just ASP.NET

You may not have known it, but the framework you've been using to develop web pages using the .NET Framework—what you probably call "ASP.NET"—can actually be broken down into two parts: the visual user interface components (aka "Web Forms") and the nonvisual "backend" web components (aka "ASP.NET"). The two parts are most easily broken down by their .NET namespaces: everything under the `System.Web.UI.*` namespaces can be considered "Web Forms" and the rest of the `System.Web.*` namespaces can be considered "ASP.NET."

Like Web Forms, ASP.NET MVC (whose classes fall under the `System.Web.Mvc.*` namespace) is built on top of the strong shoulders of the ASP.NET platform. As such, the two frameworks can be both very similar and incredibly different, depending on how you look at them. This section examines the similarities between the two frameworks, while the rest of the chapter continues on to expose their numerous differences.

Tools, Languages, and APIs

For starters, both frameworks have access to the full extent of the .NET Framework and everything it has to offer. Naturally, both frameworks rely on the .NET languages of C# and Visual Basic .NET to interact with the .NET Framework, and can access compiled assemblies developed with any other language that the .NET Framework supports.

As a nice side effect, this feature makes your existing ASP.NET code highly reusable. For instance, if you have an existing Web Forms application that accesses data stored in XML files via the System.Xml API, you'll most likely be able to reuse this code in an ASP.NET MVC application with little or no modification.

It should also come as no surprise that you'll use Visual Studio to edit ASP.NET MVC websites and the projects they depend on, just like working with Web Forms applications (or any other .NET-based applications). You may even notice a few common artifacts, such as *web.config* and *Global.asax*, both of which play a large role in both ASP.NET MVC and Web Forms applications.

HTTP Handlers and Modules

Perhaps the most notable parts of the .NET Framework that ASP.NET MVC and Web Forms share are *HTTP handlers* and *HTTP modules*. And, even though most classes in the Web Forms API (the System.Web.UI namespace) simply won't work in an ASP.NET MVC application, HTTP handlers and modules are actually part of the core ASP.NET (System.Web) API, so they are still quite functional in the context of an ASP.NET MVC application. In fact, the ASP.NET MVC pipeline itself starts out by handling incoming requests with an HTTP handler!

> Be sure to read about all of the differences between the ASP.NET MVC and Web Forms Frameworks in this chapter and consider how they apply to HTTP handlers and modules. Though HTTP handlers and modules themselves function just fine in an ASP.NET MVC application, keep in mind that there are certain aspects—such as View State—that will not work as expected.

Managing State

Managing state—the data related to a user—is an important part of any application, and the stateless nature of the Web makes this a particularly complex task within web applications.

To help deal with state management, ASP.NET Web Forms uses the *View State* mechanism, wherein state data for a request is serialized and stored in a hidden form field that gets posted back to the server with every subsequent request. View State is such a critical part of the Web Forms platform that nearly every page and component in the framework relies on it at some point. The View State abstraction also has its detriments, though, not the least of which is the fact that every request that contains View State must be a form post and that the potential size of the data in this field—data that is often not even necessary—can become quite large if it is not properly used.

As "State Management" on page 49 explains, ASP.NET MVC's approach to state management is dramatically different, and in most cases, it leaves state management up to the developer to implement (or not). Most importantly, however, ASP.NET MVC deserts View State completely.

Luckily, the ASP.NET platform offers several state management techniques in addition to View State that continue to work in exactly the same way in ASP.NET MVC. Feel free to use the ASP.NET cache and session state, or even the HttpContext.Items APIs, just as you always have to help manage state in ASP.NET MVC applications.

Deployment and Runtime

ASP.NET MVC websites get deployed to the same kind of production environment as Web Forms applications. This means that just about everything you've already learned about deploying and maintaining an ASP.NET application—e.g., to do with Internet Information Server (IIS), .NET application pools, tracing, troubleshooting, and even deploying assemblies' *bin* folders—continues to be quite relevant to deploying and maintaining ASP.NET MVC applications. Though ASP.NET MVC and Web Forms applications follow quite different architectures, in the end it's all .NET code that gets deployed and executed to process HTTP requests.

More Differences than Similarities

The number of similarities that the previous section pointed out may have you thinking that ASP.NET MVC and Web Forms seem almost like the same framework. As you analyze the two frameworks more deeply, however, it becomes quite clear that they are much more different than their numerous similarities make them seem.

Table 2-1 illustrates this fact, comparing and contrasting a number of the frameworks' core components.

Table 2-1. Fundamental differences between ASP.NET MVC and Web Forms

Web Forms	ASP.NET MVC
Views tightly coupled to logic	View and logic kept very separate
Pages (file-based URLs)	Controllers (route-based URLs)
State management (View State)	No automatic state management
Web Forms syntax	Customizable syntax (Razor as default)
Server controls	HTML helpers

Web Forms	ASP.NET MVC
Master pages	Layouts
User controls	Partial views

 Please note that—especially since both frameworks are built on top of the ASP.NET platform—in many ways it is quite possible to make Web Forms behave more like ASP.NET MVC, and vice versa. That is to say, you are certainly able to apply many MVC techniques to Web Forms applications, and vice versa.

However, keep in mind that the comparisons made throughout this chapter refer to the standard development practices for each framework, i.e., the way you see things done in "official" channels such as the API documentation and tutorials.

Separation of Application Logic and View Logic

The most important difference between ASP.NET MVC and Web Forms is the fundamental architectural concepts they each employ.

For instance, Web Forms was introduced (ironically enough) to provide a better separation of concerns than its predecessor, the ASP Framework, which effectively forced developers to combine their business logic and markup in one single file. Web Forms not only gave developers the ability to separate their business logic from their markup, it also provided a much more powerful development platform—the .NET Framework—in which to write the code that drove that business logic. But despite all of the advantages that Web Forms provided over traditional ASP scripts, the Web Forms architecture is still very much focused on "the page"; though the code is moved to another location, it is still quite difficult to truly separate the business logic that handles a request from the view that the user sees.

ASP.NET MVC, on the other hand, is built from the ground up on the concept of separation of concerns driven by loosely coupled components that work together to process a request. This approach not only benefits the development lifecycle by increasing the ability to develop individual components in relative isolation, as well as the ability to test those components, but it also provides the ability to handle requests much more dynamically, as the next section demonstrates.

URLs and Routing

Under the Web Forms architecture, every one of a website's external URLs is represented by a physical *.aspx* page, and each of those pages is tightly coupled to a single optional class (aka "code-behind") that contains the logic for the page. Pages cannot dynamically choose the class they are bound to, and code-behind classes cannot render alternate views.

The Web Forms page-based approach stands in stark contrast to the way that ASP.NET MVC handles requests, relying instead on potentially complex routing rules to dynamically map external URLs to the appropriate controller actions and allowing the controller action logic to dictate which view will be displayed to the user.

For instance, the pipeline may respond differently to a user navigating to the URL /auctions/details/123 in her browser than it responds to an AJAX request to that same URL, simply based on the fact that the AJAX request contains a special header that identifies it as an AJAX request. In the case of the user navigating directly to the URL, the server may return a full web page complete with HTML, JavaScript, and CSS, whereas the server may respond to the AJAX request with only the serialized data for the requested Auction and nothing more. What's more, the server may even choose to serialize the Auction data in different formats—e.g., JSON or XML—based on aspects of the request such as the value of a query string parameter.

This kind of dynamic processing is simply not something that the Web Forms Framework easily supports without resorting to the use of HTTP modules or HTTP handlers.

 ASP.NET's routing functionality is not limited to ASP.NET MVC applications—it can also be used to customize the URLs in a Web Forms application.

The primary difference between the two uses is that routing is such a critical component in the ASAP.NET MVC architecture that the framework could not operate without it, whereas Web Forms applications primarily use routing to avoid page file path restrictions and to gain better control over their URLs.

State Management

Perhaps the most controversial difference between Web Forms and ASP.NET MVC is how they each handle the user's state across requests—specifically, ASP.NET MVC ditches View State. How can something so fundamental be completely removed? The short answer is that ASP.NET MVC embraces the stateless nature of the Web. However, to gain a better idea of what this really means, let's revisit the history of Web Forms one more time.

In addition to providing a better development platform than ASP, one of the original goals for the Web Forms Framework was to bring "thick," native client application development techniques—such as "drag and drop" and other Rapid Application Development (RAD) concepts—to the Web.

In order to bring the Web and native client development experiences closer together, Web Forms had to create a layer of abstraction on top of fundamental web development concepts such as HTML markup and styling. One of the most significant concepts in native application development is that a native application is *stateful*, which means that the application is aware of the state of its interaction with the user and can even persist that state in order to reuse it across instances of the application.

The Web, on the other hand, is based on HTTP requests, with each request involving a single client request and a single server response. A web server must handle every HTTP request in isolation, unaware of any previous or future messages that may be exchanged with a given client—in effect, preventing the server and the client from having an on-going conversation in which the server is able to remember its previous interactions with the client.

In order to apply stateful interactions across a stateless medium, an abstraction must be applied—thus View State was born. Simply put, View State serializes the state of the interaction between the client and the server and stores that information in a hidden form field on every page that the server sends to the client. It's then the client's responsibility to pass along this serialized state on every subsequent request in the conversation.

Rather than attempt to duplicate this abstraction, ASP.NET MVC embraces the stateless nature of the Web and provides no out-of-the-box alternative to View State other than server-side techniques such as caching and session state. Instead, ASP.NET MVC expects requests to include all the data that the server needs in order to process them. For instance, rather than retrieving an Auction from the database and serializing the whole object down to the client so the client can send the Auction object back during subsequent requests, ASP.NET MVC responses might reply with simply the Auction's ID. Then, subsequent requests will include just the Auction's ID, which the ASP.NET MVC controller processing the request uses to retrieve the Auction from the database for each request.

Clearly, both approaches have their benefits and trade-offs. Whereas View State makes many ongoing client interactions much simpler, the data contained within it can quickly and easily become unwieldy, using up a significant amount of bandwidth for data that may never be used. In other words, View State is meant to make developers' lives easier without their having to think about it, but it comes at the cost of increased bandwidth, particularly when developers do not stop to consider what data their pages are storing.

ASP.NET MVC's approach, on the other hand, may decrease page sizes, but at the cost of increased backend processing and (perhaps) database requests in order to fully rehydrate the request's state on the server.

Rendering HTML

Every website is different, but one thing all websites have in common is that their need to generate HTML. One of the primary requirements for any web application framework is the ability to help developers render that HTML as productively as possible. Both ASP.NET MVC and Web Forms do this very well—but they do so in drastically different ways.

Web Forms views are easily distinguishable at a glance; just about everything in Web Forms views—from <label> tags to partially rendered AJAX sections—uses server tags to render HTML.

For instance, here's an example of the HTML view of a typical Web Forms page:

```
<%@ Page Title="EBuy Auction Listings" Language="C#" AutoEventWireup="true"
    MasterPageFile="~/Layout.master"
    CodeBehind="Default.aspx.cs" Inherits="EBuy.Website._Default" %>
<%@ Register TagPrefix="uc" TagName="SecondaryActions"
    Src="~/Controls/SecondaryActions.ascx" %>

<asp:Content ID="HeaderContent" runat="server" ContentPlaceHolderID="HeadContent">
    <uc:SecondaryActions runat="server" />
</asp:Content>

<asp:Content ID="BodyContent" runat="server" ContentPlaceHolderID="MainContent">

<div class="container">
    <header>
        <h3>Auctions</h3>
    </header>

    <asp:Repeater id="auctions" runat="server" DataSource="<%# Auctions %>">

    <HeaderTemplate>
        <ul id="auctions">
    </HeaderTemplate>

    <ItemTemplate>
        <li>
        <h4 class="title">
        <asp:HyperLink runat="server"
            NavigateUrl='<%# DataBinder.Eval(Container.DataItem, "Url") %>'>
            <%# Container.DataItem("title") %>
        </asp:HyperLink>
        </h4>
        </li>
    </ItemTemplate>

    <FooterTemplate>
        </ul>
    </FooterTemplate>

    </asp:Repeater>

</div>

<script type="text/javascript"
        src="<%: RelativeUrl("~/scripts/jquery.js") %>"></script>
</asp:Content>
```

Now, compare that view to its Razor equivalent:

```
@model IEnumerable<Auction>
```

```
@{
    ViewBag.Title = "EBuy Auction Listings";
}

@section HeaderContent {
    @Html.Partial("SecondaryActions")
}

<div class="container">
    <header>
        <h3>Auctions</h3>
    </header>

    <ul id="auctions">

    @foreach(var auction in Model.Auctions) {
        <li>
            <h4 class="title">
                <a href="@auction.Url">@auction.Title</a>
            </h4>
        </li>
    }

    </ul>
</div>

<script type="text/javascript" src="~/scripts/jquery.js"></script>
```

Both examples effectively render the same HTML, though they do it in very different ways.

Notice how Razor takes a much more code-focused approach to HTML generation, relying on code constructs like foreach loops rather than on special server-side HTML tags such as the <asp:Repeater> control.

For instance, compare how Web Forms and Razor each render a simple anchor tag to an arbitrary URL. Here's how it's done in Web Forms:

```
<asp:HyperLink runat="server" NavigateUrl='<%# auction.Url %>'>
    <%: auction.Title %>
</asp:HyperLink>
```

And in Razor:

```
<a href="@auction.Url">@auction.Title</a>
```

These two examples are representative of the differences in the approaches of the two frameworks: Razor helps developers write HTML themselves, whereas Web Forms views lean on declarative markup on server controls to render HTML for them.

HTML helpers versus server controls

Let's revisit that last sentence for a second, because it's pretty important. Using the Web Forms abstraction, it is actually possible to write an entire web page without writing any HTML by using the full suite of *server controls*—HTML-rendering components exposed in the form of declarative markup (such as the `<asp:Hyperlink>` tag shown earlier) that the framework provides out of the box in order to take care of most HTML needs.

Meanwhile, ASP.NET MVC's approach to rendering markup is nearly the opposite of the Web Forms approach, because it expects developers to write the bulk of the HTML that gets sent to the browser. This doesn't mean that ASP.NET MVC can't help generate some of that HTML, however. It does this through *HTML helpers*—HTML-rendering logic exposed via *extension methods* that developers can call in their views to generate HTML where it's needed.

Logically, HTML helpers and server controls are practically the same: they are both code-based components that are executed within a view in order to generate HTML so developers don't have to write it themselves.

The primary difference between HTML helpers and server controls comes in the technical implementation: whereas server controls are full-blown classes that derive from a particular base class, HTML helpers are exposed in the form of extension methods that extend the `HtmlHelper` object present in ASP.NET MVC views.

Yet another important difference between HTML helpers and server controls is something that we've covered a few times in this chapter already: most server controls leverage View State in some way, whereas HTML helpers must function without it.

Outside of these differences, most of the common server controls that you're used to using have an HTML helper equivalent.

As opposed to the Web Forms `<asp:HyperLink>` tag, for instance, ASP.NET MVC offers the `Html.ActionLink()` method. For example:

```
@Html.ActionLink(auction.Title, "Details", "Auction")
```

In this example we are passing three parameters to the `Html.ActionLink()` method—the text to display to the user, and the names of the action ("Details") and controller ("Auction") that should be used to build the URL—which renders the following:

```
<a href="/Auction/Details/">My Auction Title</a>
```

Unlike Web Forms, ASP.NET MVC doesn't offer HTML helpers to generate all your markup, but it does provide helpers to address the majority of nontrivial markup generation scenarios.

 In the same manner as Web Forms server controls, you are free to create your own HTML helpers in order to encapsulate bits of highly reusable rendering logic.

Partial views versus user controls

Just as HTML helpers are equivalent to Web Forms server controls, ASP.NET MVC *partial views* and Web Forms *user controls* are essentially the same thing: sections of a view that are stored in separate files, allowing developers to break one view into many smaller views and then reassemble them by combining them at runtime. Like user controls, partial views offer a great way to encapsulate portions of a view, and even to reuse those sections in multiple views.

Layouts versus master pages

Finally, we come to one of the most important and fundamental view concepts of all: the ability to define the structure, layout, and overall theme of a site and share that definition with all of the pages in the site. Yes, we're referring to *master pages*, or as they are called in the ASP.NET MVC world, *layouts*.

ASP.NET MVC layouts let developers specify a bunch of HTML that will be wrapped around the content on every page. Like master pages, ASP.NET MVC layouts allow developers to specify the content in multiple sections of the page. And, like Web Forms content pages, ASP.NET MVC views typically indicate which layout they expect to render within, but there is one major difference: this setting merely acts as a "recommendation" to the ASP.NET MVC pipeline, which is free to change the view's layout to whatever it likes—including removing it completely to render the view without a layout at all (as in the case of an AJAX request).

Authoring ASP.NET MVC Views Using Web Forms Syntax

Now that we're reaching the end of the chapter, it's time to let you in on a secret we've been keeping from you: Razor is not the only way to author ASP.NET MVC views. In fact, if you're not quite ready to leave behind your Web Forms roots completely, ASP.NET MVC gives you the option to continue writing ASP.NET MVC views using the Web Forms syntax.

Now, before you get too excited about the prospect, keep in mind that you'll only be using the Web Forms *syntax* and not the Web Forms *Framework*. In other words, everything in this chapter remains true no matter which syntax you are using: URL routes still choose which controllers to run, which in turn choose which view to display; ASP.NET server controls still will not work as you expect them to and, perhaps most important, `ViewState` will remain unpopulated.

What all that really means is that authoring ASP.NET MVC views using the Web Forms syntax effectively just means using the `<% %>` code syntax (as opposed to Razor's @ syntax) within *.aspx*, *.ascx*, and even master files (*.master*). Master pages are the exception to this rule, however—they continue to work almost exactly as they work in Web Forms applications, so ASP.NET MVC views can still take advantage of separating site-wide markup from markup generated by individual content pages.

Not only does ASP.NET MVC support views in both Razor and Web Forms syntax, you can even mix and match them! For instance, a Razor view may call `@Html.Partial("MyPartial")`, referring to the *MyPartial* view, which happens to be a Web Forms user control. However, you cannot mix and match layout styles: the Razor layout and Web Forms master pages approaches are not compatible with each other, which means that Razor views cannot refer to Web Forms master pages, and Web Forms content pages cannot refer to Razor layouts.

A Word of Caution

Although we've spent the bulk of this chapter discussing how much of your current Web Forms skill set you'll be able to use when you start using ASP.NET MVC, you need to consider that there is a downside to learning ASP.NET MVC after building years of experience with Web Forms: for all of their commonality and similarities, the architecture and goals that drive the ASP.NET MVC and Web Forms Frameworks are fundamentally very different. And this can create problems if you are used to doing things "the Web Forms way" and then you try to apply those approaches to ASP.NET MVC.

As discussed earlier, the most important and "dangerous" difference between the frameworks is that Web Forms tries its hardest to introduce and maintain state, while ASP.NET MVC does not. From a technical standpoint, what this boils down to is that you no longer have View State when you move from Web Forms to ASP.NET MVC, and most of those "stateful" things that Web Forms does for you will not work.

Likewise, you need to be mindful of what kinds of things you were putting into View State to begin with. Oftentimes, the convenience of View State turns it into a dumping ground for data that will be reused across requests. When this is the case, you may need to figure out "the ASP.NET MVC way" to accomplish the same task and find other places to temporarily persist this data, such as *session state* or the *application cache*.

The next-largest difference is the way that you author view markup. Whereas Web Forms relies on tag-based server controls and user controls, ASP.NET MVC leverages HTML helpers and partial views. While conceptually very similar, the two approaches are not interchangeable and they should not (and often *cannot*) be mixed together.

Using the Razor syntax helps to avoid this issue by making it very obvious that you are not writing Web Forms pages. However, ASP.NET does offer the *ASPX view engine*, which lets you use the Web Forms syntax to create ASP.NET MVC views. While the ASPX view engine does a fine job at rendering HTML, if you are not careful you may find yourself trying to use parts of the Web Forms Framework—much to your chagrin. To avoid confusion by showing something that looks like Web Forms, all views shown in this book will use the Razor syntax.

Though they are very real concerns, these issues should not keep you from learning and using ASP.NET MVC, or even from using the ASPX view engine if you feel more comfortable with the Web Forms syntax. Just keep in mind the concepts mentioned in this chapter as you implement ASP.NET MVC functionality. If you keep asking yourself, "Does this fit into the MVC approach?" or "Am I using the features of the ASP.NET MVC framework to their full extent?" you should be able to fully capitalize on your Web Forms skill set while avoiding these mistakes.

Summary

Because the ASP.NET MVC and Web Forms Frameworks share such a common base, Web Forms developers have a real leg up when it comes to learning ASP.NET MVC. This chapter demonstrated the similarities in the two frameworks, while also showcasing how differently they handle certain scenarios. Later in the book, Appendix A will show you how to capitalize on the core functionality the frameworks share, with examples of how to easily migrate and port existing Web Forms applications to ASP.NET MVC.

## CHAPTER 3

Working with Data

It's rare to find an application that doesn't deal with data in some way, so it's probably no surprise that ASP.NET MVC provides excellent support at all levels of the framework to make working with data much easier. In this chapter, we'll take a look at the tools that provide that support and show you how to leverage them in your data-driven scenarios by adding this functionality to the EBuy reference application.

Since EBuy is an auction site, the site's most important scenario is allowing users to create auction listings that contain the details of the items they would like to sell. So, let's take a look at how ASP.NET MVC can help us support this important scenario.

Building a Form

The concept of an HTML form is as old as the Web itself. Though browsers have gotten more advanced, to the point that you can style an HTML form to look just about any way you like and apply JavaScript to make it behave in ways you wouldn't have believed possible five years ago, underneath it all is still just a bunch of plain old form fields ready to be populated and posted back to the server.

While ASP.NET MVC encourages you to author much of your HTML markup "by hand," the framework offers an array of HTML helpers to help generate HTML form markup, such as `Html.TextBox`, `Html.Password`, and `Html.HiddenField`, just to name a few. ASP.NET MVC also offers a few "smarter" helpers, such as `Html.LabelFor` and `Html.EditorFor`, that dynamically determine the appropriate HTML based on the name and type of the model property that is passed in.

It's these helpers that we'll leverage in the sample EBuy website to build the HTML form that allows users to post to the `AuctionsController.Create` action to create new auctions. To see these helpers in action, add a new view called *Create.cshtml* and populate it with the following markup:

```
<h2>Create Auction</h2>

@using (Html.BeginForm()) {
```

```
<p>
    @Html.LabelFor(model => model.Title)
    @Html.EditorFor(model => model.Title)
</p>
<p>
    @Html.LabelFor(model => model.Description)
    @Html.EditorFor(model => model.Description)
</p>
<p>
    @Html.LabelFor(model => model.StartPrice)
    @Html.EditorFor(model => model.StartPrice)
</p>
<p>
    @Html.LabelFor(model => model.EndTime)
    @Html.EditorFor(model => model.EndTime)
</p>
<p>
    <input type="submit" value="Create" />
</p>
}
```

Then add the following actions to the controller to render this view:

```
[HttpGet]
public ActionResult Create()
{
  return View();
}
```

This view renders the following HTML to the browser:

```
<h2>Create Auction</h2>

<form action="/auction/create" method="post">
    <p>
        <label for="Title">Title</label>
        <input id="Title" name="Title" type="text" value="">
    </p>
    <p>
        <label for="Description">Description</label>
        <input id="Description" name="Description" type="text" value="">
    </p>
    <p>
        <label for="StartPrice">StartPrice</label>
        <input id="StartPrice" name="StartPrice" type="text" value="">
    </p>
    <p>
        <label for="EndTime">EndTime</label>
        <input id="EndTime" name="EndTime" type="text" value="">
    </p>
    <p>
        <input type="submit" value="Create">
    </p>
</form>
```

The user can then populate the values in this form and submit it to the */auctions/create* action. Though from the browser's point of view it seems like the form is posting back to itself (the URL to render this form initially is also */auctions/create*), this is where the second Create controller action with the HttpPostAttribute comes into play, telling ASP.NET MVC that it is this overload that handles the POST action of a form post.

Once you've verified all this, it's time to actually *do* something with those submitted form values—but what?

Handling Form Posts

Before you can work with values that are getting posted to a controller, you first need to retrieve them from the request. As you may remember from "Action Parameters" on page 21, the simplest way is to use a model as an action parameter and, lucky for us, we happen to have created a model already: refer back to the Auction class from "Models" on page 34.

To bind to the Auction class we created earlier, simply specify a parameter of type Auction as one of the Create controller action's parameters:

```
[HttpPost]
public ActionResult Create(Auction auction)
{
    // Create Auction in database

    return View(auction);
}
```

The most important aspect of the Auction model at this point is the fact that the property names (Title, Description, etc.) match the form field names that get posted to the Create action. These property names are crucial, as ASP.NET MVC model binding attempts to populate their values from the form fields with matching names.

If you run the application, submit your form post, and refresh the page, you'll see that the Auction model is populated with the values that you entered. For now, the action just returns the populated auction parameter back to the view, which you might use to display the form values back to the user to confirm his submission.

This is helpful because it gets us one step closer to actually achieving something useful with our application, but there is still more that we need to do, starting with actually *saving* the data.

Saving Data to a Database

Though the ASP.NET MVC Framework does not have any kind of data access built directly into it, there are many popular .NET data access libraries that can help make working with a database easier.

Microsoft's *Entity Framework*—also known as "EF"—is one such library. Entity Framework is a simple and flexible *object relational mapping* (ORM) framework that helps developers query and update data stored in a database in an object-oriented way. What's more, Entity Framework is actually part of the .NET Framework, with Microsoft's full support and a wealth of available documentation to back it.

Entity Framework offers a few different approaches to define a data model and use that model to access a database, but perhaps the most intriguing technique is an approach labeled *Code First*. Code First development refers to the development mindset wherein your application's model is the central focus and primary driver behind everything that happens during development.

Entity Framework Code First: Convention over Configuration

Using Code First development, database interaction is performed via the simple model classes (aka **P**lain **O**ld **CLR** **O**bjects, or POCOs). Entity Framework's Code First approach even goes so far as to generate a database schema from your model and use that schema to create a database and its entities (tables, relations, etc.) when you run the application.

Code First does this by following certain conventions that automatically evaluate the various properties and classes that make up your model layer to determine how information in those models should be saved and even how the relations between the various model classes can be best represented in terms of database relationships.

For example, in the EBuy reference application, the `Auction` class maps to an *Auctions* database table and each of its properties represent columns in that table. These table and column names are derived automatically from the names of the class and its members.

The `Auction` model shown earlier is pretty simple, but as the needs of our application grow, so will the complexity of our model: we'll add more properties, business logic, and even relationships to other models. This is no concern for Entity Framework Code First, however, because it is usually able to figure out these more complex models just as easily as the simple models. Chapter 8 builds on the simple `Auction` model shown in this chapter to add more realistic complexity and shows how Entity Framework Code First is able cover these more advanced mappings—and also what to do when it can't.

Creating a Data Access Layer with Entity Framework Code First

At the center of the Entity Framework Code First approach lies the `Sys tem.Data.Entity.DbContext` class. It's this class (or, rather, the classes that you create that derive from this class) that acts as your gateway to the database, providing all of the data-related actions you might need.

To begin using the `DbContext` class, you need to create your own class that derives from it, which, as it turns out, is pretty easy:

```
using System.Data.Entity;

public class EbuyDataContext : DbContext
{
    public DbSet<Auction> Auctions { get; set; }
}
```

In this example (*EbuyDataContext.cs*), we created a custom data context class named `EbuyDataContext` that derives from `DbContext`. This particular class defines a `Sys tem.Data.Entity.DbSet<T>` property, where `T` is the *entity* that is going to be edited and saved in the database. In the above example, we defined `System.Data.Entity.DbSet<Auc tion>` to indicate that the application needs to save and edit instances of the `Auction` class in the database. You can define more than one entity in the data context, though, and as we progress, we'll be adding more entities (or `DbSet` properties) to our `EbuyDa taContext` class.

If creating a custom data context is easy, using it is even easier, as the following example demonstrates. The following snippet revises the `Create` controller action to save the posted `Auction` object to the database simply by adding the `Auction` object to the `Ebuy DataContext.Auctions` collection and saving the changes:

```
[HttpPost]
public ActionResult Create(Auction auction)
{
    var db = new EbuyDataContext();
    db.Auctions.Add(auction);
    db.SaveChanges();

    return View(auction);
}
```

This time when you run the application and submit the populated form, the Auctions table in the database will have a new row containing the information posted in the form.

If you continue to play with this example and experiment with some different values in the form fields, you may start to notice that ASP.NET MVC's model binding is very forgiving, letting users enter just about anything and failing silently when it is unable to convert the form post values to strong types (e.g., when the user enters "ABC" to populate an `int` property). If you need more strict control over what kind of data gets saved into your database, you must apply data validation to your model.

Validating Data

When it comes to data, there are usually a number of rules and constraints that apply, such as fields that should never be empty or whose values need to be within a certain range in order to be considered "valid." Naturally, ASP.NET MVC recognizes such an important concept by integrating it right into the processing of each request.

As part of the process of executing a controller action, the ASP.NET MVC Framework validates any data that is passed to that controller action, populating a ModelState object with any validation failures it finds and passing that object to the controller. Then, controller actions can query the ModelState to discover whether the request is valid and react accordingly; for example, saving the valid object to the database, or returning the user back to the original form to correct the validation errors from an invalid request.

Here is an example of AuctionsController.Create updated to check the ModelState dictionary, applying the "save or correct" logic just described:

```
[HttpPost]
public ActionResult Create(Auction auction)
{
    if (ModelState.IsValid)
    {
        var db = new EbuyDataContext();
        db.Auctions.Add(auction);
        db.SaveChanges();
        return RedirectToAction("Index");
    }

    return View(auction);
}
```

Though it does a great job of it, the ASP.NET MVC Framework is not the only thing that can add validation errors to ModelState. Developers are free to execute their own logic to discover issues that the framework doesn't catch and manually add those errors directly using the ModelState.AddModelError(string key, string message) method.

Let's say, for example, that we require auctions to last at least one day. In other words, the auction's EndTime must be greater than the current time + 1 day. The AuctionsController.Create action can explicitly check for this before proceeding in its attempt to save the auction, and save a custom error message should this situation arise:

```
[HttpPost]
public ActionResult Create(Auction auction)
{
    if (auction.EndTime <= DateTime.Now.AddDays(1))
    {
        ModelState.AddModelError(
            "EndTime",
            "Auction must be at least one day long"
        );
    }

    if (ModelState.IsValid)
    {
        var db = new EbuyDataContext();
        db.Auctions.Add(auction);
        db.SaveChanges();
        return RedirectToAction("Index");
    }
```

```
            return View(auction);
    }
```

While this approach works quite well, it does tend to break the application's separation of concerns. Namely, controllers should not contain business logic such as this: business logic belongs in the model. So, let's move the business logic to the model!

Specifying Business Rules with Data Annotations

The practice of ensuring quality data—*data validation*—is such a common application development task that it's only natural for developers to turn to one of the many frameworks available to help them define and execute data validation logic in the most effective way possible.

This need is so common, in fact, that Microsoft ships a very effective and easy-to-use data validation API called *Data Annotations* in the core .NET Framework. As its name implies, the Data Annotations API provides a set of .NET attributes that developers can apply to data object class properties. These attributes offer a very declarative way to apply validation rules directly to a model.

What's more, ASP.NET MVC's model binding provides support for data annotations without any additional configuration. To see ASP.NET MVC data annotation support in action, let's walk through the process of applying validation to the Auction class. To begin applying validation logic, first consider what you'd expect the values of the Auction class's properties to be. Which fields should be required? Do any of the fields have particular ranges that would make them valid or invalid?

Required fields

Since an auction's Title and Description are crucial for describing the item being sold, we'll apply the RequiredAttribute data annotation to those two fields to mark them as fields that are required to have data in order to be considered valid:

```
[Required]
public string Title { get; set; }

[Required]
public string Description { get; set; }
```

In addition to marking a field as "Required," you can also ensure that string values meet a minimum length by applying the StringLengthAttribute. For example, we've decided that auction titles should be kept short, enforcing a maximum of 50 characters:

```
[Required, StringLength(50)]
public string Title { get; set; }
```

Now if a user submits the form with a Title longer than 50 characters, ASP.NET MVC model validation will fail.

Valid ranges

Next, consider the auction's starting price: it's represented by the `StartPrice` property using the `decimal` type. Since `decimal` is a value type, the `StartPrice` property will always at least default to 0, so it is redundant to mark it as a required field. However, auction starting prices have logic beyond just requiring a value: those values must never be negative, because a negative starting price would mean that the seller would owe the *buyer* money! To address this concern, apply the `RangeAttribute` to the `StartPrice` field and specify a minimum value of 1. Since the `RangeAttribute` requires a maximum value, specify an upper limit as well.

```
[Range(1, 10000]
public decimal StartPrice { get; set; }
```

This example shows a range using a `double`, but the `RangeAttribute` annotation also has an overload (`Range(Type type, string min, string max)`) to support a range of any type that implements `IComparable` and can be created by parsing or converting the string values. A good example of this is validating a date range; for instance, guaranteeing that a date is later than a certain point in time:

```
[Range(typeof(DateTime), "1/1/2012", "12/31/9999"]
public DateTime EndTime { get; set; }
```

This example ensures that the value of the `EndTime` property is at least later than January 1, 2012.

> The .NET attribute parameters must be compile-time values and cannot be evaluated at runtime, excluding the use of values such as `Date Time.Now` to ensure a date in the future. Instead, we must settle on picking an arbitrary date such as `1/1/2012`, which may not ensure a date after the time the form value is posted but can at least avoid dates in the distant past.
>
> This lack of accuracy is a trade-off we have chosen to be able to leverage the `RangeAttribute`. If your situation demands greater accuracy, you will have to fall back to the `CustomValidationAttribute`, which enables you to execute arbitrary code to validate properties. While the ability to execute arbitrary code via the `CustomValidatorAttribute` is certainly powerful, it is a less declarative approach that limits the information available to other components, such as the ASP.NET MVC client validation framework.

Custom error messages

Lastly, it's important to note that all of the data annotations provide an `ErrorMessage` property that you can use to specify an error message that will be shown to the user instead of the default error message generated by the Data Annotations API. Go ahead and specify a value for this property for each of the data annotations we've added to the model.

The final class—updated to include all of the data annotations discussed in this section—should look something like this:

```
public class Auction
{
  [Required]
  [StringLength(50,
    ErrorMessage = "Title cannot be longer than 50 characters")]
  public string Title { get; set; }

  [Required]
  public string Description { get; set; }

  [Range(1, 10000,
    ErrorMessage = "The auction's starting price must be at least 1")]
  public decimal StartPrice { get; set; }

  public decimal CurrentPrice { get; set; }
  public DateTime EndTime { get; set; }
}
```

Now that all of the validation logic is safely defined in the model, let's jump back to the controller and view and see how to display these validation errors to the user.

Displaying Validation Errors

You can tell that the validation rules you've added are working by setting a breakpoint in the Create action, submitting invalid values, and inspecting the ModelState property to see that the validation errors are, in fact, getting added. The fact that the controller returns the *Create* view instead of adding the new auction and redirecting you to another page is further proof that your validation rules are correct and the validation framework is working. The problem is, though the *Create* view may show the invalid fields with a red border to show that they are invalid, it still doesn't show any of the error messages to indicate to the user exactly what went wrong. So, let's take care of that!

As a refresher, this is what the markup for the Title property currently looks like:

```
<p>
    @Html.LabelFor(model => model.Title)
    @Html.EditorFor(model => model.Title)
    @ViewData.ModelState["Title"]
</p>
```

What we need to do is add one more line to that markup to display any Title-related validation messages that may occur. The simplest way to find out if the Title property has any validation errors is to query ModelState directly—we can get to it via View Data.ModelState, and ViewData.ModelState["Title"] returns an object that contains a collection of errors that apply to the Title property.

You can then iterate over this collection to render the error messages to the page:

```
<p>
    @Html.LabelFor(model => model.Title)
    @Html.EditorFor(model => model.Title)
    @foreach(var error in ViewData.ModelState["Title"].Errors)
    {
        <span class="error">@error.ErrorMessage</span>
    }
</p>
```

Though this works just fine, ASP.NET MVC offers an even better approach to render all of the errors for a given property: the `Html.ValidationMessage(string modelName)` helper. The `Html.ValidationMessage()` helper lets you replace the entire `foreach` loop shown above with a single method call to accomplish the same result:

```
@Html.ValidationMessageFor(model => model.Title)
```

Add a call to the `Html.ValidationMessage()` for each of the properties in your model. ASP.NET MVC will now render all of the validation issues that may have occurred, right inline with the form fields to which they apply.

In addition to the property-level `Html.ValidationMessage()` helper, ASP.NET MVC also provides the `Html.ValidationSummary()` helper. `Html.ValidationSummary()` lets you render all of the validation exceptions for the form in one place (e.g., at the top of the form), to give the user a summary of all the issues she needs to correct in order to submit the form successfully.

This helper is incredibly simple to use—just make a call to `Html.ValidationSummary()` anywhere you'd like the summary to appear:

```
@using (Html.BeginForm())
{
    @Html.ValidationSummary()

    <p>
        @Html.LabelFor(model => model.Title)
        @Html.EditorFor(model => model.Title)
        @Html.ValidationMessageFor(model => model.Title)
    </p>

    <!-- The rest of the form fields... -->
}
```

Now, when you submit invalid form field values, you'll see any error messages in two places (as in Figure 3-1): in the validation summary (from the call to `Html.Validation Summary()`) and next to the value itself (from the call to `Html.ValidationMessage()`).

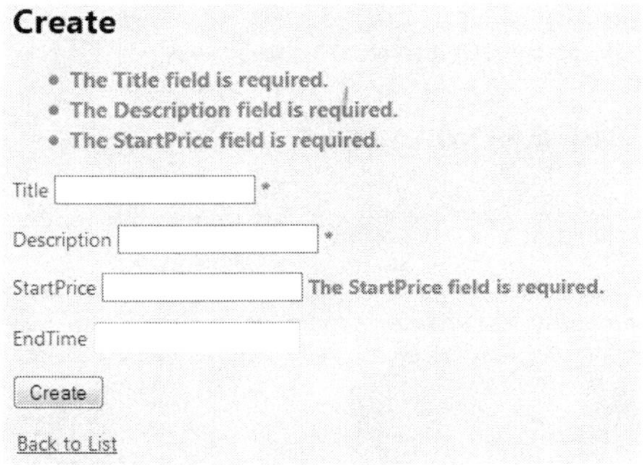

Figure 3-1. Showing errors via the Html.ValidationSummary() helper

If you'd like to avoid displaying duplicate error messages, you can modify the calls to `Html.ValidationMessage()` and specify a shorter, custom error message such as a simple asterisk:

```
<p>
    @Html.LabelFor(model => model.Title)
    @Html.EditorFor(model => model.Title)
    @Html.ValidationMessageFor(model => model.Title, "*")
</p>
```

Here is the full markup for the *Create* view after we've applied all of the validation markup:

```
<h2>Create Auction</h2>

@using (Html.BeginForm())
{
    @Html.ValidationSummary()

    <p>
        @Html.LabelFor(model => model.Title)
        @Html.EditorFor(model => model.Title)
        @Html.ValidationMessageFor(model => model.Title, "*")
    </p>
    <p>
        @Html.LabelFor(model => model.Description)
        @Html.EditorFor(model => model.Description)
        @Html.ValidationMessageFor(model => model.Description, "*")
    </p>
    <p>
        @Html.LabelFor(model => model.StartPrice)
        @Html.EditorFor(model => model.StartPrice)
        @Html.ValidationMessageFor(model => model.StartPrice)
    </p>
    <p>
```

```
        @Html.LabelFor(model => model.EndTime)
        @Html.EditorFor(model => model.EndTime)
        @Html.ValidationMessageFor(model => model.EndTime)
    </p>
    <p>
        <input type="submit" value="Create" />
    </p>
}
```

All of the validation shown thus far is *server-side validation*, requiring a full round-trip between the browser and the server and requiring the server to process each potentially invalid request and respond with a fully rendered view.

While this approach works, it is certainly not optimal. Chapter 4 shows how to implement *client-side validation* to take this approach one step further and perform most—if not all—of the validation right in the browser. This avoids any additional requests to the server, saving both bandwidth and server resources.

Summary

In this chapter, we talked about using the Entity Framework Code First approach to create and maintain the application's database. You saw how easy it is with Entity Framework to set up the database through a few lines of code, without having to draw a schema diagram first or write SQL queries to model and create the database. We talked about how Entity Framework works automagically by following conventions and what some the basic conventions are. We also touched upon taking advantage of ASP.NET MVC's model binder feature to automatically populate the state objects from the incoming request.

## CHAPTER 4

Client-Side Development

The Internet has come a long way from web pages consisting of simple HTML markup and JavaScript. Popular web applications such as Gmail and Facebook have transformed users' expectations of websites: they are no longer satisfied with basic text but instead demand rich, interactive experiences that rival those provided by native desktop applications. As users' demands grow, modern browsers fight to keep up and do their best to implement features and specifications—such as HTML 5 and CSS3—that make these kinds of applications possible.

Though most of this book focuses on the server-side aspects of developing web applications with the ASP.NET MVC Framework, this chapter takes a break to explore the fundamentals of creating rich web applications, showing how to use *jQuery* library to simplify client-side development.

Working with JavaScript

Browser incompatibilities have plagued web developers for decades. The differences in functionality and lack of standards between browsers have given rise to numerous client-side libraries and frameworks that attempt to address these problems by abstracting away the differences between browsers to provide a truly standard cross-browser API.

Emerging as the overwhelming favorite of these numerous libraries is the jQuery JavaScript Library (*http://jquery.com*), which, following its mantra of "Write less, Do more," greatly simplifies HTML Document Object Model (DOM) traversal, event handling, animation, and AJAX interactions. As of version 3 of the ASP.NET MVC Framework, the jQuery Library is included in the ASP.NET MVC web application project templates, making it quite easy to get up and running and leverage jQuery with minimum work.

To see how jQuery helps abstract browser inconsistencies, take a look at the following code, which tries to find out the width and the height of the browser window:

```
var innerWidth = window.innerWidth,
    innerHeight = window.innerHeight;
```

```
alert("InnerWidth of the window is: " + innerWidth);
alert("InnerHeight of the window is: " + innerHeight);
```

This script shows `alert` dialogs with the correct height and width in most browsers, but it will throw an error in Internet Explorer 6-8. Why? Well, it turns out that these versions of Internet Explorer (IE) provide the same information with `document.DocumentElement.clientWidth` and `document.DocumentElement.clientHeight` properties instead.

So, in order to make this snippet of code work properly across all browsers, it must be tweaked to address IE's inconsistency, as shown in the following listing:

```
var innerWidth, innerHeight;

// all browsers except IE < 9
if (typeof window.innerWidth !== "undefined") {
  innerWidth = window.innerWidth;
  innerHeight = window.innerHeight;
}
else {
  innerWidth = document.documentElement.clientWidth,
  innerHeight = document.documentElement.clientHeight
}

alert("InnerWidth of the window is: " + innerWidth);
alert("InnerHeight of the window is: " + innerHeight);
```

With these changes in place, the script now works correctly in all major browsers.

Due to noncompliance with or different interpretations of W3C standards, browsers are full of quirks like this. Older browsers are notorious for not complying with the standards, or complying only partially. And while newer specifications like HTML 5 and CSS3 are still in a draft state, modern browsers are rushing to provide draft implementation of these by using their own vendor-specific twists. Imagine factoring all of these variations into your application for almost every single DOM element that you might access—not only would your code become lengthy and unwieldy, but it would constantly need updating as browsers and standards evolve and gaps in the specification are plugged, leading to a maintenance nightmare.

A good way to isolate your application code from such inconsistencies is to use a framework or library that acts as a layer between your application and the DOM access and manipulation code. jQuery is an excellent and lightweight framework that greatly reduces this friction. jQuery's simple APIs make accessing and manipulating the DOM easy and intuitive and reduce the amount of code you need to write, allowing you to focus on your application's functionality rather than worrying about browser inconsistencies and writing repetitive boilerplate code.

Consider the snippet we just looked at, rewritten using jQuery:

```
var innerWidth = $(window).width(),
    innerHeight = $(window).height();
```

```
alert("InnerWidth of the window is: " + innerWidth);
alert("InnerHeight of the window is: " + innerHeight);
```

This code looks fairly similar to the pure JavaScript code, with the following minor changes:

- The `window` object is wrapped in the special `$()` function, which returns a jQuery-fied object (more on this special function later).
- It makes function calls to `.width()` and `.height()` instead of accessing the `.height` and `.width` properties.

You can see the benefits of using jQuery—the code is quite similar to regular JavaScript, making it easier to learn and understand, yet it's powerful enough to abstract away all cross-browser issues. Furthermore, with all of our cross-browser headaches taken care of by jQuery, the amount of code required to achieve the same functionality is reduced to just one line per property.

Not only does jQuery make it easy to *get* property values, it also makes it easy to *set* them:

```
// set the width to 480 pixels
$(window).width("480px");

// set the height to 940 pixels
$(window).height("940px");
```

Notice that the same functions are used to both set and get property values, the only difference being that the setter function call takes a parameter with the new value. Using a single API in different ways to get and set values makes the jQuery syntax easy to remember as well as easier to read.

Selectors

The first step in manipulating DOM elements is to get a reference to the desired element. You can do this in many ways: through its ID, its class name, or one of its attributes, or by using JavaScript logic to navigate the DOM's tree structure and manually locate the element.

For example, the following shows how to use standard JavaScript code to search for a DOM element by its ID:

```
<div id="myDiv">Hello World!</div>

<script type="text/javascript">
  document.getElementById("myDiv").innerText = "Hello jQuery";
</script>
```

In this simple example, you get a reference to the `<div>` element by calling the `document.getElementById()` method, passing it the ID element's ID, and then changing the inner text to "Hello jQuery". This code will work exactly the same way in every browser, because document.getElementById() is part of the JavaScript language and is supported by all major browsers.

Consider another scenario where you want to access an element by its class name:

```
<div class="normal">Hello World!</div>

<script type="text/javascript">
  document.getElementsByClassName("normal")[0].innerText = "Hello jQuery";
</script>
```

This seems straightforward—instead of document.getElementById(), you use docu ment.getElementsByClassName() and access the first element of the array to set the innerText property. But wait, where did the array come from? document.getElements ByClassName() returns an array containing all elements that have the same class name. Luckily, in the example above we have only one <div>, so we know that the first element is the one we're looking for.

In a real-world application, though, the page will likely contain several elements that may or may not have IDs, and there may be more than one element with the same class name (and some elements without any class name at all). Elements will be nested in container elements such as <div>, <p>, and <span>, as per the page design. Since the DOM is nothing but a hierarchal tree structure, what you end up having is elements nested inside one another and everything nested inside the root: document.

Consider the following example:

```
<div class="normal">
  <p>Hello World!</p>
  <div>
    <span>Welcome!</span>
  </div>
</div>
```

To access the <span> and change its content, you would have to grab the outermost <div> (having class="normal"), traverse through its child nodes, check each node to see if it is a <span>, and then do some manipulation on the <span>.

A typical JavaScript code to grab the <span> would look like:

```
var divNode = document.getElementsByClassName("normal")[0];

for(i=0; i < divNode.childNodes.length; i++) {
  var childDivs = divNode.childNodes[i].getElementsByTagName("div");
  for(j=0; j < childDivs.childNodes.length; j++) {
    var span = childDivs.childNodes[j].getFirstChild();
    return span;
  }
}
```

All this code to grab just one <span>! Now what if you wanted to access the <p> tag? Can this code be reused? Certainly not, because the <p> element is at a different node in the tree. You would need to write similar code to grab the <p> element, or tweak it with conditions to find that element. And what if there were other `<span>` tags within the child `<div>`? How would you get to a specific `<span>`? Answering these questions will make this code grow bigger and bigger, as you fill it with all sorts of conditional logic.

What if you then wanted to repeat this exercise in a different place that has a slightly different structure? Or if, in the future, the markup changes a little bit, altering the structure? You'd have to adjust all of your functions to take the new hierarchy into account. Clearly, if we continue in this manner, the code will soon become unwieldy, lengthy, and invariably error prone.

jQuery selectors help us tidy up the mess. By using predefined conventions, we can traverse the DOM in just a few lines of code. Let's take a look now to see how these conventions reduce the amount of code needed to perform the same actions as in the previous examples.

Here's how we can rewrite the traversing logic with jQuery selectors. Selecting an element by ID becomes:

```
$("#myDiv").text("Hello jQuery!");
```

We call jQuery's `$()` function, passing in a predefined pattern. The "#" in the pattern signifies an ID selector, so the pattern `#myDiv` is the equivalent of saying `document.getElementById("myDiv")`.

Once you get a reference to the element, you can change its inner text via jQuery's `text()` method. This is similar to setting the `innerText` property, but it's less verbose.

An interesting thing to note here is that almost all jQuery methods return a jQuery object, which is a wrapper around the native DOM element. This wrapping allows for "chaining" of calls—e.g., you can change the text and the color of an element in one go by saying:

```
$(".normal > span")      // returns a jQuery object
  .contains("Welcome!")  // again returns a jQuery object
  .text("...")           // returns a jQuery object again
  .css({color: "red"});
```

Because each call (`.text()`, `.css()`) returns the same jQuery object, the calls can be made successively. This style of chaining calls makes the code "fluent," which makes it easy to read, and since you do not have to repeat the element access code, the amount of overall code that you write is reduced.

Similar to the ID pattern, selecting by class name becomes:

```
$(".normal").text("Hello jQuery!");
```

The pattern for a class-based selector is `".className"`.

Recall that getElementsByClassName() returns an array—in this case, jQuery will change the text on all elements in array! So, if you have multiple elements with the same class name, you need to put additional filters in place to get to the right element.

Now, let's see how easy it is to access elements with a parent-child relation and grab the <span> from our original example:

```
$(".normal > span").text("Welcome to jQuery!");
```

The ">" indicates the parent > child relation. We can even filter based on the content of the span (or any element):

```
$(".normal > span").contains("Welcome!").text("Welcome to jQuery!");
```

The .contains() filters out elements that contain the specified text. So, if there are multiple spans, and the only way to differentiate (in the absence of ID, class name, etc.) is by checking for content, jQuery selectors make that easy, too.

jQuery offers many more selector patterns. To learn about them, check out the jQuery documentation site (*http://api.jquery.com/category/selectors*).

Responding to Events

Every DOM element on the HTML page is capable of raising events, such as "click," "mouse move," "change," and many more. Events expose a powerful mechanism to add interaction to the page: you can *listen* for events, and perform one or more actions in response, enhancing the user experience.

For example, consider a form with many fields. By listening for the onClick event on the Submit button, you can perform validation on the user's input and show any error messages without refreshing the page.

Let's add a button that alerts "hello events!" when clicked. In traditional HTML/Java-Script, the code would look like:

```
<input id="helloButton" value="Click Me" onclick="doSomething();">

<script type="text/javascript">
  function doSomething() {
    alert("hello events!");
  }
</script>
```

The onclick event handler (or *listener*) is specified in the markup: onclick="doSome thing();". When this button is clicked, this code will show the standard message box displaying the text "hello events!"

You can also attach event handlers in a nonintrusive manner, like this:

```
<input id="helloButton" value="Click Me">

<script type="text/javascript">
  function doSomething() {
    alert("hello events!");
  }

  document.getElementById("helloButton").onclick = doSomething;
</script>
```

Notice how the markup does not specify the `onclick` behavior anymore? Here, we've separated presentation from behavior, attaching the behavior outside the presentation logic. This not only results in cleaner code, but also ensures that we can reuse the presentation logic and behaviors elsewhere without making many changes.

This is a very simple example to show how basic event handling works. In the real world, your JavaScript functions will look much more complicated and may do more than display a simple alert to the user.

Now, let's look at the corresponding jQuery code for specifying event handlers:

```
<input id="helloButton" value="Click Me">

<script type="text/javascript">
  function doSomething() {
    alert("hello events!");
  }

  $(function() {
    $("#helloButton").click(doSomething);
  });
</script>
```

With jQuery, you first get a reference to the button using the `$("#helloButton")` selector, and then call `.click()` to attach the event handler. `.click()` is actually shorthand for `.bind("click", handler)`.

`$(function)` is a shortcut that tells jQuery to attach the event handlers once the DOM is loaded in the browser. Remember that the DOM tree is loaded in a top-to-bottom fashion, with the browser loading each element as it encounters it in the tree structure.

The browser triggers a `window.onload` event as soon as it is done parsing the DOM tree and loading all the scripts, style sheets, and other resources. The `$()` listens for this event and executes the function (which is actually an event handler!) that attaches various element event handlers.

In other words, `$(function(){...})` is the jQuery way of scripting:

```
window.onload = function() {
  $("#helloButton").click(function() {
    alert("hello events!");
  });
}
```

You can also specify the event handler *inline*, like this:

```
$(function() {
  $("#helloButton").click(function() {
    alert("hello events!");
  });
});
```

Interestingly, if you don't pass a function to `.click()`, it triggers a click event. This is useful if you want to programmatically *click* the button:

```
$("#helloButton").click();  // will display "hello events!"
```

DOM Manipulation

jQuery offers a simple and powerful mechanism to manipulate the DOM, or alter properties of the DOM itself or any element.

For example, to alter CSS properties of an element:

```
// will turn the color of the button's text to red
$("#helloButton").css("color", "red");
```

You've already seen some of this in action; remember the "height" example from earlier in the chapter?

```
// will return the height of the element
var height = $("#elem").height();
```

In addition to simple manipulations like these, jQuery allows you to create, replace, and remove any markup from a group of elements or the document root with ease.

The following example demonstrates adding a group of elements to an existing `<div>`:

```
<div id="myDiv">
</div>

<script type="text/javascript">
  $("#myDiv").append("<p>I was inserted <i>dynamically</i></p>");
</script>
```

This results in:

```
<div id="myDiv">
  <p>I was inserted <i>dynamically</i></p>
</div>
```

It is just as easy to remove any element (or a set of elements):

```
<div id="myDiv">
  <p>I was inserted <i>dynamically</i></p>
</div>

<script type="text/javascript">
  $("#myDiv").remove("p");  // will remove the <p> and its children
</script>
```

This code results in:

```
<div id="myDiv">
</div>
```

jQuery provides several methods to control the placement of markup, as Table 4-1 illustrates.

Table 4-1. Commonly used DOM manipulation methods

Method	Description
.prepend()	Inserts at the beginning of the matched element
.before()	Inserts before the matched element
.after()	Inserts after the matched element
.html()	Replaces all the HTML inside the matched element

AJAX

AJAX (Asynchronous JavaScript and XML) is a technique that enables a page to request or submit data without doing a refresh or postback.

Using asynchronous requests to access data behind the scenes (on demand) greatly enhances the user experience because the user does not have to wait for the full page to load. And since the full page doesn't have to reload, the amount of data requested from the server can be significantly smaller, which results in even faster response times.

At the heart of AJAX is the XmlHttpRequest object, which was originally developed by Microsoft for use in Outlook Web Access with Exchange Server 2000. It was soon adopted by industry heavyweights such as Mozilla, Google, and Apple and is now a W3C standard (*http://www.w3.org/TR/XMLHttpRequest/*).

A typical AJAX request with XmlHttpRequest object would look like:

```
// instantiate XmlHttpRequest object
var xhr = new XMLHttpRequest();

// open a new 'GET' request to fetch google.com's home page
xhr.open("GET", "http://www.google.com/", false);

// send the request with no content (null)
xhr.send(null);

if (xhr.status === 200) {    // The 200 HTTP Status Code indicates a successful request

    // will output reponse text to browser's console (Firefox, Chrome, IE 8+)
    console.log(xhr.responseText);
}
else {  // something bad happened, log the error
    console.log("Error occurred: ", xhr.statusText);
}
```

This example creates a *synchronous* request (the third parameter in `xhr.open()`), which means that the browser will *pause* the script execution until the response comes back. You typically want to avoid these kinds of synchronous AJAX requests at all costs because the web page will be unresponsive until the response comes back, resulting in a very poor user experience.

Luckily, it's quite easy to switch from a synchronous request to an asynchronous request: simply set the third parameter in `xhr.open()` to true. Now, because of the asynchronous nature, the browser will not stop; it will execute the next line (the `xhr.status` check) immediately. This will most likely fail because the request may not have completed executing.

To handle this situation, you need to specify a *callback*—a function that gets called as soon as the request is processed and a response is received.

Let's look at the modified code now:

```
// instantiate XmlHttpRequest object
var xhr = new XMLHttpRequest();

// open a new asynchronous 'GET' request to fetch google.com's home page
xhr.open("GET", "http://www.google.com/", true);

// attach a callback to be called as soon as the request is processed
xhr.onreadystatechange = function (evt) {

  //  as the request goes through different stages of processing,
  //  the readyState value will change
  //  this function will be called every time it changes,
  //  so readyState === 4 checks if the processing is completed
  if (xhr.readyState === 4) {
    if (xhr.status === 200) {
      console.log(xhr.responseText)
    }
    else {
      console.log("Error occurred: ", xhr.statusText);
    }
  }
};

// send the request with no content (null)
xhr.send(null);
```

This code is almost identical to the synchronous version, except that it has a callback function that gets executed whenever the server sends back any information.

 You must attach any callbacks *before* issuing `xhr.send()`, or they will not be called.

Let's look at the equivalent jQuery code. jQuery offers an `.ajax()` method and various shorthands for accomplishing common tasks using AJAX.

Here's the jQuery version:

```
$.ajax("google.com")  // issue a 'GET' request to fetch google.com's home page
  .done(function(data) { // success handler (status code 200)
      console.log(data);
  })
  .fail(function(xhr) {  // error handler (status code not 200)
      console.log("Error occurred: ", xhr.statusText);
  });
```

The first line specifies the URL from which you want to request data. The code then specifies the callback functions for the success and error conditions (jQuery takes care of checking for `readyState` and the status code).

Notice how we didn't have to specify the type of request (GET) or whether it is asynchronous or not. This is because jQuery uses GET by default and `$.ajax()` is asynchronous by default.

You can override these parameters (and more) to fine-tune your request:

```
$.ajax({
  url: "google.com",
  async: true,        // false makes it synchronous
  type: "GET",           // 'GET' or 'POST' ('GET' is the default)
  done: function(data) {    // success handler (status code 200)
        console.log(data);
      },
  fail: function(xhr) {    // error handler (status code not 200)
        console.log("Error occurred: ", xhr.statusText);
      }
});
```

jQuery AJAX (*http://api.jquery.com/jQuery.ajax*) offers many more parameters than what's shown here. See the jQuery documentation site for details.

 `.done()` and `.fail()` were introduced in jQuery 1.8. If you're using an older version of jQuery, use `.success()` and `.error()`, respectively.

Client-Side Validation

In Chapter 3, you were introduced to server-side validation techniques. In this section, you'll see how you can enhance the user experience by performing some of the same validations purely on the client side (without making a round-trip to the server), with the help of jQuery and the jQuery validation plug-in.

ASP.NET MVC (starting with version 3) offers unobtrusive client-side validation out of the box. Client validation comes enabled by default, but you easily enable or disable it by tweaking these two settings in your *web.config* file:

```
<configuration>
  <appSettings>
    <add key="ClientValidationEnabled" value="true"/>
    <add key="UnobtrusiveJavaScriptEnabled" value="true"/>
  </appSettings>
</configuration>
```

The good part about performing client-side validation with the jQuery validation plug-in is that it can take advantage of the DataAnnotation attributes defined in your model, which means that you have to do very little to start using it.

Let's revisit the Auction model from Chapter 3 to see how data annotations were used in input validation:

```csharp
public class Auction
{
    [Required]
    [StringLength(50,
        ErrorMessage = "Title cannot be longer than 50 characters")]
    public string Title { get; set; }

    [Required]
    public string Description { get; set; }

    [Range(1, 10000,
        ErrorMessage = "The auction's starting price must be at least 1")]
    public decimal StartPrice { get; set; }

    public decimal CurrentPrice { get; set; }
    public DateTime EndTime { get; set; }
}
```

And here's the view that renders out the validation messages:

```
<h2>Create Auction</h2>

@using (Html.BeginForm())
{
  @Html.ValidationSummary()

  <p>
      @Html.LabelFor(model => model.Title)
      @Html.EditorFor(model => model.Title)
      @Html.ValidationMessageFor(model => model.Title, "*")
  </p>
  <p>
      @Html.LabelFor(model => model.Description)
      @Html.EditorFor(model => model.Description)
      @Html.ValidationMessageFor(model => model.Description, "*")
  </p>
  <p>
      @Html.LabelFor(model => model.StartPrice)
```

```
        @Html.EditorFor(model => model.StartPrice)
        @Html.ValidationMessageFor(model => model.StartPrice)
    </p>
    <p>
        @Html.LabelFor(model => model.EndTime)
        @Html.EditorFor(model => model.EndTime)
        @Html.ValidationMessageFor(model => model.EndTime)
    </p>
    <p>
        <input type="submit" value="Create" />
    </p>
}
```

The validation we're performing is quite simple, yet with server-side validation, the page has to be submitted via a postback, inputs have to be validated on the server, and, if there are errors, the messages need to be sent back to the client and, after a full page refresh, shown to the user.

With client-side validation, the inputs are checked as soon as they are submitted, so there is no postback to the server, there's no page refresh, and the results are shown instantly to the user!

To begin with client-side validation, go ahead and reference the jQuery validation plug-in scripts in the view:

```
<script src="@Url.Content("~/Scripts/jquery.validate.min.js")"
        type="text/javascript"></script>
<script src="@Url.Content("~/Scripts/jquery.validate.unobtrusive.min.js")"
        type="text/javascript"></script>
```

 If you use Visual Studio's "Add View" wizard to generate Create or Edit views, you may choose the "Reference script libraries" option to have Visual Studio add these references automatically. Instead of the <script> tag references shown above, however, Visual Studio will achieve the same thing through a reference to the ~/bundles/jquery-val script bundle toward the bottom of the view. See "Bundling and Minification" on page 289 for more information about script bundling.

If you run the application now and inspect the Create Auction page's source (using "View Source"), you'll see the following markup being rendered (with unobtrusive JavaScript and client-side validation enabled):

```
<form action="/Auctions/Create" method="post" novalidate="novalidate">
  <div class="validation-summary-errors" data-valmsg-summary="true">
    <ul>
      <li>The Description field is required.</li>
      <li>The Title field is required.</li>
      <li>Auction may not start in the past</li>
    </ul>
  </div>
  <p>
    <label for="Title">Title</label>
```

```
      <input class="input-validation-error"
        data-val="true"
        data-val-length="Title cannot be longer than 50 characters"
        data-val-length-max="50"
        data-val-required="The Title field is required."
        id="Title" name="Title" type="text" value="">

      <span class="field-validation-error"
        data-valmsg-for="Title"
        data-valmsg-replace="false">*</span>
   </p>
   <p>
      <label for="Description">Description</label>

   <input class="input-validation-error"
        data-val="true"
        data-val-required="The Description field is required."
        id="Description" name="Description" type="text" value="">

      <span class="field-validation-error"
        data-valmsg-for="Description"
        data-valmsg-replace="false">*</span>
   </p>
   <p>
      <label for="StartPrice">StartPrice</label>

      <input data-val="true"
        data-val-number="The field StartPrice must be a number."
        data-val-range="The auction's starting price must be at least 1"
        data-val-range-max="10000"
        data-val-range-min="1"
        data-val-required="The StartPrice field is required."
        id="StartPrice" name="StartPrice" type="text" value="0">

      <span class="field-validation-valid"
        data-valmsg-for="StartPrice"
        data-valmsg-replace="true"></span>
   </p>
   <p>
      <label for="EndTime">EndTime</label>

      <input data-val="true"
        data-val-date="The field EndTime must be a date."
        id="EndTime" name="EndTime" type="text" value="">

      <span class="field-validation-valid"
        data-valmsg-for="EndTime"
        data-valmsg-replace="true"></span>
   </p>
   <p>
      <input type="submit" value="Create">
   </p>
</form>
```

With unobtrusive JavaScript and client-side validation enabled, ASP.NET MVC renders the validation criteria and corresponding messages as `data-val-` attributes. The jQuery validation plug-in will use these attributes to figure out the validation rules and the corresponding error messages that will be displayed if the rules are not satisfied.

Go ahead now and try to submit the form with some invalid values. You'll see that the "submit" did not actually submit the form; instead, you'll see error messages next to the invalid inputs.

Behind the scenes, the jQuery validation plug-in attaches an event handler to the form's `onsubmit` event. Upon form submit, the jQuery validation plug-in scans through all the input fields and checks for errors against the given criteria. When it finds an error, it shows the corresponding error message.

Being unobtrusive in nature, the jQuery validation plug-in doesn't emit any code to the page, nor is anything required on your part to wire up the client-side validation logic with the page's events. Rather, the code to attach to the `onsubmit` event, as well as the validation logic, is part of the *jquery.validate.js* and *jquery.validate.unobtrusive.js* files.

The good thing about being unobtrusive is that if you forget to include these two scripts, the page will still render without any errors—only, the client-side validation will not happen client side!

This section was meant to show you how easy it is to start taking advantage of client-side validation and was kept simple and minimal purposefully. The jQuery validation plug-in is quite complex and offers many more features and customizations. You're encouraged to learn more about the plug-in at the official documentation page (*http://docs.jquery.com/Plugins/Validation*).

Summary

jQuery makes cross-browser development a joyful experience. ASP.NET MVC's support of jQuery out of the box means you can quickly build a rich and highly interactive client-side user interface (UI) with very few lines of code. With client-side validation and unobtrusive JavaScript, validating user input can be done with minimal effort. All of these techniques combined can help you develop highly interactive and immersive web applications with ease.

## PART II

Going to the Next Level

## CHAPTER 5

Web Application Architecture

The first few chapters of this book introduced you to several core concepts that are essential to understanding how to use the ASP.NET MVC Framework. This chapter builds upon those core concepts, elaborating on the fundamental design patterns and principles used to build the ASP.MVC Framework and exploring how to apply these patterns and principles to build an ASP.NET MVC web application.

The Model-View-Controller Pattern

The Model-View-Controller (MVC) pattern is a user interface architecture pattern that promotes separation of concerns across multiple application layers. Instead of putting all the logic and data access code for an application in a single place, MVC promotes separating the application's logic into specific classes, each with a small, specific set of responsibilities.

The MVC pattern is not a new concept, and it's certainly not specific to the .NET Framework or even to web development; in fact, it was originally created by the programmers at Xerox PARC in the late 1970s and applied to applications that used the SmallTalk programming language. Since that time, many have considered MVC one of the most misquoted patterns ever created. This is because MVC is a very high-level pattern that has engendered many related implementations and subpatterns.

Separation of Concerns

Separation of concerns is a computer science principle that promotes separating the responsibility for an application or use case across multiple components, where each component has a distinct, small set of responsibilities. A "concern" can be associated with a specific set of features or behaviors. Separation of concerns is traditionally achieved by using encapsulation and abstraction to better isolate one set of concerns from another. For example, separation of concerns may be applied to application architecture by separating the different layers of the application into presentation, business, and data access layers, each of which is logically and physically separate.

Separation of concerns is a powerful principle that is frequently used in the design of platforms and frameworks. For example, web pages in the early days of the Web contained markup that combined the layout, style, and even data all in the same document. Over the years, standards based on separation of concerns emerged, and what was once one document is now split into three parts: an HTML document, which mainly focuses on the structure of content; one or more CSS stylesheets that define the style of the document; and JavaScript to attach behaviors to the document.

In the context of the Model-View-Controller (MVC) pattern, separation of concerns is used to define the responsibilities of the key components: model, view, and controller.

Figure 5-1 shows the interaction between the different MVC components and their core responsibilities.

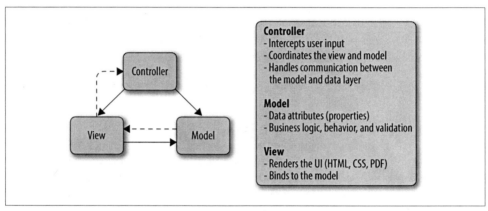

Figure 5-1. MVC separation of concerns

It is important to note that while each individual component has its own responsibilities, components can and do rely on each other. For example, in MVC, controllers are responsible for retrieving data from the model and syncing changes from a view back into the model. A controller can be associated with one or more views. Each of these views is responsible for displaying data in a particular way, but it relies on the controller to process and retrieve that data. While components may rely quite heavily on other components, it is critical for each component to concentrate on its own responsibilities and leave the other responsibilities to other components.

MVC and Web Frameworks

The original MVC pattern was designed with the assumption that the view, controller, and model were all within the same context. The pattern relies heavily on each component being able to directly interact with the others and share state across user interactions. For example, controllers would use the *observer* pattern to monitor changes to the view and react to user input. This approach works great when the controller, view, and model all exist under the same memory context.

In a web application things are stateless, and the view (HTML) runs on a client inside of a browser. A controller can't use the observer pattern to monitor changes; instead, an HTTP request needs to be sent from the view to a controller. To address this, the *front controller* pattern (Figure 5-2) has been adopted. The main concept behind this pattern is that when an HTTP request is sent, a controller intercepts and processes it. The controller is responsible for determining how to process the request and for sending the result back to the client.

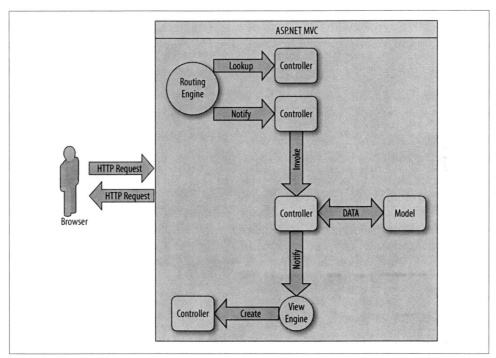

Figure 5-2. The front controller pattern

The power of the front controller pattern becomes apparent when you consider that modern web applications are often expected to execute the same logic for multiple requests, yet potentially return different content for each individual request. For instance, the same controller action can process both a normal browser request and an AJAX request, yet the browser expects a fully rendered web page (with layout, stylesheets, scripts, etc.), whereas the AJAX request might expect a partial HTML view or even raw JSON data. In all of these instances, the controller logic remains the same and the view can remain unaware of where its data came from.

In an ASP.NET MVC application, the routing and view engines are involved with processing an HTTP request. When a request URI (e.g., */auctions/detail/25*) is received, the ASP.NET MVC runtime looks it up in the route table and invokes the corresponding controller action. The controller handles the request and determines what type of result to return. When a view result is returned, the ASP.NET MVC Framework delegates to the view engine the task of loading and rendering the corresponding requested view.

Architecting a Web Application

The core design of the ASP.NET MVC Framework is driven by the principle of separation of concerns. In addition to routing and view engines, the framework promotes the use of action filters, which are used to handle cross-cutting concerns such as security, caching, and error handling. When designing and architecting an ASP.NET MVC web application, it's important to understand how the framework uses this principle and how to design your application to take advantage of it.

Logical Design

The logical (conceptual) architecture of an application focuses on the relationships and interactions between components, and those components are grouped into logical layers that support specific sets of features.

Components should be designed to enforce the separation of concerns and use abstraction for cross-component communication. Cross-cutting concerns such as security, logging, and caching should be isolated into different application services. These services should support a plug-and-play module approach. Switching between different security authentication types or implementing different logging sources should have no impact on other parts of the application.

ASP.NET MVC Web Application Logical Design

The ASP.NET MVC Framework was designed to promote this type of logical design. In addition to isolating the view, controller, and model, the framework includes several action filters that handle different types of cross-cutting concerns and multiple action result types for views, JSON, XML, and partial pages. Since the framework supports endless extensibility, developers can create and plug in their own custom action filters and results.

`SingleSignOnAttribute` is an example of a custom `ActionFilter` that has been created for supporting Single Sign On Authentication across multiple ASP.NET Web applications:

```
public class SingleSignOnAttribute : ActionFilterAttribute, IActionFilter
{
    void OnActionExecuted(ActionExecutedContext filterContext)
    {
        // Verify security token and authenticate user
    }

    void OnActionExecuting(ActionExecutingContext filterContext)
    {
```

```
        // Preprocessing code used to verify if security token exists
    }
}
```

The best way to communicate the logical design of an application is to create a visual representation of each component and its corresponding layer. Figure 5-3 shows the typical logical design of an ASP.NET MVC web application. Take note of how cross-cutting concerns have been separated into different application services.

Table 5-1 describes the different elements in Figure 5-3.

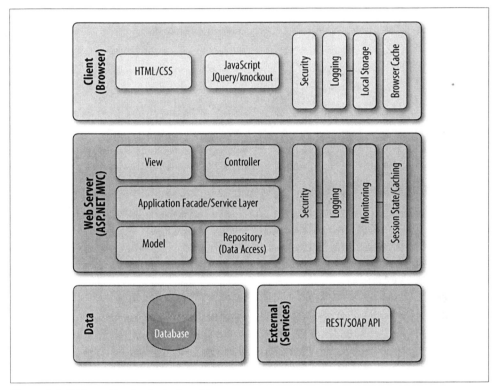

Figure 5-3. Web application logical architecture

Table 5-1. Component descriptions

Name	Layer	Description
HTML/CSS	Client	The UI elements used to describe the layout and style of the application
JavaScript	Client	Any client-side logic used for validation and business processing
Security	Client	Security token (cookie)
Logging	Client	Local service used for logging and monitoring

Name	Layer	Description
Local Storage	Client	HTML 5 local storage (used for caching/offline storage)
Browser Cache	Client	Cache provided by the browser, used for storing HTML, CSS, images, etc.
View	Web Server	Server-side view used to render HTML
Controller	Web Server	Application controller, handles user input and orchestration
Model	Web Server	A collection of classes representing the business domain model for the application
Service Layer	Web Server	Service layer used for encapsulating complex business processes and persistence
Repository	Web Server	Data access components (object relational mapper)
Security	Web Server	Security service used for authenticating and authorizing users
Logging	Web Server	Application service used for logging
Monitoring	Web Server	Application service used for health monitoring
Session/Caching	Data	Application service used for managing transit state
External Service	Data	Any external systems the application depends on

Logical Design Best Practices

A layered application design such as the one shown in Figure 5-3 offers the most flexible application architecture. Each layer deals with a specific set of responsibilities, and layers are only dependent on layers lower down the stack. For example, the data access repository exists at the same layer as the model, so it's perfectly acceptable for it to have a dependency. The model is isolated from the underlying data store; it doesn't care how the repository handles persistence or even if it saves to a local file or database.

A common debate when architecting a web application is the issue of where to enforce business and validation rules. The MVC pattern promotes that the model should be responsible for business logic. This is true, though in a distributed application, each layer should share some level of responsibility for validating user input. Ideally, input should always be checked before sending it across the wire to another layer.

Each layer should take responsibility for the level of validation it can enforce. Downstream layers should never assume that a calling layer has verified everything. On the client side, JavaScript (JQuery) should be used to verify required fields and restrict input for common UI controls (Numeric, DateTime, etc...). The application business model should enforce all business and validation rules, while the database layer should use strongly typed fields and enforce constraints to prevent foreign key violations.

What you want to avoid is duplicating complex business logic across each layer. If a screen has special logic or features for an administrator as compared to a normal user, the business model should identify which features are enabled or disabled and provide a flag to hide or disable administration fields for normal users.

Physical Design

The role of physical architecture design is to define the physical components and deployment model for the web application. Most web applications are based on the *N-Tier* model. The client tier consists of HTML, CSS, and JavaScript that runs inside a web browser. The client makes HTTP requests to retrieve HTML content directly or executes an AJAX request (which returns a partial HTML page, XML, or JSON data). The application layer includes the ASP.NET MVC Framework (running under the IIS web server) and any custom or third-party assemblies used by the application. The data layer may consist of one or more relational or NoSQL databases, or one or more external SOAP or REST-based web services or other third-party application programming interfaces (APIs).

Project Namespace and Assembly Names

Before an ASP.NET MVC web application can be deployed, the developer needs to decide how to physically separate the application code into different namespaces and assemblies. There are many different approaches to take when designing an ASP.NET MVC application. A developer can decide to keep all the application's components inside the website assembly, or separate components into different assemblies. In most cases it's a good idea to separate the business and data access layers into different assemblies than the website. This is typically done to better isolate the business model from the UI and make it easier to write automated test that focuses on the core application logic. In addition, using this approach makes it possible to reuse the business and data access layers from other applications (console applications, websites, web services, etc.).

A common root namespace (e.g., *company.{ApplicationName}*) should be consistently used across all assemblies. Each assembly should have a unique sub-namespace that matches the name of the assembly. Figure 5-4 shows the project structure of the Ebuy reference application. The functionality for the application has been divided into three projects: *Ebuy.WebSite* contains the view, controllers, and other web-related files; *Ebuy.Core* contains the business model for the application; and the *CustomExtensions* project contains the custom extensions used by the application for model binding, routing, and controllers. In addition, the project has two testing projects (not shown): *UnitTests* and *IntegrationTests*.

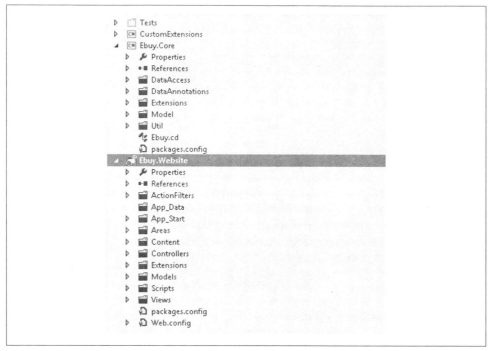

Figure 5-4. Visual Studio project structure

Deployment Options

Once the Visual Studio solution and project structure have been defined, a developer can use an automated or manual process to deploy the compiled application to a web server. See Chapter 19 for additional details on how to deploy ASP.NET MVC web applications.

Figure 5-5 shows an ASP.NET MVC web application that has been configured to use a multiserver web farm and clustered SQL Server database. ASP.NET MVC web applications support all kinds of deployment models. The application can be self-contained and use a local SQL Server Express database or use an Enterprise N-Tier model.

Physical Design Best Practices

There are no silver bullets to architecting a web application, and every choice has trade-offs. It's important that an application design be flexible and include proper monitoring, so real-time data can be used to make informed decisions on how to best tweak the application. This is one of the areas where the ASP.NET MVC Framework shines. It was designed with flexibility and extensibility in mind. The framework makes it easy

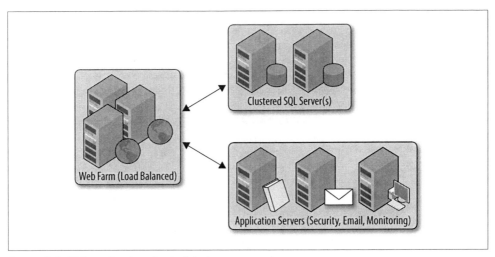

Figure 5-5. Web application physical design

to take advantage of the services built into IIS and ASP.NET, and it offers lots of extensibility and the ability to plug in different components and services.

There are many factors that you need to consider when designing a web application. Four of the more important ones are performance, scalability, bandwidth, and latency. Choices made to address one or more of these concerns can have an impact on the other factors. Setting up a monitoring strategy is a good way to properly evaluate how the application is working, especially under load, and determine the proper balance factors.

Performance and scalability

Choices to address either performance or scalability can very easily significantly affect the other factor. If the design for an application requires a large amount of data to be kept cached, this can have an impact on the memory usage requirement for the application. The IIS worker process needs to be properly configured to take into account the memory usage requirement: if too much memory gets allocated, the worker process will get recycled. Understanding how the .NET garbage collector frees resources can have a significant impact, too. Continually loading a large collection or data set into session state can cause the object to get pushed into the .NET garbage collector generation 2 or the large object heap.

Using a web farm is a good way to increase the scalability of a web application. It's critical that this be addressed by the application's technical design. Using a farm affects how the application handles transient state. If the load balancing hardware and software supports it, a sticky session approach can be used to ensure that a user will always be routed back to the server that established her original session.

An alternative approach is using a session state server or persisting session state to a database. It is always a good idea to minimize the use of session state and make sure to have defined timeout rules for cached data.

Since the location of where session state and data are cached is configurable, it's important to make sure all classes that might be used have been properly set up for serialization. This can be done by using the .NET `SerializableAttribute`, implementing the `ISerializeable` interface, or using Windows Communication Foundation (WCF) data contract serialization or one of the other supported .NET serialization methods.

Bandwidth and latency

Dealing with bandwidth and latency can be extremely tricky. Latency is usually a fixed constraint; if a server is located in New York and the user browses the site from Japan, there can be a significant (potentially five-second) latency for each request. There are plenty of things that can be done to address this, including compressing JavaScript files, using image maps, and limiting the number of requests. Bandwidth is usually more variable, but it can incur a significant cost if the application requires large amounts of data to be sent across the wire. The best option to address these factors is to minimize the number of requests and keep the payload size small. Good strategies to use are enabling paging for large result sets, sending only the necessary fields across the wire, and utilizing client-side validation and caching where possible.

Design Principles

When designing an application, framework, or class, it's important to think about the extensibility of your code and not just the best way to implement an initial set of features. This idea was baked into the design of the ASP.NET MVC Framework. Throughout, the framework uses and promotes the fundamental principles and best practices of object-oriented design.

SOLID

SOLID is an acronym that describes a particular set of application development principles that drive proper object-oriented design and development. When applied across an entire application, these techniques work together to create modular components that are easy to test and resilient to change.

SOLID consists of the following principles.

The Single Responsibility Principle

The *Single Responsibility Principle* (SRP) states that objects should have a single responsibility and all of their behaviors should focus on that one responsibility. A good example of this is having different controllers for different screens. For instance, the

---

`HomeController` should only contain operations related to the home page, while the `ProductController` should only handle the operations for the product pages. Likewise, views should focus on rendering the UI and avoid any data access logic.

The `ErrorLoggerManager` class shown below is a common example of a class that breaks SRP. The class has two methods, one for logging errors to the event log and one for logging errors to a file. While at first it may seem harmless to group these methods together, this class currently has too many responsibilities; this will become more apparent when additional logging methods are introduced. A common code smell to watch out for is any class named `xxxManager`. It more than likely has too many responsibilities.

```
public class ErrorLoggerManager
{
    public void LogErrorToEventLog(Exception e)
    {
        // Logging code
    }

    public void LogErrorToFile(Exception e)
    {
        // Logging code
    }
}
```

The Open/Closed Principle

The *Open/Closed Principle* (OCP) encourages components that are *open* for extension, but *closed* for modification. This complements SRP by pointing out that, rather than adding more and more behavior and responsibility to a class, you should instead choose to inherit from the class to extend its capabilities. A good example of this would be a cross-cutting service such as error logging: instead of adding the ability to log errors to a database and to a file in the same class, you should create an abstraction from which the different methods of logging can inherit. By doing this you isolate the inner working of logging to a database or a file from the other implementations.

Looking back over the `ErrorLoggerManager` class one more time, it should be easy to see how the class breaks both SRP and OCP. The class currently has two methods that are very specific to their implementation: `LogErrorToEventLog` for logging errors to the event log, and `LogErrorToFile` for logging errors to a file. When additional error logging types are required, the maintainability of this class will quickly get out of hand.

```
public class ErrorLoggerManager
{
    public void LogErrorToEventLog(Exception e)
    {
            // Logging code
    }

    public void LogErrorToFile(Exception e)
    {
```

```
            // Logging code
        }
    }
```

Here is the updated version of the ErrorLogger class designed to enforce SRP and OCP. An interface called ILogSource has been introduced that each type of logging implements. Two additional classes have also been created: EventLogSource and FileLog Source. Both classes deal with a specific type of logging. Now when additional logging types are introduced, none of the existing classes needs to be changed.

```
public class ErrorLogger
{
    public void Log(ILogSource source)
    {
    // Logging code
    }
}

public interface ILogSource
{
    LogError(Exception e);
}

public class EventLogSource : ILogSource
{
    public void LogError(Exception e)
    {
    LogError(Exception e);
    }
}

public class FileLogSource : ILogSource
{
    public void LogError(Exception e)
    {
    LogError(Exception e);
    }
}
```

At this point, you might be thinking to yourself that while this approach may seem cleaner, it also requires a lot more code. While this may be true, the examples throughout this book will show the many benefits that come from loosely coupled components that follow this pattern.

The Liskov Substitution Principle

The *Liskov Substitution Principle* (LSP) states that objects should be easily replaceable by instances of their subtypes without influencing the behavior and rules of the objects. For example, though it may seem to be a good idea to have a common base class or interface, this approach may indirectly introduce code that breaks LSP.

Take a look at ISecurityProvider and the classes that implement this interface. Everything looks good, until the UserController goes to call RemoveUser on the

`ActiveDirectoryProvider` class. In this example, only the `DatabaseProvider` class supports removing users. One way to address this issue would be to add type-specific logic, which is what the `UserController` is currently doing. But this approach has a big drawback in that it breaks LSP. Raising an exception in this case is a bad idea and forces the introduction of type-specific code. One way to resolve this issue is to utilize the SOLID Interface Segregation Principle, discussed next.

```
public interface ISecurityProvider
{
    User GetUser(string name);
    void RemoveUser(User user);
}

public class DatabaseProvider : ISecurityProvider
{

    public User GetUser(string name)
    {
            // Code to add a new user
    }

    public void RemoveUser(User user)
    {
            // Code to save a user
    }

}

public class ActiveDirectoryProvider : ISecurityProvider
{

    public User GetUser(string name)
    {
            // Code to add a new user
    }

    public void RemoveUser(User user)
    {
            // AD does not allow users to be removed
            throw new NotImplementedException();
    }

}

public class UserController : Controller
{
    private ISecurityProvider securityProvider;

    public ActionResult RemoveUser(string name)
    {
            User user = securityProvider.GetUser(name);

            if (securityProvider is DatabaseProvider) // Breaks LSP
                    securityProvider.Remove(user);
```

```
        }
    }
```

The Interface Segregation Principle

The *Interface Segregation Principle* (ISP) encourages the use—and at the same time,
limits the size—of interfaces throughout an application. In other words, instead of one
superclass interface that contains all the behavior for an object, there should exist multiple, smaller, more specific interfaces. A good example of this is how .NET has separate
interfaces for serialization and for disposing. A class would implement the interfaces
`ISerializable` and `IDisposable`, while a consumer who is only concerned with serialization would only care about the methods implemented by the `ISerializable` interface.

The following code is an example of ISP being used properly. Two separate interfaces
have been created—one (`ISearchProvider`) only contains methods for searching, while
the other (`IRepository`) defines methods for persisting an entity. Note how the `Search`
`Controller` is only concerned with the behavior for searching and only references the
`ISearchProvider` interface. This is powerful because you can use this technique to enforce a level of security. For example, say you allow anyone to search for a product, but
only admins can add/remove products. By using ISP you can ensure that the `Search`
`Controller` that allows anonymous access can only search for products and not add/
remove them.

```
public interface ISearchProvider
{
    IList<T> Search<T>(Criteria criteria);
}

public interface IRepository<T>
{
    T GetById(string id);
    void Delete(T);
    void Save(T)
}

public class ProductRepository< : ISearchProvider, IRepository<Product>
{
    public IList<Product> Search(Criteria criteria)
    {
        // Search code
    }

    public Product GetById(string id)
    {
        // Data access code
    }

    public void Delete(Product product)
    {
        // Data access code
    }
```

```
        public void Save(Product product)
        {
                // Data access code
        }
}

public class SearchController : Controller
{
    private ISearchProvider searchProvider;

    public SearchController(ISearchProvider provider)
    {
            this.searchProvider = provider;
    }

    public ActionResult SearchForProducts(Criteria criteria)
    {
            IList<Products> products = searchProvider.Search<Product>(criteria);
            return view(products);
    }
}
```

The Dependency Inversion Principle

The *Dependency Inversion Principle* (DIP) says that components that depend on each other should interact via an abstraction and not directly with a concrete implementation. A good example of this would be a controller relying on an abstract class or interface to communicate with a data access layer, as opposed to creating an instance of a specific type of data access object itself.

There are several advantages to this principle: using abstraction allows different components to be developed and changed independently of each other, it's possible to introduce new implementations of the abstraction, and it makes it easier to test since the dependency can be mocked.

In the next section, we will dig deeper into how a particular implementation of DIP—the Inversion of Control (IoC) principle—makes this easier by using a separate component to manage the creation and lifetime of this abstraction.

The following code is an example of DIP being used. The SearchController class has a dependency on the ISearchProvider interface. Instead of directly creating an instance of the ProductRepository, the controller uses the instance of the ISearchProvider passed in to its controller. The next section will cover how an IoC container can be used to manage dependencies.

```
public class SearchController : Controller
{
    private ISearchProvider searchProvider;

    public SearchController(ISearchProvider provider)
    {
            this.searchProvider = provider;
```

```
        }
    }

    public class ProductRepository : ISearchProvider
    {
    }
```

Inversion of Control

Now that you have grasped the concepts of the SOLID design principles, it's time to dig into the magic that glues all of these concepts together: *Inversion of Control*. IoC is a design principle that promotes loosely coupled layers, components, and classes by inverting the control flow of the application.

Compared with traditional procedural code where a single routine explicitly controls the flow between itself and subroutines, IoC uses the concept of separating the execution of code from problem-specific code. This approach allows the different components of the application to be developed independently of each other. For example, in an MVC application, the model, view, and controller layers can be designed and built independently.

Two popular implementations of the IoC design principle are *dependency injection* and *service location*. Both of these use the same basic concept of a central container to manage the lifetime of a dependency. The major difference between the two implementations revolves around how dependencies are accessed: a service locator relies on the caller to invoke and ask for a dependency, while dependency injection is done by injecting a dependency into a class by either populating its constructor, setting one of its properties, or executing one of its methods.

Understanding dependencies

Understanding the different types of dependencies and how to manage the relationship between dependencies is critical to minimizing the complexity of an application. Dependencies come in many forms: one .NET assembly can have one or more references to other .NET assemblies; an MVC controller must inherit from the base ASP.NET MVC controller class; and an ASP.NET application requires an IIS web server to host it.

Figure 5-6 shows the relationship between a controller and a repository class. In this scenario, the controller directly creates an instance of the repository class. The controller currently has a tight coupling to the repository class. Any change to the repository public interface potentially affects the controller class. For instance, if a developer decides to change the default constructor for the repository class to require one or more parameters, this change will affect the controller class.

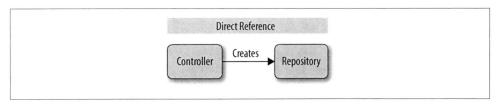

Figure 5-6. Managing dependencies

In order to make the relationship between the controller and repository more loosely coupled, a developer can introduce an abstraction `IRepository` and move the creation of the repository class to a factory (pattern). Figure 5-7 illustrates this configuration. The controller now is only dependent on the `IRepository` interface, and any changes to the repository class constructor will not require changes to the controller class. While this eliminates the tight coupling between the controller and the repository, it introduces a new coupling between the controller and the factory class.

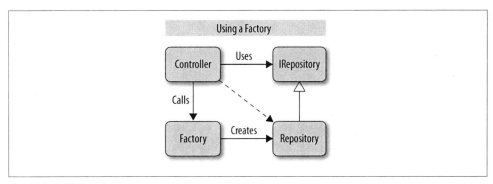

Figure 5-7. Using abstraction

Figure 5-8 shows how an IoC container can replace the factory class as a means to manage the dependency between the controller and the repository classes. This implementation still has the controller using an interface `IRepository` for abstraction. Only now, the controller knows nothing about how the repository is created—the IoC container is responsible for both creating and "injecting" (i.e., passing) the repository instance into the controller. Using an IoC container provides an additional level of functionality over the factory, in that the IoC container allows the lifetime management of the class to be configured.

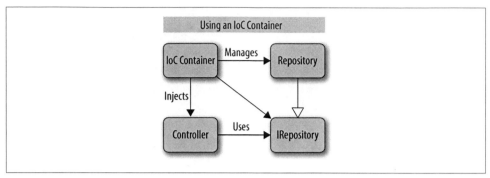

Figure 5-8. Managing dependencies with IoC

Service location

Using the service locator pattern is easy. A developer just needs to ask the IoC container for a specific service class. The container looks to see if the requested class has been configured, and based on the lifetime management rules for the class, it will either create a new instance or return a previously created instance to the requester.

The service locator pattern works great if you need to directly access a particular service in a single method or need to request a service by name, not just interface. The major drawback to using this pattern is that your code needs direct access to the IoC container, which could introduce a tight coupling between your code and the API of the IoC container. One way to minimize this coupling is to abstract the IoC container away, behind a custom interface.

The following is an example of a class directly asking the IoC container for a specific service based on its registered interface:

```
public class AuctionsController : Controller
{
    private readonly IRepository _repository;

    public AuctionsController()
    {
        IRepository repository = Container.GetService<IRepository>();
        _repository = repository;
    }
}
```

Dependency injection

The dependency injection (DI) pattern promotes a more loosely coupled approach, compared to the service locator pattern. DI uses an approach where dependencies are passed in via constructors, properties, or methods. Typically, most developers use constructor injection since in most cases the dependency is needed right away.

However, certain IoC containers allow a lazy-loading approach for property injected dependencies. In this case the dependency is not loaded until a property gets invoked.

The `AuctionsController` class has been set up to use constructor injection. The class depends on a data repository to persist and retrieve auction-related data; however, the controller has no direct reference to an actual implementation of a repository. Instead, the controller relies on the `IRepository` interface and the IoC container determines the appropriate `IRepository` implementation and "injects" it at runtime:

```
public class AuctionsController : Controller
{
    private readonly IRepository _repository;

    public AuctionsController(IRepository repository)
    {
        _repository = repository;
    }
}
```

Dependency injection really starts to shine in situations that involve multiple levels of dependencies, i.e., when dependencies themselves have other dependencies. When the IoC container goes to inject a dependency, it will check to see if it already has a previously loaded instance of the dependency. If it hasn't, it will create a new instance and check to see if it has any dependencies that need to be injected. In this scenario, as the IoC container walks down the dependency tree, it creates the necessary dependencies.

The following example shows how chaining dependencies works. When the IoC container creates an instance of the `AuctionsController`, it will detect that the class has a dependency on an `IRepository`. The container will look to see if an instance of the `IRepository` class has been registered and create an instance of the `AuctionsReposi tory` class. Since the class has its own dependency, the container will create an instance of the `ErrorLogger` class and inject it into the `AuctionsRepository`:

```
public class AuctionsController : Controller
{
    private readonly IRepository _repository;

    public AuctionsController(IRepository repository)
    {
        _repository = repository;
    }
}

public interface IRepository<T>
{
    T GetById(string id);
    void Delete(T);
    void Save(T)
}

public class AuctionsRepository : IRepository<Auction>
{
```

```
    private readonly IErrorLogger _logger;

    public AuctionsRepository(IErrorLogger logger)
    {
        _logger = logger;
    }

    public Auctions GetById(string id)
    {
            // Data access code
    }

    public void Delete(Auctions auction)
    {
            // Data access code
    }

    public void Save(Auctions auction)
    {
            // Data access code
    }
}

public class ErrorLogger : IErrorLogger
{
    public void Log(Exception e)
    {
            // Logging code
    }
}

public interface IErrorLogger
{
    Log(Exception e);
}
```

Picking an IoC container

When using Inversion of Control, a developer needs to keep a couple of things in mind:
performance and error handling. Using an IoC container to manage and inject dependencies can be costly. Dependencies need to have an appropriate lifetime cycle. If a
dependency is configured as a singleton, cross-threading issues could be introduced
and any external resources (e.g., connection strings) need to be properly managed. It
is critical to avoid using an IoC container to create a large collection; it would be a really
bad idea to use DI to create a 1,000-item collection. Missing or unregistered
dependencies can be a nightmare to debug. A developer needs to keep track of the
dependencies required and make sure they all get registered during the loading of the
application.

Since most of the IoC containers are very similar, choosing a particular container is
usually more about developer preference than an in-depth comparison of features.

There are several containers available for .NET, each offering different approaches for injecting and managing dependencies. Popular .NET IoC containers include:

1. Ninject: *http://www.ninject.org*
2. Castle Windsor: *http://www.castleproject.org/container/index.html*
3. Autofac: *http://code.google.com/p/autofac/*
4. StructureMap: *http://structuremap.net/structuremap/index.html*
5. Unity: *http://unity.codeplex.com*
6. MEF: *http://msdn.microsoft.com/en-us/library/dd460648.aspx*

For the EBuy reference application, we chose the Ninject container, because of the popularity of the container in the ASP.NET MVC developer community. The container includes a number of custom-built extensions for working with ASP.NET and supports an easy-to-use fluent interface style for setting up and registering dependencies.

To initialize and use the Ninject IoC container, you need to set up its bootstrapper. The bootstrapper is responsible for managing the modules registered with Ninject. The important module to examine is the `BindingsModule`. Note the static `Start()` and `Stop()` methods of the bootstrapper. These methods need to be called from the *Global.asax* application start and end methods. Here's how to set up the Ninject bootstrapper:

```
private static readonly Bootstrapper bootstrapper = new Bootstrapper();

/// <summary>
/// Starts the application
/// </summary>
public static void Start()
{
    DynamicModuleUtility.RegisterModule(typeof(OnePerRequestModule));
    DynamicModuleUtility.RegisterModule(typeof(HttpApplicationInitializationModule));
    bootstrapper.Initialize(CreateKernel);
}

/// <summary>
/// Stops the application.
/// </summary>
public static void Stop()
{
    bootstrapper.ShutDown();
}

/// <summary>
/// Creates the kernel that will manage your application.
/// </summary>
/// <returns>The created kernel.</returns>
private static IKernel CreateKernel()
{
    var kernel - new StandardKernel();
    RegisterServices(kernel);
    return kernel;
```

```
    }

    /// <summary>
    /// Load your modules or register your services here!
    /// </summary>
    /// <param name="kernel">The kernel.</param>
    private static void RegisterServices(IKernel kernel)
    {
        kernel.Load(new BindingsModule());
    }
```

The `BindingsModule` inherits from the Ninject base module class and contains the dependency registration needed by the ASP.NET MVC Framework. Observe how the controller and route dependencies have been defined using a singleton scope. This means that both dependencies will be managed as a singleton and only one instance will ever be created. Any custom dependencies should be registered in the `Load()` method:

```
public class BindingsModule : Ninject.Modules.NinjectModule
{
    public override void Load()
    {
        Bind<ControllerActions>()
            .ToMethod(x => ControllerActions.DiscoverControllerActions())
            .InSingletonScope();

        Bind<IRouteGenerator>().To<RouteGenerator>().InSingletonScope();

        Bind<DataContext>().ToSelf().InRequestScope()
            .OnDeactivation(x => x.SaveChanges());

        Bind<IRepository>().To<Repository>().InRequestScope()
            .WithConstructorArgument("isSharedContext", true);
    }
}
```

When you register your own dependencies, you can define how the container should manage their lifetime, choose which arguments to pass to a constructor, and define what behavior to perform when a dependency is deactivated.

Using Inversion of Control to extend ASP.NET MVC

The ASP.NET MVC Framework relies heavily on the Inversion of Control principle. Out of the box, the framework contains a default controller factory that handles the creation of your application's controller by intercepting the input request execution, reading its MVC route and creating the specific controller, and calling a method on the controller based on the route definition. The other major area where IoC comes into play is in managing the view engine for your application and controlling the execution between the controller and its corresponding view(s).

The real power of IoC emerges when you extend the ASP.NET Framework by overriding its dependency resolver with your own IoC to gain direct control over the way

ASP.NET MVC manages dependencies and creates instances of objects. Overriding ASP.NET MVC's default dependency resolver is as simple as implementing the IDependencyResolver interface and registering your custom dependency resolver with the ASP.NET MVC Framework.

To see this in action, let's take a look at how to build a custom dependency resolver that uses the Ninject IoC. First, implement the IDependencyResolver interface, passing these calls through to an instance of IKernel (Ninject's IoC container class):

```
public class CustomDependencyResolver : IDependencyResolver
{
    private readonly Ninject.IKernel _kernel;

    public CustomDependencyResolver(Ninject.IKernel kernel)
    {
        _kernel = kernel;
    }

    public object GetService(Type serviceType)
    {
        return _kernel.TryGet(serviceType);
    }

    public IEnumerable<object> GetServices(Type serviceType)
    {
        return _kernel.GetAll(serviceType);
    }
}
```

Then, register this implementation by calling the static SetResolver() method on the System.Web.Mvc.DependencyResolver class, like so:

```
Ninject.IKernel kernel = new Ninject.StandardKernel();
DependencyResolver.SetResolver(new CustomDependencyResolver(kernel));
```

Notice how we first had to create a Ninject IKernel instance to pass in to the CustomDependencyResolver. Though every IoC container is implemented differently, most IoC frameworks require you to configure the container before it is able to create and resolve dependencies. In this example, Ninject's StandardKernel provides the same default configuration.

The snippet above will not work yet, however—you must first tell the StandardKernel about the classes and interfaces you want it to manage. With Ninject, this is done using the Bind<T>() method. For example, the call to tell Ninject to use the concrete implementation ErrorLogger whenever an IErrorLogger is required resembles:

```
kernel.Bind<IErrorLogger>().To<ErrorLogger>();
```

Here is an example of adding a new binding for the ErrorLogger class:

```
// Register services with container
kernel.Bind<IErrorLogger>().To<ErrorLogger>();
```

Don't Repeat Yourself

Don't Repeat Yourself (DRY) is a design principle, closely related to the SOLID principles, that encourages developers to avoid duplicating code that is the same or very similar.

Take a look at the SearchController class below; do you see any potential violations of the DRY principle? Everything looks good until you consider that there may be dozens of controllers in an application that all contain code exactly the same as or similar to this. At first, it may seem like a good idea to move the CheckUserRight() method to a base controller that all the controllers share. This approach would work, but the ASP.NET MVC Framework offers an even better option: a developer can create a custom ActionFilter to handle this behavior.

```
public class SearchController : Controller
{
    public ActionResult Add(Product product)
    {
        if (CheckUserRights())
            // Code for adding product

        return View();
    }

    public ActionResult Remove(Product product)
    {
        if (CheckUserRights())
            // Code for removing product

        return View();
    }

    private bool CheckUserRights()
    {
        // Code to verify if the user can perform the operation
    }
}
```

Summary

This chapter covered the key design patterns and principles used during the design of the ASP.NET MVC Framework. A developer can take advantage of these same principles (separation of concerns, Inversion of Control, and SOLID) to build a flexible and maintainable ASP.NET MVC web application. Using these principles goes beyond just writing better code. They are the fundamental building blocks for architecting a web application.

## CHAPTER 6

Enhancing Your Site with AJAX

The concept of a web application has changed greatly over the last 20 years. HTML was originally designed as a way to expose text-based content and easily link to other text-based pages via the Internet. After a little while, however, users and content producers alike wanted more from their web pages, so many websites began using JavaScript and Dynamic HTML techniques in order to make their static HTML content more interactive. Asynchronous JavaScript and XML—or, as it's more commonly known, *AJAX*—is a catchall term that refers to making asynchronous requests to the web server, avoiding the need to navigate to a new page in order to get fresh data.

Rather than transmitting and redrawing the entire page, AJAX techniques request content asynchronously and then use that content to update various sections of the page. AJAX techniques typically request one of two types of content: server-generated HTML markup that the browser injects directly into the page, and raw serialized data that client-side JavaScript logic uses to create new HTML or to update existing markup in the browser.

In this chapter, we will take a look at how to take advantage of the powerful features in ASP.NET MVC that help you incorporate AJAX techniques into your web applications.

Partial Rendering

The concept of making an HTTP request to a server and receiving HTML markup in response is the foundation of the World Wide Web. Therefore, making yet another request for more server-generated HTML markup in order to update or replace a section of the original page seems like a logical choice. This approach is called *partial rendering*, and it's a very effective option for powering simple and effective AJAX behaviors.

The partial rendering technique involves making an asynchronous request to the server, which replies with a chunk of HTML markup that is ready to insert right into the current page.

For example, let's say that you have the following document, *ajax_content.html*, that you'd like to asynchronously insert into a page:

```
<h2>This is the AJAX content!</h2>
```

And here's the page into which you want to insert this content:

```
<html>
<body>
<h1>Partial Rendering Demo</h1>
<div id="container" />
</body>
</html>
```

This example uses the `<div id="container" />` element to mark where you want to insert the dynamic content. You can then populate the `<div id="container" />` element with the server-side content in *ajax_content.html* using the jQuery `.load()` method:

```
$("#container").load('ajax_content.html')
```

The `.load()` method makes an asynchronous request for the server-side content, then injects it into the `#container` element. After the call, the DOM will include the dynamically retrieved server-side content:

```
<html>
<body>
<h1>Partial Rendering Demo</h1>
<div id="container">
  <h2>This is the AJAX content!</h2>
</div>
</body>
</html>
```

As this example shows, the partial rendering approach is a simple and effective way to dynamically update sections of your web pages. What's more, it's incredibly easy to implement in an ASP.NET MVC application!

Rendering Partial Views

For the most part, ASP.NET MVC treats a partial rendering request the same as any other request—the request is routed to the appropriate controller action, and the controller action performs any logic that it needs to.

The difference occurs toward the end of the request, when it comes time to render the view. Whereas the normal course of action might be to use the `Controller.View()` helper method to return a `ViewResult`, you instead call the `Controller.Partial()` helper to return a `PartialViewResult`. This is very similar to the `ViewResult`, except that it only renders the content of the view—it does not render the view's layout.

To demonstrate the difference, let's compare the rendered markup from a partial view of an `Auction` with the rendered markup generated for the "normal" view of an `Auction`.

Rendering a "normal" view

The following controller action (*AuctionsController.cs*) calls the `Controller.View()` helper method that you're already familiar with:

```
public class AuctionsController : Controller
{
  public ActionResult Auction(long id)
  {
    var db = new DataContext();
    var auction = db.Auctions.Find(id);

    return View("Auction", auction);
  }
}
```

Its corresponding *Auction* view (*Auction.cshtml*) looks like this:

```
@model Auction

<div class="title">@Model.Title</div>

<div class="overview">
    <img src="@Model.ImageUrl" alt="@Model.Title" />
    <p>
        <strong>Current Price: </strong>
        <span class="current-price">@Model.CurrentPrice</span>
    </p>
</div>

<h3>Description</h3>
<div class="description">
    @Model.Description
</div>
```

This combination produces the final rendered HTML shown in Example 6-1.

Example 6-1. Rendered markup for "normal" Auction view

```
<!DOCTYPE html>
<html>
<head>
    <meta charset="utf-8" />
    <link href="/Content/Site.css" rel="stylesheet" type="text/css" />
    <link href="/Content/themes/base/jquery.ui.all.css" rel="stylesheet" type="text/css" />
    <script src="/Scripts/jquery-1.7.1.min.js" type="text/javascript"></script>
    <script src="/Scripts/jquery-ui-1.8.16.js" type="text/javascript"></script>
    <script src="/Scripts/modernizr-2.0.6.js" type="text/javascript"></script>
    <script src="/Scripts/AjaxLogin.js" type="text/javascript"></script>
</head>

<body>
    <header>
      <h1 class="site-title"><a href="/">EBuy: The ASP.NET MVC Demo Site</a></h1>
      <nav>
          <ul id="menu">
                  <li><a href="/categories/Electronics">Electronics</a></li>
```

```
                <li><a href="/categories/Home_and_Outdoors">Home/Outdoors</a></li>
                <li><a href="/categories/Collectibles">Collectibles</a></li>
            </ul>
        </nav>
    </header>

    <section id="main">

<div class="title">Xbox 360 Kinect Sensor with Game Bundle</div>

<div class="overview">
    <img src="/Content/images/products/kinect.jpg"  alt="Xbox 360 Kinect Sensor with Game ↵
    Bundle" />
    <p>
        Closing in <span class="time-remaining">4 days, 19 hours</span>
    </p>
    <div>
        <a class="show-bid-history"  href="/auctions/764cc5090c04/bids">Bid History</a>
    </div>
    <p>
        <strong>Current Price: </strong>
        <span class="current-price">$43.00</span>
    </p>
</div>

<h3>Description</h3>
<div class="description">
    You are the controller with Kinect for Xbox 360!
</div>

    </section>

    <footer>
        <p>&copy; 2012 - EBuy: The ASP.NET MVC Demo Site</p>
    </footer>
</body>
</html>
```

Rendering a partial view

Notice how the *Auctions.cshtml* view is rendered inside the site's layout. This is exactly
what users need to see when they browse to the page for the first time. But what if we
want to reuse the layout markup that effectively stays the same for every page in the
site, and update just the auction information in order to display the details of another
auction without the user being required to navigate to another page?

The answer is to use the `Controller.PartialView()` method to create a `PartialViewRe
sult` instead of the `ViewResult` that the `Controller.View()` method generates:

```
public class AuctionsController : Controller
{
  public ActionResult Auction(long id)
  {
    var db = new DataContext();
```

```
    var auction = db.Auctions.Find(id);

    return View("Auction", auction);
  }

  public ActionResult PartialAuction(long id)
  {
    var db = new DataContext();
    var auction = db.Auctions.Find(id);

    return PartialView("Auction", auction);
  }
}
```

Notice how nothing else has changed except the switch from the View() method to the
PartialView() method. The PartialViewResult can even use exactly the same views
that the ViewResult depends on. In fact, the PartialViewResult and ViewResult are
nearly identical, except for one very important difference: the PartialViewResult renders *only* the markup in the view itself and does not render any layout or master page
that the view may specify. What's more, partial views behave the same way as normal
views, so you are free to use any type of syntax you like (such as the Razor syntax) and
make full use of ASP.NET MVC view functionality such as HTML helpers.

 Since partial pages do not execute the layout, you may have to include
some dependencies, such as CSS or JavaScript, directly in the partial
view rather than including them in the page's layout.

This means that—using the same view shown in *Auction.cshtml* in the previous section
—the PartialView result will render the markup in Example 6-2.

Example 6-2. Rendered markup for the partial auction view

```
<div class="title">Xbox 360 Kinect Sensor with Game Bundle</div>

<div class="overview">
    <img src="/Content/images/products/kinect.jpg"  alt="Xbox 360 Kinect Sensor with Game ↵
    Bundle" />
    <p>
        Closing in <span class="time-remaining">4 days, 19 hours</span>
    </p>
    <div>
        <a class="show-bid-history" href="/auctions/764cc5090c04/bids">Bid History</a>
    </div>
    <p>
        <strong>Current Price: </strong>
        <span class="current-price">$43.00</span>
    </p>
</div>

<h3>Description</h3>
<div class="description">
```

```
    You are the controller with Kinect for Xbox 360!
</div>
```

With these changes, you can now use the following jQuery client-side code to load the HTML for new auctions without having to navigate to a new page:

```
function showAuction(auctionId) {
  $('#main').load('/Auctions/PartialAuction/' + auctionId);
}
```

 If you write the previous snippet inside of a Razor view, you can leverage the ASP.NET MVC `UrlHelper` to generate the correct route to the `AuctionsController.Auction` action.

Simply replace this:

`'/Auctions/PartialAuction/' + auctionId`

with:

`'@Url("PartialAuction", "Auctions")/' + auctionId`

Managing complexity with partial views

The previous example showed how you can use partial views to display a page without its layout. Partial views needn't always be full pages, however—splitting a page into multiple partial views is often a very good way to help simplify an otherwise overwhelming and complex view.

Perhaps the best example of managing complexity with partial views is when you need to display something in a foreach loop, as in the list of auctions shown in the following snippet:

```
@model IEnumerable<Auction>

<h1>Auctions</h1>
<section class="auctions">

@foreach(var auction in Model) {
  <section class="auction">
    <div class="title">@auction.Title</div>

    <div class="overview">
        <img src="@auction.ImageUrl" alt="@auction.Title" />
        <p>
            <strong>Current Price: </strong>
            <span class="current-price">@auction.CurrentPrice</span>
        </p>
    </div>

    <h3>Description</h3>
    <div class="description">
        @auction.Description
    </div>
```

```
        </section>
    }

    </section>
```

Take a close look at the markup inside of the `foreach` loop—does it remind you of something you've seen before? It's *exactly the same markup* from *Auctions.cshtml* that we used as a partial rendering result!

That means we should be able to replace that whole section with a call to the `Html.Partial()` helper to render the partial view we've already created:

```
@model IEnumerable<Auction>

<h1>Auctions</h1>
<section class="auctions">

@foreach(var auction in Model) {
    <section class="auction">
        @Html.Partial("Auction", auction)
    </section>
}

</section>
```

Notice how we can specify the model that the partial view renders by passing it as the second parameter to the `Html.Partial()` helper. This allows us to iterate through the entire list of `Auction` objects and apply the same view to each instance.

As the examples in this section show, effectively applying partial views can not only help simplify each individual view and reduce the amount of duplicate code in your application, it is also a great way to maintain consistency throughout your site.

JavaScript Rendering

Although the prerendered HTML approach is very easy and effective, it can also be quite wasteful to transmit both the data you'd like to display and the markup to display it, when the browser is perfectly capable of creating that markup itself. Thus, the alternative to retrieving prerendered HTML from the server is to retrieve the raw data that you'd like to display, then use that data to create and update HTML elements by manipulating the DOM directly.

In order to implement a client-side rendering approach, you must have two things: a server that can produce the serialized data, and client-side logic that knows how to parse the serialized data and convert it into HTML markup.

Rendering JSON Data

Let's tackle the server-side piece first: responding to an AJAX request with serialized data. Before we can do this, however, we must decide what technique we are going to use to serialize that data.

JavaScript Object Notation (JSON) is a simple and very effective format for transmitting data over the Web. JSON objects leverage two types of data structures to represent data: collections of name/value pairs, and ordered lists of values (aka arrays). And, as its name implies, JavaScript Object Notation is based on a subset of the JavaScript language, so all modern browsers already understand it.

ASP.NET MVC offers native JSON support in the form of the `JsonResult` action result, which accepts a model object that it serializes into the JSON format. In order to add AJAX support to your controller actions via JSON, simply use the `Controller.Json()` method to create a new `JsonResult` containing the object to be serialized.

To show the `Json()` helper and `JsonResult` in action, let's add a `JsonAuction` action to the `AuctionsController`:

```
public ActionResult JsonAuction(long id)
{
    var db = new DataContext();
    var auction = db.Auctions.Find(id);

    return Json(auction, JsonRequestBehavior.AllowGet);
}
```

This new controller action responds to requests with the JSON-serialized version of the auction data. For example:

```
{
  "Title": "XBOX 360",
  "Description": "Brand new XBOX 360 console",
  "StartTime": "01/12/2012 12:00 AM",
  "EndTime": "01/31/2012 12:00 AM",
  "CurrentPrice": "$199.99",
  "Bids": [
    {
      "Amount"   : "$200.00",
      "Timestamp": "01/12/2012 6:00 AM"
    },
    {
      "Amount"   : "$205.00",
      "Timestamp": "01/14/2012 8:00 AM"
    },
    {
      "Amount"   : "$210.00",
      "Timestamp": "01/15/2012 12:32 PM"
    }
  ]
}
```

This snippet is a great example of JSON's simplicity and elegance—notice how [and] define arrays and how property values can be simple data types or complex data types represented by JSON objects themselves. This syntax also has the positive side effect of making JSON data very human-readable.

Avoiding JSON hijacking with JsonRequestBehavior

Notice that the Json() method's second parameter is JsonRequestBehavior.AllowGet, which explicitly informs the ASP.NET MVC Framework that it's acceptable to return JSON data in response to an HTTP GET request.

The JsonRequestBehavior.AllowGet parameter is necessary in this case because, by default, ASP.NET MVC disallows returning JSON in response to an HTTP GET request in order to avoid a potentially dangerous security vulnerability known as *JSON hijacking*. This vulnerability takes advantage of a glitch in the way that many browsers handle JavaScript <script> tags that can lead to exposing sensitive information if the data in the request includes a JSON array.

Though it is somewhat complex, all you really need to know to avoid this vulnerability is that you should never return data from a GET request that you would not want shared with the world. Therefore, ASP.NET MVC makes you deliberately opt in to delivering JSON data through this insecure way when you are returning publicly accessible (non-sensitive) data by leveraging the JsonRequestBehavior.AllowGet option.

In scenarios where you need to transmit sensitive information via a JSON response, you can protect yourself from this vulnerability by restricting access to your controller method to HTTP POST requests only by applying the HttpPostAttribute:

```
[HttpPost]
public ActionResult JsonAuction(long id)
{
    var db = new DataContext();
    var auction = db.Auctions.Find(id);

    return Json(auction);
}
```

Requesting JSON Data

With the server-side functionality in place, we now need to make a request to retrieve the JSON data so that we can use it to build markup in the client. Luckily, jQuery makes this very easy to do.

To request JSON data from an ASP.NET MVC controller action, simply make an $.ajax() call to the controller action URL and specify a success function to handle the response. The first parameter of the success function (named "result" in the example below) contains the deserialized object returned from the server.

The following snippet demonstrates this by calling our new `JsonAuction` controller action and using jQuery's `.val()` and `.html()` methods to update the DOM with the JSON-serialized `Auction` data that the controller action returns:

```
function updateAuctionInfo(auctionId) {
  $.ajax({
    url: "/Auctions/JsonAuction/" + auctionId,
    success: function (result) {
      $('#Title').val(result.Title);
      $('#Description').val(result.Description);
      $('#CurrentPrice').html(result.CurrentPrice);
    }
  });
}
```

While this client-side rendering approach may require a bit more code, it allows you to send the least amount of data over the wire, which generally makes it a much more efficient method of transmitting and displaying AJAX data.

Client-Side Templates

While the string concatenation approach shown above is an effective way to generate client-side markup, it is really only suitable for small sections of markup. As the amount of markup grows, it adds to the complexity of the code that needs to concatenate it, resulting in something that is increasingly difficult to maintain.

Client-side templates are a powerful alternative to simple string concatenation that let you quickly and efficiently transform JSON data into HTML in a very maintainable way. Client-side templates define reusable sections of markup by combining simple HTML with data expressions that can range from simple placeholders to be replaced with data values, to full-blown JavaScript logic that can perform even more powerful data processing directly within the template.

Note that the concept of client-side templates is not part of any official specification, so in order to take advantage of this approach, you will need to rely on a JavaScript library to help you out. Though the exact syntax will differ between the various libraries, the fundamental concept remains the same: the library will take client template markup and parse it into a function that knows how to produce HTML markup from a JSON object.

The following examples use the Mustache template syntax (*http://mustache.github .com/*) to define the client template markup and the *mustache.js* JavaScript library (*https: //github.com/janl/mustache.js*) to parse and execute the client templates in the browser. However, there are plenty of client template libraries available for you to choose from, so be sure to research each of them and choose the one that best fits the needs of your application.

To see client-side templates in action, let's rewrite the *Auction* view from earlier in the chapter into client template syntax:

```
<div class="title">{{Title}}</div>

<div class="overview">
  <img src="{{ImageUrl}}" alt="{{Title}}" />
  <p>
    <strong>Current Price: </strong>
    <span class="current-bid">{{CurrentPrice}}</span>
  </p>
</div>

<h3>Description</h3>
<div class="description">
  {{Description}}
</div>
```

Notice how the markup of the client template looks almost identical to the final output. In fact, the only difference is that the client template has data placeholders instead of actual data. Also note that this is a very simple example to show the fundamental concept of client templating—most client template libraries offer *far more* functionality than simple placeholders.

The second step is to *compile* the client template, or convert the client template HTML into an executable JavaScript function.

 Since compiling the template is often the most expensive operation in the process, it's often a good idea to compile it once and save the compiled function in a variable.

This way, you can execute the compiled template multiple times while only performing the compilation once.

Finally, we invoke the compiled template by passing it the data that we wish to convert into HTML. The compiled template then returns formatted HTML, which we can insert into the DOM wherever we like.

Take a look at Example 6-3 for an end-to-end example of a page that leverages client templates.

Example 6-3. A complete client template example

```
@model IEnumerable<Auction>

<h2>Auctions</h2>

<ul class="auctions">
    @foreach(var auction in Model) {
        <li class="auction" data-key="@auction.Key">
            <a href="#">
            <img src="@auction.ThumbnailUrl" />
            <span>@auction.Title</span>
            </a>
        </li>
```

```
        }
    </ul>

    <section id="auction-details">
        @Html.Partial("Auction", Model.First())
    </section>

    <script id="auction-template" type="text/x-template">
        <div class="title">{{Title}}</div>

        <div class="overview">
            <img src="{{ImageUrl}}" alt="{{Title}}" />
            <p>
                <strong>Current Price: </strong>
                <span class="current-bid">{{CurrentPrice}}</span>
            </p>
        </div>

        <h3>Description</h3>
        <div class="description">
            {{Description}}
        </div>
    </script>

    <script type="text/javascript" src="~/scripts/mustache.js"></script>

    <script type="text/javascript">
      $(function() {
        var templateSource = $('#auction-template').html();
        var template = Mustache.compile(templateSource);

        $('.auction').click(function() {
          var auctionId = $(this).data("key");
          $.ajax({
            url: '@Url.Action("JsonAuction", "Auctions")/' + auctionId,
            success: function(auction) {
              var html = template(auction);
              $('#auction-details').html(html);
            }
          });
        });
      });
    </script>
```

While it looks like there is quite a bit going on in this example, it is actually quite simple:

1. When the page loads, the script block at the bottom retrieves the client template markup from the inner HTML of the auction-template element.

2. The script then passes the client template markup to the Mustache.compile() method to compile it into a JavaScript function, which it saves to the template variable.

3. The script block then listens for the click event on each `Auction` element in the list of `Auction+s`, which triggers an AJAX request to retrieve the JSON-serialized data for that +Auction.

   - Upon successfully retrieving the `Auction` data, the `success` handler executes the previously compiled client template (stored in the `template` variable) to produce markup from the JSON data.

   - Finally, the `success` handler calls the `.html()` method to replace the content of the `auction-details` element with the markup generated from the `template` function.

 The "`text/x-template`" MIME type is an arbitrary, made-up type—you are free to use just about any invalid MIME type value here.

Browsers ignore script tags that specify MIME types that the browser doesn't understand, so wrapping the template markup in a script tag and setting its MIME type to an "invalid" value such as "`text/x-tem plate`" prevents the browser from rendering it as normal HTML with the rest of the page.

While the client template approach may seem like a lot of work, in most cases the ease of maintenance and the lower bandwidth costs that it allows make it well worth the up-front cost. When your application relies on lots of AJAX interactions that result in complex client-side markup, client templates are often a great choice.

Reusing Logic Across AJAX and Non-AJAX Requests

The Model-View-Controller pattern that drives the ASP.NET MVC Framework leverages a strong separation of concerns to help ensure that individual components are isolated from each other. Though our `PartialAuction` and `JsonAuction` controller actions might do exactly what we want them to, if we take a step back to scrutinize them, we begin to see that we've broken several of the patterns and practices that are so fundamental to the MVC philosophy.

When done right, MVC application logic should not be tied to a particular view. Why, then, do we have *three* controller actions (shown in Example 6-4) that perform the same logic and only differ in the way that they return the content to the browser?

Example 6-4. AuctionsController.cs with three ways to retrieve an Auction

```
public class AuctionsController : Controller
{
  public ActionResult Auction(long id)
  {
    var db = new DataContext();
    var auction = db.Auctions.Find(id);
```

```
        return View("Auction", auction);
    }

    [HttpPost]
    public ActionResult JsonAuction(long id)
    {
        var db = new DataContext();
        var auction = db.Auctions.Find(id);

        return Json(auction);
    }

    public ActionResult PartialAuction(long id)
    {
      var db = new DataContext();
      var auction = db.Auctions.Find(id);

      return PartialView("Auction", auction);
    }
}
```

Responding to AJAX Requests

In order to help alleviate this duplication of logic and code, ASP.NET MVC provides
the Request.IsAjaxRequest() extension method, which lets us know whether or not the
request is an AJAX request. We can then use this information to determine what format
the requester expects to receive its response in and which action result we should choose
to generate that response.

 The Request.IsAjaxRequest() method is quite simple: it merely checks
the HTTP headers for the incoming request to see if the value of the X-
Requested-With header is XMLHttpRequest, which is automatically ap-
pended by most browsers and AJAX frameworks.

If you ever need to trick ASP.NET MVC into thinking that a request is
an AJAX request, simply add the X-Requested-With: XMLHttpRequest
HTTP header.

To demonstrate the Request.IsAjaxRequest() method in action, let's first try to merge
the Auction and PartialAuction controller actions together. The combined controller
action should retrieve the auction instance from the data context, then choose which
way to display it. If the request is an AJAX request, use the PartialView() method to
return a PartialViewResult, and otherwise, use the View() method to return a
ViewResult:

```
    public ActionResult Auction(long id)
    {
      var db = new DataContext();
      var auction = db.Auctions.Find(id);
```

```
  if (Request.IsAjaxRequest())
    return PartialView("Auction", auction);

  return View("Auction", auction);
}
```

With this change in place, the `Auction` controller action is able to respond to both "normal" HTTP `GET` requests and AJAX requests with the appropriate view, using the same application logic.

Responding to JSON Requests

Unfortunately, ASP.NET does not provide a helpful method such as `Request.IsAjax Request()` to help determine whether the requester expects JSON data. However, with a little creativity we can easily implement this logic ourselves.

We'll start with perhaps the simplest solution: adding a custom parameter to the controller action to indicate that the request expects JSON data in response.

For instance, we can look for a request parameter named `format` and return a `JsonRe sult` whenever the value of this parameter is `"json"`:

```
public ActionResult Auction(long id)
{
  var db = new DataContext();
  var auction = db.Auctions.Find(id);

  if (string.Equals(request["format"], "json"))
    return Json(auction);

  return View("Auction", auction);
}
```

Clients may then request auction data from this action in JSON format by appending the query string "?format=json" to their request; for example, */Auctions/Auction/1234? format=json*.

We can also take this one step further by moving this logic into its own extension method so that we can call it from anywhere, just like the `Request.IsAjaxRequest()` extension method:

```
using System;
using System.Web;

public static class JsonRequestExtensions
{
  public static bool IsJsonRequest(this HttpRequestBase request)
  {
    return string.Equals(request["format"], "json");
  }
}
```

With the `IsJsonRequest()` extension method, the previous snippet can be cleaned up as follows:

```
public ActionResult Auction(long id)
{
  var db = new DataContext();
  var auction = db.Auctions.Find(id);

  if (Request.IsJsonRequest())
    return Json(auction);

  return View("Auction", auction);
}
```

Applying the Same Logic Across Multiple Controller Actions

If we combine the partial rendering and JSON conditional approaches shown above into the same controller action, we end up with a very flexible approach that is able to produce different outputs based on the same application logic. Take a look at the optimized *AuctionsController.cs*:

```
public class AuctionsController : Controller
{
  public ActionResult Auction(long id)
  {
    var db = new DataContext();
    var auction = db.Auctions.Find(id);

    // Respond to AJAX requests
    if (Request.IsAjaxRequest())
      return PartialView("Auction", auction);

    // Respond to JSON requests
    if (Request.IsJsonRequest())
      return Json(auction);

    // Default to a "normal" view with layout
    return View("Auction", auction);
  }
}
```

The code that drives this controller action may be flexible, but the fact that it is defined inside the `Auction` controller action means that no other actions are able to leverage it. Luckily, ASP.NET MVC offers the perfect mechanism to reuse logic across multiple controller actions: *action filters*.

To move this logic into an action filter that can be applied to other controller actions, begin by creating a class that implements the `System.Web.Mvc.ActionFilterAttribute` type and override its `OnActionExecuted()` method. This will allow us to modify the result of the action after the action has executed, but before the action result has been executed:

```
public class MultipleResponseFormatsAttribute : ActionFilterAttribute
{
    public override void OnActionExecuted(ActionExecutedContext filterContext)
    {
        // We will add the logic here
    }
}
```

Then, move the logic from the Auction controller action into this new class and use it to replace the action result that the controller originally returned (filterCon text.Result) when the request is an AJAX or JSON request:

```
using System;
using System.Web.Mvc;

public class MultipleResponseFormatsAttribute : ActionFilterAttribute
{
  public override void OnActionExecuted(ActionExecutedContext filterContext)
  {
    var request = filterContext.HttpContext.Request;
    var viewResult = filterContext.Result as ViewResult;

    if (viewResult == null)
        return;


    if (request.IsAjaxRequest())
    {
      // Replace result with PartialViewResult
      filterContext.Result = new PartialViewResult
          {
              TempData = viewResult.TempData,
              ViewData = viewResult.ViewData,
              ViewName = viewResult.ViewName,
          };
    }
    else if (Request.IsJsonRequest())
    {
      // Replace result with JsonResult
      filterContext.Result = new JsonResult
          {
              Data = viewResult.Model
          };
    }
  }
}
```

Now you can easily apply the MultipleResponseFormatsAttribute action filter to any controller action in your website, instantly adding the ability to dynamically choose between returning a view, partial view, or JSON response, depending on the incoming request.

Sending Data to the Server

The first half of this chapter concentrated on requesting content and data *from* the server via AJAX. Now it's time to take a look at the other half of the equation: sending data *to* the server via AJAX.

The two most popular ways to "send" data to any web server are through URL query string parameters (generally via an HTTP GET request) and form post data (generally via an HTTP POST request). The first chapter of the book introduced the concept of ASP.NET MVC model binding, showing off ASP.NET MVC's ability to "automagically" populate controller action parameters from values in the request.

What the introductory chapter didn't show is that, in addition to mapping query string and "normal" HTTP form post values, ASP.NET MVC's model binding framework also knows how to bind JSON objects to action parameters. This means that you do not need to do anything at all to your controller actions to make them accept JSON data—it just works out of the box!

So, now we'll skip over to the client side, where jQuery's `$.post()` method makes it very easy to post JSON data to our controller actions. To post an object to the server, simply provide the URL that you'd like to post to and the object containing what you'd like to send—jQuery takes care of serializing the object to JSON and attaching it as the request's form post data.

To see this in action, take a look at this example, which populates a new `Auction` object via JavaScript and posts it to the `Create` controller action (shown in the example that follows):

```
var auction = {
  "Title": "New Auction",
  "Description": "This is an awesome item!",
  "StartPrice": "$5.00",
  "StartTime": "01/12/2012 6:00 AM",
  "EndTime": "01/19/2012 6:00 AM"
};

$.post('@Url.Action("Create", "Auctions")', auction);
```

Remember, the controller action doesn't need to do anything special—the JSON data is automatically bound to the `auction` controller action parameter. All that's left for the controller action to do is perform its logic (i.e., adding the auction to the database) and return a result. The `Create` controller action looks like this:

```
[HttpPost]
public ActionResult Create(Auction auction)
{
  if(ModelState.IsValid)
  {
    var db = new DataContext();
    db.Auctions.Add(auction);
```

```
        return View("Auction", auction);
    }

    return View("Create", auction);
}
```

Posting Complex JSON Objects

The default JSON model binding logic does have one important limitation: it is implemented as an all-or-nothing approach. That is, the factory expects the *entire* response to include a single JSON object and does not support the ability for individual fields to deliver data in JSON format.

Let's look at an example where the default approach will lead to trouble. Suppose we have a collection of Bid objects, each with two properties, Amount and Timestamp:

```
Bid[0].Timestamp="01/12/2012 6:00 AM" &
Bid[0].Amount=100.00 &

Bid[1].Timestamp="01/12/2012 6:42 AM" &
Bid[1].Amount=73.64
```

Here is how that same request would be represented in JSON format:

```
[
    { "Timestamp":"01/12/2012 6:00 AM", "Amount":100.00 },
    { "Timestamp":"01/12/2012 6:42 AM", "Amount":73.64 }
]
```

Not only is the JSON array much cleaner, simpler, and smaller, it's also much easier to build and manage using JavaScript in the browser. This simplicity is particularly helpful when building a form dynamically, for example, allowing the user to bid on multiple auctions at one time.

However, in order to represent the Bid field as JSON using the DefaultModelBinder, you'd need to post the entire object as a JSON object. For example:

```
{
    Bids:
    [
        { "Timestamp":"01/12/2012 6:00 AM", "Amount":100.00 },
        { "Timestamp":"01/12/2012 6:42 AM", "Amount":73.64 }
    ],
}
```

On the surface, posting JSON objects to be used for model binding looks like a great idea. However, this approach has a number of downsides.

First, the client must build the entire request dynamically, and this logic must know how to explicitly manage every field that must be sent down—the HTML form ceases to become a form and simply becomes a way for the JavaScript logic to collect data from the user.

Then, on the server side, the JSON value provider ignores all HTTP requests except those with the Content Type header set to "application/json", so this approach will not work for standard GET requests; it only works for AJAX requests that contain the correct header. Finally, when the default validation logic fails for even just one field, the model binder considers the *entire object* to be invalid!

To help reduce these drawbacks, we can introduce an alternative to the built-in JSON model binding logic by creating our own custom JSON model binder, shown in Example 6-5. JsonModelBinder differs from the JSON value provider factory in that it allows each individual field to contain JSON, eliminating the need to send the entire request as a single JSON object. Since the model binder binds each property separately, you can mix and match which fields contain simple values and which fields support JSON data. As with most custom model binders, the JSON model binder derives from DefaultModelBinder so that it can fall back to the default binding logic when fields do not contain JSON data.

Example 6-5. JsonModelBinder

```
public class JsonModelBinder : DefaultModelBinder
{
    public override object BindModel
        (
            ControllerContext controllerContext,
            ModelBindingContext bindingContext
        )
    {
        string json = string.Empty;

        var provider = bindingContext.ValueProvider;
        var providerValue = provider.GetValue(bindingContext.ModelName);

        if (providerValue != null)
            json = providerValue.AttemptedValue;

        // Basic expression to make sure the string starts and ends
        // with JSON object ( {} ) or array ( [] ) characters
        if (Regex.IsMatch(json, @"^(\[.*\]|{.*})$"))
        {
            return new JavaScriptSerializer()
                    .Deserialize(json, bindingContext.ModelType);
        }

        return base.BindModel(controllerContext, bindingContext);
    }
}
```

Model Binder Selection

Given ASP.NET MVC's focus on extensibility, it is probably no surprise to find out that there are quite a few ways to specify which model binder should be used for any given model. In fact, the comments in the source code for the `ModelBinderDiction` `ary.GetBinder()` method literally spell out how the framework discovers the appropriate model binder for each type:

```
private IModelBinder GetBinder(Type modelType, IModelBinder fallbackBinder) {

    // Try to look up a binder for this type. We use this order of precedence:
    // 1. Binder returned from provider
    // 2. Binder registered in the global table
    // 3. Binder attribute defined on the type
    // 4. Supplied fallback binder
```

Let's tackle this list from the bottom up.

Replacing the default (fallback) binder

With no additional configuration, ASP.NET MVC will bind all models using the `DefaultModelBinder`. You can replace this global default handler by setting the `Model` `Binders.Binders.DefaultBinder` property to a new model binder. For example:

```
protected void Application_Start()
{
    ModelBinders.Binders.DefaultBinder = new JsonModelBinder();
    // ...
}
```

With this setting in place, the instance of `JsonModelBinder` will act as the new fallback binder, handling the binding of all models that haven't specified otherwise.

Adorning models with custom attributes

Perhaps the most elegant approach for specifying model binders is to use the abstract `System.Web.Mvc.CustomModelBinderAttribute` to decorate both classes and individual properties in a nicely declarative way. Though you can apply this approach to any model that you wish to bind, it is best combined with the request model approach because the model binding is the sole reason the request model exists!

In order to leverage the `CustomModelBinderAttribute` approach, you first need to create an implementation. The following code shows an example of a `CustomModelBinder` `Attribute` and how it can be applied to the `CreateProductRequest` model:

```
[AttributeUsage(AttributeTargets.Class | AttributeTargets.Enum |
                AttributeTargets.Interface | AttributeTargets.Parameter |
                AttributeTargets.Struct | AttributeTargets.Property,
                AllowMultiple = false, Inherited = false)]
public class JsonModelBinderAttribute : CustomModelBinderAttribute
{
    public override IModelBinder GetBinder()
```

```
        {
            return new JsonModelBinder();
        }
    }

    public class CreateProductRequest
    {
        // ...

        [Required]
        [JsonModelBinder]
        public IEnumerable<CurrencyRequest> UnitPrice { get; set; }
    }
```

Decorating `CreateProductRequest.UnitPrice` with the `JsonModelBinderAttribute` indicates that the model binder should use the `JsonModelBinder` (created with a call to `JsonModelBinderAttribute.GetBinder()`) to bind the `CreateProductRequest.UnitPrice` property.

That is, unless a global handler or model binder provider has been registered for the `CurrencyRequest` type...

Registering a global binder

In much the same way that you can set the default model binder as the fallback for all model types, you can register model binders for individual types as well. Like setting the default model binder, the syntax is very simple.

This example tells the framework to use the `JsonModelBinder` for every `Currency` model it comes across:

```
ModelBinders.Binders.Add(typeof(Currency), new JsonModelBinder());
```

This approach allows you to associate a model binder with a particular type across the entire application in a single line. It's also an effective way to control how business models are bound without having to decorate those models with custom model binder attributes.

Sending and Receiving JSON Data Effectively

JSON is a fundamental building block for building rich, interactive AJAX-based web applications, so it's important to understand how to properly utilize it. As the following section shows, jQuery makes it easy for you to work with JSON data and query HTML elements.

One of the most challenging things to deal with when working with JSON data is serialization. Complex objects that have many relationships or are tightly coupled to a specific data access technology such as Entity Framework may present problems. When returning a JSON result, if the object passed in cannot be serialized, a 500 internal server error will be returned.

The other major drawback to working with complex objects is that they may be heavy or challenging to work with via JavaScript. A good practice to help avoid these challenges is to create a special, lightweight version of the entity called a *data transfer object* (DTO) that is more easily converted into JSON. DTOs should use simple data structures and avoid complex multilevel relationships.

Additionally, DTOs should contain only the fields that the application or request requires, and no more. It is perfectly acceptable to have multiple DTO classes—even for the same entity—to act as the responses for various requests.

The following code shows an example of a simple DTO object. Its simplified data structure is specifically designed to make it easier to work with in JavaScript. What's more, the fact that the DTO is smaller than the `Auction` model makes it an optimal data structure for an AJAX response:

```
public class AuctionDto
{
    public string Title { get; set; }
    public string Description { get; set; }
}
```

Cross-Domain AJAX

By default, web browsers restrict AJAX calls to be made only to the web application's site of origin. This restriction is a good thing to prevent nasty security issues like cross-site scripting (XSS) attacks. Sometimes, though, applications require the ability to interact with externally hosted Representational State Transfer (REST) API(s) like Twitter or Google.

For these scenarios to work, the externally hosted web application must support JSONP requests or Cross-Origin Resource Sharing (CORS). Out of the box, ASP.NET MVC does not offer any direct support for either option; adding these features requires a little bit of coding and configuration.

JSONP

JSONP (which stands for "JSON with Padding") is a clever trick that takes advantage of the Cross-Site Request Forgery exploit on page 199, allowing you to make cross-domain AJAX calls even when browsers are trying as hard as they can to keep you from doing so.

From a high level, a JSONP interaction involves several steps:

1. The client creates a JavaScript function that it expects to be called upon receiving the JSONP response from the server; e.g., updateAuction.

2. The client dynamically adds a `<script>` tag to the DOM, tricking the browser into thinking it is making a standard script include and taking advantage of the fact that browsers allow `<script>` references to other domains.

3. The `<script>` tag references a call to a data service that supports JSONP and the client specifies the name of the callback function created in step 1 in the URL; e.g., `<script href="http://other.com/auctions/1234?callback=updateAuction" />`.

4. The server processes the request and proceeds to render it just as it would any other JSON request, with one important distinction: instead of returning the JSON object as the full content of the response, it wraps the object in a call to the client-side *callback* function name that the client provided (as shown in the example below).

Note that the server neither knows nor cares about what the callback function does. The server's only responsibility is to call the function and assume that the function exists on the client side:

```
updateAuction({
  "Title": "XBOX 360",
  "Description": "Brand new XBOX 360 console",
  "StartTime": "01/12/2012 12:00 AM",
  "EndTime": "01/31/2012 12:00 AM",
  "CurrentPrice": "$199.99",
  "Bids": [
    {
      "Amount"   : "$200.00",
      "Timestamp": "01/12/2012 6:00 AM"
    },
    {
      "Amount"   : "$205.00",
      "Timestamp": "01/14/2012 8:00 AM"
    },
    {
      "Amount"   : "$210.00",
      "Timestamp": "01/15/2012 12:32 PM"
    }
  ]
});
```

It's very important to note that the JSONP approach describes a different method of client/server data exchange. Rather than returning raw JSON data (as is the case in normal AJAX responses), in a JSONP response the server wraps the raw JSON data in a call to the specified client-side function (JSONP responses are, after all, JavaScript script files, and accordingly, they can execute client-side logic). Consequently, the only way to access data returned via a JSONP call is within the client-side function—it cannot be accessed directly.

In the above example, for instance, the JSONP response consisted merely of a call to the client-side callback that passed the serialized JSON object. The JSONP response could just as well have executed other logic prior to executing the callback, however: for example, converting the timestamps into the user's local time zone before displaying them on the screen:

```javascript
var data = {
  "Title": "XBOX 360",
  "Description": "Brand new XBOX 360 console",
  "StartTime": "01/12/2012 12:00 AM",
  "EndTime": "01/31/2012 12:00 AM",
  "CurrentPrice": "$199.99",
  "Bids": [
    {
      "Amount"   : "$200.00",
      "Timestamp": "01/12/2012 6:00 AM"
    },
    {
      "Amount"   : "$205.00",
      "Timestamp": "01/14/2012 8:00 AM"
    },
    {
      "Amount"   : "$210.00",
      "Timestamp": "01/15/2012 12:32 PM"
    }
  ]
};

/* Convert times to local time */

function toLocalTime(src) {
  return new Date(src+" UTC").toString();
}

bid.StartTime = toLocalTime(bid.StartTime);
bid.EndTime = toLocalTime(bid.EndTime);

for(var i = 0; i < data.Bids.length; i++) {
  var bid = data.Bids[i];
  bid.Timestamp = toLocalTime(bid.Timestamp);
}


/* Execute the callback */
updateAuction(data);
```

Making a JSONP request

The jQuery `$.ajax` method offers first-class support for JSONP requests. All you have to do is pass in the `dataType` and `jsonpCallback` options to specify the `jsonp` data type and the name of the client-side callback function (respectively).

The following example shows a jQuery `$.ajax` JSONP request in action:

```
function updateAuction(result) {
  var message = result.Title + ": $" + result.CurrentPrice;
  $('#Result').html(message);
}

$.ajax({
  type: "GET",
  url: "http://localhost:11279/Auctions/Auction/1234",
  dataType: "jsonp",
  jsonpCallback: "updateAuction"
});
```

Note that because it is a query string parameter and not an actual JavaScript function like the ones you register with the `.success()` and `.error()` events, the callback method *must* be a globally accessible, uniquely named function. Otherwise, the JSONP script will not be able to execute it.

Adding JSONP support to ASP.NET MVC controller actions

ASP.NET MVC has no built-in support for JSONP, so in order to leverage this approach you will need to implement everything yourself. Luckily, JSONP results are little more than a modified version of the ASP.NET MVC Framework's `JsonResult` action result.

Perhaps the best way to add support for JSONP to your controller actions is to create a custom `ActionResult`. Example 6-6 shows an example.

Example 6-6. JsonpResult: custom JSONP action result

```
using System.Web.Mvc;

public class JsonpResult : JsonResult
{
  public string Callback { get; set; }

  public JsonpResult()
  {
    JsonRequestBehavior = JsonRequestBehavior.AllowGet;
  }

  public override void ExecuteResult(ControllerContext context)
  {
    var httpContext = context.HttpContext;
    var callback = Callback;

    if(string.IsNullOrWhiteSpace(callback))
        callback = httpContext.Request["callback"];

    httpContext.Response.Write(callback + "(");
    base.ExecuteResult(context);
    httpContext.Response.Write(");");
  }
}
```

You may have noticed that the JsonpResult hardcodes the JsonRequestBehavior property to JsonRequestBehavior.AllowGet. This is because—by definition—all JSONP requests are GET requests.

 Thus, every JSONP request is subject to the aforementioned security vulnerability, so you must avoid sending sensitive information via JSONP!

Then, to provide a JSONP response to a JSONP request, simply return an instance of the JsonpResult:

```
public ActionResult Auction(long id)
{
  var db = new DataContext();
  var auction = db.Auctions.Find(id);

  return new JsonpResult { Data = auction };
}
```

Enabling Cross-Origin Resource Sharing

When it's supported, the preferred method for cross-domain AJAX calls is to use *Cross-Origin Resource Sharing* (CORS). Unlike JSONP, CORS does not take advantage of security holes; instead, it uses a special HTTP header to let the browser know that the server allows cross-domain AJAX calls. Avoiding "hacks" also makes a CORS approach much more straightforward, because it does not require a JavaScript callback method or custom action result class.

To enable CORS support, simply set the Access-Control-Allow-Origin header value for each request that requires CORS support. You can set the value of this header to a "whitelist" of allowed domains, or simply "*" to grant access from any domain:

```
HttpContext.Response.AppendHeader("Access-Control-Allow-Origin", "*");
```

Alternatively, you can enable CORS for the entire application by adding the HTTP header to the system.webServer > httpProtocol > customHeaders configuration section:

```
<system.webServer>
  <httpProtocol>
    <customHeaders>
      <add name="Access-Control-Allow-Origin" value="*" />
    </customHeaders>
  </httpProtocol>
</system.webServer>
```

Then, make a "normal" jQuery $.ajax() request:

```
$.ajax({
  type: "GET",
  url: "http://localhost:11279/Auctions/Auction/1234",
  dataType: "json",
  success: function (result) {
```

```
        var message = result.Title + ": $" + result.CurrentPrice;
        $('#Result').html(message);
    },
    error: function (XMLHttpRequest, textStatus, errorThrown) {
        alert("Error: " + errorThrown);
    }
});
```

With CORS support in place, we are back to a simple and effective AJAX call and all the hoops that we have to jump through in order to make JSONP requests are a thing of the past.

CORS Browser Support

At the time of this writing, Cross-Origin Resource Sharing (CORS) is still a working draft, so it's not yet fully supported by all the major browsers. Therefore, before using this approach be sure to verify whether it works with the browsers your website targets.

Summary

Understanding when and how to use AJAX properly is an important tool for developers who want to offer a better user experience to their users. This chapter outlined the different ways you can use AJAX to enhance your web applications, featuring an in-depth overview of the ways ASP.NET MVC supports handling AJAX requests. We also explored how jQuery's powerful APIs make it very easy to add AJAX communication to your site.

## CHAPTER 7

The ASP.NET Web API

As your application's client-side UI grows beyond a few simple AJAX requests, you may begin to find that ASP.NET MVC's `JsonResult`-based controller actions don't quite meet the needs of an advanced AJAX frontend. When this happens, it may be time to look for a more simple and elegant way to handle advanced AJAX requests. It may be time to start using the *ASP.NET Web API*.

The ASP.NET Web API Framework leverages both web standards—such as HTTP, JSON, and XML—and a standard set of conventions to provide a simple way to build and expose REST-based data services. From an architectural standpoint, the ASP.NET Web API is very similar to ASP.NET MVC in that it leverages some of the same core concepts, such as routing, controllers, and even controller action results. It uses these concepts, however, to support a very different set of scenarios: scenarios that involve working with data as opposed to generating HTML markup.

This chapter gives you a basic introduction to the ASP.NET Web API Framework, showing you how to create and expose ASP.NET Web API services, then consume those services via AJAX from a browser.

Building a Data Service

Adding an ASP.NET Web API controller to your application is almost exactly like adding an ASP.NET MVC controller. The following sections walk you through the process by showing how you can add a Web API controller to the Ebuy reference application.

Before you begin, you'll need a folder in which to store your new Web API controller. Web API controllers can live just about anywhere, so it's really up to you to come up with a convention that works for you. For instance, we prefer to create a new folder named *Api* in the root of the website, but you can feel free to store your Web API controllers in the *Controllers* folder right next to the ASP.NET MVC controllers—as long as you don't have any naming conflicts, ASP.NET will be able to tell them apart just fine.

To add a new Web API controller, simply right-click on the folder you'd like to add the service to (in our case, the *Api* folder) and choose the "Controller..." context menu item. This will bring up the same Add Controller dialog that you use to create ASP.NET MVC controllers (Figure 7-1), only this time you will choose the "API controller with empty read/write actions" template rather than one of the ASP.NET MVC controller templates. (For more on the available options, refer back to "Controller templates" on page 36.) To begin, give the new controller a name. For this example, we'll use the name *AuctionsController.cs*.

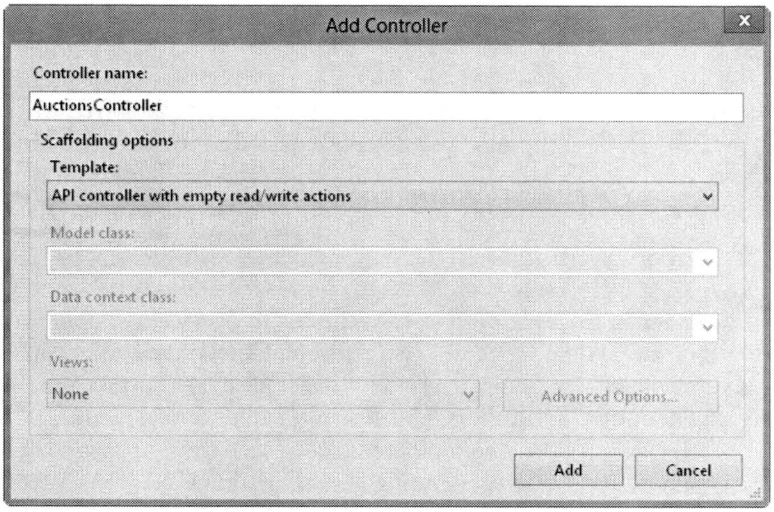

Figure 7-1. Adding a Web API controller

When you're done, click the Add button to add the Web API controller to your project. Example 7-1 contains the code for the new Web API controller.

Example 7-1. Web API controller

```
using System;
using System.Collections.Generic;
using System.Linq;
using System.Net;
using System.Net.Http;
using System.Web.Http;

namespace Ebuy.Website.Api
{
    public class AuctionsDataController : ApiController
    {
```

```
// GET api/auctions
public IEnumerable<string> Get()
{
    return new string[] { "value1", "value2" };
}

// GET api/auctions/5
public string Get(int id)
{
    return "value";
}

// POST api/auctions
public void Post(string value)
{
}

// PUT api/auctions/5
public void Put(int id, string value)
{
}

// DELETE api/auctions/5
public void Delete(int id)
{
}
    }
}
```

Registering Web API Routes

Before we can use this new controller, however, we must register it with the ASP.NET routing framework so that it can begin to receive requests.

As with ASP.NET MVC, ASP.NET Web API requests are based on routing URLs to their corresponding controller actions. In fact, ASP.NET Web API routes are registered in *almost* exactly the same way as ASP.NET MVC routes are registered. The only difference is that instead of the RouteTable.MapRoute() helper extension, Web API routes use the RouteTable.MapHttpRoute() extension.

```
routes.MapHttpRoute(
    name: "DefaultApi",
    routeTemplate: "api/{controller}/{id}",
    defaults: new { id = RouteParameter.Optional }
);
```

This is because the Web API Framework figures out the controller action to execute using *convention over configuration*.

You are not required to begin your route with the literal *api* path segment —feel free to change the Web API route pattern to whatever route you like, as long as it doesn't conflict with any other routes registered in the same application.

The same rules that apply to ASP.MVC routing also apply to Web API data services—be careful that your route patterns aren't too specific, or overly vague.

Leaning on Convention over Configuration

Like ASP.NET MVC, ASP.NET Web API makes heavy use of convention over configuration to lighten the workload involved in creating web data services. For example, instead of requiring you to annotate each method with an attribute such as `HttpPost Attribute` to identify what type of requests an action may handle (as you must do with ASP.NET MVC controller actions), `ApiController` methods rely on names that correspond to the standard HTTP actions.

Using this convention makes it really easy to perform CRUD (Create, Read, Update, Delete) operations on a resource (entity). The standard HTTP actions and their corresponding CRUD operations are:

`GET` *(Read)*
    Retrieves the representation of the resource

`PUT` *(Update)*
    Updates an existing resource (or creates a new instance)

`POST` *(Create)*
    Creates a new instance of a resource

`DELETE` *(Delete)*
    Deletes a resource

The `PUT` method will replace the entire entity. To support partial updating, the `PATCH` method should be used instead.

Interacting with an ASP.NET Web API data service is incredibly easy.

For example, the snippet below shows how to use the jQuery `$.getJSON()` method to make a `GET` request to the */api/auction* service, which returns a collection of auctions serialized in JSON format:

```
<script type="text/javascript">

    $(function () {
        $.getJSON("api/auction/",
        function (data) {
```

```
        $.each(data, function (key, val) {
            var str = val.Description;
            $('<li/>', { html: str }).appendTo($('#auctions'));
        });
    });
});

</script>
```

Overriding Conventions

It's important to note that the controller action naming convention only applies when the name corresponds to one of the standard REST actions (*GET, POST, PUT,* and *DELETE*). However, if you'd like to name your methods differently but still leverage the rest of the Web API's functionality, you can apply the AcceptVerbsAttribute—or its aliases, such as HttpGetAttribute or HttpPostAttribute—to the Web API controller methods, just as you would apply the attribute on an ASP.NET MVC controller action.

The following code snippet shows this in action:

```
[HttpGet]
public Auction FindAuction(int id)
{
}
```

In this example, we've decided to break the REST convention and name our controller action FindAuction rather than using the conventional Get method name. In order to do this, we applied the HttpGetAttribute to the FindAuction controller action to indicate that this action handles GET requests.

Hooking Up the API

Now let's walk through setting up the Web API controller that we created earlier so it can perform CRUD operations on auctions.

In order to access the Ebuy database, an instance of the application's data repository class is passed in to the AuctionsDataController constructor:

```
public class AuctionsDataController : ApiController
{
    private readonly IRepository _repository;

    public AuctionsDataController(IRepository repository)
    {
        _repository = repository;
    }
}
```

By default, Web API controllers require a default (empty parameter) constructor. Since an IRepository needs to be passed in to the controller, a custom dependency resolver class needs to be initialized during application startup:

```
GlobalConfiguration.Configuration.DependencyResolver =
new NinjectWebApiResolver(kernel);
```

Here is an example of a custom dependency resolver that is using a Ninject IoC container. Since Web API controllers are created per request, the custom resolver needs to create a new dependency scope (e.g., `NinjectWebApiScope`) for each request:

```
using System.Web.Http.Dependencies;
using Ninject;

public class NinjectWebApiResolver : NinjectWebApiScope, IDependencyResolver
{
    private IKernel kernel;

    public NinjectWebApiResolver(IKernel kernel) : base(kernel)
    {
        this.kernel = kernel;
    }

    public IDependencyScope BeginScope()
    {
        return new NinjectWebApiScope(kernel.BeginBlock());
    }
}
```

Here are the contents of the custom Ninject scope class. When a Web API controller is requested, the `GetService()` method will be called; `Resolve()` will handle injecting the repository when it creates an instance of the controller:

```
using System;
using System.Collections.Generic;
using System.Linq;
using System.Web.Http.Dependencies;
using Ninject.Activation;
using Ninject.Parameters;
using Ninject.Syntax;

public class NinjectWebApiScope : IDependencyScope
{

    protected IResolutionRoot resolutionRoot;

    public NinjectWebApiScope(IResolutionRoot resolutionRoot)
    {
        this.resolutionRoot = resolutionRoot;
    }

    public object GetService(Type serviceType)
    {
        return resolutionRoot.Resolve(this.CreateRequest(serviceType)).SingleOrDefault();
    }

    public IEnumerable<object> GetServices(Type serviceType)
    {
        return resolutionRoot.Resolve(this.CreateRequest(serviceType))
```

```
    }

    private IRequest CreateRequest(Type serviceType)
    {
        return resolutionRoot.CreateRequest(serviceType,
                                            null,
                                            new Parameter[0],
                                            true,
                                            true);
    }

    public void Dispose()
    {
        resolutionRoot = null;
    }
}
```

The following code shows the fully implemented Web API controller that has been
updated to use the repository to peform CRUD operations on the Auctions class:

```
public class AuctionsDataController : ApiController
{
    private readonly IRepository _repository;

    public AuctionsDataController(IRepository repository)
    {
        _repository = repository;
    }

    public IEnumerable<Auction> Get()
    {
        return this._repository.All<Auction>();
    }

    public Auction Get(string id)
    {
        return _repository.Single<Auction>(id);
    }

    public void Post(Auction auction)
    {
        _repository.Add<Auction>(auction);
    }

    public void Put(string id, Auction auction)
    {
        var currentAuction = _repository.Single<Auction>(id);

        if (currentAuction != null)
        {
            currentAuction = Mapper.DynamicMap<Auction>(auction);
        }
    }
```

```
    public void Delete(string id)
    {
        _repository.Delete<Auction>(id);
    }
}
```

Paging and Querying Data

One of the most powerful aspects of the ASP.NET Web API Framework is its support for paging and filtering data via the Open Data Protocol (OData) for expression queries via web URL parameters. For example, the URI */api/Auction?$top=3&$orderby=CurrentBid* returns the top three auctions, ordered by the value of their CurrentBid property.

Table 7-1 lists a few of the common query parameters that OData understands.

Table 7-1. Supported OData query string parameters

Query string parameter	Description	Example
$filter	Filters entities that match the Boolean expression	*/api/Auction?$filter=CurrentBid gt 2*
$orderby	Returns a group of entities ordered by the specified field	*/api/Auction?$orderby=Description*
$skip	Skips the first *n* entities	*/api/Auction?$skip=2*
$top	Returns the first *n* entities	*/api/Auction?$top=3&*

 See the OData website (*http://www.odata.org/*) to learn more about the Open Data Protocol (OData) specification.

To support paging and filtering, a Web API controller action must return an IQueryable<T> result. When data is not in IQueryable<T>, you can use the AsQueryable() LINQ extension. The Web API then takes the IQueryable<T> result and converts the OData query string into a LINQ expression that it uses to filter the items in the IQueryable<T> collection.

Next, the Web API Framework takes the result of the LINQ expression and converts it to a JSON object, which gets delivered via an HTTP result:

```
public IQueryable<Auction> Get()
{
    return _repository.All<Auction>().AsQueryable();
}
```

Exception Handling

Developers building AJAX-based applications need to take extra care when handling exceptions. By default, if an error occurs on the server while processing an AJAX request an internal server (500) error will be returned. This can introduce a number of problems.

First, telling the user there was an internal server error is not very valuable. Plus, returning error messages offers limited information for developers to use to debug and track down the problem. But perhaps most important of all is that sending error messages to users without "sanitizing" them in some way has the potential to be a serious security risk: the error message could contain exception call stacks or other information an attacker could use to compromise your site!

Figure 7-2 is an example of an internal server error returned from the Web API controller. The message returned doesn't contain anything useful other than a call stack.

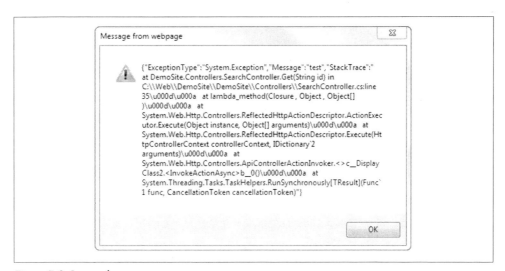

Figure 7-2. Internal server error

Fortunately, ASP.NET Web API offers some options for handing exceptions and returning more meaningful information to the client application. For instance, the HttpResponseException class gives you much more control over the HTTP status codes and response messages sent back to the client than traditional error handling approaches.

The following example demonstrates using the HttpResponseException class to set the HTTP status code (404) and customize the content of the error message returned to the client:

```
public Auction Get(string id)
{
    var result = _repository.Single<Auction>(id);
    if (result == null)
    {
        var errorMessage = new HttpResponseMessage(HttpStatusCode.NotFound);
        errorMessage.Content = new StringContent
            (string.Format("Invalid id, no auction available for id: {0}.", id));
        errorMessage.ReasonPhrase = "Not Found";

        throw new HttpResponseException(errorMessage);
    }
    return result;
}
```

In addition to using `HttpResponseException`, the ASP.NET WEB API allows you to create exception filters. Exception filters get invoked when unhandled exceptions that are not of type `HttpResponseException` are raised from a controller.

To create an exception filter, you can directly implement the `System.Web.Http.Filters.IExceptionFilter` interface or inherit from `ExceptionFilterAttribute`. Creating a custom attribute is the easy and preferred way of creating exception filters. This approach only requires you to override the `OnException()` method:

```
using System.Diagnostics;
using System.Web.Http.Filters;

public class CustomExceptionFilter  : ExceptionFilterAttribute
{
    public override void OnException(HttpActionExecutedContext context)
    {
        base.OnException(context);
    }
}
```

It is also possible to override the HTTP response sent back to the client. You can do this by modifying the `HttpActionExecutedContext` parameter:

```
using System.Web.Http.Filters;
using System.Net.Http;
using System.Net;

public class CustomExceptionFilter  : ExceptionFilterAttribute
{
    public override void OnException(HttpActionExecutedContext context)
    {
        if (context.Response == null)
        {
            context.Response = new HttpResponseMessage();
        }
        context.Response.StatusCode = HttpStatusCode.NotImplemented;
        context.Response.Content = new StringContent("Custom Message");
        base.OnException(context);
    }
}
```

After a custom exception filter has been created, it must be registered. There are two ways to register an exception filter: you can register it globally by adding it to the `GlobalConfiguration.Configuration.Filters` collection, or you can add it as an attribute to a Web API controller method. Globally registered exceptions will be executed for all exceptions raised except `HttpResponseException`, across all Web API controllers.

Registering global exception filters is easy—just add any custom filters to the `Global Configuration.Configuration.Filters` collection during the application's startup phase:

```
public class MvcApplication : System.Web.HttpApplication
{
    static void ConfigureApi(HttpConfiguration config)
    {
        config.Filters.Add(new CustomExceptionFilter());
    }

    protected void Application_Start()
    {
        ConfigureApi(GlobalConfiguration.Configuration);
    }
}
```

Alternatively, a Web API controller method can be annotated directly using the custom exception filter attribute:

```
[CustomExceptionFilter]
public Auction Get(string id)
{
    var result = _repository.Single<Auction>(id);
    if (result == null)
    {
        throw new Exception("Item not Found!");
    }
    return result;
}
```

ASP.NET Web API exception filters are similar to ASP.NET MVC filters except that they are defined in a different namespace and behave slightly differently. For example, the ASP.NET MVC `HandleErrorAttribute` class cannot handle exceptions thrown from Web API controllers.

Media Formatters

One of the more powerful aspects of the ASP.NET Web API framework is the ability to work with many different media (MIME) types. *MIME types* are used to describe the format of the data in an HTTP request. A MIME type consists of two strings, a type and a subtype: for example, `text.html` is used for describing an HTML format.

A client can set the HTTP Accept header to tell the server which MIME types the client wants sent back. For example, the following Accept header tells the server that the client wants either HTML or XHTML returned:

```
Accept: text/html,application/xhtml+xml,application
```

The ASP.NET Web API uses the media type to determine how to serialize and deserialize the HTTP message body. It provides support for XML, JSON, and form-encoded data right out of the box.

To create a custom media formatter, simply derive from one of the MediaTypeFormatter or BufferedMediaTypeFormatter classes. MediaTypeFormatter uses an asynchronous read and write approach; BufferedMediaTypeFormatter inherits from MediaTypeFormatter and wraps the asynchronous read and write methods and exposes them as synchronous operations. While inheriting from BufferedMediaTypeFormatter is simpler, it can cause a thread blocking issue.

The following example shows how to create a custom media type for serializing an Auction item into a comma-separated values (CSV) format. To keep things simple, the custom formatter inherits from BufferedMediaTypeFormatter. In the formatter's constructor, the supported media types need to be defined:

```
using System;
using System.Collections.Generic;
using System.IO;
using System.Net;
using System.Net.Http.Formatting;
using System.Net.Http.Headers;
using DemoSite.Models;

public class AuctionCsvFormatter : BufferedMediaTypeFormatter
{
    public AuctionCsvFormatter()
    {
        this.SupportedMediaTypes.Add(new MediaTypeHeaderValue("text/csv"));
    }
}
```

To serialize or deserialize entities, the CanWriteType() and CanReadType() methods must be overwritten. These methods are used to define which types the custom formatter supports:

```
protected override bool CanWriteType(Type type)
{
    if (type == typeof(Auction))
    {
        return true;
    }
    else
    {
        Type enumerableType = typeof(IEnumerable<Auction>);
        return enumerableType.IsAssignableFrom(type);
    }
```

```
    }

    protected override bool CanReadType(Type type)
    {
        return false;
    }
}
```

When the formatter is executed, the `OnWriteToStream()` method is called for serializing a type to a stream, and `OnReadFromStream()` is called to deserialize a type from a stream. Example 7-2 shows how to serialize a single `Auction` type, or a collection of `Auction` types. Take note of how the `Encode` method is escaping out some characters. This is an important step to keep in mind when working with custom formatters.

Example 7-2. Serializing a type

```
protected override void OnWriteToStream(Type type,
        object value, Stream stream,
        HttpContentHeaders contentHeaders,
        FormatterContext formatterContext,
        TransportContext transportContext)
{
    var source = value as IEnumerable<Auction>;
    if (source != null)
    {
        foreach (var item in source)
        {
            WriteItem(item, stream);
        }
    }
    else
    {
        var item = value as Auction;
        if (item != null)
        {
            WriteItem(item, stream);
        }
    }
}

private void WriteItem(Auction item, Stream stream)
{
    var writer = new StreamWriter(stream);
    writer.WriteLine("{0},{1},{2}",
        Encode(item.Title),
        Encode(item.Description),
        Encode(item.CurrentPrice.Value));

    writer.Flush();
}
```

```
static char[] _specialChars = new char[] { ',', '\n', '\r', '"' };
private string Encode(object o)
{
    string result = "";

    if (o != null)
    {
        string data = o.ToString();
        if (data.IndexOfAny(_specialChars) != -1)
        {
            result = String.Format("\"{0}\"", data.Replace("\"", "\"\""));
        }
    }

    return result;
}
```

To use a custom media formatter, it has to be registered. Inside the *Global.asax.cs* Application_Start() method, add the custom media formatter to the GlobalConfigura tion.Configuration.Filters collection:

```
static void ConfigureApi(HttpConfiguration config)
{
    config.Formatters.Add(new AuctionCsvFormatter());
}
```

Once it's registered, the custom media formatter will execute for any request that contains the text/csv Accept header.

Summary

This chapter introduced Microsoft's new ASP.NET Web API Framework and showed how you can leverage this framework as an easy way to expose data services to your web applications.

## CHAPTER 8

Advanced Data

The main focus throughout this book so far has been on the key components of ASP.NET MVC: the model, view, and controller. This chapter switches the focus to the data access layer and shows how to leverage the repository and object relational mapping data access patterns when building ASP.NET MVC web applications.

Data Access Patterns

One of the key features of the ASP.NET MVC Framework is extensibility. The framework was designed to give developers lots of flexibility to plug in different components and frameworks. Since ASP.NET MVC is built on top of .NET 4.5, any of the popular data access frameworks—including ADO.NET, LINQ to SQL, ADO.NET Entity Framework, or NHibernate—can be used in building the data access layer for an application.

No matter which data access framework you choose, it's important to understand the key data access design patterns that complement the Model-View-Controller pattern.

Plain Old CLR Objects

A Plain Old CLR Object (POCO) is a .NET class that is used to represent a business entity (model) class. The class focuses on the key business attributes (properties) and behaviors (methods) of a business entity and its associated entities, without requiring any specific database infrastructure code.

The main goal behind using POCO classes is to design the application's business model to have *persistence ignorance* (PI). This design approach allows the application's business model to evolve independently of its data access model. Since the business model does not contain any specific data access code, it is easier to test the model in isolation, and the underlying data store can easily be swapped out to meet changing business requirements.

Here is an example of a simple POCO class that only contains properties and methods:

```
public class Product
{
    public long Id { get; set; }
    public string Name { get; set; }
    public double Price { get; set; }
    public int NumberInStock { get; set; }

    public double CalculateValue()
    {
        return Price * NumberInStock;
    }
}
```

Note that the class contains no specific database infrastructure code. Later in this chapter we will talk about how to use an object relational mapper (ORM) and the repository pattern to persist POCO classes.

The business model for an application can easily contain dozens or even hundreds of classes, in more complex scenarios. Even for simple models that only contain a few classes, it makes sense to create a base entity class that contains common properties and methods.

The following is an example of a base entity class. Note how the class and its methods are marked abstract; this is a common approach in a base entity class to enforce consistency across the model:

```
public abstract class BaseEntity
{
    public string Key { get; set; }

    public abstract void GenerateKey();

}
```

Using the Repository Pattern

The *respository pattern* is a data access pattern that promotes a more loosely coupled approach to data access. Instead of having a controller or the business model contain the data access logic, a separate class or set of classes called a *repository* takes on the responsibility of persisting the application's business model.

The repository pattern nicely complements the key design principle of the MVC pattern —separation of concerns. By using this pattern, we isolate the data access layer from the rest of the application and take advantage of the benefits of using POCO classes.

There are several different approaches to designing a repository:

One per business model
> The most straightforward way is to create a repository for each business model class. While this approach is easy, it can lead to problems, such as duplicate code or complexity, when multiple repositories need to interact with each other.

Using aggregate root

An *aggregate root* is a class that can exist by itself and is responsible for managing the associations to other related classes. For example, in an ecommerce application, you would have an `OrderRepository` that would handle the creation of an order and its related order detail items.

Generic repository

Instead of creating specific repository classes, a developer can instead take advantage of .NET generics to build a common repository that can be used across multiple applications. The Ebuy reference application includes an example of a *generic repository*.

Here is the structure of a stubbed-out repository class:

```
public class ModelRepository
{

    public ModelRepository()
    {
    }


    public void Add(Model instance)
    {
    }

    public void Update(Model instance)
    {
    }

    public void Delete(Model instance)
    {
    }

    public Model Get(string id)
    {
    }

    public ICollection<Model> GetAll()
    {
    }

}
```

In addition to performing the CRUD (Create, Read, Update, and Delete) operations for an entity, a repository sometimes takes on the responsibility of caching entities. Caching works great for entities that are fairly static, such as lookup values for dropdown lists, but it can be problematic for entities that are frequently updated.

See Chapter 12 for additional details about caching data.

In ASP.NET MVC controllers interact with repositories to load and persist an application business model. By taking advantage of dependency injection (DI), repositories can be injected into a controller's constructor. Figure 8-1 shows the relationship between the repository and the Entity Framework data context, in which ASP.NET MVC controllers interact with the repository rather than directly with Entity Framework.

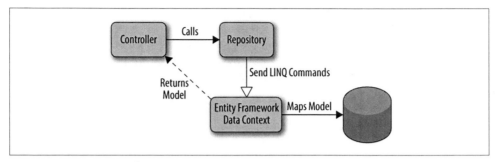

Figure 8-1. Interactions when using a repository

The following example shows how a repository is injected into a controller using the dependency injection technique and how the controller uses the injected repository to retrieve a list of auctions. Using dependency injection makes it easier to test the controller by mocking out the repository passed in:

```
public class AuctionsController : Controller
{
    private readonly IRepository _repository;

    public AuctionsController(IRepository repository)
    {
        _repository = repository;
    }

    public ActionResult Index()
    {
        var auctions = _repository.GetAll<Auction>();
        return auctions;
    }
}
```

Object Relational Mappers

An *object relational mapper* (ORM) is a data access pattern that supports mapping entities between classes (.NET Framework types) and a relational database model. The main reason for using this pattern is that there can be a significant disconnect between the structure of the application business model and the database model. This disconnect is called the *object relational impedance mismatch*, which is just a fancy way of saying that the best structures for the application's business layer and data access layer are usually not compatible.

It is easy to fall into the trap of just reflecting the relational database model in the business layer. The problem with this approach is that it limits your ability to take advantage of the full power of the .NET platform.

Here are the main pain points of the object relational impedance mismatch:

Granularity

Sometimes your model will contain more classes than the number of matching tables in the database. A good example of this is an `Address` class, because there can be different behaviors associated with the different kinds of addresses that exist in the real world—a billing address may be handled differently than a shipping address, for example. Even though it is often a good idea to represent these differences using different classes to contain each specific set of behaviors, they may all contain (mostly) the same data, so you may want to store all `Address` types in a single database table.

Inheritance

The concept of inheritance—or classes deriving from other classes in order to share common logic—is one of the most important aspects of object-oriented development. Regardless of its importance in object-oriented development, however, relational databases generally don't understand the concept of inheritance. For example, while your relational database may have a single *Customers* table with a special column that determines whether the customer is domestic or international, your business domain model may express this relationship via a base `Customer` class and several subclasses—such as `DomesticCustomer` and `InternationalCustomer`— to represent the different kinds of customers your business interacts with.

Identity

Relational databases rely on a single table column (i.e., the table's *primary key*) to act as a unique identifier for each row. This often conflicts with the .NET Framework world, in which objects can be identified both by their object identity (a == b) and by their object equality (`a.Equals(b)`), neither of which depends on the object having a single unique property or field.

Associations

A relational database uses primary and foreign keys to establish the association between entities. Meanwhile, the .NET Framework represents object associations as unidirectional references. For example, in a relational database it's possible to query data across tables in either direction. However, in .NET the association is owned by only one class, so to get bidirectional support you would need to copy the association. In addition, it's impossible to know the multiplicity of an association in a class. The concepts of "one to many" and "many to many" are indistinguishable.

Data navigation

The way you access data in a .NET Framework class is fundamentally different from the way you would do it inside a relational database. In a domain model implemented using .NET, you walk one associate relationship to another across the whole model object graph, while typically you try to minimize the number of SQL queries required by loading several entities using JOIN(s) and specific SELECT statements.

While developers may use the model to perform data access operations such as loading and saving data, the importance and responsibility of the database is still paramount. The traditional data access design rules should still be followed. Each table should have a single primary key, one-to-many relationships should be defined using foreign keys, etc. For example, to represent the relationship between students and teachers, there should be a third table (e.g., *Class*), since students and teachers both can have one or more classes.

Entity Framework Overview

Crafting an ORM by hand can be an impossible journey. Fortunately, instead of building everything themselves, developers can look to one of the myriad ORM frameworks available. These include a couple provided by Microsoft—such as LINQ to SQL and ADO.NET Entity Framework—and the many popular third-party commercial or open source frameworks, such as nHibernate (*http://www.nhibernate.com*).

The *ADO.NET Entity Framework* (simply known as EF) is an object relational mapper included with the .NET framework. When using EF, a developer interacts with an entity model instead of the application's relational database model. This abstraction allows the developer to focus on the business behavior and the relationships between entities, instead of on the details of storing entities into a relational data model. To interact with the entity model, the developer uses the Entity Framework data context to perform queries or persist the model. When one of these operations is invoked, EF will generate the necessary SQL to perform the operation.

One of the more controversial subjects when switching from traditional data access approaches (e.g., ADO.NET Datasets) to an object relational mapping approach is deciding what role stored procedures should play, if any. Since the entity model is the primary focus when using an ORM, developers are encouraged to let the framework handle mapping entities, instead of worrying about writing SQL queries themselves. Fortunately, if you work in an organization that requires stored procedures, or you need to interact with an existing database that leverages stored procedures, ADO.NET Entity Framework offers support for calling stored procedures. See *http://msdn.micro soft.com/en-us/library/bb399203(v=VS.90).aspx* for additional details.

Here is an example of how to use the Entity Framework data context for adding and saving new products. When the SaveChanged() method is called, Entity Framework will generate the SQL for inserting two new products:

```
using (var db = new ProductModelContainer())
{
    db.Product.Add(new Product { Id = "173", Name = "XBox 360" });
    db.Product.Add(new Product { Id = "225", Name = "Halo 4" });
    db.SaveChanges()
}
```

Choosing a Data Access Approach

Microsoft recognizes that a one-size-fits-all approach for data access does not work. Some developers prefer a more data-centric approach that focuses on designing the database first, then generating the business model for their application, largely driven by the structure of the database. Other developers want to use POCO classes to define the structure of the business model and either generate the database from the POCO classes or hook up the model to an existing database.

As a result, the ADO.NET Entity Framework allows developers to choose between three different styles:

Database First

> For developers who prefer a more data-centric design or starting from an existing database, Entity Framework is able to generate a business model based on the tables and columns in a relational database. Entity Framework uses a special configuration file (stored with the *.edmx* file extension) to store the information about the database schema, the conceptual data model, and the mapping between them. Developers can use the Entity Framework designer included with Visual Studio to generate, display, and edit the conceptual model used by Entity Framework.

Model First

> For developers who do not have an existing database, Entity Framework offers a designer that can be used to create a conceptual data model. As with the Database First model, Entity Framework uses a schema file to store the information related to mapping the model to a database schema. After the model has been created, the EF designer can generate the database schema that can be used to create a database.

Code First

> Developers who want to use more of a persistence ignorance approach can create the business model directly in code. Entity Framework provides a special mapping API and supports a set of conventions to make this approach work. Under the Code First approach, Entity Framework does not leverage any kind of external configuration file to store the database schema, because the mapping API uses these conventions to generate the database schema dynamically at runtime.

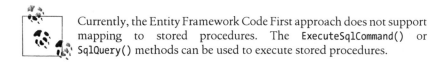 Currently, the Entity Framework Code First approach does not support mapping to stored procedures. The `ExecuteSqlCommand()` or `SqlQuery()` methods can be used to execute stored procedures.

Database Concurrency

Handling *concurrency conflicts* is one of the most important aspects developers need to manage when building web applications. A concurrency conflict occurs when multiple users try to change the same data simultaneously. By default, unless you configure Entity Framework to detect conflicts, the "last in" rule applies. For example, if user one and user two load the same product, the user who clicks the submit button last will be the one who wins, and that user's data will override the first user's data without any warning being given to either user.

Depending on the type of the application and the volatility of its data, a developer can decide if the cost of programming for concurrency outweighs its benefits. Two approaches can be taken to handle concurrency:

Pessimistic concurrency
> The pessimistic concurrency approach requires the use of database locks to prevent multiple users from overriding each other's changes. When a row of data is retrieved, a read-only lock is applied and kept until the same user updates the data or removes the read-only lock. This approach can cause a lot of issues in web applications since the Web relies heavily on a stateless model. The major issue to watch out for is managing when read-only locks get removed; since a web browser is used to access the web application, there is no guarantee of when and if the user will perform an action that can trigger the removal of a read-only lock.

Optimistic concurrency
> Instead of relying on database locks, the optimistic concurrency approach chooses to verify that the data to be updated has not been modified since it was originally retrieved. This is typically accomplished by adding a timestamp field to the table that tracks the last time each row was updated. Then, prior to applying any updates to the row, the application checks the timestamp field to see if the row has been changed by anyone since the user retrieved the data.

ADO.NET Entity Framework does not offer support for pessimistic concurrency out of the box. Instead, it is recommended that optimistic concurrency be used. Entity Framework offers two ways to utilize optimistic concurrency: by adding a timestamp property to an entity and by handling any `OptimisticConcurrencyException` exceptions returned from the Entity Framework data context.

Here is an example of using the `Timestamp` attribute to add a timestamp field to an entity. When this attribute is applied, the corresponding database column will be added as a condition to the SQL `Where` clause during any `UPDATE` or `DELETE` operations:

```
[Timestamp]
public Byte[] Timestamp { get; set; }
```

To trap `OptimisticConcurrencyException` errors, use normal .NET `try/catch` techniques to retrieve and compare the state of the entity the user is trying to save, along with the current state of the entity saved in the database:

```
try
{
    dbContext.Set<Product>().Add(instance);
    dbContext.SaveChanges();
}
catch (DbUpdateConcurrencyException ex)
{
    var entry = ex.Entries.Single();
    var databaseValues = (Product)entry.GetDatabaseValues().ToObject();
    var clientValues = (Product)entry.Entity;

    if (databaseValues.Name != clientValues.Name)
        //Log concurrency exception

}
catch (DataException ex)
{
    //Log data exception errors
}
catch (Exception ex)
{
    //Log general exception errors
}
```

Building a Data Access Layer

Picking the design of the data access layer is a critical decision that can influence the rest of the application. For the Ebuy reference application, the Entity Framework Code First approach was chosen. The main reasons for this choice were that the Ebuy business model is designed using the concepts of domain-driven design (*http://www.do maindrivendesign.org*) and that the development team wanted to use a persistence ignorance approach to ensure that the application would be able to easily support multiple types of persistence models, including rational databases, cloud storage, and NoSQL databases.

Using Entity Framework Code First

The driving force behind the Code First approach is the ability to use POCO (Plain Old CLR Objects) classes. Under the Database First or Model First approaches, the EF-generated model classes inherit from the `EntityObject` base class, which provides the necessary plumbing to map the class to its underlying database schema. Because the Database First and Model First approaches require persisted classes to inherit from the `EntityObject` class, they do not support persistence ignorance.

Instead of using a base entity class for mapping, Code First uses a set of conventions to map POCO classes:

- Table names are defined using the pluralized form of the entity class name.
- Column names are derived from the property names.
- Primary keys are based on properties named `ID` or `classNameID`.
- The default connection string matches the name of the `DataContext` class.

Code First data annotations

Entity Framework includes several data annotation attributes developers can use to control how the framework handles mapping entities (see Table 8-1). Note that the ASP.NET MVC Framework uses some of the same attributes for field-level validation.

Table 8-1. Code First data annotations

Property	Description
Column	The database column name, ordinal position, and data type to map the property to.
ComplexType	Used on classes that do not contain keys and cannot be managed by Entity Framework. Typically used to manage scalar properties in related entity.
ConcurrencyCheck	Used to specify whether a property should participate in optimistic concurrency checks.
DatabaseGenerated	Used to mark a property that should be generated by the database.
ForeignKey	Used to identify a related entity; represents the foreign key constraint used between tables.
InverseProperty	Used to identify a property that represents the other end of a relationship.
Key	One or more properties used to uniquely identify an entity.
MaxLength	The maximum length for the property (column).
MinLength	The minimum length for the property (column).
NotMapped	Marks a property that will not be mapped by Entity Framework.
Required	Marks a property as being required (non-nullable).
StringLength	Defines the minimum and maximum length of a field.
Table	Used to define the table name to use for an entity.
Timestamp	Marks a property (column) that contains a timestamp that is checked prior to saving changes.

Overriding conventions

While conventions aim to enhance developer productivity, Entity Framework recognizes that there may be times when you need to break one or more of the conventions it applies and exposes an API that allows developers to bypass its conventions.

Here is an example of an entity class that has been configured to use the `Key` attribute, a data annotation that overrides the default primary key mapping:

```
public class Product
{
    [Key]
    public string MasterKey { get; set; }
    public string Name { get; set; }
}
```

In addition to using attributes to override Entity Framework conventions, developers may also choose to remove any of the default conventions or even enhance the default conventions by creating their own.

The following code shows how to remove the `PluralizingTableNameConvention` so singular names can be used for tables:

```
public class ProductEntities : DbContext
{
    protected override void OnModelCreating(DbModelBuilder modelBuilder)
    {
        // Modify the Code First conventions to not use PluralizingTableName
        modelBuilder.Conventions.Remove<PluralizingTableNameConvention>();
    }
}
```

The EBuy Business Domain Model

The business model of the Ebuy reference application is made up of several POCO classes that have been designed using the principles of domain-driven design. Each POCO entity inherits from a base entity class that contains common behaviors and attributes shared across all classes in the business model.

Since EBuy has been designed with the SOLID design principles in mind (see "SOLID" on page 96), the `Entity` base class implements two interfaces: the custom `IEntity` interface, which defines the naming rules for the URL-safe key name for an entity, and the .NET Framework `IEquatable` interface, which compares different instances of the same entity type to each other. The base class looks like this:

```
public interface IEntity
{
    /// <summary>
    /// The entity's unique (and URL-safe) public identifier
    /// </summary>
    /// <remarks>
    /// This is the identifier that should be exposed via the Web, etc.
    /// </remarks>
```

```
        string Key { get; }
    }

    public abstract class Entity<TId> : IEntity, IEquatable<Entity<TId>>
    where TId : struct
    {
        [Key]
        public virtual TId Id
        {
            get
            {
                if (_id == null && typeof(TId) == typeof(Guid))
                    _id = Guid.NewGuid();

                return _id == null ? default(TId) : (TId)_id;
            }
            protected set { _id = value; }
        }
        private object _id;

        [Unique, StringLength(50)]
        public virtual string Key
        {
            get { return _key = _key ?? GenerateKey(); }
            protected set { _key = value; }
        }
        private string _key;

        protected virtual string GenerateKey()
        {
            return KeyGenerator.Generate();
        }
    }
```

A class that inherits from the Entity class must define the type used for its ID. Take note of the other behaviors defined in the class, such as how the Key property must contain a unique value and that value must be 50 characters or less. Notice, too, how the class overrides the equal operators to properly compare multiple instances of the same model object.

The Payment model inherits from the base Entity class; it uses a GUID-based identifier and contains both primitive and complex properties. Complex properties are used to represent relationships to other entities in the model. For example, Payment includes relationships to an Auction and to the User object:

```
public class Payment : Entity<Guid>
{
    public Currency Amount { get; private set; }
    public Auction Auction { get; private set; }
    public DateTime Timestamp { get; private set; }
    public User User { get; set; }

    public Payment(User user, Auction auction, Currency amount)
```

```
    {
        User = user;
        Auction = auction;
        Amount = amount;
        Timestamp = Clock.Now;
    }

    private Payment()
    {
    }
}
```

One important concept of working with a domain model is to divide the model into one or more contexts, wherein each context is defined as an aggregate cluster that is made up of associated objects that act as a single logical unit. Each cluster contains a single aggregate root that is the main entity that all other entities are associated with and that the other entities cannot exist without.

The EBuy reference application's aggregate root is the Auction class. The Auction class represents the main entity in the application that all other classes can't exist without.

Figure 8-2 shows the core classes that make up the EBuy domain model and the associations between them. Since Auction is the aggregate root, it has relationships to the other core entities—including Bid, which is a collection of bids made by different users for an auction, the User class, which represents two different roles (auctioneer and bidder), and a Payment class that represents the payment the winning bidder makes to an auctioneer.

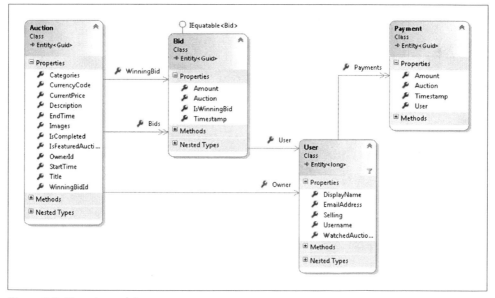

Figure 8-2. Domain model

The following code shows the inner workings of the Auction class, along with all its related entities and behaviors. The ICollection<T> type is used to define the different related classes, including Bid, Category, and Image. The main behaviors of the class are related to posting new bids:

```
public class Auction : Entity<Guid>
{
    public virtual string Title { get; set; }
    public virtual string Description { get; set; }
    public virtual DateTime StartTime { get; set; }
    public virtual DateTime EndTime { get; set; }
    public virtual Currency CurrentPrice { get; set; }

    public Guid? WinningBidId { get; set; }
    public virtual Bid WinningBid { get; private set; }

    public bool IsCompleted
    {
        get { return EndTime <= Clock.Now; }
    }

    public virtual bool IsFeaturedAuction { get; private set; }

    public virtual ICollection<Category> Categories { get; set; }

    public virtual ICollection<Bid> Bids { get; set; }

    public virtual ICollection<WebsiteImage> Images { get; set; }

    public long OwnerId { get; set; }
    public virtual User Owner { get; set; }

    public virtual CurrencyCode CurrencyCode
    {
        get
        {
            return (CurrentPrice != null) ? CurrentPrice.Code : null;
        }
    }

    public Auction()
    {
        Bids = new Collection<Bid>();
        Categories = new Collection<Category>();
        Images = new Collection<WebsiteImage>();
    }

    public void FeatureAuction()
    {
        IsFeaturedAuction = true;
    }

    public Bid PostBid(User user, double bidAmount)
    {
        return PostBid(user, new Currency(CurrencyCode, bidAmount));
```

```
        }

        public Bid PostBid(User user, Currency bidAmount)
        {
            Contract.Requires(user != null);

            if (bidAmount.Code != CurrencyCode)
                throw new InvalidBidException(bidAmount, WinningBid);

            if (bidAmount.Value <= CurrentPrice.Value)
                throw new InvalidBidException(bidAmount, WinningBid);

            var bid = new Bid(user, this, bidAmount);

            CurrentPrice = bidAmount;
            WinningBidId = bid.Id;

            Bids.Add(bid);

            return bid;
        }

    }
```

Working with a Data Context

The ADO.NET Entity Framework Code First data access approach requires the developer to create a data access context class that inherits from DbContext. This class must contain properties for each of the entities in the domain model. The custom data context class can override the methods of the base context class to handle any special logic for queries and saving data, along with any custom logic for mapping entities.

Here is an Entity Framework Code First data context that contains two entities: Categories and Products. Below the definition of the data context class, a LINQ query is used to retrieve a list of products for a specific category:

```
public partial class DataContext : DbContext
{
    public DbSet<Category> Categories { get; set; }
    public DbSet<Product> Products { get; set; }
}

public IList<Product> GetProductsByCategory(Category item)
{
    IList<Product> result = null;

    var db = new DataContext();
    result = db.Products.Where(q => q.Category.Equals(item)).ToList();

    return resut;
}
```

To handle special entity mappings such as many-to-many relationships, the OnModel Creating() method of the data context needs to be overridden. Below is an example of setting up a many-to-many relationship between the *Bids* and *Auctions* database tables:

```
protected override void OnModelCreating(DbModelBuilder modelBuilder)
{
    modelBuilder.Entity<Bid>()
        .HasRequired(x => x.Auction)
        .WithMany()
        .WillCascadeOnDelete(false);
}
```

By default, Entity Framework will look in the ASP.NET MVC web application's *web.config* file for a connection string that has the same name as the custom data access class:

```
<connectionStrings>
    <add name="Ebuy.DataAccess.DataContext" providerName="System.Data.SqlClient"
        connectionString="Data Source=.\SQLEXPRESS;AttachDbFilename=
                |DataDirectory|\Ebuy.mdf;Initial Catalog=Ebuy; ↵
                Integrated Security=True;User Instance=True; ↵
                MultipleActiveResultSets=True"
    />
</connectionStrings>
```

Instead of working directly with the Entity Framework data context, the developer can use the repository pattern. This will give a level of abstraction between the application's controllers and Entity Framework. Having the repository class implement an interface (IRepository) allows the developer to use an IoC container to inject the repository into the controller.

Here is an example of a repository that has been set up to abstract away the Entity Framework data context:

```
public class Repository : IRepository
{
    private readonly DbContext _context;

    public Repository(DbContext context)
    {
        _context = context;
        _isSharedContext = isSharedContext;
    }
}
```

Sorting, Filtering, and Paging Data

In order to support the sorting, filtering, and paging of data, the ADO.NET Entity Framework relies on Language Integrated Query (LINQ) queries to interact with the database.

Developers create and invoke LINQ queries against the Entity Framework data context. Once a LINQ query has been defined, a developer calls one of the LINQ methods, such as `ToList()`, to invoke the query. Entity Framework converts the LINQ commands into their corresponding SQL syntax and executes the query. When the query is done executing, the returned result is converted into a strongly typed collection based on the entity type defined by the query.

The EBuy reference application's search page (Figure 8-3) shows several of these methods working together to provide filtering, sorting, and paging of search results. Users can enter a keyword to search for, change the property to sort on, and page through the search results returned from the database, all through simple LINQ queries.

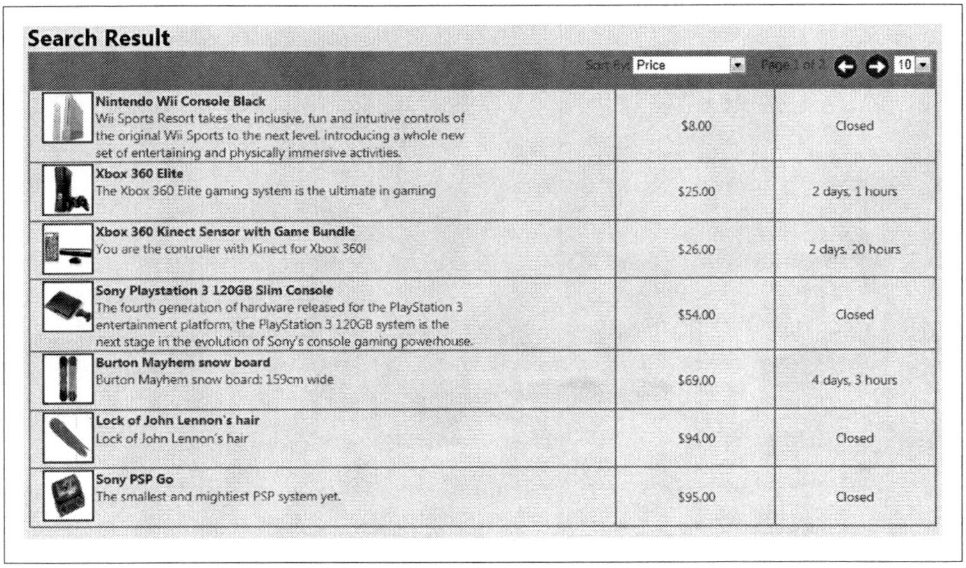

Figure 8-3. EBuy search page

After a user enters a keyword and clicks submit, the `SearchController` will be invoked. The `Index` method accepts a `SearchCriteria` parameter. This class contains all the key fields that the user can change on the search screen: the keyword, the field to sort by, and the number of items to display per page.

When the method is invoked, the ASP.NET MVC model binder magic will map the search form's fields to the `SearchCriteria` class. In addition to fields on the search page, the class contains a few helper methods to make it easier to get the sort by field and number of items to display per page:

```
public class SearchCriteria
{
    public enum SearchFieldType
    {
        Keyword,
```

```
        Price,
        RemainingTime
    }

    public string SearchKeyword { get; set; }
    public string SortByField { get; set; }
    public string PagingSize { get; set; }
    public int CurrentPage { get; set; }

    public int GetPageSize()
    {
        int result = 5;

        if (!string.IsNullOrEmpty(this.PagingSize))
        {
            int.TryParse(this.PagingSize, out result);
        }

        return result;
    }

    public SearchFieldType GetSortByField()
    {
        SearchFieldType result = SearchFieldType.Keyword;

        switch (this.SortByField)
        {
            case "Price":
                result = SearchFieldType.Price;
                break;
            case "Remaining Time":
                result = SearchFieldType.RemainingTime;
                break;
            default:
                result = SearchFieldType.Keyword;
                break;
        }

        return result;
    }
}
```

The *Search* view (Example 8-1) involves a number of important concepts that should be familiar by now. The view leverages jQuery events to trap the events associated with the search criteria fields, so when one of these fields changes, the hidden field for tracking the current page is updated and the form is submitted to the SearchControl ler. The view also uses a SearchViewModel class that contains properties for setting the search criteria and results.

Example 8-1. The Search view

```
@model SearchViewModel

@{
```

```
        ViewBag.Title = "Index";
}

<script type="text/javascript">

    $(function () {
        $("#SortByField").change(function () {
            $("#CurrentPage").val(0);
            SubmitForm();
        });

        $("#PagingSize").change(function () {
            $("#CurrentPage").val(0);
            SubmitForm();
        });

        $("#Previous").click(function () {
            var currentPage = $("#CurrentPage").val();
            if (currentPage != null && currentPage > 0) {
                currentPage--;
                $("#CurrentPage").val(currentPage);
            }
            SubmitForm();
        });

        $("#Next").click(function () {
            var currentPage = $("#CurrentPage").val();
            if (currentPage) {
                currentPage++;
                $("#CurrentPage").val(currentPage);
            }
            SubmitForm();
        });

    });

    function SubmitForm() {
        document.forms["SearchForm"].submit();
    }

</script>

@using (Html.BeginForm("Index", "Search", FormMethod.Post,   new { id = "SearchForm" }))
{

    <div class="SearchKeyword">
        @Html.TextBoxFor(m => m.SearchKeyword, new {@class="SearchBox"})
        <input id="Search" type="submit" value=" " class="SearchButton" />
    </div>

    <h2>Search Result</h2>

    <div>
        <div class="SearchHeader">
            @Html.Hidden("CurrentPage", @Model.CurrentPage)
```

```
<div class="PagingContainer">
    <span class="CurrentPage">Page @Model.CurrentPage of @Model.MaxPages</span>
    <img id="Previous" src="@Url.Content("~/Content/Images/PagingPrevious.png")"↵
    class="PagingButton" />
    <img id="Next" src="@Url.Content("~/Content/Images/PagingNext.png")" ↵
    class="PagingButton" />
    <div class="PageSize">
        @Html.DropDownListFor(m => m.PagingSize, new SelectList↵
        (Model.PagingSizeList))
    </div>
</div>
<div class="SortingContainer">
    <span>Sort By:</span>
    @Html.DropDownListFor(m => m.SortByField, new SelectList↵
    (Model.SortByFieldList))
</div>
</div>
<div class="SearchResultContainer">
    <table>
        @foreach (var item in @Model.SearchResult)
        {
            var auctionUrl = Url.Auction(item);
            <tr>
                <td class="searchDescription">
                    <div class="fieldContainer">
                        <a href="@auctionUrl">@Html.SmallThumbnail(@item.Image, ↵
                        @item.Title)</a>
                    </div>
                    <div class="fieldContainer">
                        <div class="fieldTitle">@item.Title</div>
                        <div class="fieldDescription">
                            @item.Description
                        </div>
                    </div>
                </td>
                <td class="centered-field">@item.CurrentPrice</td>
                <td class="centered-field">@item.RemainingTimeDisplay</td>
            </tr>
        }
    </table>
    </div>
</div>

}
```

After the user enters a search keyword or changes one of the search criteria fields, the
SearchController is invoked. The Index action handles the incoming requests and
checks to see if the search criteria input model contains any criteria data. If the user
enters a keyword, it is used to filter the auction items returned in the search result. The
Query() method in the repository is used for sending the filter data (e.g., keyword) to
the Entity Framework data context, which builds an SQL query and returns the filtered
data to the controller:

```
public ActionResult Index(SearchCriteria criteria)
{
    IQueryable<Auction> auctionsData = null;

    // Filter auctions by keyword
    if (!string.IsNullOrEmpty(criteria.SearchKeyword))
        auctionsData = _repository.Query<Auction>(q => q.Description.Contains↵
        (criteria.SearchKeyword));
    else
        auctionsData = _repository.All<Auction>();

    // Code for loading view model

    return View(viewModel);
}
```

When the user changes the sort by field, the SearchController will be invoked. The controller checks the SearchCriteria class to determine which field to sort the search result by. To sort data, LINQ OrderBy command is called, passing in the field to sort by (q ⇒ q.CurrentPrice.Value):

```
switch (criteria.GetSortByField())
{
    case SearchCriteria.SearchFieldType.Price:
        auctionsData = auctionsData.OrderBy(q => q.CurrentPrice.Value);
        break;
    case SearchCriteria.SearchFieldType.RemainingTime:
        auctionsData = auctionsData.OrderBy(q => q.EndTime);
        break;
    case SearchCriteria.SearchFieldType.Keyword:
    default:
        auctionsData = auctionsData.OrderBy(q => q.Description);
        break;
}
```

When the user clicks on the previous or next page button or changes the number of items to display per page, the SearchController is invoked. The controller checks the criteria parameter to determine how many pages to display and gets the previous or next page of search results. The PageSearchResult() method then calls the custom Page() extension method to see how many auctions to display after all the search filters have been applied.

If the number of auctions is greater than the requested page count, the search result for the current page is returned. If the page size is greater than or equal to the number of auctions, however, the method returns all the auctions that matched the search request:

```
private IEnumerable<Auction> PageSearchResult(SearchCriteria criteria, IQueryable ↵
<Auction>auctionsData)
{
    IEnumerable<Auction> result = null;

    var NumberOfItems = auctionsData.Count();

    if (NumberOfItems > criteria.GetPageSize())
```

```
    {
        var MaxNumberOfPages = NumberOfItems / criteria.GetPageSize();

        if (criteria.CurrentPage > MaxNumberOfPages)
            criteria.CurrentPage = MaxNumberOfPages;

        result = auctionsData.Page(criteria.CurrentPage, criteria.GetPageSize());
    }
    else
    {
        result = auctionsData.ToArray();
    }

    return result;
}
```

To make paging data easier, a C# extension method for IEnumerable<T> types has been created. The method uses the LINQ Skip and Take commands to return only the number of items specified by the current page index and page size parameters:

```
public static class CollectionExtensions
{
    public static IEnumerable<T> Page<T>(this IEnumerable<T> source, ↵
    int pageIndex, int pageSize)
    {
        Contract.Requires(pageIndex >= 0, "Page index cannot be negative");
        Contract.Requires(pageSize >= 0, "Page size cannot be negative");

        int skip = pageIndex * pageSize;

        if (skip > 0)
            source = source.Skip(skip);

        source = source.Take(pageSize);

        return source;
    }
}
```

Summary

This chapter outlined the common data access patterns and how to apply them using the ADO.NET Entity Framework, exploring the different data access approaches supported by Entity Framework and how to use the Code First approach to build a data access layer. It also looked at how to use the POCO classes and the repository pattern when building an ASP.NET MVC web application.

## CHAPTER 9

Security

This chapter discusses the details of how to build secure ASP.NET MVC web applications, including guidance on how to secure web applications; the differences that need to be taken into account when securing Internet, intranet, or extranet applications; as well as how to take advantage of functionality built right into the .NET Framework that can help prevent the common security issues that most web applications face.

Building Secure Web Applications

Benjamin Franklin once said that "an ounce of prevention is worth a pound of cure." This statement conveys the philosophy that you should embrace when it comes to securing your web applications: the world is a dangerous place and web applications often represent attractive targets for would-be attackers, so you're going to want to be prepared.

Unfortunately, there are no silver bullets when it comes to web application security. It isn't as simple as including a library or making a method call. Security is something that needs to be baked into an application right from the start and not an afterthought that is tacked on at the last minute.

There are, however, a few security principles that we will explain over the next few sections that can have a great impact on creating more secure ASP.NET MVC web applications. If you keep these principles in mind as you design and implement your web applications, you have a much greater chance of avoiding some of the more common and serious security mistakes.

Defense in Depth

Just because a website is the only application layer that directly interacts with the outside world doesn't mean that it is the only layer responsible for enforcing security. Much to the contrary, secure systems are based on the notion that each application layer and subsystem is responsible for its own security and should act as its own gatekeeper—it is often assumed that a particular layer will only be called from another, trusted layer, but that is not always the case! Instead, each layer should act as if it is always interacting directly with the outside world, authenticating and authorizing users before allowing them to perform any actions.

Never Trust Input

Any input from a user or another system should always be treated as a potential threat, so always be sure to validate any input before using it. Don't ever assume that you can trust the data because it has already been validated elsewhere.

For example, client-side form validation using JavaScript in the browser helps to create a more enjoyable user experience, but this should not be your only line of defense, since it is very easy for a would-be attacker to submit a form post directly to the server and bypass any client validation you may have in place. Client validation should be considered a convenience feature—not a security feature—and controllers should always validate the data they accept.

Enforce the Principle of Least Privilege

Execute code using an account with only those privileges that are required for the task at hand (the principle of least privilege) and design your application not to require elevated rights unless they are really necessary. In scenarios that do require elevated rights, restrict those rights by granting them for as short a period of time as possible: complete the work, and then immediately remove the rights. For example, instead of running an entire website under an administrator account just to allow disk access to save uploaded files, create a user account that has no direct access to the local machine, except to a specific folder where the account has access to create new files but not to delete, update, or execute them.

Assume External Systems Are Insecure

It's just as important to authenticate and authorize a computer or an external application as it is a human end user. When systems need to interact with each other, consider using different system accounts for each external system that your application communicates with, then restrict each account's permissions so that it can only access operations that the external system needs to perform.

Reduce Surface Area

Avoid exposing information or operations unnecessarily. For instance, ASP.NET MVC controllers should minimize the number of actions that they expose and restrict those actions' input parameters only to the data that is necessary for each action to do what it needs to.

ASP.NET MVC's model binding `BindAttribute` provides `Include` and `Exclude` properties that allow you to specify a comma-delimited list of model properties that should be bound or ignored, respectively.

Likewise, log and handle any exceptions that your application generates, making sure to never return system details such as file paths, account names, or database schema information that an attacker could use to take advantage of the system.

Disable Unnecessary Features

The most common attacks are automated attacks that target widely known vulnerabilities in popular platforms or services. To avoid becoming a target of this type of attack, it is a good idea to reduce your exposure by uninstalling or disabling features or services that your application does not require.

For instance, if your application does not send email, you should disable all email on the host machine.

Securing an Application

Web applications often deal with several kinds of users. For example, your application may interact with end users, who are the primary audience of your application; administrators, who perform tasks related to monitoring and deploying the application; and application or service account "users," which are accounts that are used to communicate between different layers of an application or interact with external services.

At a high level, the first thing you need to consider when designing an ASP.NET web application is the authentication model your site requires; then you can divide the features of your application into different security authorization roles. Before we go any further, let's define these terms:

Authentication
> Authentication is the process of identifying who is accessing the application. Authentication provides an answer to the following questions: who is the current user and does that user represent who it says it does? Both ASP.NET and ASP.NET MVC allow you to choose between either *Windows Authentication* or *Forms Authentication*.

Authorization
> Authorization is the process of determining what level of rights an authenticated user should have for accessing secured resources. The ASP.NET MVC Framework allows you to declaratively add the `AuthorizeAttribute` to controller actions (or entire controllers) to programmatically check to see if a user is in a specific role.

Once you have defined the security model that your application will use for end users, it is time to decide how the various application layers will communicate with each other.

One of the most popular ways to enable interapplication communication is to create an *application service account* that is granted the least amount of privileges required for the layers to communicate with each other.

For example, if a web application only requires the ability to search and report on data and not modify it, the service account would only be granted read access to the web server's local filesystem and the application's database.

In cases where read and write access is required, the attack surface can still be minimized by granting the service account very fine-grained access to specific systems and features —for instance, restricting uploads to a single folder and only granting the service account write access to the specific database tables the application needs to update or insert into.

Securing an Intranet Application

Both intranet and extranet web applications are most often configured to use Windows Authentication. Under this approach, a user's Windows security token is sent with the HTTP request as the user navigates through the web application.

The application then uses this token to verify that the user has a valid account on the local machine (or domain), as well as evaluating the roles that the user belongs to in order to validate that user's ability to perform a given action. When users are not properly authenticated or authorized, they are prompted by the web browser to enter their security credentials.

Setting up Windows Authentication

ASP.NET MVC makes it easy to create a web application that uses Windows Authentication. All you need to do is create a new ASP.NET MVC 4 application using the Intranet Application template, as shown in Figure 9-1. This template sets the authentication mode `<authentication mode="Windows" />` in the application's *web.config* file.

In order to deploy an ASP.NET MVC intranet application, you must first configure Windows Authentication on the web server that will be hosting your application. The following sections explain how to configure both the Internet Information Server (IIS) and IIS Express web servers.

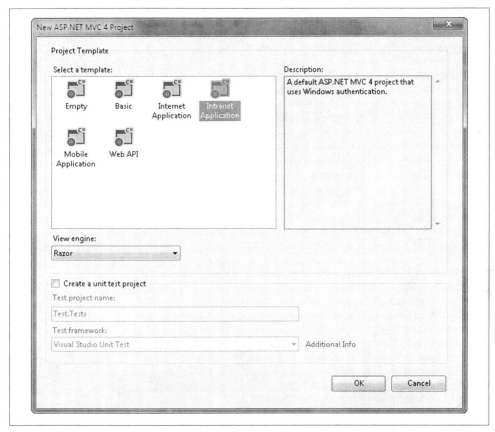

Figure 9-1. Creating a new ASP.NET MVC intranet application

 Visual Studio's built-in web server is great for local development, but it does not handle Windows Authentication failures the same way IIS does. So, in order to develop and test web application functionality that requires Windows Authentication, you must use an IIS Express or IIS 7.0+ web server.

Configuring IIS Express

The following steps outline how to configure IIS Express to host an ASP.NET web application that requires Windows Authentication:

1. In the Solution Explorer, right-click the ASP.NET web project and select "Use IIS Express..." from the menu (Figure 9-2). Say yes to the IIS Express dialog that is displayed.

2. Back in the Solution Explorer, select your project and hit F4 to display the project's properties. Then, set Anonymous Authentication to *Disabled* and set Windows Authentication to *Enabled*, as shown in Figure 9-3.

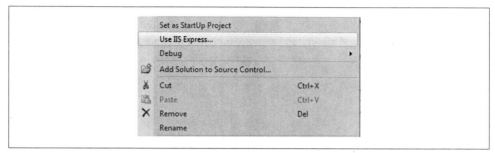

Figure 9-2. Choosing IIS Express

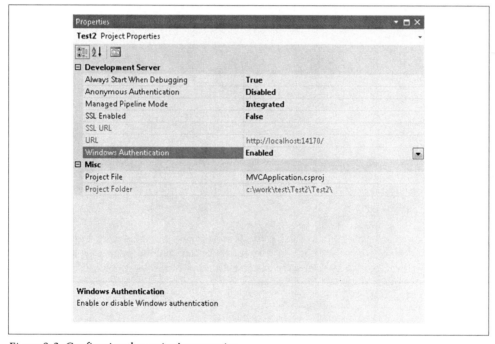

Figure 9-3. Configuring the project's properties

Configuring IIS 7

Configuring Windows Authentication in IIS 7 is a bit different than configuring it in IIS Express. The following steps outline how to enable Windows Authentication on IIS 7:

1. Load IIS 7.0 Manager, right-click on one of the websites (e.g., "Default Web Site"), as shown in (Figure 9-4), and select "Add Web Application."

2. In the Add Application dialog (Figure 9-5), choose an alias, an application pool (make sure to select an ASP.NET 4.0 application pool), and a physical path that will act as the website's root folder.

3. Select the newly created web application and click on the Authentication option, then disable Anonymous Authentication and enable Windows Authentication, as shown in Figure 9-6:

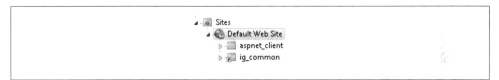

Figure 9-4. Choosing a website on which to configure Windows Authentication

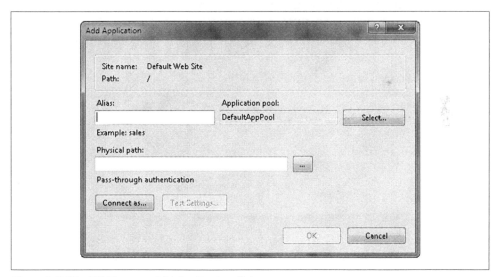

Figure 9-5. The IIS Manager Add Application dialog

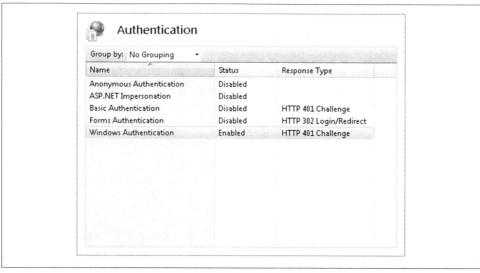

Figure 9-6. Configuring the authentication options

Using the AuthorizeAttribute

The AuthorizeAttribute allows you to declaratively restrict access to a controller action by rejecting requests whenever a user tries to access a controller action that the user doesn't have rights to.

 If the Visual Studio built-in web server is hosting the application a blank page will be returned, since it doesn't support Windows Authorization failures.

Table 9-1 lists the available AuthorizeAttribute properties.

Table 9-1. AuthorizeAttribute properties

Properties	Description
Order	Defines the order in which the action filter is executed (inherited from FilterAttribute)
Roles	Gets or sets the roles required to access the action
Users	Gets or sets the usernames allowed to access the action

The following code snippet shows how to configure an action that is only available to certain users. In this example, only the *Company\Jess* and *Company\Todd* users are able to access the `AdminProfile` controller action; all other users will be denied:

```
[Authorize(Users = @"Company\Jess, Company\Todd")]
public ActionResult AdminProfile()
{
    return View();
}
```

Though this example specifies a list of explicit usernames, it is generally a better idea to use Windows Groups instead. This makes application access management significantly easier, since the same Windows Group name can be used in multiple places and the members of the Windows Group can be modified using standard Windows tools.

In order to leverage Windows Groups instead of usernames, simply populate the `Roles` property with the Windows Group names:

```
[Authorize(Roles = "Admin, AllUsers")]
public ActionResult UserProfile()
{
    return View();
}

[Authorize(Roles = "Executive")]
public ActionResult ExecutiveProfile()
{
    return View();
}
```

Forms Authentication

The limitations of the Windows Authentication approach can become really clear as soon as your application's user base extends outside of your local domain. In these scenarios—that is, most publicly accessible Internet sites—you'll want to use ASP.NET's *Forms Authentication* instead.

Using the Forms Authentication approach, ASP.NET issues an encrypted HTTP cookie (or query string value, if the user has cookies disabled) to identify authenticated users across all future requests. This cookie is tightly coupled to the user's ASP.NET session, such that when the session times out or the user closes the web browser, the session and cookie will become invalid and the user will need to log in again to establish another session.

It's highly recommended that you use SSL in conjunction with Forms Authentication whenever possible. SSL encryption will automatically encrypt the user's sensitive credentials, which would otherwise be sent to the server in clear, human-readable text.

To learn more about setting up SSL, visit *http://learn.iis.net/page.aspx/ 144/how-to-set-up-ssl-on-iis/*.

Since it is by far the most commonly used authentication technique, most of the ASP.NET MVC web application templates (all except the Intranet Application template) come preconfigured to use Forms Authentication.

ASP.NET MVC's Internet Application template even goes so far as to provide a default implementation right out of the box, generating a controller class named `AccountCon troller` and its associated login and new user registration views.

Figure 9-7 shows the default login form that ships with the ASP.NET Internet template. The form includes the typical features of a login form, including fields for the user's username and password, a "Remember me?" checkbox, and a Register link for new users.

Figure 9-7. The ASP.NET Internet Application template's default login form

The default New User Registration Form (Figure 9-8) also includes built-in password validation to verify that the two password fields match and that users enter passwords that are at least six characters long.

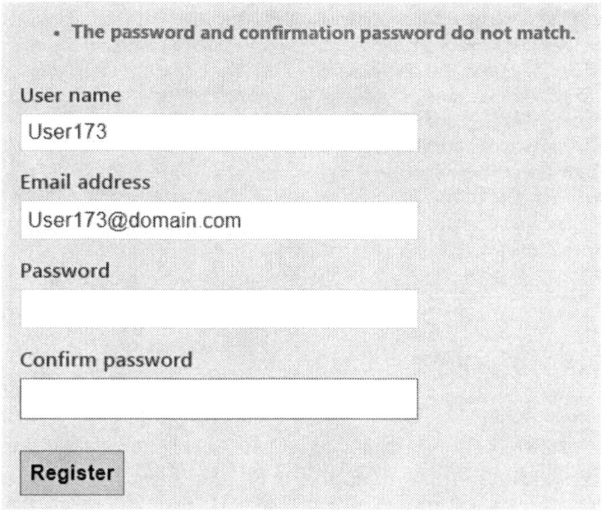

Figure 9-8. The default registration form for new users

Consider these views as a starting point for your website and feel free to modify them to meet your application's particular needs.

AccountController

The AccountController comes fully equipped for supporting typical ASP.NET form-based authentication scenarios. Out of the box, supports registering new users with the site, authenticating existing users, and even includes logic that lets users change their passwords.

Under the covers, the controller uses the standard ASP.NET membership and roles providers, as configured in the application's *web.config* file. The default ASP.NET membership provider configuration stores the site's membership data in an SQL Express database called *ASPNETDB.MDF*, located under the application's */App_Data* folder. Since SQL Express is generally only suitable for development scenarios, however, you will probably want to switch to a more production-ready data store, such as the full version of Microsoft SQL Server or even Active Directory. Alternatively, you can create and register your own custom providers in order to extend the capabilities of the membership provider to include additional fields or to provide additional features that the default providers do not offer.

Luckily, changing the settings for the default membership provider or even switching to a custom membership provider is only a matter of configuration. To change the membership provider configuration, simply update the <membership> section of the application's *web.config*:

```
<membership defaultProvider="DefaultMembershipProvider">
    <providers>
        <add name="DefaultMembershipProvider" type="System.Web.Providers.DefaultMembership↵
            Provider, System.Web.Providers, Version=1.0.0.0, Culture=neutral, PublicKey↵
            Token=31bf3856ad364e35"
            connectionStringName="DefaultConnection" enablePasswordRetrieval="false" ↵
            enablePasswordReset="true"
            requiresQuestionAndAnswer="false" requiresUniqueEmail="false" maxInvalid↵
            PasswordAttempts="5"
            minRequiredPasswordLength="6" minRequiredNonalphanumericCharacters="0" password↵
            AttemptWindow="10" applicationName="/" />
    </providers>
</membership>
```

Authenticating users

When a user tries to access a secure section of a web application, he or she will be redirected to the login form. The `AccountController` leverages the `AllowAnonymous` `Attribute` to indicate that the `Login` action is an exception to the authorization rules and that unauthenticated users may access it. If this were not the case, users would never be able to see the login form in order to authenticate themselves!

Since the `Login` controller action is accessible both by standard HTML login forms and by AJAX-based forms, the action looks at the `content` property of the query string to determine which one of these it is being called from. When the `content` parameter is not null, the action returns the AJAX version of the login form; otherwise, it is assumed that the request is a standard full-page browser request and the action returns the full login form view. The user login code looks like this:

```
[AllowAnonymous]
public ActionResult Login()
{
    return ContextDependentView();
}

private ActionResult ContextDependentView()
{
    string actionName = ControllerContext.RouteData.GetRequiredString("action");
    if (Request.QueryString["content"] != null)
    {
        ViewBag.FormAction = "Json" + actionName;
        return PartialView();
    }
    else
    {
        ViewBag.FormAction = actionName;
        return View();
    }
}
```

After the user enters his security credentials and hits submit, the login form posts the credentials back to the `HttpPost` version of the `Login` action in order to try to authenticate the user.

Authenticating users using ASP.NET Forms Authentication is a two-step process:

1. First, the `Login` action calls the `Membership.ValidateUser()` method to see if the user is valid.
2. Then, if the membership provider says that the credentials are valid, the action calls `FormsAuthentication.SetAuthCookie()` to create the user's security token.

Finally, if the user is successfully logged in, he will be either redirected to the URL that originally failed authentication or, if he navigated directly to the login page, returned to the application's home page. If an error occurs during authentication, the user is returned back to the login form to try again. The code to handle all of this looks like the following:

```
[AllowAnonymous]
[HttpPost]
public ActionResult Login(LoginModel model, string returnUrl)
{
    if (ModelState.IsValid)
    {
        if (Membership.ValidateUser(model.UserName, model.Password))
        {
            FormsAuthentication.SetAuthCookie(model.UserName, model.RememberMe);
            if (Url.IsLocalUrl(returnUrl))
            {
                return Redirect(returnUrl);
            }
            else
            {
                return RedirectToAction("Index", "Home");
            }
        }
        else
        {
            ModelState.AddModelError("", "The user name or password provided is ↵
            incorrect.");
        }
    }

    // If we got this far, something failed; redisplay form
    return View(model);
}
```

Registering new users

Before users are able to authenticate themselves with the site, they must first have an account. Though it is possible for website administrators to manage user accounts manually, the much more common approach is to allow users to register their own accounts. In the ASP.NET MVC Internet Application template, it's the `Register` controller action's job to interact with the user and collect all the data necessary to create a new user account with the membership provider.

At a glance, the `Register` action looks a lot like the `Login` action we saw previously—the `AllowAnonymous` attribute allows users to access the action, and it leverages context-specific logic to return a partial view or a full view, depending on whether the request is an AJAX request or not.

Instead of authenticating users, however, form posts to the `Register` action tell the application to register a new user with the ASP.NET membership provider using its `Membership.CreateUser()` API method.

When the new user is successfully registered, the action uses the same `FormsAuthentication.SetAuthCookie()` method shown in the `Login` action to automatically authenticate the new user, then redirects the user to the application's home page:

```
[AllowAnonymous]
public ActionResult Register()
{
    return ContextDependentView();
}

[AllowAnonymous]
[HttpPost]
public ActionResult Register(RegisterModel model)
{
    if (ModelState.IsValid)
    {
        // Attempt to register the user
        MembershipCreateStatus createStatus;
        Membership.CreateUser(model.UserName, model.Password, model.Email, password↵
        Question: null, passwordAnswer: null, isApproved: true, providerUserKey: null, ↵
        status: out createStatus);

        if (createStatus == MembershipCreateStatus.Success)
        {
            FormsAuthentication.SetAuthCookie(model.UserName, createPersistentCookie: ↵
        false);
            return RedirectToAction("Index", "Home");
        }
        else
        {
            ModelState.AddModelError("", ErrorCodeToString(createStatus));
        }
    }

    // If we got this far, something failed; redisplay form
    return View(model);
}
```

Changing passwords

The `AccountController` provides one additional action that is typical in most Forms Authentication web applications: `ChangePassword`.

The process begins with a request to the ChangePassword action from a user who wants to change her password. The controller attempts to locate the user's account using the Membership.GetUser API to get an instance of MembershipUser, which contains the user's authentication information.

If it successfully locates the user's account, the ChangePassword action then calls the ChangePassword() method on the MembershipUser, passing in the user's new password.

After the password is successfully changed, the user is redirected to the *ChangePasswordSuccess* view, confirming to the user that everything went well and that the password has been changed:

```
public ActionResult ChangePassword()
{
    return View();
}

[HttpPost]
public ActionResult ChangePassword(ChangePasswordModel model)
{
    if (ModelState.IsValid)
    {

        // ChangePassword will throw an exception rather
        // than return false in certain failure scenarios.
        bool changePasswordSucceeded;
        try
        {
            MembershipUser currentUser = Membership.GetUser(User.Identity.Name, ↵
            userIsOnline: true);
            changePasswordSucceeded = currentUser.ChangePassword(model.OldPassword, ↵
            model.NewPassword);
        }
        catch (Exception)
        {
            changePasswordSucceeded = false;
        }

        if (changePasswordSucceeded)
        {
            return RedirectToAction("ChangePasswordSuccess");
        }
        else
        {
            ModelState.AddModelError("", "The current password is incorrect or the new ↵
            password is invalid.");
        }
    }

    // If we got this far, something failed; redisplay form
    return View(model);
}
```

Interacting via AJAX

In addition to the standard HTML GET/POST model, the AccountController also supports logging in and registering users via AJAX. The following code snippet shows the AJAX methods for these features:

```
[AllowAnonymous]
[HttpPost]
public JsonResult JsonLogin(LoginModel model, string returnUrl)
{
    if (ModelState.IsValid)
    {
        if (Membership.ValidateUser(model.UserName, model.Password))
        {
            FormsAuthentication.SetAuthCookie(model.UserName, model.RememberMe);
            return Json(new { success = true, redirect = returnUrl });
        }
        else
        {
            ModelState.AddModelError("", "The user name or password provided is ↵
            incorrect.");
        }
    }

    // If we got this far, something failed
    return Json(new { errors = GetErrorsFromModelState() });
}

[AllowAnonymous]
[HttpPost]
public ActionResult JsonRegister(RegisterModel model)
{
    if (ModelState.IsValid)
    {
        // Attempt to register the user
        MembershipCreateStatus createStatus;
        Membership.CreateUser(model.UserName, model.Password, model.Email, ↵
        passwordQuestion: null, passwordAnswer: null, isApproved: true, ↵
        providerUserKey: null, status: out createStatus);

        if (createStatus == MembershipCreateStatus.Success)
        {
            FormsAuthentication.SetAuthCookie(model.UserName, createPersistentCookie: ↵
            false);
            return Json(new { success = true });
        }
        else
        {
            ModelState.AddModelError("", ErrorCodeToString(createStatus));
        }
    }

    // If we got this far, something failed
    return Json(new { errors = GetErrorsFromModelState() });
}
```

If you think these methods look familiar, you're right—the only major difference between the AJAX-based actions and the GET-based actions is that the controller returns a JSON response (via a `JSONResult`) rather than an HTML response (via a `ViewResult`).

User authorization

User authorization works the same in Forms Authentication as it does with Windows Authentication—placing the `AuthorizeAttribute` on a controller action restricts the action to only authenticated users:

```
[Authorize]
public ActionResult About()
{
        return View();
}
```

When a non-authenticated user attempts to access the controller action, ASP.NET MVC will reject the request by redirecting the user to the login page instead.

When this happens, the original request page is passed as a parameter (`ReturnUrl`) to the login page, e.g., */Account/LogOn?ReturnUrl=%2fProduct%2fCreateNew*. After the user successfully logs in, he will be redirected to the original requested view.

When working with Forms Authentication, certain pages, such as the application's home or Contact Us page, may be accessible to all users. The `AllowAnonymous` attribute grants access to nonauthenticated users:

```
[AllowAnonymous]
public ActionResult Register()
{
    return ContextDependentView();
}
```

In addition to declaratively authorizing the user using the `User` or `Groups` properties of the `AuthorizeAttribute`, you may also access the logged-in user directly by calling the `User.Identity.Name()` or `User.IsInRole()` method to check if the user is authorized to perform a given action:

```
[HttpPost]
[Authorize]
public ActionResult Details(int id)
{
    Model model = new Model();

    if (!model.IsOwner(User.Identity.Name))
        return View("InvalidOwner");

    return View();
}
```

Guarding Against Attacks

Managing user security is just the first step in securing a web application. The second, more important challenge is guarding against attacks from potential intruders.

While most users do not typically go around trying to hack the applications they use, people using your application are very good at discovering bugs that can lead to security holes. What's more, intruders come in many forms, from a simple attacker out to have some fun to sophisticated automated attacks that leverage worms and viruses designed to attack known vulnerabilities.

Regardless of the type of intruder, the most important weapons that you have at your disposal to defend against attacks are planning and implementing the security principles discussed in this chapter. It is also important that proper monitoring and auditing are carried out, so if an attack occurs, the operation and development teams can identify its cause and guard against future attacks.

The next few sections discuss the most common types of web application attacks and what steps you can take to protect yourself against them.

SQL Injection

A SQL injection attack occurs when an attacker tricks the web application into accepting parameters that cause a query you may not have planned for that uses untrusted data to be run. For demonstration purposes, the examples given here are simple and straightforward. Keep in mind, though, that attackers generally do not leverage simple logic; instead, they try to create complex algorithms that identify exploits and then attack those exploits.

Let's start with a simple example that is vulnerable to an SQL injection attack. All the examples use the database schema from the EBuy reference application, which includes tables such as *Auctions* and *Categories*. The *Auctions* and *Categories* tables (Figure 9-9 and Figure 9-10) have a many-to-many relationship, managed by the *CategoryAuctions* table (Figure 9-11).

	Column Name	Data Type	Allow Nulls
🔑	Id	uniqueidentifier	☐
	Title	nvarchar(500)	☐
	Description	nvarchar(MAX)	☐
	StartTime	datetime	☐
	EndTime	datetime	☐
	CurrentPrice_Code	nvarchar(MAX)	☑
	CurrentPrice_Value	float	☐
	WinningBidId	uniqueidentifier	☑
	IsFeaturedAuction	bit	☐
	OwnerId	bigint	☐
	[Key]	nvarchar(50)	☐
	User_Id	bigint	☑
			☐

Figure 9-9. EBuy Auctions table

	Column Name	Data Type	Allow Nulls
🔑	Id	bigint	☐
	Name	nvarchar(100)	☐
	ParentId	bigint	☑
	[Key]	nvarchar(50)	☐
			☐

Figure 9-10. EBuy Categories table

	Column Name	Data Type	Allow Nulls
🔑	Category_Id	bigint	☐
🔑	Auction_Id	uniqueidentifier	☐
			☐

Figure 9-11. EBuy CategoryAuctions table

Here is an example of a controller class that accepts an ID and queries the *Categories* table:

```
public ActionResult Details(string id)
{
    var viewModel = new CategoriesViewModel();

    var sqlString = "SELECT * FROM Categories WHERE id = " + id;
    var connString = WebConfigurationManager.ConnectionStrings["Ebuy.DataAccess. ↵
DataContext"].ConnectionString;
    using (var conn = new SqlConnection(connString))
    {
        var command = new SqlCommand(sqlString, conn);
        command.Connection.Open();

        IDataReader reader = command.ExecuteReader();

        while (reader.Read())
        {
            viewModel.Categories.Add(new Category { Name = reader[1].ToString()});
        }
    }

    return View(viewModel);
}
```

When users navigate to the view *~/category/details/1%20or%201=1* under normal circumstances, everything works as expected—the controller loads a single category based on the ID passed in via the query string (Figure 9-12).

Figure 9-12. SQL injection attack view

However, by simply modifying the query string to *~/category/details/1 or 1=1*, a security hole is exposed. Now, instead of a single category being displayed, all of the records in the *Categories* table are returned (Figure 9-13).

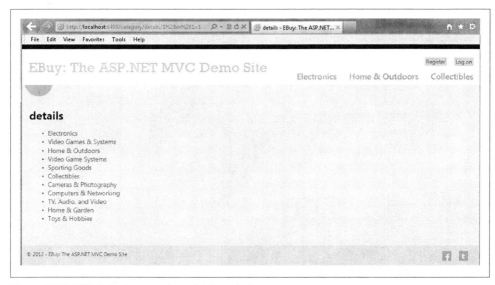

Figure 9-13. SQL injection attack exploiting a hole

When attackers successfully identify holes such as this, they will start seeing what else they can discover by modifying the query string to use other types of SQL statements. In fact, the entire process can be automated so that the attacker doesn't even have to be at the keyboard.

The following are some examples of really dangerous SQL statements that allow an attacker to not only discover what other tables the application uses, but modify the contents of those tables as well.

The first thing an attacker will try to discover is which fields exist in the table being displayed. This is very useful because it allows the attacker to discover foreign keys that can be used to grab data from other tables. In this example, the attacker submits a query that includes a *CategoryName* column *~/category/details/1 or categoryname=\"*. And, since the *Categories* table does not have this column, the database responds with an exception (Figure 9-14).

Displaying the full details of the error—the default, in any ASP.NET application—is just about the worst thing to do, because it exposes the call stack and other sensitive application information that the attacker can use to locate and exploit other security holes in the application.

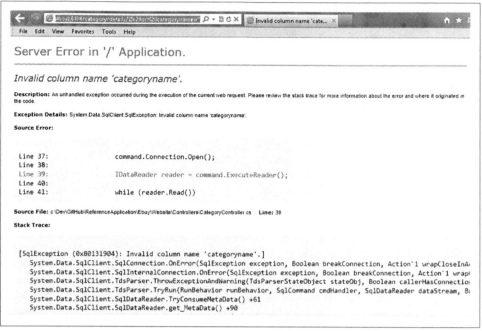

Figure 9-14. SQL injection attack missing field

Here is another sequence of queries an attacker might try to send to a web application she has exploited. The first query is used to discover what other tables exist. Once an attacker knows a table exists, she can then try to insert, update, or even delete data from the application's SQL database, as shown in the second query:

```
1 OR 1=(SELECT COUNT(1) FROM Auctions)

1; INSERT INTO Auctions VALUES (1, "Test", "Description")
```

Fortunately, there are many techniques you can use to guard against SQL injection attacks, so you are not defenseless against this kind of threat. The best option to deflect a would-be attacker is to treat all input as evil. This includes data from query strings, HTML forms, request headers, and any other input that comes into your system.

From a high level, there are two approaches you can take to validate input data:

Blacklists

> A blacklist-based approach depends on validating incoming data against a list of known values to exclude. Blacklists often seem like a good starting point because they actively guard against known threats. However, the effectiveness of a blacklist approach is only as good as the data you give it, and it can often provide a false sense of security as potentially malicious input changes and new values are able to sneak through.

Whitelists

Whitelist-based approaches follow the opposite mind-set, wherein incoming data is only considered valid when it matches values included in the list of known values. In other words, whitelists block all values except values that are explicitly allowed. This makes whitelist approaches generally much safer, by placing tighter control over the data that is allowed to flow into the system.

While both whitelist and blacklist approaches require care and maintenance of the values they allow or disallow, the possible effects of allowing malicious input (as is the danger with a blacklist approach) typically far outweigh the effects of blocking input that should be considered valid but is not explicitly allowed (as in the whitelist approach).

To see a whitelist approach in action, check out the code below, which shows an example of verifying that the input parameter passed in is a numeric value:

```
var message = "";
var positiveIntRegex = new Regex(@"^0*[1-9][0-9]*$");
if (!positiveIntRegex.IsMatch(id))
{
    message = "An invalid Category ID has been specified.";
}
```

 Though object-relational mappers such as LINQ to SQL and Entity Framework automatically take care of many SQL injection issues, these frameworks can't protect against everything.

Here is the guidance from Microsoft (*http://http://msdn.microsoft.com/ en-us/library/cc716760.aspx*) on how to handle SQL injection attacks when working with Entity Framework:

Entity SQL injection attacks:

> SQL injection attacks can be performed in Entity SQL by supplying malicious input to values that are used in a query predicate and in parameter names. To avoid the risk of SQL injection, you should never combine user input with Entity SQL command text.

Entity SQL queries accept parameters everywhere that literals are accepted. You should use parameterized queries instead of injecting literals from an external agent directly into the query. You should also consider using query builder methods to safely construct Entity SQL.

LINQ to Entities injection attacks:

> Although query composition is possible in LINQ to Entities, it is performed through the object model API. Unlike Entity SQL queries, LINQ to Entities queries are not composed by using string manipulation or concatenation, and they are not susceptible to traditional SQL injection attacks.

Cross-Site Scripting

Like SQL injection attacks, *cross-site scripting* (XSS) attacks represent a serious threat to web applications that accept input from users.

The root cause of these types of attacks is insufficient validation of input data. XSS attacks usually occur when the attacker is able to trick the user into viewing fake pages that look similar to the target web application, or uses embedded links in innocent-looking emails that take the user to an unexpected location.

Web applications that contain sensitive data are highly susceptible to XSS attacks. Attackers often try to hijack cookies that may contain a user's login credentials or session IDs, since they can use these cookies to try to get access to the user's information or trick the user into doing something harmful, such as submitting extra HTML content or malicious JavaScript.

Fortunately, Microsoft recognizes the threat of cross-site scripting and has built basic protection right into the framework in the form of *request validation*. When ASP.NET receives a request, it will examine it to look for markup or scripts submitted in the request (such as form field values, headers, cookies, etc.). If suspicious content is detected, ASP.NET rejects the request by throwing an exception. In addition, the popular Microsoft XSS library has been included in ASP.NET 4.5.

In some scenarios, applications such as content management systems (CMSs), forums, and blogs need to support the input of HTML content. To this end, ASP.NET 4.5 introduces the ability to use deferred (or "lazy") request validation, and methods for accessing unvalidated request data. It is important to use these features with caution, though, and remember that when you do so, you assume the responsibility of validating input on your own.

To configure ASP.NET to use deferred request validation, update the `httpRuntime` > `requestValidationMode` attribute in *web.config* to 4.5:

```
<httpRuntime requestValidationMode="4.5" />
```

When deferred request validation is enabled, the validation process will get triggered the first time the application calls the request collection (e.g., `Request.Form["post_con tent"]`). To skip the input validation, use the `HttpRequest.Unvalidated()` helper method to access an unvalidated collection:

```
using System.Web.Helpers;

var data = HttpContext.Request.Unvalidated().Form["post_content"];
```

Microsoft has included a portion of the popular Microsoft Anti-XSS Library in ASP.NET 4.5. The encoding features are part of the `AntiXSSEncoded` class, which is in the `System.Web.Security.AntiXss` namespace. The library can be used directly by calling one of the static encoding methods in the `AntiXSSEncoded` class.

An easy way to utilize the new anti-XSS functionality is to set up an ASP.NET web application to use the class by default. This is done by setting the `encoderType` in *web.config* to `AntiXssEncoded`. When this is turned on, all output encoding will automatically use the new XSS encoding functionality:

```
<httpRuntime ...
    encoderType="System.Web.Security.AntiXss.AntiXssEncoder,System.Web, Version=4.0.0.0, ↵
    Culture=neutral, PublicKeyToken=b03f5f7f11d50a3a" />
```

Here are the features from the Anti-XSS library included in ASP.NET 4.5:

- `HtmlEncode`, `HtmlFormUrlEncode`, and `HtmlAttributeEncode`
- `XmlAttributeEncode` and `XmlEncode`
- `UrlEncode` and `UrlPathEncode` (new to ASP.NET 4.5!)
- `CssEncode`

Cross-Site Request Forgery

The Web is not a safe place, and no matter how secure you try to make your applications, there will always be someone who tries to get around the restrictions you put in place. While cross-site scripting and SQL injection attacks get a lot of attention, there is another—potentially more serious—issue that a lot of web developers overlook: *Cross-Site Request Forgery* (CSRF).

The reason CSRF is such a potential security risk is that it exploits how the Web works. Here is an example of a controller that is susceptible to a CSRF attack. Everything looks straightforward and fairly innocent, but the controller is a prime target for a CSRF attack:

```
public class ProductController : Controller
{
    public ViewResult Details()
    {
        return View();
    }

    public ViewResult Update()
    {
        Product product = DbContext.GetProduct();

        product.ProductId = Request.Form["ProductId"];
        product.Name = Request.Form["Name"];
        SaveUProduct(product);

        return View();
    }
}
```

To exploit the controller, all a resourceful attacker needs to do is set up a page that targets it. Once the attacker persuades a user to visit his page, that page will try to post to the controller:

```
<body onload="document.getElementById('productForm').submit()">
    <form id=" productForm'" action="http://.../Product/Update" method="post">
        <input name="ProductId" value="123456" />
        <input name="Name" value="My Awesome Hack" />
    </form>
</body>
```

If the user has already been authenticated using either Windows Authentication or Forms Authentication, the controller will be oblivious to the CSRF attack. So, what's the cure to this potentially serious security risk?

There are two main ways of blocking a CSRF attack:

Domain referrer
> Check to see if the incoming request has a referrer header for your domain. This will help prevent requests submitted from external third-party sources. This approach has a couple of drawbacks: a user can disable sending a referrer header for privacy reasons, and attackers can spoof the header if the user has an older version of Adobe Flash installed.

User-generated token
> Using a hidden HTML field, store a user-specific token (e.g., generated from your server) and verify that the submitted token is valid. The generated token can be stored in the user session or in an HTTP cookie.

Using ASP.NET MVC to avoid Cross-Site Request Forgery

ASP.NET MVC includes a set of helpers that help you detect and block CSRF attacks by creating a user-specific token that is passed between the view and the controller and verified on each request. All you need to do to take advantage of this functionality is to use the @Html.AntiForgeryToken() HTML helper to add a hidden HTML field to your page that the controller will verify at each request. For increased security, the HTML helper also accepts a salted key that will be used to increase the randomization of the generated token:

```
@Html.AntiForgeryToken()
@Html.AntiForgeryToken("somerandomsalt")
```

For this antiforgery approach to work, the controller action that handles the form post needs to be aware that the form contains an antiforgery token. To ensure this, you apply the ValidateAntiForgeryTokenAttribute to it. This attribute will verify that the incoming request includes both a cookie value and a form field named RequestVerificationToken, and that both of their values match:

```
[ValidateAntiForgeryToken]
public ViewResult Update()
{
}
```

The anti-CSRF helpers included with ASP.NET MVC are very useful, but they have some limitations that you need to keep in mind as you use them:

- Legitimate users must accept cookies. If the user has cookies disabled in her web browser, the `ValidateAntiForgeryTokenAttribute` filter will reject that user's requests.

- This method only works with `POST` requests, not `GET` requests. In reality, this is not a big deal because you should be using only `GET` requests for read-only operations.

- If you have any cross-site scripting (XSS) holes in your domain, it's easy for an attacker to access and read the antiforgery token.

- Out-of-the-box web frameworks like jQuery do not automatically pass the required cookie and hidden HTML field when making AJAX requests. You have to build your own solution for passing and reading the anti-CSRF token.

Summary

This chapter outlined how to build secure ASP.NET MVC web applications. It explored the differences between using Windows Authentication and Forms Authentication, how to use the `AuthorizeAttribute` to authorize different users and groups and how to guard against SQL injection, and cross-site scripting attacks and how to use the CSRF antiforgery helpers.

## CHAPTER 10

Mobile Web Development

The mobile web offers a powerful medium to deliver your content to a greater number of users. With the increasing number of smartphones in use and the subsequent explosion in the market penetration of mobile web users, it has become increasingly important to incorporate mobile devices into your projects' initial planning and requirements phases.

The most painful part of developing for the mobile web is that not all mobile devices are created equal. Different devices have different hardware capabilities, resolutions, browsers, feature support, touch capabilities—and the list goes on. Adapting your website to deliver a consistent experience across all mobile devices is a nontrivial task.

This chapter will show you how to use the features in the ASP.NET MVC Framework —particularly the new features added in ASP.NET MVC 4—to deliver a rich and consistent experience across as many devices as possible, and to gracefully handle the scenarios where you can't.

ASP.NET MVC 4 Mobile Features

From version 3, the ASP.NET MVC Framework provides a set of features that help make mobile web development a bit more straightforward. These features were enhanced in version 4.

The following list gives a brief description of each of the mobile development features new to version 4 of ASP.NET MVC. The rest of this chapter will show you how to put these new features to use in your application.

The ASP.NET MVC 4 Mobile template

If you want to create a purely mobile web application from scratch, ASP.NET MVC 4 includes a *Mobile Application* template that allows you to jump-start your mobile application development. Just like the regular MVC web application templates, version 4 automatically adds scaffolding code to render mobile-specific views, sets up jQuery Mobile MVC NuGet packages, and creates a bare-bones application for you to build upon. "The ASP.NET MVC 4 Mobile Template" on page 224 provides an in-depth description of the new ASP.NET MVC 4 Mobile Application template.

Display modes

To make it easier to target different devices, the ASP.NET MVC 4 Framework offers *display modes*, a feature that helps detect and cater to different devices.

Different mobile devices have different resolutions, different browser behavior, and even different features for your web application to take advantage of. Instead of retrofitting all possible device variations into a single view, you can isolate different behaviors and features into separate, device-specific views.

For example, say you have a regular desktop view called *Index.cshtml* and you need to create some mobile-specific variations of it, such as a view for smartphones and another for tablets. Using display modes, you can create device-specific views such as *Index.iPhone.cshtml* and *Index.iPad.cshtml* and register them with the ASP.NET MVC 4 Framework's DisplayModeProvider on application startup. Based on your filter criteria, the ASP.NET MVC Framework can automatically look for views that contain one of these suffixes ("iPhone" or "iPad") and render them instead of the regular desktop view. (Note that ASP.NET MVC follows a simple file naming convention of "[View Name].[Device].[Extension]" for alternate views.) In "Browser-Specific Views" on page 221, you'll see how you can use this feature to serve different devices.

Overriding regular views with mobile views

ASP.NET MVC 4 introduces a simple mechanism that lets you override any view (including layouts and partial views) for any specific browser, including mobile browsers. To provide a mobile-specific view, you just need to create a view file with *.Mobile* in the filename. For example, to create a mobile *Index* view, copy *Views\Home\Index.cshtml* to *Views\Home\Index.Mobile.cshtml*, and ASP.NET will automatically render this view in a mobile browser instead of the desktop view. It is interesting to note that while display modes allow you to specifically target a particular mobile browser, this feature provides similar functionality on a more generic level. This feature is helpful if your view is generic enough for different mobile browsers, or if you use a framework like jQuery Mobile that provides a consistent experience across most mobile platforms.

jQuery Mobile

The jQuery Mobile Framework brings all the richness and goodness of jQuery and jQuery UI to mobile applications. Instead of having to deal with the browser inconsistencies for different devices, you can create a single application that works on all modern mobile devices. It brings all the virtues of progressive enhancement techniques and provides a flexible design so that older devices can still see a functional (but not as pretty or rich) application, while allowing modern devices to benefit from all the rich interactivity that comes with newer HTML 5 features. The jQuery Mobile Framework also has great theme support, which makes it very easy to create a branded site with a rich user experience that doesn't sacrifice the benefits of progressive enhancement. Throughout this chapter, you'll see how the jQuery Mobile Framework makes it easy to take your application to the next level.

Making Your Application Mobile Friendly

The topic of "mobile web development" is vast and includes a lot of things that website producers need to consider as they create their sites. Perhaps the most important issue is how best to provide information to—and interact with—your users.

Consider the desktop web experience, where the browser has a nice big screen, web access is fast and reliable, and users can interact with applications using both a keyboard and mouse. In sharp contrast, the mobile web experience is often limited to a small screen, web access is intermittent, and you only have a stylus or a couple of fingers to input data.

These limitations invariably lead to selective content and a reduced feature set as compared to desktop browser-based web applications. However, the mobile web also provides opportunities that are largely unavailable in the desktop web environment, such as location-specific data, on-the-go communication, and video and voice communication.

Understanding the needs of the target audience is the first step in formulating a mobile strategy. For example, consider these common examples of mobile device usage:

- Walking down the street, trying to catch up on emails (while glancing up occasionally to make sure you don't bump into the next pole)
- Traveling on the subway or a train, trying to read the latest news
- Holding a coffee cup in one hand and the phone in another, trying to check the balance of a bank account

The thing that all of these scenarios have in common is that the user's attention is divided—he is trying to accomplish a task as quickly as possible so that he can move on with his busy day.

What all of this means for your website is that it needs to focus on getting the user the content he needs in a manner that is quickly and easily comprehensible and highly relevant to the task at hand.

Creating the Auctions Mobile View

When developing for the mobile web, you can start by either adding mobile-specific views to your existing application, or creating a new mobile application from the ground up. Many factors can influence which path you take, and both have their own advantages and disadvantages in terms of how the development goes. Keeping this in mind, ASP.NET MVC 4 offers tools to aid in both the workflows, as you'll see as we go along in this chapter.

In this section, we begin by adding a mobile view to an existing desktop view and then slowly enhancing the mobile view with the new features that ASP.NET MVC 4 offers.

To begin, make a copy of the *Auctions.cshtml* view and name it *Auctions.Mobile.cshtml*, to indicate that it is a mobile-specific view.

To distinguish that our mobile view is being rendered, let's also change the <H1> heading in the mobile view to "Mobile Auctions".

We can verify this by running the application right now and navigating to the Auctions page from a mobile browser. The result is shown in Figure 10-1.

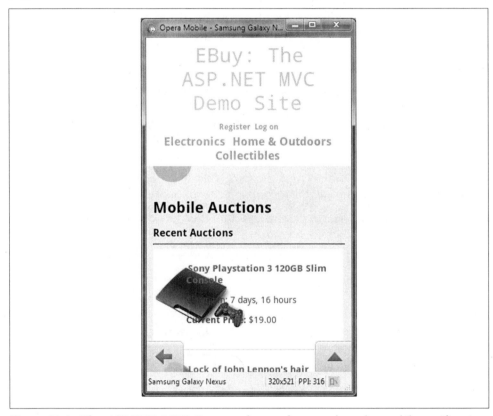

Figure 10-1. The ASP.NET MVC Framework can detect and render mobile-specific views automatically

You can see that the page heading shows "Mobile Auctions," which confirms that the mobile view is being rendered (navigating to the Auctions page from a regular browser shows the heading as "Auctions"). The display modes feature of the framework is able to detect the client browser and load the appropriate view for it.

ASP.NET MVC doesn't just automatically load "mobile" views when the request is coming from a mobile device; in fact, this extends to layouts and partial views also—

a fact that is utilized by the *jQuery.Mobile.MVC* package to create jQuery Mobile-based layouts optimized for mobile devices.

Getting Started with jQuery Mobile

jQuery Mobile allows you to quickly enhance an existing view to create a more native look and feel for mobile devices. Along with that, it allows you to "theme" the application, and its progressive enhancements ensure that older and lower-grade browsers get a reduced (and not a very pretty look and feel) but nevertheless functional and usable page.

To use jQuery Mobile, install the *jQuery.Mobile.MVC* package from the NuGet package gallery (Figure 10-2).

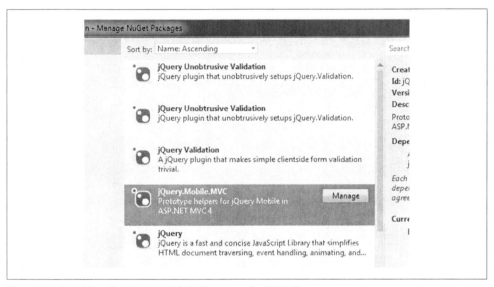

Figure 10-2. Adding the jQuery Mobile Framework via NuGet

This package adds the following files:

jQuery Mobile Framework
> A set of JavaScript (*jQuery.mobile-1.1.0.js*) and CSS (*jQuery.mobile-1.1.0.css*) files, along with their minified versions and supporting images.

/Content/Site.Mobile.css
> A new mobile-specific stylesheet.

Views/Shared/_Layout.Mobile.cshtml
> A layout optimized for mobile devices that references jQuery Mobile Framework files (JS and CSS). ASP.NET MVC will automatically load this layout for mobile views.

The view-switcher component

Consists of the *Views/Shared/_ViewSwitcher.cshtml* partial view and the *View-SwitcherController.cs* controller. This component shows a link on mobile browsers to enable users to switch to the desktop version of the page. We'll explore how this works in "Switching between desktop and mobile views" on page 212.

 jQuery Mobile is under constant development, so you may see a newer version number in the files.

To allow the jQuery Mobile Framework to style the page accordingly, open up *Views/Shared/_Layout.Mobile.cshtml* and modify the content as shown in the following snippet:

```
<body>
  <div data-role="page" data-theme="b">
    <header data-role="header">
      <h1>@Html.ActionLink("EBuy: The ASP.NET MVC Demo Site", "Index", "Home")</h1>
    </header>
    <div id="body" data-role="content">
      @RenderBody()
    </div>
  </div>
</body>
```

And then modify *Auctions.Mobile.cshtml* to optimize it for mobile layout:

```
@model IEnumerable<AuctionViewModel>
<link href="@Url.Content("~/Content/product.css")" rel="stylesheet" type="text/css" />
@{
  ViewBag.Title = "Auctions";
}

<header>
  <h3>Mobile Auctions</h3>
</header>

<ul id="auctions">
  @foreach (var auction in Model)
  {
    <li>
        @Html.Partial("_AuctionTile", auction);
    </li>
  }
</ul>
```

When you're finished, build and run the application, then navigate to the application's home page using a mobile browser to see the changes. You should see something like Figure 10-3.

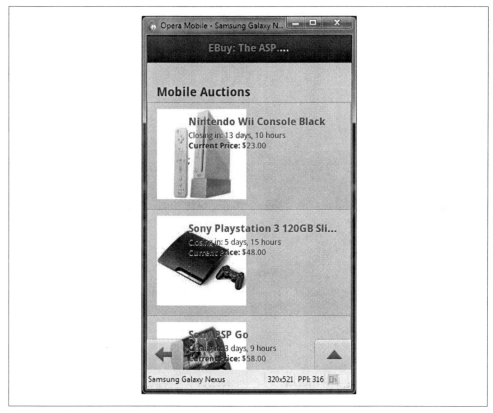

Figure 10-3. The EBuy application, optimized for mobile layout

You can see how the *Auctions* view changes to adapt to the mobile browser. While the appearance is not perfect, the *jQuery.Mobile.MVC* package provides a foundation upon which you can quickly and easily build your mobile views.

Enhancing the View with jQuery Mobile

The *jQuery.Mobile.MVC* package does a lot of groundwork for us, but the UI still doesn't look and feel like a native mobile application. However, jQuery Mobile offers a lot of components and styles to make your application look like a true mobile application.

Improving the auctions list with jQuery Mobile's "listview"

Let's start by enhancing the auctions list by using jQuery Mobile's "listview" component. jQuery Mobile operates on `data-role` attributes to perform most of its mobile transformations, so to render the auctions as a listview, add the `data-role="list view"` attribute to the Auction's `<ul>` tag:

```
<ul id="auctions" data-role="listview">
  @foreach (var auction in Model.Auctions)
  {
    <li>
      @Html.Partial("_AuctionTileMobile", auction);
    </li>
  }
</ul>
```

and modify the _AuctionTileMobile_ partial view as follows:

```
@model AuctionViewModel
@{
  var auctionUrl = Url.Auction(Model);
}

<a href="@auctionUrl">
  @Html.Thumbnail(Model.Image, Model.Title)
  <h3>@Model.Title</h3>
  <p>
    <span>Closing in: </span>
    <span class="time-remaining" title="@Model.EndTimeDisplay">↵
    @Model.RemainingTimeDisplay</span>
  </p>
  <p>
    <strong>Current Price: </strong>
    <span class="current-bid-amount">@Model.CurrentPrice</span>
    <span class="current-bidder">@Model.WinningBidUsername</span>
  </p>
</a>
```

Navigating to the *Auctions* view on a mobile browser now produces the much nicer view shown in Figure 10-4.

Given the fact that `<ul>` is already a list element, you may find it redundant to add the "listview" role. The `<ul>` will display a list, but the link area would be too small to tap on a mobile device with a small screen. What `data-role="listview"` actually does is make the list items easier to "tap" by displaying a larger link area!

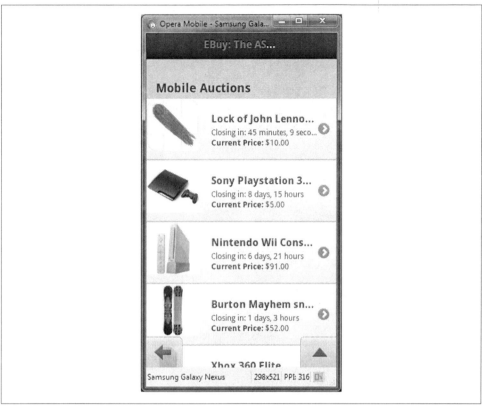

Figure 10-4. Rendering the auctions <ul> as a listview with jQuery Mobile

Making the auctions list searchable with jQuery Mobile's "data-filter"

Next, let's make the view bit more friendly by adding a handy Search box that allows users to quickly filter the list of auctions. The jQuery Mobile framework makes this very easy—simply add the `data-filter="true"` attribute to the auctions `<ul>` tag:

```
<ul id="auctions" data-role="listview" data-filter="true">
  @foreach (var auction in Model.Auctions)
  {
    <li class="listitem">
      @Html.Partial("_AuctionTileMobile", auction);
    </li>
  }
</ul>
```

Refresh the mobile browser to see the Search text box at the top (Figure 10-5).

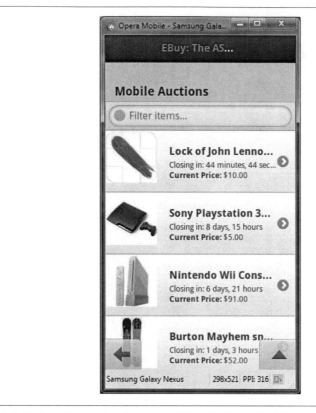

Figure 10-5. Making the auctions list searchable with jQuery Mobile

Try typing in the Search text box to see how jQuery Mobile automatically filters the list to show only the entries that match the text you've entered (Figure 10-6).

You've seen how jQuery Mobile makes it super easy to transform any page to look and behave like a native view. In addition to these features, jQuery Mobile comes with many other handy components that you can use to make any view in your site more accessible to mobile users. To see a comprehensive list of such attributes, check out the ever-evolving API docs (*http://jquerymobile.com/test/docs/api/data-attributes.html*).

Switching between desktop and mobile views

Whenever you provide a mobile-specific version of your website, it's generally a good idea to automatically direct mobile users to your mobile site, but also to provide them with the ability to switch to the full site should they feel the need to.

Notice that the top of the mobile view that's included in the default ASP.NET MVC Mobile Application template displays a link that allows users to switch to the "desktop

Figure 10-6. jQuery Mobile automatically filters the list based on the search text

view." This is known as the `ViewSwitcher` widget and is installed as part of the *jQuery.Mobile.MVC* NuGet package.

To see how the widget works under the hood, let's take a deep dive into its components.

Taking a look at the new partial view, *_ViewSwitcher.cshtml*, shows us the following markup:

```
@if (Request.Browser.IsMobileDevice && Request.HttpMethod == "GET")
{
  <div class="view-switcher ui-bar-a">
    @if (ViewContext.HttpContext.GetOverriddenBrowser().IsMobileDevice)
    {
      @: Displaying mobile view
      @Html.ActionLink("Desktop view", "SwitchView", "ViewSwitcher",
      new { mobile = false, returnUrl = Request.Url.PathAndQuery },
      new { rel = "external" })
    }
    else
    {
      @: Displaying desktop view
      @Html.ActionLink("Mobile view", "SwitchView", "ViewSwitcher",
```

```
        new { mobile = true, returnUrl = Request.Url.PathAndQuery },
        new { rel = "external" })
    }
  </div>
}
```

The GetOverriddenBrowser() method returns an HttpBrowserCapabilities object listing the capabilities of the overridden browser, or the actual browser if not overridden, which allows you to check whether the requesting device is a mobile device or not. The widget then checks to see if it is being rendered in a desktop view or a mobile view and renders appropriate links to switch between the desktop and mobile views.

As a bonus, it also sets the property mobile in the RouteValue dictionary to indicate whether the mobile or the desktop view is active.

Next we'll take a look at the ViewSwitcherController class, which contains the logic that performs the switching action:

```
public class ViewSwitcherController : Controller
{
  public RedirectResult SwitchView(bool mobile, string returnUrl) {
    if (Request.Browser.IsMobileDevice == mobile)
      HttpContext.ClearOverriddenBrowser();
    else
      HttpContext.SetOverriddenBrowser(mobile ? BrowserOverride.Mobile
                                        : BrowserOverride.Desktop);

    return Redirect(returnUrl);
  }
}
```

Depending on whether or not the request originates from a mobile device (as indicated by the Request.Browser.IsMobileDevice property), the controller uses the ClearOver riddenBrowser() and SetOverriddenBrowser() methods to tell ASP.NET MVC how to treat the request, as a mobile browser and display the mobile version of the site, or as a desktop browser and display the full version of the site.

Add the following snippet before the closing <body> tag in *Layout.mobile.cshtml* to render the *ViewSwitcher* partial view as a footer (Figure 10-7):

```
<div data-role="footer">
  @Html.Partial("_ViewSwitcher")
</div>
```

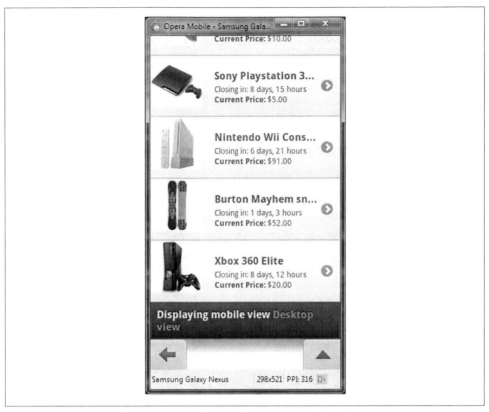

Figure 10-7. View switcher in action in the page footer

If you click the "Desktop view" link, you'll see the regular desktop *Auctions* view. Notice how the desktop view does not have a link to switch to the mobile view, though. To fix that, open up the *_Layout.cshtml* shared view and add this line of code:

```
@Html.Partial("_ViewSwitcher")
```

Run the application and navigate to any page from a mobile browser—you'll see that the view switcher widget shows links to render the mobile view and the full desktop view (Figure 10-8).

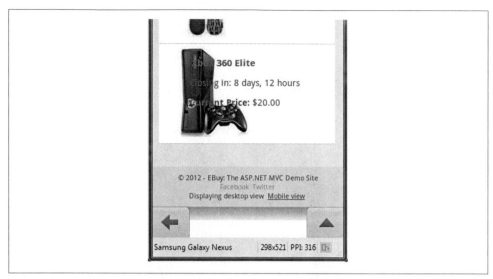

Figure 10-8. View switcher in desktop view

Avoiding Desktop Views in the Mobile Site

You will notice how, in the absence of a mobile view, ASP.NET MVC renders the desktop view in a mobile layout.

Adhering to standards-based markup does help in displaying a somewhat usable view, but there may be cases where you simply want to turn this feature off.

In order to do so, set RequireConsistentDisplayMode to true:

```
@{
    Layout = "~/Views/Shared/_Layout.cshtml";
    DisplayModeProvider.Instance.RequireConsistentDisplayMode = true;
}
```

This will disable any default (non-mobile) view from rendering inside a mobile layout. You can also do it globally for all views by setting this property to true in the */Views/_ViewStart.cshtml* file.

Improving Mobile Experience

Mobile browsers are capable of displaying HTML pages, to varying degrees. However, relying on the browser to make the display good may not provide the best user experience, given that browsers can only operate at a generic level of resizing pages and images. As the content author, only you can decide what elements are the most relevant, and consequently which ones should be highlighted on a smaller screen and which ones can be dropped. Therefore, the onus is on you to make your site look pretty and keep it functional across different browsers.

Fortunately, you can use techniques like adaptive rendering and progressive enhancements to improve your site's display, and ASP.NET MVC 4 and jQuery Mobile allow you to do so easily. We'll look at these next.

Adaptive Rendering

Adaptive rendering is the technique that allows your view to "adapt" to the browser's capabilities. For example, say you have a bunch of tabs on the page and each tab, when clicked, makes an AJAX call to fetch the content and display it. If JavaScript is disabled, the tab would normally fail to display any content. However, using adaptive rendering, the tab will simply point to a URL with the content, so the user can still see the content.

Another example would be a navigation bar that displays a horizontal list of links. While this looks good in a desktop view, it can be overwhelming on the smaller screen of a mobile device. Using adaptive rendering, the navigation bar can render as a dropdown to present the same functionality adapted to the smaller device.

The benefit of using this technique is that it allows you to present a "functional" or "usable" site to different browsers and devices with different capabilities. The level of service may vary based on the device's capabilities, but nevertheless, your site remains useful.

Remember, if you want your users to return to your site again and again, you need to ensure that their experience remains enjoyable, regardless of the device they are using.

ASP.NET MVC 4 includes such adaptive techniques primarily via the jQuery Mobile Framework.

The Viewport Tag

In computer graphics, "viewport" means a rectangular viewing region. When applied to browsers, it is the browser window in which the HTML document displays. In other words, it is the imaginary construct that contains the <html> tag, which in turn is the root element for all your markup.

What happens when you zoom in or zoom out of the browser window? And what happens when you change the orientation of the device—does it change the viewport?

In mobile devices, the answer is slightly tricky, because in actuality, there exists not one but two viewports—the "layout" viewport and the "visual" viewport.

The "layout" viewport never changes—it is the imaginary construct that constrains the <html> of your page. What changes with zoom level or orientation is the "visual" viewport, and that affects what is visible through the borders of the device's frame.

You need to consider the role of the viewport as a way to provide a functional and usable experience to your end users. When your page is rendered on the mobile device, it is important that the width of the page is not too large or too small, but rather fits nicely on the screen. And when it fits, the page should not appear as a micro, shrunken version of the full page; rather, it should be a readable view of the actual page.

In modern browsers, it is not CSS but the meta viewport tag that allows you to configure the dimensions of the visual viewport.

You can set the size of the viewport using the viewport meta tag like this:

```
<meta name="viewport" content="width=device-width" />
```

The "width=device-width" value used here is a special value that says to set the viewport width to whatever the device's actual width is. This is the most flexible and frequently used value.

You can also set the content property to a fixed value if your content is better adapted that way:

```
<meta name="viewport" content="width=320px" />
```

Now, irrespective of how wide the device's screen is, the content will always be displayed at 320 pixels wide, which means that on larger screens the user may want to zoom in, and on smaller screens he may have to zoom out.

The <meta name="viewport"> tag is a de facto industry standard, but it is not actually part of the W3C standard.

The feature was first implemented in the iPhone's web browser, and pretty soon—due to the iPhone's overwhelming popularity—every other manufacturer began to support it.

Mobile Feature Detection

Since every mobile device supports a different set of features, you can never safely assume that a particular feature will be available in every browser.

For instance, let's say your application uses HTML 5's Web Storage, which many smartphones (such as iPhone, Android, Blackberry, and Windows Phone devices) support, but others do not.

Traditionally, developers have relied on techniques like browser detection to check if their application can be run on a particular browser or not.

Rather than checking whether Web Storage is supported, a classical approach is to check if the target browser is Opera Mini.

This approach has several major pitfalls, though, not the least of which are:

- The potential to exclude browsers that you did not explicitly include, but that support the feature
- The possibility that your site will not function properly if the user visits it from a another device

Here's an example of this approach:

```
// Warning: do not use this code!
if (document.all) {
  // Internet Explorer 4+
  document.write('<link rel="stylesheet" type="text/css" src="style-ie.css">');
}
else if (document.layers) {
  // Navigator 4
  document.write('<link rel="stylesheet" type="text/css" src="style-nn.css">');
}
```

Note how the above example only provides stylesheets for Internet Explorer and Netscape Navigator 4; even then, the browser must have JavaScript support enabled. This means that other browsers, such as Netscape 6, Netscape 7, CompuServe 7, Mozilla, and Opera may not be able to view the site properly.

Even if you do add explicit support for most browsers, you may still miss out on a new browser version that gets released with support for the feature you're looking for.

Another potential problem is wrongly identifying the browser.

Since browser detection largely involves guessing based on a user agent string and certain properties, it is quite possible that you may wrongly identify a particular browser:

```
// Warning: do not use this code!
if (document.all) {
  // Internet Explorer 4+
  elm = document.all['menu'];
}
else {
  // Assume Navigator 4
  elm = document.layers['menu'];
}
```

Note how the previous example assumed that any browser that was not Internet Explorer was Navigator 4 and attempted to use layers.

This is a common source of problems when using browsers based on Gecko and Opera.

Due to all of these reasons, it's generally a good idea to explicitly check for the existence of a feature rather than assuming that a set of known browser versions does or does not support that feature.

Here is the same example as above, refactored to use feature detection rather than browser detection:

```
// if localStorage is present, use that
if (('localStorage' in window) && window.localStorage !== null) {
```

```
    // easy object property API
    localStorage.wishlist = '["Unicorn","Narwhal","Deathbear"]';

} else {

    // without sessionStorage we'll have to use a far-future cookie
    //   with document.cookie's awkward API :(
    var date = new Date();
    date.setTime(date.getTime()+(365*24*60*60*1000));
    var expires = date.toGMTString();
    var cookiestr = 'wishlist=["Unicorn","Narwhal","Deathbear"];'+
                    ' expires='+expires+'; path=/';
    document.cookie = cookiestr;
}
```

Not only is this much more robust, it is also future-proof—any browser that adds support for Web Storage will automatically get the new features.

CSS Media Queries

CSS media queries are a progressive enhancement technique that lets you adapt or display alternate styles based on different browser conditions.

Version 2 of the CSS specification (aka "CSS2") allows you to specify styles based on media type, such as screen and print.

Version 3 of the CSS specification (aka "CSS3") provides the concept of *media queries*, a technique that expands on this concept to help detect browser features in a standard way.

> Unfortunately, the CSS3 specification is still in the "candidate recommendation" phase, which means that media queries—and the other new features in version 3 of the CSS specification—are not necessarily well supported across all browsers.
>
> Therefore, it is important to have default styles to provide browsers that don't support these features with something to fall back on.

You have seen how the viewport tag can define a default width based on device size. While the viewport makes the page looks good at the default zoom level, it does not help when the user zooms in or out on the device.

As the layout width changes, you need a way to tell the browser to restrict your content to a certain width so that it displays properly at all times.

Let's take a look at a simple example to see how this can be done with a CSS media query:

```
body {background-color:blue;}
@media only screen and (max-width: 800px) {
    body {background-color:red;}
}
```

Since CSS rules are evaluated top to bottom, we start out by specifying a general rule that the body background will be blue.

We then surround a device-specific rule with a media query and override the background color to red on devices whose screen width is narrower than 800 pixels.

On devices where CSS3 media queries are supported and the width is narrower than 800 pixels, the background will be shown in red; otherwise, it will be blue. (Note that changing the background color as the user zooms in or out is not something you'd normally do in a real application; rather, the focus of this example is to show how to use a CSS media query to apply different styles based on certain conditions.)

It is very important to start with a general rule and then enhance that rule with the support of media queries and feature detection.

This will allow your site to present a rich experience on browsers that support the newer features and, at the same time, still render a useful display on older browsers.

Browser-Specific Views

The new display modes feature in ASP.NET MVC 4 allows us to load different views based on predefined conditions. A simple example of this feature would be to create separate views for smartphones, which have smaller screens, and tablets, which sport a larger display than mobile devices but a smaller one than desktops. Creating different views for these classes of device enables us to make optimum use of the screen space and provide an efficient and rich user experience that is customized, keeping the device's capabilities in mind.

First, register the display modes on application startup:

```
using System.Web.WebPages;

// register iPhone-specific views
DisplayModeProvider.Instance.Modes.Insert(0, new DefaultDisplayMode("iPhone")
{
    ContextCondition = (ctx => ctx.Request.UserAgent.IndexOf(
        "iPhone", StringComparison.OrdinalIgnoreCase) >= 0)
});

// register Windows Phone-specific views
DisplayModeProvider.Instance.Modes.Insert(0, new DefaultDisplayMode("WindowsPhone")
{
    ContextCondition = (ctx => ctx.Request.UserAgent.IndexOf(
        "Windows Phone", StringComparison.OrdinalIgnoreCase) >= 0)
});
```

Now, create an iPhone-specific view by copying *Auctions.mobile.cshtml* and renaming it to *Auctions.iPhone.cshtml*. Then change the title to "iPhone Auctions" to distinguish it from the mobile view. Run the application using a mobile browser emulator (the examples shown here use Firefox's User Agent Switcher (*https://addons.mozilla.org/en-US/firefox/addon/user-agent-switcher/*) add-on to emulate the iPhone's browser) to see this in action (Figure 10-9).

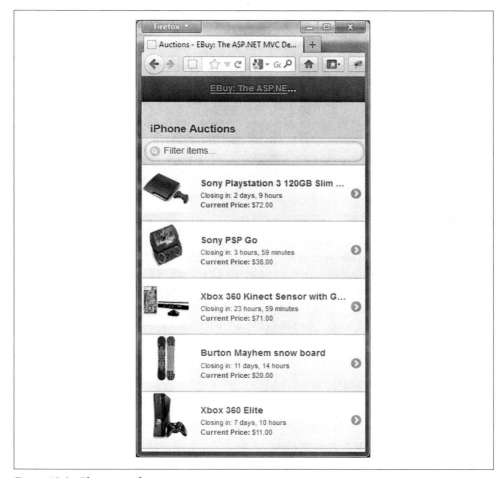

Figure 10-9. iPhone-specific view

To see the Windows Phone version of the page, create another copy of *Auctions.mobile.cshtml* and rename it *Auctions.WindowsPhone.cshtml*. Then change the title to "Windows Phone Auctions" to distinguish it from the other mobile views. Run the application using a mobile browser emulator to see this in action (Figure 10-10).

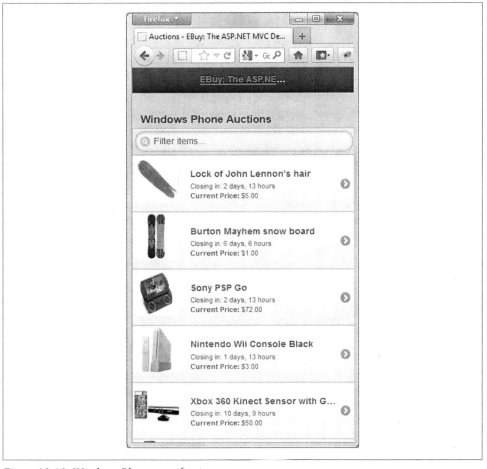

Figure 10-10. Windows Phone-specific view

To see whether the request is coming from a mobile device or not, internally ASP.NET checks it against a predefined set of well known mobile browser definitions.

It provides a whole lot of information about the browser's capabilities through `HttpBrowserCapabilities` (*http://msdn.microsoft.com/en-us/library/system.web.httpbrowsercapabilities.aspx*), which is accessible through the `Request.Browser` property.

Or, rather than relying on the built-in browser definitions, you can use a service like 51Degrees.mobi (*http://51degrees.mobi/Support/Blogs/tabid/212/EntryId/26/51Degrees-mobi-and-MVC4.aspx*), which maintains a much more up-to-date bank of information about various mobile devices.

Creating a New Mobile Application from Scratch

ASP.NET MVC 4 makes it easy to add mobile views to your existing application, but you can create a mobile application from scratch just as easily. This is helpful if you don't have an existing application to use as a starting point or if, for whatever reason, you do not want to mix your mobile and desktop sites.

ASP.NET MVC 4 includes a Mobile Application template that lets you get off the ground quickly with your mobile application development. The template relies heavily on jQuery Mobile for most of its magic, so to build an effective application, you need to understand jQuery Mobile first.

The jQuery Mobile Paradigm Shift

Perhaps the most important distinction while working with jQuery Mobile is the notion of a "page." In traditional web development, a page refers to a single HTML document or an *.aspx* page in ASP.NET Web Forms or a *.cshtml* view in ASP.NET MVC. These files contain the markup and logic to render a single page to the browser.

However, in the jQuery Mobile Framework, a single file can contain multiple mobile "pages." Technically speaking, a jQuery Mobile page is really just a `<div>` tag with the `data-role="page"` attribute. You can put as many of those as you like in a single view file, and jQuery will turn them into multiple pages showing one at a time.

Since a single, regular desktop view can lead to smaller chunks of multiple views on a mobile device (mainly due to the redesign of the page to make it suitable for mobile navigation), this approach helps in reducing the file cutter that would otherwise be created with the small chunks of the desktop view.

The ASP.NET MVC 4 Mobile Template

To create a new mobile web application, you begin the same way as you would for any other ASP.NET MVC web application: select the `File > New > Project` menu option and choose the "ASP.NET MVC 4 Web Application" type (Figure 10-11).

At the next screen (Figure 10-12), select the Mobile Application template.

This creates a new ASP.NET MVC application with example controllers and views that showcase ASP.NET MVC's mobile features and helps you get started quickly.

Figure 10-11. Creating a new project

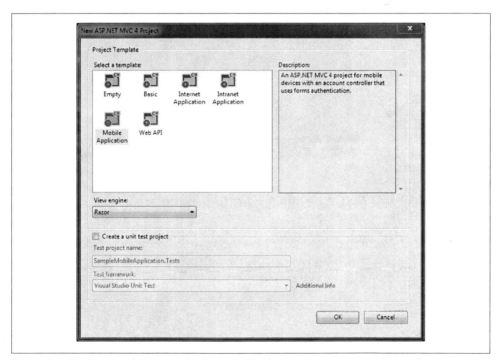

Figure 10-12. Choosing the Mobile Application template

Run this project by hitting F5 or by choosing the Debug > Start menu option. This will build the solution and start a browser instance pointing to the website's mobile-friendly home page (Figure 10-13).

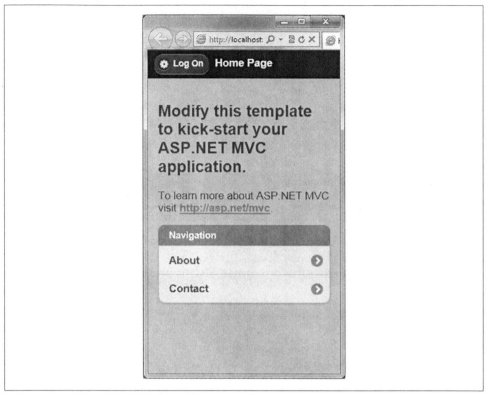

Figure 10-13. Mobile application default start page

Using the ASP.NET MVC 4 Mobile Application Template

As you can see, a lot of scaffolding code has already been written for us. The project structure is very similar to the one we saw for the regular website, with a few additions:

- The *Content* folder now includes stylesheets for jQuery Mobile, as shown in Figure 10-14:
    —*jquery.mobile-1.1.0.css* (and its minified version)
    —*jquery.mobile.structure-1.1.0.css* (and its minified version)

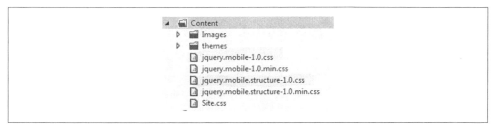

Figure 10-14. The new project's Content folder

- The *Scripts* folder contains two new files, as you can see in Figure 10-15:
    — *jquery.mobile-1.1.0.js*
    — *jquery.mobile-1.1.0.min.js*

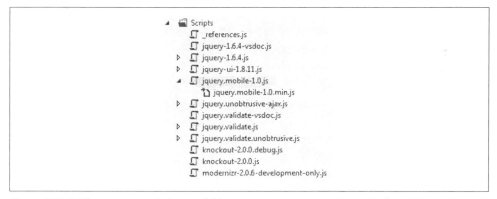

Figure 10-15. The new project's Scripts folder

These new files are part of the jQuery Mobile Framework, a JavaScript framework that brings all the jQuery and jQuery UI goodness to mobile devices.

Now take a look at the modified *_Layout.cshtml*. The head tag contains few new lines.

The meta viewport tag specifies the size of the viewport. This is important because, while most browsers allow users to zoom in or out as they please, setting an initial width for your content provides a better user experience. As mentioned earlier, the "width-device-width" value automatically sets the content width to the width of the device's screen:

```
<meta name="viewport" content="width=device-width" />
```

Alternatively, you can set the viewport's width to any value you like by specifying a fixed value in pixels. For example, this code sets the initial width of the page to 320 pixels:

```
<meta name="viewport" content="width=320px" />
```

The following tag includes jQuery Mobile styles onto the page. It also enables you to configure themes via the jQuery Theming framework (*http://jquerymobile.com/demos/1.0/docs/api/themes.html*):

```
<link rel="stylesheet" a href="@Url.Content("~/Content/jquery.mobile-1.0b2.min.css")" />
```

Finally, this script tag includes the jQuery Mobile Framework on the page. This enables scripting support such as performing AJAX operations, animations, validations, and so on:

```
<script type="text/javascript" src="@Url.Content("~/Scripts/jquery.mobile-1.0b2.min.js")">
</script>
```

Now let's take a look at the modified HTML on the page, which includes a few new attributes. jQuery Mobile identifies various elements, such as pages, buttons, listviews, etc., by `data-role` attributes. Looking at the `body` tag, you can see how the default template has decorated certain `<div>`+s with these +`data-role` attributes:

```
<body>
  <div data-role="page" data-theme="b">
    <div data-role="header">
      @if (IsSectionDefined("Header")) {
        @RenderSection("Header")
      } else {
        <h1>@ViewBag.Title</h1>
        @Html.Partial("_LogOnPartial")
      }
    </div>

    <div data-role="content">
        @RenderBody()
    </div>
  </div>
</body>
```

The first `<div>` has the `data-role="page"` attribute, which identifies the `<div>` as a single page in the mobile application. Similarly, the page header is identified by the `data-role="header"` attribute and the body content is identified by the `data-role="content"` attribute.

jQuery Mobile defines various attributes for known HTML elements, such as `<H1>`, `<H2>`, `<P>`, and `<table>`, as well as list and form elements such as buttons, text fields, select lists, etc. As further reading, visit the jQuery Mobile (*http://jQueryMobile.com*) website for in-depth documentation, demos, and a lot more!

Summary

This chapter talked about various aspects of programming for the mobile web, such as what, exactly, "the mobile web" really means and how mobile websites differ from desktop websites. We also explored the various development frameworks and techniques at your disposal to help make your mobile web development more productive, and we looked at how you can provide the best possible user experience by leveraging the various browser capabilities that are available to you.

This includes all of the mobile features in ASP.NET MVC 4, such as:

- Improvements to the default Mobile Application template
- Ability to customize the default template by overriding the layout, views, and partial views
- Browser-specific support (such as iPhone-specific views) and ability to override browser capabilities
- Enhancing the mobile view by using the jQuery Mobile Framework

Going Above and Beyond

Parallel, Asynchronous, and Real-Time Data Operations

The web application programming model has traditionally been based on synchronous client/server communication, in which the browser makes an HTTP request and waits for the server to return a response. While this model works well for a majority of scenarios, it can be very inefficient in handling long-running or complex transactions.

This chapter shows you how to take advantage of the powerful asynchronous and parallel processing capabilities in ASP.NET MVC to deal with more complex scenarios, such as asynchronous request processing and the use of real-time communication to send and receive messages to/from many simultaneously connected clients at once.

Asynchronous Controllers

When a request arrives, ASP.NET grabs one of the threads from the pool to handle the request. If the process is synchronous, the thread will be blocked from handling other incoming requests until the current process is complete.

In most scenarios, the process being executed is short-lived enough that ASP.NET can handle a few blocked threads. However, if the application needs to handle a large number of incoming requests or there are too many long-running requests, the thread pool might become depleted, and a condition known as *thread starvation* will occur. When this happens, the web server will start queuing new incoming requests. At some point, the queue will fill up and any new requests will be rejected, returning an HTTP 503 (server too busy) status code.

To prevent the thread pool from being fully utilized, ASP.NET MVC controllers can be set up to execute asynchronously instead of synchronously (the default). Using an asynchronous controller does not change the amount of time the request will take. It just frees up the thread executing the request so it can be allocated back into the ASP.NET thread pool.

Here are the steps for handling an asynchronous request. ASP.NET grabs a thread from the thread pool and executes it to handle the incoming request. After invoking the ASP.NET MVC action asynchronously, it returns the thread to the thread pool so it can handle other requests. The asynchronous operation executes on a different thread; when it's done it notifies ASP.NET. ASP.NET grabs a thread (which may be different than the original thread) and invokes it to finish processing the request. This includes rendering the process (output).

Creating an Asynchronous Controller

Creating an asynchronous controller is fairly easy. Simply inherit from the `AsyncCon troller` base class, which provides methods to help manage asynchronous request processing:

```
public class SearchController : AsyncController
{

}
```

An asynchronous controller is required because the `SearchForBids()` method uses a complex LINQ query, which could take several seconds to process:

```
public ActionResult SearchForBids(DateTime startingRange, DateTime endingRange)
{
  var bids = _repository
               .Query<Bid>(x => x.Timestamp >= startingRange && x.Timestamp ↵
               <= endingRange)
               .OrderByDescending(x => x.Timestamp)
               .ToArray();

  return Json(bids, JsonRequestBehavior.AllowGet);
}
```

Prior to ASP.NET MVC 4, the following conventions had to be followed to create asynchronous controller methods:

Action Name `Async`
: The method has to return `void`; it starts the asynchronous process

Action Name `Completed`
: This method is called when the asynchronous process is complete; it handles returning the `ActionResult`

Here is the updated `SearchForBids()` method that has been set up to use `Background Worker` to asynchronously search for bids:

```
public void SearchForBidsAsync(DateTime startingRange, DateTime endingRange)
{
    AsyncManager.OutstandingOperations.Increment();

    var worker = new BackgroundWorker();
    worker.DoWork += (o, e) => SearchForBids(Id, e);
```

```
worker.RunWorkerCompleted += (o, e) =>
    {
        AsyncManager.Parameters["bids"] = e.Result;
        AsyncManager.OutstandingOperations.Decrement();
    };

worker.RunWorkerAsync();
}

private void SearchForBids(string Id, DoWorkEventArgs e)
{
    var bids = _repository
        .Query<Bid>(x => x.Timestamp >= startingRange && x.Timestamp <= endingRange)
        .OrderByDescending(x => x.Timestamp).ToList();

    e.Result = bids;
}

public ActionResult SearchForBidsCompleted(IEnumerable<Bid> bids)
{
    return Json(bids, JsonRequestBehavior.AllowGet);
}
```

Note how `AsyncManager.OutstandingOperations` is `Increment` prior to the operation being started and `Decrement` when the operation is completed. This is required to notify ASP.NET about how many pending operations the method contains. When the value of the `OutstandingOperations` property reaches zero, ASP.NET completes the asynchronous processing of the method and calls `SearchForBidsCompleted()`.

That's a lot of code. Fortunately, version 4.5 of the .NET Framework introduces the new `async` and `await` keywords to help make asynchronous programming much simpler.

 See the following link to get additional details about asynchronous programming in .NET 4.5: *http://msdn.microsoft.com/en-us/library/hh191443(v=vs.110).aspx*.

Here is the final `SearchForBids()` method, updated to use the new asynchronous keywords:

```
public async Task<ActionResult> SearchForBids(string Id)
{
    var bids = await Search(Id);
    return Json(bids, JsonRequestBehavior.AllowGet);
}

private async Task<IEnumerable<Bid>> Search(string Id)
{
    var bids = _repository
        .Query<Bid>(x => x.Timestamp >= startingRange && x.Timestamp <= endingRange)
```

```
        .OrderByDescending(x => x.Timestamp).ToList();
    return bids;
}
```

Controller actions that return a `Task` instance can be configured with a timeout. To set a timeout, use the `AsyncTimeout` attribute. The following example shows a controller action that has a timeout of 2,500 milliseconds. If the timeout occurs, the *AjaxTimed-Out* view will be returned:

```
[AsyncTimeout(2500)]
[HandleError(ExceptionType = typeof(TaskCanceledException), View = "AjaxTimedOut")]
public async Task<ActionResult> SearchForBids(string Id)
{
}
```

Choosing When to Use Asynchronous Controllers

There are no hard and fast rules regarding when to use asynchronous actions. The following guidelines will help make your decision about when to take advantage of asynchronous actions.

These are the typical scenarios where it's best to use synchronous actions:

- Simple and short-running operations
- Cases where simplicity is more important than efficiency
- CPU-intensive operations (asynchronous actions provide no benefit and can add overhead for such operations)

These are the typical scenarios where it's preferable to use asynchronous actions:

- Long-running operations that are causing a bottleneck in performance
- Network- or I/O-intensive operations
- When the application requires the ability for users to cancel a long-running operation

Real-Time Asynchronous Communication

The World Wide Web is an ever-changing environment; application models that worked even a few months ago may no longer meet user expectations. Instead of building monolithic web applications with dozens of pages, more and more developers are building applications using a single-page architecture approach, or a small set of pages that are dynamically updated in real time.

The adoption of real-time data techniques can be traced to the explosion of social networking and mobile devices. In today's world, people are always on the go, and they want instant access to the latest information, whether it's their favorite team's sports score, the price of a hot stock, or new posts from their friends. And since more people are accessing websites using mobile devices, it's important that a web application be able to detect network availability and gracefully handle the features of web browsers across a multitude of different devices.

Comparing Application Models

The traditional web application model relies on synchronous communication. As a user interacts with the application, the host web browser makes requests to the server, which processes them and returns a snapshot of the current state of the application. Since there is no guarantee that the user will trigger another request, there is a high potential that the content the user is looking at may become stale, leading to data conflict issues.

Using techniques like AJAX only addresses part of the problem. In most cases the user still needs to trigger a request. AJAX relies on the traditional request/response approach, where interactions are very transactional and atomic, and anything that changes outside of the current transaction cannot be communicated—in order to get "back in sync," another request must be made. As such, this approach does not handle real-time updates very well. More advanced techniques that create longer-lived conversations between the server and the browser must be applied in order to support such scenarios.

Let's take a look at the different real-time communication models available. Keep in mind that the HTTP protocol is designed around the request/response communication pattern and does not directly support the ability for the server to communicate with a client without the client first submitting a request.

HTTP Polling

Figure 11-1 involves creating an ongoing conversation by mimicking a "constant connection" with the server based on a series of standard AJAX requests. This is usually achieved by sending AJAX requests on a regular basis using a JavaScript timer.

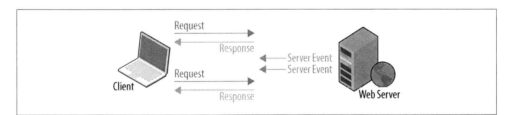

Figure 11-1. HTTP polling

Figure 11-1 shows polling in action. The most important thing about this technique is that the browser creates a new request immediately after each existing request is complete (regardless of whether the completed request actually succeeded or contained data), so fault tolerance is effectively built in.

As such, polling is one of the most reliable and fail safe "real-time" communication methods—but this reliability comes at a cost. As Figure 11-2 shows, polling produces a relatively huge amount of network traffic and server load, especially considering requests are processed regardless of whether the server has any updates (so many, if not most, of the requests will return no data).

Browser support

Polling utilizes various browser technologies that have been around essentially since the origin of the graphical web browser, so it works anywhere and everywhere that JavaScript is enabled.

Downsides

Polling has several drawbacks. The inordinate number of requests compared to the amount of actual data that is transferred makes this technique incredibly wasteful. Client requests and server events are not always in sync; it's possible for multiple server events to occur between client requests. If not kept in check, this approach can inadvertently create a denial-of-service attack on your own servers!

HTTP Long Polling

The HTTP Long Polling technique is primarily a server-side implementation wherein the browser makes an AJAX request to the server to retrieve data, and the server keeps the connection open until it has data to return. This is in stark contrast to the traditional request/response approach, wherein the server immediately responds that it has no data if it is unable to supply the data when it receives the AJAX request.

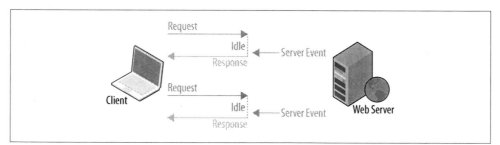

Figure 11-2. HTTP long polling

Long polling entails making a request in anticipation of a possible future server event. Instead of the server immediately returning a response, the incoming request is blocked until a server event occurs or the request times out (or the connection is broken). Then the client must initiate a new long polling request in order to start the next interaction and continue to retrieve updated data.

Browser support

Because there are many different long polling implementations, this technique works —with varying degrees of reliability—on all browsers.

Downsides

Because the Internet infrastructure is built around simple HTTP request/response interactions and not built to handle long-lived connections, long polling requests are not reliable, because they tend to get disconnected frequently. Broken connections are actually part of the long polling workflow, so handling them is the same as handling a successful request: you start a new request. However, this complexity adds to the unreliability of the approach as a whole.

Further, as with most widely supported techniques, long polling implementations are often limited to the lowest common feature set that all browsers support, which amounts to a simple HTTP GET request (the URL that can be applied to an IFRAME or `<script>` tag).

Server-Sent Events

The server-sent events (aka "EventSource") approach is quite similar to long polling in that the client makes an HTTP request to the server, and the resulting connection remains open until the server has data that satisfies the client's request. The fundamental difference between the two approaches is that the server-sent events approach does not close the connection once the initial server response is returned. Instead, the server keeps the connection open in order to send additional updates to the client as they become available (see Figure 11-3).

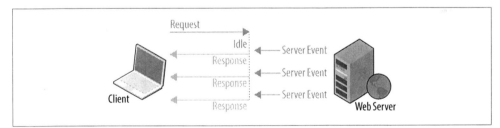

Figure 11-3. Server-sent events

Note that the server-sent events approach, as its name indicates, facilitates one-way communication from the server to the client. That is, the client is not able to send additional information back to the server after the initial request on the same connection. In order for the client to communicate back to the server, it must make additional AJAX requests. However, the client does not need to close the server-sent event channel in order to make these additional requests—the client can use standard AJAX techniques to send information to the server and the server can choose to respond to those events via the open server-sent events channel or the other AJAX request (or both).

The "EventSource" part of the name refers to the JavaScript EventSource API, a standard client-side API (defined as part of the larger HTML 5 specification) that facilitates server-sent event approach in the browser.

Browser support

Most mainstream browsers have some kind of server-sent event support, with the notable exception of Internet Explorer. Specifically, native support is available in Chrome 9+, Firefox 6+, Opera 11+, and Safari 5+.

Downsides

Though it allows the server to deliver real-time updates, this approach only allows one-way communication from the client to the server. That is, the open channel is not bidirectional. However, clients can still communicate with the server by issuing additional AJAX requests.

WebSockets

The WebSocket API is a new protocol (proposed as part of the HTML 5 specification) that effectively converts standard HTTP request connections into bidirectional, full-duplex TCP communications channels. More recent (and not widely supported) versions of the protocol also offer the option for secure communication. Figure 11-4 shows how WebSockets work.

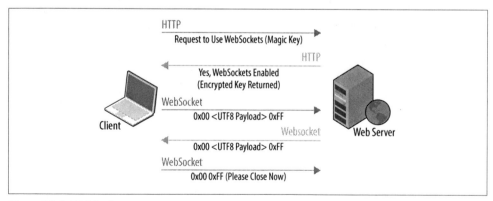

Figure 11-4. WebSockets

Browser support

Most mainstream browsers have some kind of WebSocket support, with the notable exceptions of Internet Explorer and Opera. Specifically, native support is available in IE 10, Firefox 6.0+, Chrome 4.0+, Safari 5.0+, and iOS 4.2+.

 In cases where browsers do not have a native WebSocket implementation, certain shims (such as *web-socket-js*, which uses a Flash implementation) may be used. These shims can hardly be considered "native," but they do help to fill in the gaps.

Downsides

Though browser adoption is growing, WebSocket support is not fully implemented in all major browsers just yet. Also, just having support for WebSockets doesn't guarantee they will work for every user. Antivirus programs, firewalls, and HTTP proxies may interfere with WebSocket connections, sometimes rendering them useless.

Empowering Real-Time Communication

Adding real-time communication into a web application can be a nontrivial task for developers to tackle alone. Fortunately, Microsoft has recognized the need for real-time communication and responded by including libraries for task-level parallel processing in version 4.0 of the .NET Framework and creating *SignalR*, an open source asynchronous signaling library for ASP.NET.

SignalR makes building real-time communication into a web application easy. It acts as an abstraction over an HTTP connection and gives developers two programming models to choose from: hubs and persistent connections. The library consists of a server API and client libraries for both .NET and JavaScript.

It supports several different transport models. Each model decides how to send and receive data and how the client and server connect and disconnect. By default, SignalR will choose the "best" transport model based on what the hosted browser supports (developers also have the option of choosing a specific transport).

The transport models SignalR supports are:

- WebSockets
- Server-sent events
- Forever frames
- Long polling

The easy way to get started with SignalR is to use NuGet to install its package:

```
Install-Package SignalR
```

Persistent connections

As soon as you've installed the package, you can start building a real-time communication application. Let's get started by examining how to set up a persistent connection to send messages between a client and a server.

First we need to create a custom connection object by inheriting from the `Persistent Connection` base class. The following code snippet shows an example of a custom connection class. Note the overridden `OnReceivedAsync()` method, which sends a broadcast to all the clients currently connected to the server:

```
using System.Threading.Tasks;
using SignalR;

public class EbuyCustomConnection : PersistentConnection
{
  protected override Task OnReceivedAsync(IRequest request, string connectionId,
  string data)
  {
      // Broadcast data to all clients
      return Connection.Broadcast(data);
  }
}
```

The next step is to register the custom connection by adding it to the ASP.NET MVC route table (make sure to set up the SignalR mapping before any other routes, to avoid conflicts!).

```
RouteTable.Routes.MapConnection<EbuyCustomConnection>("echo", "echo/{*operation}");
```

Now, on the client, you need to add a reference to the required SignalR JavaScript files:

```
<script src="http://code.jquery.com/jquery-1.7.js" type="text/javascript"></script>
<script src="Scripts/jquery.signalR-0.5.0.min.js" type="text/javascript"></script>
<script type="text/javascript">
```

To receive a message, initialize the connection object and subscribe to its `received` event. The final step is to start the connection by calling `connection.start()`:

```
$(function () {
  var connection = $.connection('/echo');

  connection.received(function (data) {
      $('#messages').append('<li>' + data + '</li>');
  });

  connection.start();
});
```

To send a message, call the `send()` method on the connection object:

```
connection.send("Hello SignalR!");
```

Hubs

Using hubs is much easier than creating custom low-level connection objects. Hubs provide a Remote Procedure Call (RPC) framework built on top of `PersistentConnec tion`. Hubs should be used over custom connection objects to avoid having to handle dispatching messages directly.

Unlike custom +PersistentConnection+s, hubs do not require any special routing configuration because they are accessible over a special URL (*/signalr*).

Creating a custom hub is straightforward: just create a class that inherits from the `Hub` base class and add a method for sending messages. Use the dynamically typed `Clients` instance exposed from the base class to define a custom method (e.g., `Display Message`) that will be used for communicating with the clients connected to the hub:

```
public class EbuyCustomHub: Hub
{
    public void SendMessage(string message)
    {
        Clients.displayMessage(message);
    }
}
```

To communicate with a hub, first add the necessary SignalR JavaScript files:

```
<script src="Scripts/jquery-1.6.2.min.js" type="text/javascript"></script>
<script src="Scripts/jquery.signalR-0.5.0.min.js" type="text/javascript"></script>
<script src="/signalr/hubs" type="text/javascript"></script>
```

To receive a message, create an instance of the hub's JavaScript proxy class and subscribe to one or more of the methods defined by the `Clients` dynamic object. Call `$.connection.hub.start()` to initialize the communication channel between the client and server:

```
$(function () {
    // Proxy created on the fly
    var proxy = $.connection.ebuyCustomHub;

    // Declare callback function
    proxy.displayMessage = function(message) {
        $('#messages').append('<li>' + message + '</li>');
    };

    // Start the connection
    $.connection.hub.start();
});
```

To send a message, call one of the public methods defined for the hub (e.g., `sendMes sage()`).

```
connection.sendMessage("Hello SignalR!");
```

Hubs are very extensible. It's easy to create multiple different methods for handling different types of server events. Also, in addition to sending string-based messages, it's possible to send JSON objects between the client and the server.

Here is an example of a hub that supports multiple message types:

```
public class EbuyCustomHub : Hub
{
    public void PlaceNewBid(string jsonObject)
    {
        var serializer = new JavaScriptSerializer();
        var bid = serializer.Deserialize<Bid>(jsonObject);

        Clients.newBidPosted(bid);
    }

    public void AuctionClosed(Auction auction)
    {
        Clients.auctionClosed(auction);
    }
}
```

 Out of the box .NET types sent to the `Clients` object will automatically be serialized into JSON. Incoming messages require manual deserialization using a JSON serializer.

The following code snippet shows the JavaScript used in the Ebuy reference application for receiving and sending notifications about new bids. To send a new bid, a JSON object needs to be created and serialized into a string; the incoming hub event parameter (bid) will be passed in as a JSON object:

```
$(function () {

    // Proxy created on the fly
    var proxy = $.connection.ebuyCustomHub;

    // Declare server callback methods
    proxy.newBidPosted = function (bid) {
        $('#bids').append('<li>Auction: ' + bid.Auction.Title + ' Latest Bid: ' ↵
        + bid.Amount.Value + ' </li>');
    };

    // Start the connection
    $.connection.hub.start();

    $("#postBid").click(function () {
        var bidToPost = GetBid();
        proxy.placeNewBid(bidToPost);
    });
});

function GetBid() {
```

```
    var bidPrice = $('#bidPrice').val();
    var newBid = "{ 'Code': 'USD', 'Value': '" + bidPrice + "' }";
    return "{ 'Auction': {'Id': '61fdb6eb-b565-4a63-b048-0418dcb8b28d', 'Title': ↵
    'XBOX 360'}, 'Amount': " + newBid + "}";
}
```

Configuring and Tuning

Unlike traditional web applications that require short-lived connections, real-time communication requires connections that can have a significantly longer lifespan. Proper monitoring and tuning are required to effectively tweak SignalR to get the best performance and to balance its resource requirements against the rest of the web application's needs.

Managing SignalR connections

The SignalR runtime exposes an `IConfigurationManager` interface that can be used to tweak the connection settings used by SignalR. Table 11-1 lists the configurable settings.

Table 11-1. Configurable SignalR settings

Settings	Description
ConnectionTimeout	The amount of time to keep an idle connection open before closing it (defaults to 110 seconds).
DisconnectTimeout	The amount of time to wait after a connection closes before raising a disconnected event to the client (defaults to 20 seconds).
HeartBeatInterval	The interval at which to check the state of a connection (defaults to 10 seconds).
KeepAlive	The amount of time to wait before sending a keepalive ping on an idle connection (defaults to 30 seconds). When this is active, ConnectionTimeout has no effect; set to null to disable.

Specifying the SignalR settings should be done during the initial startup of the web application, e.g.:

```
// Change the connection timeout to 60 seconds
GlobalHost.Configuration.ConnectionTimeout = TimeSpan.FromSeconds(60);
```

Configuring the environment

By default, ASP.NET and Internet Information Services (IIS) are configured to offer the best scalability for managing lots of requests per second. To support real-time communication, a few settings need to be modified to properly handle large numbers of concurrent connections.

To increase the maximum number of concurrent requests IIS will handle, open a command prompt with administrator privileges and change the directory to *%windir% \System32\inetsrv\'*. Then, run the following command to change the `appConcurrentRe questLimit` from the IIS 7 default of 5,000 connections to 100,000 connections:

```
appcmd.exe set config /section:serverRuntime /appConcurrentRequestLimit:100000
```

By default, ASP.NET 4.0 is configured to support 5,000 connections per CPU. To support additional connections per CPU, change the `maxConcurrentRequestsPerCPU` setting in *aspnet.config*:

```
<system.web>
    <applicationPool maxConcurrentRequestsPerCPU="20000" />
</system.web>
```

This file is located in the .NET Framework system directory (*%windir%\Microsoft.NET \Framework\v4.0.30319* for 32-bit and *%windir%\Microsoft.NET\Framework64\v4.0.30319* for 64-bit operating systems).

ASP.NET will start throttling requests using a queue when the total number of connections exceeds the maximum concurrent requests per CPU (i.e., `maxConcurrentRe questsPerCPU` – number of logical processors on the machine). To control the size of the throttling queue, alter the `requestQueueLimit` setting in *machine.config* (located in the same place as *aspnet.config*.

To modify the request queue limit, set the `autoConfig` attribute to `false` under the `processModel` element and update the `requestQueueLimit` size:

```
<processModel autoConfig="false" requestQueueLimit="250000" />
```

Summary

This chapter covered how to incorporate parallelization when designing and building a web application. It also introduced how to use asynchronous controllers to handle long-running requests, and how to use SignalR to incorporate real-time communication into your web application.

Caching

Just about every website serves some amount of content that changes infrequently, be it static pages that only change with an application update, or content pages that change every few days or even every few hours.

The problem is, your web application is working hard to generate this content from scratch every time it's requested, blissfully unaware that it has generated the same thing perhaps thousands of times already. Wouldn't it make more sense to try to avoid generating the same content over and over again, choosing instead to generate and store the content once, then use that same content again in response to future requests?

The concept of storing and reusing generated data is called *caching*, and it's one of the most effective ways to improve your web application's performance. Which content should be cached, however—and how long to cache it for—is not typically something a web application can figure out by itself. Instead, you must provide your application with the information it needs in order to determine which content makes a good candidate for caching.

Luckily, both the core ASP.NET Framework and the ASP.NET MVC Framework provide a number of caching APIs to meet all of your caching needs. This chapter explores the various caching techniques and APIs that are available to you and how you can leverage these techniques to improve the performance of your ASP.NET MVC applications.

Types of Caching

Web application caching techniques generally fall into one of two categories: server-side and client-side caching. While both categories have the same goal of limiting the amount of duplicate content that gets generated and transmitted over the wire, the primary difference between them is where the cached data is stored—on the server, or on the client's browser.

Server-Side Caching

Server-side caching techniques focus on optimizing the way that the server retrieves, generates, or otherwise manipulates content. The main goal in server-side caching is to limit the amount of work involved in processing a request, be it by avoiding calls to retrieve data from a database or even reducing the number of CPU cycles it takes to generate HTML—every little bit counts.

Limiting the work involved in processing requests not only lowers the time it takes to complete each request, but it also makes more server resources available to handle even more requests at the same time.

Client-Side Caching

In addition to caching content on the server, modern browsers offer several caching mechanisms of their own. Client-side techniques open up whole new opportunities for improving application performance, from intelligently avoiding duplicate requests all the way to storing content directly to a user's local environment.

Whereas the main goal of server-side caching is to handle requests as quickly and efficiently as possible, the primary goal of client-side caching techniques is to avoid making any requests at all. Not only does avoiding unnecessary requests improve the experience for the users who would have made them, it also helps to lower the overall load on the server, which improves the experience of all users of the site at the same time.

It's important to keep in mind that client-side and server-side caching techniques both have their place, and neither one is necessarily more important than the other. The most effective caching strategies typically combine the two types of caching techniques to get the best of both worlds.

Server-Side Caching Techniques

When it comes to server-side caching, there are plenty of techniques for you to choose from, ranging from simple in-memory storage to dedicated caching servers. In fact, most of the caching options available in ASP.NET MVC applications don't come from the ASP.NET MVC Framework, but from the core ASP.NET Framework.

The following sections explore the server-side caching techniques that are most commonly used within the context of ASP.NET MVC web applications.

Request-Scoped Caching

Every ASP.NET request begins with the ASP.NET Framework creating a new instance of the `System.Web.HttpContext` object to act as the central point of interaction between components throughout the request.

One of the many properties of the `HttpContext` is the `HttpContext.Items` property, a dictionary that lives throughout the lifetime of the request and which any component may manipulate.

The accessibility of this property—coupled with the fact that it is always scoped to the current request—makes the `Items` dictionary an excellent place to store data that is relevant only to the current request. Its accessibility also makes it a great way for components to pass data to each other in a loosely coupled manner, using the common `HttpContext.Items` object as the middleman rather than interacting directly with one another.

Since it's just a simple `IDictionary`, working with the `Items` collection is pretty straightforward. For instance, here's how to store data in the collection:

```
HttpContext.Items["IsFirstTimeUser"] = true;
```

Retrieving data from the dictionary is just as easy:

```
bool IsFirstTimeUser = (bool)HttpContext.Items["IsFirstTimeUser"];
```

Notice that the `Items` dictionary is not strongly typed, so you must first cast the stored object to your desired type before using it.

User-Scoped Caching

ASP.NET session state allows you to store data that persists *between* multiple requests. ASP.NET session state is a semidurable data store that applications can use to store information on a per-user basis.

When sessions are enabled, components can access the `HttpContext.Session` or `Session` property in order to save information for a future request by the same user, and to retrieve information that was stored in previous requests by that user.

 Since ASP.NET session state is scoped to the current user, it cannot be used to share information across users.

Like the `HttpContext.Item` dictionary, the `Session` object is an untyped dictionary, so you'll interact with it in the same way.

For instance, the following code shows how to store the username in a session:

```
HttpContext.Session["username"] = "Hrusi";
```

And here's how you retrieve and cast the untyped value:

```
string name = (string)HttpContext.Session["username"];
```

Session lifetime

Objects stored in the user's Session live until the session is destroyed by the server, usually after the user has been inactive for a certain period of time.

The default timeout value of 20 minutes can easily be changed by modifying the value of the system.web > sessionState timeout attribute in the application's *web.config* file.

For example, the following configuration extends the default timeout from 20 minutes to 30 minutes:

```
<system.web>
    <sessionState timeout="30" />
</system.web>
```

Storing session data

There's a lot of flexibility in terms of where session state is stored. The default behavior is to store all of the session state information in memory, but you can also choose to persist the data to the ASP.NET Session State Service, a SQL Server database, or any other data source by implementing your own custom provider.

Application-Scoped Caching

ASP.NET offers an HttpApplicationState class to store application-wide data, exposed by the HttpContext.Application property. HttpContext.Application is a key/value-based collection similar to HttpContext.Items and HttpContext.Session, except that it lives at the application-level scope so the data that is added to it is able to span users, sessions, and requests.

You can store data in HttpApplicationState like this:

```
Application["Message"] = "Welcome to EBuy!";
Application["StartTime"] = DateTime.Now;
```

And read data stored in HttpApplicationState like this:

```
DateTime appStartTime = (DateTime)Application["StartTime"];
```

Data stored in HttpApplicationState lives for the lifetime of the Internet Information Services worker process that hosts the application instance. Because it's IIS—not ASP.NET—that manages the lifetime of the worker threads, be aware that HttpApplicationState may not be a reliable way to store and retrieve persistent values.

Because of this, HttpApplicationState should only be used when the data is guaranteed to be the same across all worker processes. For example, if you are reading the contents of a file on disk or fetching values from a database and those values rarely change, you can use HttpApplicationState as a caching layer to avoid making the expensive calls to retrieve those values.

The ASP.NET Cache

A better alternative to storing application-level data in `HttpApplicationState` is to use the `System.Web.Cache` object exposed by the `HttpContext.Cache` property.

`System.Web.Cache` is a key/value store that acts just like `HttpContext.Items` and `HttpSessionState`; however, the data that it stores is not limited to individual requests or user sessions. In fact, the `Cache` is much more similar to `HttpApplicationState`, except that it is able to cross worker process boundaries and so eliminates most of the headaches inherent to `HttpApplicationState`, which generally makes it a better choice.

ASP.NET automatically manages removal of cached items, and notifies the application when such removals happen so that you can repopulate the data. ASP.NET removes cached items when any one of the following occurs:

- The cached item expires.
- The cached item's dependency changes, invalidating the item.
- The server runs on low resources and must reclaim memory.

Expiration

When you add items to the `Cache`, you can indicate how long it should keep the data around before it expires and should no longer be used. This time span can be expressed in one of two ways:

Sliding expiration
> Specifies that an item should expire a certain amount of time after it was last accessed. For example, if you cache an item with a sliding expiration of 20 minutes and the application continuously accesses the item every few minutes, the item should stay cached indefinitely (assuming the cached item has no dependencies and the server does not run low on memory). The moment the application stops accessing the item for at least 20 minutes, the item will expire.

Absolute expiration
> Specifies that an item expires at a specific moment in time, regardless of how often it is accessed. For example, if you cache an item with an absolute expiration of 10:20:00 PM, the item will no longer be available beginning at 10:20:01 PM.

> Only one type of expiration—sliding or absolute—may be specified for each item. You cannot use both expiration types on the same cached item.
>
> You can use different types of expiration for different cached items, however.

Cache dependencies

You can also configure an item's lifetime in the cache to be dependent on other application elements, such as files or databases. When the element that a cache item depends on changes, ASP.NET removes the item from the cache.

For example, if your website displays a report that the application creates from an XML file, you can place the report in the cache and configure it to have a dependency on the XML file. When the XML file changes, ASP.NET removes the report from the cache. The next time your code requests the report, the code first determines whether the report is in the cache and, if not, re-creates it. This ensures that an up-to-date version of the report is always available.

File dependency is not the only dependency that is available in ASP.NET—ASP.NET offers all of the types of dependencies listed in Table 12-1 out of the box, along with the ability to create your own dependency policies.

Table 12-1. Cache dependency policies

Dependency type	Definition
Aggregate	This type combines multiple dependencies (via the `System.Web.Caching.AggregateCacheDependency` class). The cached item is removed when any of the dependencies in the aggregate change.
Custom	The cached item depends on a custom class that derives from `System.Web.Caching.CacheDependency`. For example, you can create a custom web service cache dependency that removes data from the cache when a call to a web service results in a particular value.
File	The cached item depends on an external file and is removed when the file is modified or deleted.
Key	The cached item depends on another item in the application cache (referred to by its cache key). The cached item is removed when the target item is removed from the cache.
SQL	The cached item depends on changes in a table in a Microsoft SQL Server database. The cached item is removed when the table is updated.

Scavenging

Scavenging is the process of deleting items from the cache when memory is scarce. The items that are removed are typically those that have not been accessed in some time, or those that were marked as low priority when they were added to the cache. ASP.NET uses the `CacheItemPriority` object to determine which items to scavenge first.

In all cases, ASP.NET provides `CacheItemRemovedCallback` to notify the application that an item is being removed.

The Output Cache

While all of the caching techniques mentioned above focus on caching data, ASP.NET provides the ability to operate at a higher level, caching the HTML that is generated as a result of a request. This technique is called *output caching*, and it is a powerful feature that dates all the way back to the first version of the ASP.NET Framework.

In order to make output caching as easy as possible, the ASP.NET MVC Framework provides `OutputCacheAttribute`, an action filter that tells ASP.NET MVC to add the rendered results of the controller action to the output cache.

Opting controller actions in to output caching is as simple as adorning the controller action with the `OutputCacheAttribute`. By default, this attribute will cache the rendered HTML content with an absolute expiration of 60 seconds. On the next request to the controller action after the cached content expires, ASP.NET MVC will execute the action again and cache the HTML that it renders once more.

To see ASP.NET MVC output caching in action, try adding the `OutputCacheAttri bute` to a controller action in the EBuy reference application:

```
[OutputCache(Duration=60, VaryByParam="none")]
public ActionResult Contact()
{
  ViewBag.Message = DateTime.Now.ToString();
  return View();
}
```

When you execute this action after the output caching is in place, you'll see that the value of `ViewBag.Message` only changes every 60 seconds. For further proof, try adding a breakpoint to the controller method. You'll see that the breakpoint only gets hit the first time the page is executed (when the cached version does not exist), and anytime after the cached version expires.

Configuring the cache location

The `OutputCacheAttribute` contains several parameters that give you complete control over how and where the page's content is cached.

By default, the `Location` parameter is set to `Any`, which means content is cached in three locations: the web server, any proxy servers, and the user's web browser. You can change the `Location` parameter to any of the following values: `Any`, `Client`, `Down stream`, `Server`, `None`, or `ServerAndClient`.

The default `Any` setting is appropriate for most scenarios, but there are times when you need more fine-grained control over where data is cached.

For example, say you want to cache a page that displays the current user's name. If you use the default `Any` setting, the name of the first person to request the page will incorrectly be displayed to all users.

To avoid this, configure the output cache with the `Location` property set to `Output CacheLocation.Client` and `NoStore` set to `true` so that the data is stored only in the user's local web browser:

```
[OutputCache(Duration = 3600, VaryByParam = "none", Location = OutputCacheLocation.Client, ↵
NoStore = true)]
public ActionResult About()
{
    ViewBag.Message = "The current user name is " + User.Identity.Name;
    return View();
}
```

Varying the output cache based on request parameters

One of the most powerful aspects of output caching is being able to cache multiple versions of the same controller action based on the request parameters used to call the action.

For example, say you have a controller action named Details that displays the details of an auction:

```
public ActionResult Details(string id)
{
  var auction = _repository.Find<Auction>(id);
  return View("Details", auction);
}
```

If you use the default output caching setup, the same product details will be displayed for each request. To resolve this issue, you can set the VaryByParam property to create different cached versions of the same content based on a form parameter or query string parameter:

```
[OutputCache(Duration = int.MaxValue, VaryByParam = "id")]
public ActionResult Details(string id)
{
  var auction = _repository.Find<Auction>(id);
  return View("Details", auction);
}
```

The VaryByParam property offers quite a few options to help specify when a new version cache will be created. If you specify "none", you will always get the first cached version of the page. If you use "*", a different cached version will be created whenever any of the form or query string values vary. You can define the list of form or query string parameter caching rules by separating the entries using a query string.

Table 12-2 gives the complete list of properties available on the OutputCacheAttribute.

Table 12-2. Output caching parameters

Parameter	Description
CacheProfile	The name of the output cache policy to use
Duration	The amount of time in seconds to cache the content
Enabled	Enables/disables output cache for the current content
Location	The location of where to cache the content
NoStore	Enables/disables HTTP Cache-Control

Parameter	Description
SqlDependency	The database and table name pairs that the cache entry depends on
VaryByContentEn coding	A comma-delimited list of character sets (content encodings) that the output cache uses to vary the cache entries
VaryByCustom	A list of custom strings that the output cache uses to vary the cache entries
VaryByHeader	A comma-delimited list of HTTP header names used to vary the cache entries
VaryByParam	A semicolon-delimited list of form POST or query string parameters that the output cache uses to vary the cache entry

Output cache profiles

Instead of adorning every controller action with an `OutputCacheAttribute`, you can create global output caching rules through the use of *output cache profiles* in your application's *web.config* file.

The fact that output cache profiles live in a single location makes it very easy to tweak and maintain the output caching logic for your entire site all at once. As an added benefit, none of these changes require recompiling and redeploying the application in order to take effect.

To use output cache profiles, you need to add the output caching section to your application's *web.config*. Then, define one or more cache profiles and the parameters associated with each caching profile.

For example, the following `ProductCache` profile caches a page's content for an hour and varies each cache by the `"id"` request parameter:

```
<caching>
  <outputCacheSettings>
    <outputCacheProfiles>
      <add name="ProductCache" duration="3600" varyByParam="id"/>
    </outputCacheProfiles>
  </outputCacheSettings>
</caching>
```

You can use this caching profile as follows:

```
[OutputCache(Duration = 0, VaryByParam = "none")]
public JSONResult Index()
{
  User user = new User { FirstName = "Joe", LastName = "Smith"};
  return Json(user);
}
```

Donut Caching

In a complex dynamic web application, you'll often come across the need to cache an entire page but continue to generate specific portions of the page.

For example, in the EBuy application, it makes sense to cache most of the home page, but not the portions of the page that change based on the logged in user, such as the login section that displays the current user's username—clearly, you don't want one user's username to be shown for all users!

If you think the answer is to use `OutputCache` with `VaryByParam` and vary by user ID, think again. `OutputCache` stores the entire page, so with this approach, you would store the entire page every time for each user with a different username (or whatever your dynamic section is). Barring a few tidbits, most of that data is simply redundant.

This is where *donut caching* comes into play. Donut caching is a server-side caching technique in which the entire page gets cached, except for small portions that remain dynamic. These small portions are like holes in the cached content, much like in a donut (hence the technique's name).

While ASP.NET MVC's Razor view engine does not have first-class support for donut caching, ASP.NET Web Forms offers the `Substitution` control to carve out the "holes" or dynamic sections, like this:

```
<header>
    <h1>Donut Caching Demo</h1>

    <div class="userName">
        <asp:Substitution runat="server" MethodName="GetUserName" />
    </div>
</header>

<!-- Rest of the page with cacheable content goes here -->
```

This control registers a callback event within the ASP.NET output cache, which then invokes a static method on your page when the cached page is requested:

```
partial class DonutCachingPage : System.Web.UI.MasterPage
{
  public static string GetUserName(HttpContext Context)
  {
    return "Hello " + Context.User.Identity.Name;
  }
}
```

Whenever `DonutCachingPage` is requested, the entire cached page is returned except for the username section, which continues to get generated for each request.

Leveraging the fact that ASP.NET MVC is built on top of ASP.NET, we can use the APIs that the `Substitution` control uses to implement something similar in ASP.NET MVC: the `HttpResponse` class has a `WriteSubstitution()` method, which is what the `Substitution` control uses behind the scenes.

Using this method, you can write a custom `HtmlHelper` to duplicate this same logic:

```
public delegate string CacheCallback(HttpContextBase context);

public static object Substitution(this HtmlHelper html, CacheCallback ccb) {
```

```
    html.ViewContext.HttpContext.Response.WriteSubstitution(
        c => HttpUtility.HtmlEncode(
            ccb(new HttpContextWrapper(c))
        ));
    return null;
}
```

With this extension method in place, we can rewrite the previous example to use the new helper:

```
<header>
    <h1>MVC Donut Caching Demo</h1>

    <div class="userName">
      Hello @Html.Substitution(context => context.User.Identity.Name)
    </div>
</header>

<!-- Rest of the page with cacheable content goes here -->
```

Now the entire view is cached except for the section within the `<div class="user Name">` tag, bringing functionality similar to the Web Forms `Substitution` control to ASP.NET MVC.

The MvcDonutCaching NuGet Package

The example used here shows a simplified version of donut caching and is not well suited to more advanced scenarios. While donut caching is still not available out of the box with ASP.NET MVC 4, the *MvcDonutCaching* NuGet package (*http://mvcdonut caching.codeplex.com/*) can help you implement more advanced scenarios with ease.

This package adds several extensions to existing HTML helper methods, and also adds a custom `DonutOutputCacheAttribute` that can be placed on any action that needs donut caching.

Donut Hole Caching

Donut hole caching is the inverse of donut caching: while the donut caching technique caches the entire page, leaving out only a few small sections, donut hole caching caches only one or a few portions of the page (the donut "holes").

For example, the Ebuy reference application contains a list of auction categories that do not change often, so it makes sense to render all of the categories just once and cache the resulting HTML.

Donut hole caching is very useful in these kinds of scenarios, where most of the elements in your page are dynamic, with the exception of a few sections that rarely change, or are changed based on a request parameter. And, unlike donut caching, ASP.NET MVC has great support for donut hole caching through the use of child actions.

Let's see donut hole caching in action by applying it to the Ebuy auction categories example mentioned above. Here is the partial view that we will be caching:

```
@{
    Layout = null;
}

<ul>
    @foreach(var category in ViewBag.Categories as IEnumerable<Category>)
        <li>@Html.ActionLink(@category.Name, "category", "categories",
                                    new { categoryId = category.Id })</li>
</ul>
```

This partial view enumerates through all the categories and renders each one as a list item in an unordered list. Each item in the list is a link to the Category action in the Categories controller, passing the category's Id as an action parameter.

Next, create a child action that displays this view:

```
[ChildActionOnly]
[OutputCache(Duration=60)]
public ActionResult CategoriesChildAction()
{
    // Fetch Categories from the database and
    // pass it to the child view via its ViewBag
    ViewBag.Categories = Model.GetCategories();

    return View();
}
```

Notice how the OutputCacheAttribute caches the result of this method for 60 seconds.

Then you can call this new action from a parent view by calling @Html.Action("Catego riesChildAction"), as shown in the following example:

```
<header>
  <h1>MVC Donut Hole Caching Demo</h1>
</header>

<aside>
  <section id="categories">
    @Html.Action("CategoriesChildAction")
  </section>
</aside>

<!-- Rest of the page with non cacheable content goes here -->
```

Now when the page is rendered, the Categories child action is called to generate the list of categories.

The results of this call get cached via the OutputCacheAttribute, so when the page is rendered the next time, the Categories list is rendered from the cache while the rest of the page is generated from scratch.

Distributed Caching

In cases where multiple instances of your application are running on more than one web server, requests to the application may be served by any one of those servers. And every time a request goes to a new server, the cached items have to be regenerated if they have not been generated on that server already.

Depending on how complex a process it is to generate the cached items, it may be terribly inefficient to regenerate the same data again and again. Instead, it can be much more efficient to generate the data once and store it in multiple servers or web farms. This technique of caching data on one application instance and sharing it with other instances is known as *distributed caching*, and it is the most elaborate of all caching techniques.

Distributed caching is an extension of normal caching techniques by which data from a database or session is stored in a central location that all instances of an application have access to.

There are a number of benefits to using a distributed caching layer, such as:

Performance
> Because a high volume of data can be stored in memory on the servers, read performance improves significantly, which benefits all pages downstream by making them load faster.

Scalability
> Scalability becomes a function of adding more capacity or nodes to the clusters, allowing the application to scale to higher demands and load easily. Combined with cloud storage, nodes can be spun up on demand and freed when not required, increasing cost efficiency.

Redundancy
> Redundancy ensures that if one node or server fails, the whole application does not suffer. Instead, another failover node can simply pick up the request and serve it without any manual intervention. Failover and redundancy are essential features of many distributed caching solutions.

Distributed caching solutions

There are a number of distributed caching products available today, and although each of these products offer very different APIs and ways of working with the data they manage, the basic concepts of distributed caching remain the same. In order to give you an idea of how to implement a distributed caching solution, the next few sections show how to implement Microsoft's distributed caching solution, called Velocity, within the Ebuy reference application.

Installing Velocity. Velocity is the Windows AppFabric (aka Microsoft Application Server) caching layer. So in order to install Velocity, you must download Windows

AppFabric (*http://msdn.com/appfabric*) or install it via the Web Platform Installer (*http://www.microsoft.com/web/downloads/platform.aspx*).

After you've started the installer and gotten to the Feature Selection page (shown in Figure 12-1), select the "Caching Services" and "Cache Administration" features. If you are using Windows 7, install the IIS 7 Manager for Remote Administration (*http://www.iis.net/download/IISManager*) extension, which will let you manage remote IIS servers from the Windows 7 machine.

 If you just want to use the caching part, perform an automated (*http://msdn.microsoft.com/en-us/library/ff637714.aspx*) installation or use `SETUP /i CACHINGSERVICE`.

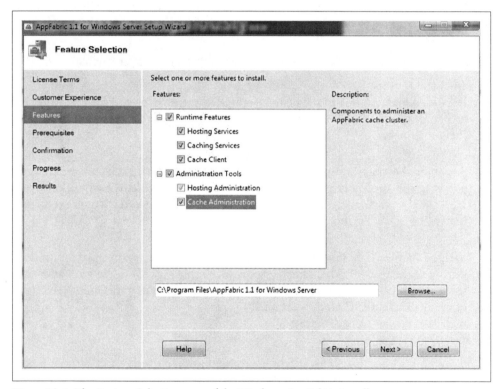

Figure 12-1. The Feature Selection page of the Windows AppFabric installer

Once Windows AppFabric is installed it will display a configuration wizard to help walk you through the rest of the process, starting with where to store Velocity's configuration information.

For this demo, choose the database option and click Next to configure the database options (Figure 12-2):

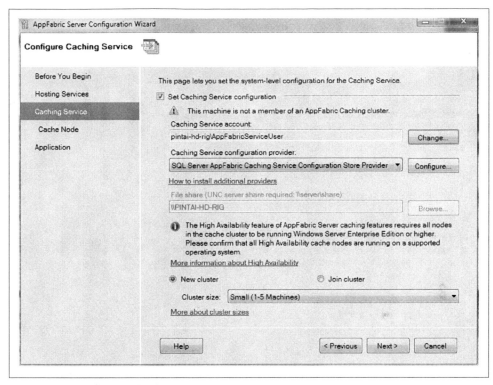

Figure 12-2. Configuring the database options

Administering your memory cluster from PowerShell. The next step is to administer the cache using PowerShell. At this point, you should have a new item called "Caching Administration Windows PowerShell" in your Programs menu.

Using this console, you can manage your caches, check the activity, and create new ones.

Before you begin, you must "start" a cache cluster. In your PowerShell console, issue the following command:

```
C:\> Start-CacheCluster
```

Next, run the following command to grant your user account access to the cache cluster as a client:

```
C:\> Grant-CacheAllowedClientAccount 'domain\username'
```

To verify that your user account has been granted access, use the `Get-CacheAllowed ClientAccounts` command.

If you want to see all the cache-related commands that are available, use the command get-command *cache*.

Using the cache. The cache can be hooked up in the *web.config* file or from code. Here's a code example where the helper method does this manually:

```
using Microsoft.ApplicationServer.Caching;
using System.Collections.Generic;

public class CacheUtil
{

  private static DataCacheFactory _factory = null;
  private static DataCache _cache = null;

  public static DataCache GetCache()
  {
    if (_cache != null)
      return _cache;

    //Define array for 1 cache host
    List<DataCacheServerEndpoint> servers = new List<DataCacheServerEndpoint>(1);

    // Specify cache host details
    //   Parameter 1 = host name
    //   Parameter 2 = cache port number
    servers.Add(new DataCacheServerEndpoint("mymachine", 22233));

    //Create cache configuration
    DataCacheFactoryConfiguration configuration = new DataCacheFactoryConfiguration();

    //Set cache host(s)
    configuration.Servers = servers;

    //Set default properties for local cache (local cache disabled)
    configuration.LocalCacheProperties = new DataCacheLocalCacheProperties();

    //Disable tracing to avoid informational/verbose messages on the web page
    DataCacheClientLogManager.ChangeLogLevel(System.Diagnostics.TraceLevel.Off);

    //Pass configuration settings to cacheFactory constructor
    _factory = new DataCacheFactory(configuration);

    //Get reference to named cache called "default"
    _cache = _factory.GetCache("default");

    return _cache;
  }
}
```

Once your cache is set up, it's trivial to use. Here's how to add an item to the Cache object created in the previous listing:

```
var cache = CacheUtil.GetCache();

cache.Add(orderid, order);
```

Retrieving the cached item is also straightforward:

```
Order order = (Order)cache.Get(orderid);
```

As is updating an existing object:

```
cache.Put(orderid, order);
```

You can also swap out the default session provider with AppFabric caching.

Here's a sample *web.config*:

```
<?xml version="1.0" encoding="utf-8" ?>
<configuration>

  <!--configSections must be the FIRST element -->
  <configSections>
    <!-- required to read the <dataCacheClient> element -->
    <section name="dataCacheClient"
        type="Microsoft.ApplicationServer.Caching.DataCacheClientSection,
          Microsoft.ApplicationServer.Caching.Core, Version=1.0.0.0,
          Culture=neutral, PublicKeyToken=31bf3856ad364e35"
        allowLocation="true"
        allowDefinition="Everywhere"/>
  </configSections>

  <!-- cache client -->
  <dataCacheClient>
    <!-- cache host(s) -->
    <hosts>
      <host
        name="CacheServer1"
        cachePort="22233"/>
    </hosts>
  </dataCacheClient>

  <system.web>
    <sessionState mode="Custom" customProvider="AppFabricCacheSessionStoreProvider">
      <providers>
        <!-- specify the named cache for session data -->
        <add
          name="AppFabricCacheSessionStoreProvider"
          type="Microsoft.ApplicationServer.Caching.DataCacheSessionStoreProvider"
          cacheName="NamedCache1"
          sharedId="SharedApp"/>
      </providers>
    </sessionState>
  </system.web>
</configuration>
```

As you can see, AppFabric offers elaborate features that allow it to range from being a simple caching mechanism to replacing the default session state provider with ease.

You can learn more about AppFabric's concepts, features, and architecture on its MSDN page (*http://msdn.microsoft.com/en-us/library/ff383731%28v=azure.10%29*).

Client-Side Caching Techniques

Browsers display web pages to the user by fetching HTML, data, and supporting resources such as CSS files, images, JavaScript files, cookies, Flash media, etc. But no matter how fast the user's Internet connection is, it is always faster to display something by fetching it from the user's hard disk, rather than having to travel across the Internet.

Browser designers know this, and employ caching to store resources on the disk to avoid network access whenever possible. The process is simple: anytime you access a web page, the browser checks the local disk to see if it has local copies of any files that are part of the page. If not, it downloads the resources from the server. For the first visit to a page, this amounts to everything. For subsequent visits, the browser should load the page faster, given that it already has local access to the resources required to display the page (unless the page requests new or different resources).

The browser caches the resources by storing them locally on the hard disk in a preallocated area of predefined size. Users can control how much disk space is allocated to this storage. The browser takes care of clearing out old items and managing the resources without any intervention or input required from the user.

Next, let's take a look at how we can leverage client-side caching or the browser cache to speed up our application.

Understanding the Browser Cache

The resources that are cached locally by the browser are controlled by three basic mechanisms: *freshness*, *validation*, and *invalidation*. They are part of HTTP itself and are defined by HTTP headers.

Freshness allows a response to be used without rechecking it on the origin server, and can be controlled by both the server and the client. For example, the Expires response header gives a date when the document becomes stale, and the Cache-Control: max-age directive tells the cache how many seconds the response is fresh for.

The following code shows how to set these headers via server-side code:

```
public ActionResult CacheDemo()
{
        // Sets the Cache-Control header to one of the values of
        http://msdn.microsoft.com/en-us/library/system.web.httpcacheability(v=vs.110).aspx
        [HttpCacheability]

        // Sets Cache-Control: public to specify that the response is cacheable by
        clients and shared (proxy) caches.
        Response.Cache.SetCacheability(HttpCacheability.Public);
```

```
        // Sets the Cache-Control: max-age header to 20 minutes.
        Response.Cache.SetMaxAge(DateTime.Now.AddMinutes(20));

        // Sets the Expires header to 11:00 P.M. local time on the current expiration
        day.
        Response.Cache.SetExpires(DateTime.Parse("11:00:00PM"));

        return View();
}
```

Validation is used to check whether a cached response is still good after it becomes
stale. For example, if the response has a `Last-Modified` header, a cache can make a
conditional request using the `If-Modified-Since` header to see if the content has
changed. This is a fairly weak form of validation, however; if you want stronger validation you can use the ETag (entity tag) mechanism instead.

The following code demonstrates both approaches:

```
public ActionResult CacheDemo()
{
        // Sets the Last-Modified HTTP header to the DateTime value supplied.
        Response.Cache.SetLastModified(DateTime.Parse("1/1/2012 00:00:01AM"));

        // Sets the ETag HTTP header to the specified string.
        Response.Cache.SetETag("\"someuniquestring:version\"");

        return View();
}
```

Invalidation is usually a side effect of another request that passes
through the cache. For example, if the URL associated with a cached
response subsequently gets a `POST`, `PUT`, or `DELETE` request, the cached
response will be invalidated.

Although it's a great feature to help the pages load faster, the browser-based cache has
had its own share of issues over the years. Bugs, security concerns, and the lack of fine-
grained control over what gets cached have presented numerous challenges to web
developers. Further, the inability to invalidate the cache when an item on the server
has changed often requires you to implement special techniques (also known as
"hacks") that inherently lead to messy code.

The new HTML 5 specification aims to eliminate some of these concerns by providing
developers with new techniques and more granular control over the client-side cache.

App Cache

The HTML 5 specification defines the ApplicationCache (*http://www.whatwg.org/
specs/web-apps/current-work/#applicationcache*) (or AppCache) API to give developers
direct access to the local browser content cache.

In order to enable the App Cache in your application, you need to complete three steps:

1. Define the manifest.
2. Reference the manifest.
3. Serve the manifest to the user.

Let's take a detailed look at each of these steps to see how you can implement them.

Define the manifest

Defining the manifest file is as simple as creating a text file with a *.manifest* extension:

```
CACHE MANIFEST

# version 0.1

home.html
site.css
application.js
logo.jpg
```

This is a simple manifest file that tells the browser to cache the four files mentioned in it. The first line of the file must contain the text "CACHE MANIFEST".

As this slightly more complex example demonstrates, you have fine-grained control over what gets cached:

```
CACHE MANIFEST
# Generated on 04-23-2012:v2

# Cached entries.
CACHE:
/favicon.ico
home.html
site.css
images/logo.jpg
scripts/application.js

# Resources that are "always" fetched from the server
NETWORK:
login.asmx

# Serve index.html (static version of home page) if /Home/Index is inaccessible
# Serve offline.jpg in place of all images in images/ folder
# Serve appOffline.html in place of all other routes
FALLBACK:
/Home/Index /index.html
images/ images/offline.jpg
* /appOffline.html
```

You can see that the manifest file utilizes few basic conventions:

- Lines starting with # are comment lines.
- The CACHE section lists resources that will be cached after the website is accessed for the first time.
- The NETWORK section lists resources the browser must always fetch from the server —in other words, these resources are never cached.
- The FALLBACK section defines resources that should be served if the corresponding resource is inaccessible or unavailable. This is completely optional and supports wildcards.

The next step is to tell the browser about this manifest file for your application.

Reference the manifest

To reference the manifest file, simply define the manifest attribute on the <html> tag:

```
<!DOCTYPE html>
<html manifest="site.manifest">
...
</html>
```

When the browser sees the manifest attribute, it recognizes that your application defines a cache manifest and attempts to download the manifest file automatically.

Serve the manifest correctly

The key to using this manifest is to serve it with the correct MIME type ("text/cache-manifest"):

```
Response.ContentType = "text/cache-manifest";
```

Without this MIME type specified, the browser won't recognize this file as a manifest file, and AppCache will not be enabled for your site.

With AppCache enabled for your application, the browser will fetch server resources only in these three cases:

1. When the user clears the cache, which removes all the cached content.
2. When the manifest file changes on the server. Simply updating a comment and saving the file can trigger an update.
3. When the cache is updated programmatically via JavaScript.

As you can see, AppCache gives you complete control over what gets cached and allows you to trigger updates when needed, without resorting to any workarounds or hacks.

The next section will explore yet another new feature of the HTML 5 specification that allows you to cache items on the browser, albeit differently than AppCache.

Local Storage

Another new feature introduced in the HTML 5 specification is the support for an offline, browser-based storage mechanism called *Local Storage*. You can think of Local Storage as a "super cookie" that is not limited by the size of normal browser cookies: it allows you to persist large amounts of data to the user's device.

The Local Storage API consists of two endpoints for managing local data storage: localStorage and sessionStorage. While localStorage and sessionStorage both expose similar methods, the key difference between the two is that the data stored in local Storage is available indefinitely, whereas data stored in sessionStorage is wiped out when the page in the browser is closed.

 Like most server-side caching objects, Local Storage uses a string-based dictionary data structure. So, if you are retrieving anything other than strings, you may need to use functions like parseInt() or parse Float() to cast the data back to native JavaScript data types.

To store an item in localStorage, you can use setItem():

```
localStorage.setItem("userName", "john");
localStorage.setItem("age", 32);
```

Or, you can use square bracket syntax:

```
localStorage[userName"] = "john";
localStorage["age"] = 32;
```

Retrieving an item is straightforward as well:

```
var userName = localStorage.getItem("userName");
var age = parseInt(localStorage.getItem("age"));

// or use square brackets...

var userName = localStorage["userName"];
var age = parseInt(localStorage["age"]);
```

You can also use the removeItem() function to remove any individual item from storage:

```
localStorage.removeItem("userName");
```

Or, you can clear all keys at once:

```
localStorage.clear();
```

The memory allocated to Local Storage is not infinite; there is a limit to how much you can store. This limit is arbitrarily set to 5 megabytes in the draft specification, although browsers can implement a higher limit. An application can request more storage, which results in a prompt being shown to the user. This puts the user in control of whether or not more storage is allowed.

Local Storage offers APIs to detect how much space is remaining in the quota, and to request more storage. `localStorage.remainingSpace()` gives you the amount of disk space remaining, in bytes. When the amount of data you have stored exceeds the set limit, the browser can throw a `QuotaExceededError` exception or request the user to allow for more storage.

Most modern browsers support `localStorage`; regardless, it is always a good practice to detect whether or not a particular browser feature exists prior to using it. The following snippet shows how to check whether or not `localStorage` is supported in the current browser:

```
function IsLocalStorageSupported() {
  try {
    return 'localStorage' in window && window['localStorage'] !== null;
  } catch (e) {
    return false;
  }
}
```

Summary

Caching is an important aspect of building highly scalable and performant applications. This chapter showed you several caching techniques and discussed their practical usage scenarios. Apart from built-in caching mechanisms such as `HttpContext.Application`, `HttpContext.Session`, and `OutputCache`, you can also use a distributed caching layer to achieve greater efficiency. Donut and donut hole caching techniques provide some interesting variations to regular caching and can be very effective in appropriate scenarios. Finally, caching is not limited to the server side. With the new features added in HTML 5, you can extend the idea of caching to the client side as well. The HTML 5 specification brings two new, highly flexible mechanisms to enable client-side or browser caching, putting you and the users in direct control over the cached data. Further, the new client-side storage options available under the HTML 5 specification make it easier than ever to support an "offline" mode, enabling your application to continue to work without an active Internet connection.

Client-Side Optimization Techniques

The ultimate performance goal of any developer is to have a web page that loads as quickly as possible. The faster your page loads, the more responsive your site appears, and the happier your users are. *Client-side optimization* collectively refers to the set of techniques that can help you speed up the page load time.

This chapter focuses on the few basic techniques that give you the most bang for your buck. While no single technique is a silver bullet, following these rules should help any fairly well designed page achieve a boost in its load time.

Most of the techniques presented here will not require you to rewrite a significant amount of your code; rather, they can be applied to any well-designed application outside of code.

Why optimize? A page that loads quickly also appears more responsive in limited-bandwidth scenarios. If your target audience is on a slow network, it helps even more to have a leaner page that the user can see quickly.

Anatomy of a Page

In order to understand what affects the page load times, let's look at how the browser renders a page.

A web page primarily consists of HTML, JavaScript files, and stylesheets, but also contains images and possibly other media, such as Flash or Silverlight objects.

Browsers follow a top-down approach to rendering a web page: they start at the top of the HTML and start downloading resources as they appear in the markup (Figure 13-1). The page is not rendered or displayed completely until all resources have been downloaded, which means that even if all the HTML for the page has been downloaded, users will still see a blank screen until the browser has finished downloading and loading other resources on the page (such as images, stylesheets, and JavaScript files).

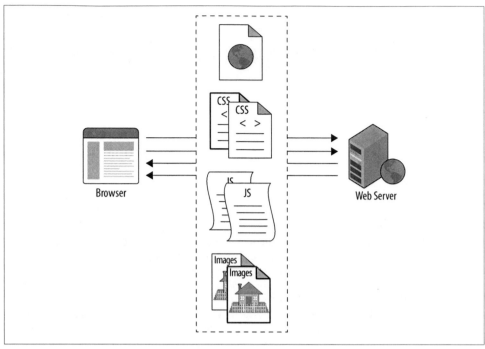

Figure 13-1. Anatomy of a page

To sum it up:

- Having fewer resources cuts down on page load times.
- Rearranging the resources in your page can make a difference in when the page (or part of it) is displayed.

Anatomy of an HttpRequest

More requests make a page slower. But why? Let's look at what happens when a resource is requested to see what affects the download times. These are the steps:

1. *DNS lookup.* The first step is to resolve the domain name for the request:
   - First, the browser or client sends a DNS query to the local ISP's DNS server.
   - Then, the DNS server responds with the IP address for the given hostname.
2. *Connect.* The client establishes a TCP connection with the IP address of the hostname.
3. *Initiate* `HttpRequest`. The browser sends the HTTP request to the web server.
4. *Wait.* The browser then waits for the web server to respond to the request:

- On the server side, the web server processes the request, which includes finding the resource, and sends the response to the client.
- The browser then receives the first byte of the first packet from the web server, which contains the HTTP response headers and content.

5. *Load*. The browser loads the content of the response.
6. *Close*. After receiving the last byte, the browser then requests the server to close the connection.

These steps (illustrated in Figure 13-2) are repeated for every request not already present in the browser cache. If the requested resource is present in the browser cache, the browser simply loads the resource from the cache and doesn't go to the server to download the resource. The browser also tries to cache the resource locally once it has downloaded it from the server.

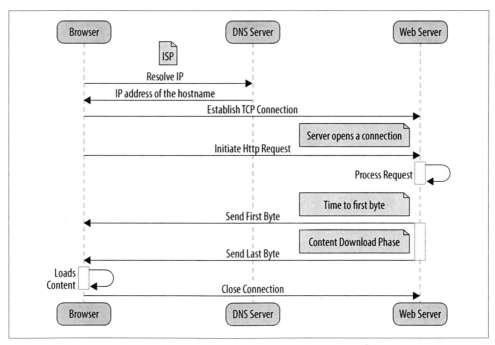

Figure 13-2. Anatomy of an HttpRequest

Optimizing parts of these steps can help you bring down the response time.

Best Practices

Yahoo!'s Exceptional Performance team identifies 35 best practices that help improve web page performance. They start with 13 simple rules and then expand the rule set to

35 rules spanning 7 categories. The complete list can be found at the team's developer blog (*http://developer.yahoo.com/performance/rules.html*).

Google also came up with its own set of rules to enhance the performance of websites. Google's recommendation (*https://developers.google.com/speed/docs/best-practices/rules_intro*) spans over 30 rules across 6 categories.

The next few sections will present a quick summary of some of the basic rules that can help you in creating a highly responsive website.

Make Fewer HTTP Requests

Some 80% of the end-user response time is spent on the frontend. Most of this time is tied up in downloading the components in the page, such as images, stylesheets, scripts, Flash, etc. Reducing the number of components in turn reduces the number of HTTP requests (see Figure 13-3). This is the key to faster pages.

You can redesign your page to reduce the number of components in the page, or combine the number of external resources (JavaScript files, stylesheets, images) to reduce the number of components that get downloaded to the client. ASP.NET MVC 4 offers "bundling" out of the box that can help you combine several JavaScript files and stylesheets into a "bundled" resource, which in turn reduces the number of downloaded components. "Bundling and Minification" on page 289 explains this feature in detail.

This technique reduces the number of script and stylesheet requests, but it cannot be applied to images as such. If your page has a lot of images, consider using CSS Sprites (*http://www.alistapart.com/articles/sprites*) to reduce the number of image requests. Another technique is to have *inline* images or image data embedded in the page or stylesheet using the `data:` URL scheme (*http://tools.ietf.org/html/rfc2397*), but be aware that these are not supported across all major browsers (*http://en.wikipedia.org/wiki/Data_URI_scheme#Web_browser_support*).

Use a Content Delivery Network

A *content delivery network* (CDN) is a collection of web servers distributed across multiple locations to deliver content more efficiently to users. Which server is selected for delivering content to a specific user is typically based on network proximity: the server with the fewest network hops or the quickest response time is chosen. Switching to a CDN is a relatively easy change that will dramatically improve the speed of your website.

Further, you can maximize the number of images, stylesheets, and scripts that are downloaded by using multiple subdomains on the server or CDN. A browser limits the number of connections to download resources per domain. By scattering resources on multiple subdomains, you're essentially increasing the number of parallel downloads,

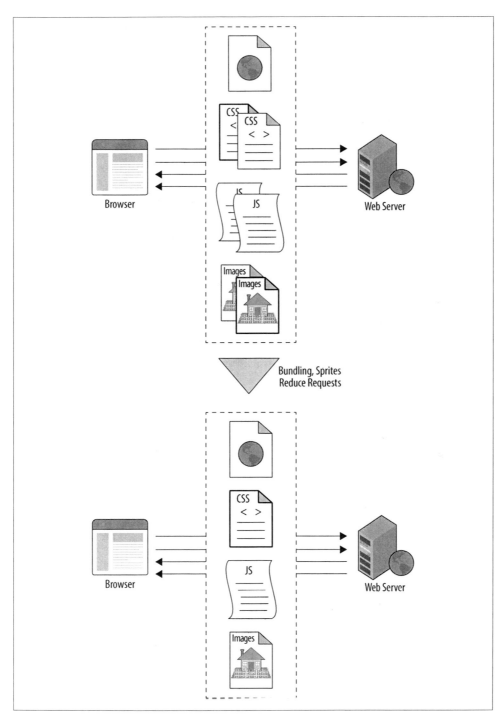

Figure 13-3. Fewer requests help the page load faster

because the browser treats them as separate domains and uses more connections for different domains (see Figure 13-4).

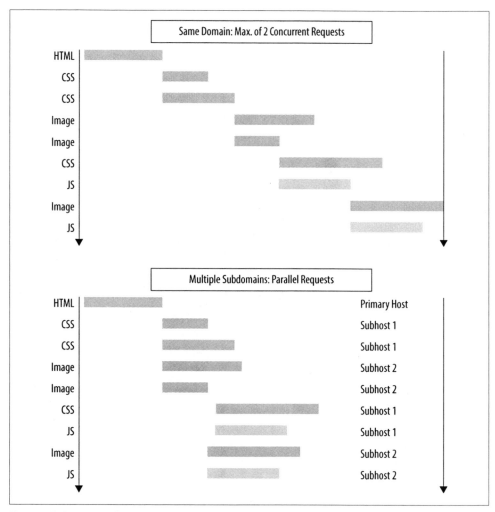

Figure 13-4. Using a CDN

Add an Expires or a Cache-Control Header

According to research (*http://yuiblog.com/blog/2007/01/04/performance-research-part -2/*), 40-60% of daily visitors to your site come in with an empty cache. The previous techniques (fewer HTTP requests, using a CDN) help speed up the first-time experience, and using Expires or a Cache-Control header helps speed up subsequent page visits by enabling caching on the client side.

Browsers (and proxies) use a cache to reduce the number and size of HTTP requests, making web pages load faster. A web server uses the `Expires` header in the HTTP response to tell the client how long a component can be cached. This is a far-future `Expires` header, telling the browser that this response won't be stale until May 20, 2013:

```
Expires: Wed, 20 May 2013 20:00:00 GMT
```

You can add the `Expires` and `Cache-Control` headers in IIS, or programmatically through ASP.NET MVC.

Set up client caching in IIS

IIS 7 allows you to set up client caching (*http://www.iis.net/ConfigReference/system .webServer/staticContent/clientCache*) headers with the `<clientCache>` element of the `<staticContent>` element.

The `httpExpires` attribute adds the HTTP `Expires` header, which specifies a date and time when the content should expire. `Cache-Control` headers can be added with the `cacheControlMaxAge` attribute (note that its behavior depends on the `cacheControl Mode` attribute).

Set up client caching through ASP.NET MVC

You can also add Expires and Cache-Control headers programmatically by calling `Cache.SetExpires()` and `Cache.SetMaxAge()`, respectively.

The following snippet shows an example:

```
// Sets the Cache-Control: max-age header to 1 year.
Response.Cache.SetMaxAge(DateTime.Now.AddYears(1));

// Sets the Expires header to 11:00 P.M. local time on the current expiration day.
Response.Cache.SetExpires(DateTime.Parse("11:00:00PM"));
```

You can find in-depth coverage of the `Cache-Control: max-age` and `Expires` headers in "Understanding the Browser Cache" on page 264.

Note that it is redundant to specify both `Expires` and `Cache-Control` headers—specify only one of them for each resource.

Cache busting

If you use a far-future `Expires` header, you have to notify the browser when cached content changes. If you fail to do so, the browser will continue to use the stale, cached copy of the content.

Since the browser caches the component by its URL, you have to change the URL in some way. Usually this is done by appending a "version" query string parameter. In fact, ASP.NET MVC's bundling and minification feature provides a built-in "cache-busting" feature that takes care of this automatically whenever any component changes.

Using a far-future `Expires` header affects page views only after a user has already visited your site. It has no effect on the number of HTTP requests when a user visits your site for the first time and the browser's cache is empty. Therefore, the performance impact of this improvement depends on how often users hit your pages with a "primed" cache, when the browser already contains all of the components in the page.

GZip Components

Compressing text-based content such as HTML, JavaScript, CSS, and even JSON data reduces the time required to transfer a component over the wire, thereby improving the response time significantly.

On average, compressing components with GZip compression generally reduces the response time by about 70%. Older browsers and proxy servers are known to have issues with compressed content because they may see a mismatch in what is expected and what is received. These are edge cases, though, and with older browser support dropping off, this should not be a major concern.

 Some proxies and antivirus software are known to remove the `Accept-Encoding: gzip, deflate` header from HTTP requests, causing the server to simply return the uncompressed content. This is generally innocuous, however. It causes no side effects other than reduced performance.

The web server can be configured to compress content based on file or MIME types, or it can figure it out on the fly. While it is worthwhile to enable compression on any text-based response, it is often counterproductive to enable compression on binary components such as images, audio, and PDFs that are already compressed. In these cases, attempting to compress them further may actually *increase* the file size.

Compressing as many file types as possible is an easy way to reduce overall page weight, which will make your pages load faster, improving the user's experience.

In IIS 7, the `<httpCompression>` (*http://www.iis.net/ConfigReference/system.webServer/httpCompression*) element specifies the HTTP compression settings. Compression is enabled by default, provided the Performance module is installed.

The following snippet shows the default configuration of this element in the *ApplicationHost.config* (*http://learn.iis.net/page.aspx/124/introduction-to-applicationhostconfig/*) file:

```
<httpCompression
    directory="%SystemDrive%\inetpub\temp\IIS Temporary Compressed Files">
  <scheme name="gzip" dll="%Windir%\system32\inetsrv\gzip.dll" />
  <dynamicTypes>
    <add mimeType="text/*" enabled="true" />
    <add mimeType="message/*" enabled="true" />
    <add mimeType="application/javascript" enabled="true" />
```

```
            <add mimeType="*/*" enabled="false" />
        </dynamicTypes>
        <staticTypes>
            <add mimeType="text/*" enabled="true" />
            <add mimeType="message/*" enabled="true" />
            <add mimeType="application/javascript" enabled="true" />
            <add mimeType="*/*" enabled="false" />
        </staticTypes>
    </httpCompression>
```

You can override some or all of the values by specifying your own `<httpCompression>` element under `<system.webserver>` in your application's *web.config* file.

Note that dynamic compression can increase CPU usage, since it performs the compression for every request. The results cannot be cached effectively because they are dynamic in nature.

> If your dynamic content is relatively static (in other words, it doesn't change per request), you can still cache it by setting the `dynamicCompres` `sionBeforeCache` attribute of the `<urlCompression>` (*http://www.iis.net/ ConfigReference/system.webServer/urlCompression*) element.

Put Stylesheets at the Top

Putting stylesheets in the document head allows the page to render progressively.

Since you care about performance, you want the page to load progressively, that is, you want the browser to display whatever content it has as soon as possible. This is especially important for pages with a lot of content and for users on slower Internet connections.

In our case, the HTML page *is* the progress indicator! When the browser loads the page progressively, the header, the navigation bar, the logo at the top, and other elements such as these all serve as visual feedback to the user that the page is loading.

The problem with putting stylesheets near the bottom of the document is that it prohibits progressive rendering in many browsers, including Internet Explorer. These browsers block rendering to avoid having to redraw elements of the page if their styles change, which usually means that users get stuck viewing a blank page.

Put Scripts at the Bottom

Scripts block parallel downloads. The HTTP/1.1 specification (*http://www.w3.org/Pro tocols/rfc2616/rfc2616-sec8.html#sec8.1.4*) suggests that browsers download no more than two (although newer browsers allow slightly more) components in parallel per hostname. If you serve your images from multiple hosts, you can get more than two downloads to occur in parallel. While a script is downloading, however, the browser won't start any other downloads, even on different hosts (Figure 13-5).

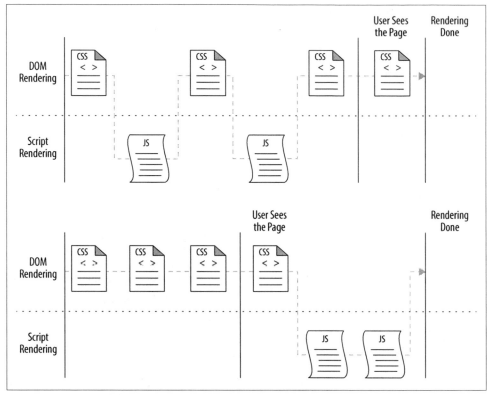

Figure 13-5. Effect of browser rendering with scripts at the bottom

In some situations, it's not easy to move scripts to the bottom. If, for example, the script uses document.write to insert part of the page's content, it can't be moved lower in the page. In many cases, though, there are ways to work around these situations. We'll look at a few of those next.

Defer script execution

The parsing of a script block can be *deferred* by using the DEFER attribute in the <script> tag. The DEFER attribute is a clue to browsers that they can continue rendering.

However, different browsers process this attribute differently, making it fairly unreliable. The good news is that if a script can be deferred, it can also be moved to the bottom of the page, which makes the web page render faster.

Lazy loading scripts

Some applications, such as Gmail, use the lazy loading technique (*http://googlecode.blogspot.com/2009/09/gmail-for-mobile-html5-series-reducing.html*) to render the JavaScript inside comment blocks. The browser simply ignores the comments and continues rendering the page. When a script block is needed (on some user action), the module's script is accessed by stripping out the comment tags and then using `eval()` to parse the JavaScript. While certainly not elegant, this technique can be more beneficial than putting scripts at the bottom or deferring them.

Make Scripts and Styles External

Placing styles and scripts in separate external files, as opposed to inline with the markup in the HTML document, enables browsers to cache them. This makes subsequent page loads faster, as illustrated in Figure 13-6:

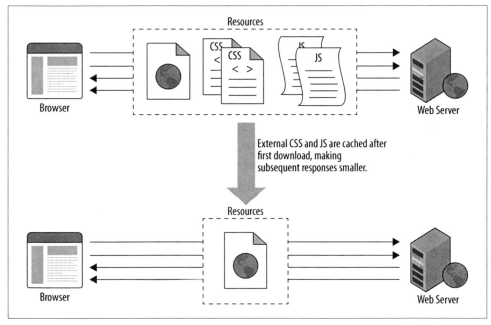

Figure 13-6. External styles and scripts

Including styles and scripts inline makes them noncacheable and increases the size of the response. However, it also reduces the number of HTTP requests, because everything gets downloaded as a single resource.

So the question is, what offers greater benefits: reducing the number of requests or making them external and cacheable? The answer to this question will vary for different applications. While it can be tricky to quantify the benefits, they can be estimated and measured to some extent. For example, if your application reuses resources across different pages, making them external will offer more benefits. However, if your application only has a few pages or uses different resources for each page, rendering them inline may offer greater benefits (although external files will still help here).

A middle ground is to load the resources on the landing page inline and dynamically load the external resources (using asynchronous loading techniques such as AJAX or the async attribute for `<script>` tags (*http://davidwalsh.name/html5-async*)). This makes the initial page load faster, and subsequent page views will be able to benefit from the cached resources. This technique is employed by Yahoo! on its home page.

Reduce DNS Lookups

DNS lookup is the process of resolving a hostname to its IP address. On average, it takes 20–120 milliseconds per request, and during this time the browser cannot perform any other tasks, so it is effectively blocked.

Reducing the number of HTTP requests minimizes this issue, but you will still end up having some resources on the page (such as images, stylesheets, and JavaScript files) that need to be requested. Reducing the number of unique hostnames in a page allows you to optimize this process, since browsers typically cache the results of DNS lookups. Figure 13-7 illustrates this effect.

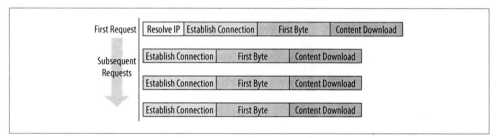

Figure 13-7. Reducing DNS lookups improves performance

Reducing the number of unique hostnames leads to the side effect of having fewer parallel downloads. There is therefore a trade-off between the number of unique hostnames and the number of subdomains for parallel downloading. Yahoo!'s team recommends splitting these resources between two, three, or four hosts for the optimum balance.

Minify JavaScript and CSS

Minification is the practice of removing unnecessary characters from code to reduce its size, thereby improving load times. When code is minified, all comments are removed, along with unneeded whitespace characters (spaces, newlines, and tabs). Figure 13-8 illustrates the result. In the case of JavaScript, this improves response times because the size of the downloaded file is reduced. Two popular tools for minifying JavaScript code are JSMin and YUI Compressor. The YUI Compressor can also minify CSS.

Figure 13-8. Minifying scripts and styles improves response times

Obfuscation is an alternative optimization that can be applied to source code. In a survey of 10 top U.S. websites, minification achieved a 21% size reduction versus 25% for obfuscation. However, while obfuscation may result in a greater reduction in the size of the code, minifying JavaScript is less risky. Obfuscation is more complex than minification and thus more likely to generate bugs as a result of the obfuscation step itself.

In addition to minifying external scripts and styles, in-lined `<script>` and `<style>` blocks can and should be minified. Even if you GZip your scripts and stylesheets, minifying them will still reduce their size by 5% or more. As the use and size of JavaScript and stylesheets increases, so will the savings gained by minifying your code.

Avoid Redirects

A *redirect* happens when a browser opens a different URL than the one that is requested. It is accomplished using HTTP status codes 301 and 302.

Redirects are considered bad performance-wise, because their results are usually not cached (unless caching explicitly indicated by `Expires` or `Cache-Control` headers) and they incur the same processing delay as a new request. Figure 13-9 illustrates what happens when redirects are made.

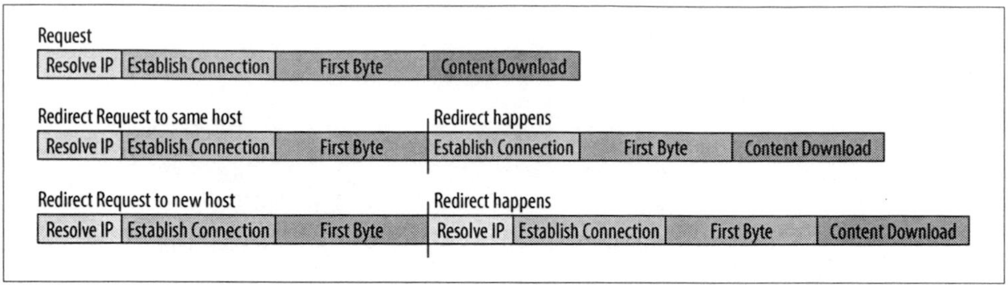

Figure 13-9. Redirects should be avoided in most cases

Redirects can be useful in fixing broken links (e.g., when old pages are moved to a new location), in URL-shortening services, or for redirecting users from multiple (but somewhat similar) domain names to a single domain (such as from *wikipedia.net* to *wikipedia.com*).

While the above are legitimate uses for redirects and cannot be avoided, many times redirects happen without the developer's knowledge. For instance, in your ASP.NET MVC application (or any application running in IIS), a call to *http://www.ebuy.biz/Home/About* will cause a redirection to *http://ebuy.biz/Home/About/"*—the same action but with a trailing "/".

This can be fixed by making the redirect "permanent" (HTTP status code 301).

Here's how sample HTTP headers look in a 301 response:

```
HTTP/1.1 301 Moved Permanently
Location: http://yourhostname.com/Home/About
Content-Type: text/html
```

There are many ways to handle this, such as:

- Writing your own `HttpModule`
- Doing the redirection on your controller
- Using the IIS URL Rewrite (*http://www.iis.net/download/urlrewrite*) module to rewrite the URL

The IIS Rewrite module is an HTTP module that is built right into IIS. You can configure the IIS Rewrite module using the `system.webServer` > `rewrite` element in your *web.config* file.

The following snippet shows an example of doing such a redirection:

```
<rewrite>
  <rules>
    <!-- remove the trailing slash from the URL -->
    <rule name="Strip trailing slash" stopProcessing="true">
      <match url="(.*)/$" />
      <conditions>
        <add input="{REQUEST_FILENAME}" matchType="IsFile" negate="true" />
        <add input="{REQUEST_FILENAME}" matchType="IsDirectory" negate="true" />
```

```
            </conditions>
            <action type="Redirect" redirectType="Permanent" url="{R:1}" />
        </rule>
    </rules>
</rewrite>
```

The above snippet adds rules that leverage regular expressions to detect if the request contains a trailing slash. If found, the trailing slash is stripped out and a permanent redirect response header is returned back, with the rewritten URL without the trailing slash.

Remove Duplicate Scripts

It hurts performance to include the same JavaScript file twice in one page—and this isn't as unusual as you might think. A review of 10 top U.S. websites showed that two of them contained a duplicated script. Two main factors increase the odds of a script being duplicated in a single web page: team size and number of scripts. When it does happen, it can hurt performance.

Duplicated scripts will result in unnecessary HTTP requests in Internet Explorer (but not in Firefox). In Internet Explorer, if an external script is included twice and is not cacheable, it will generate two HTTP requests during page loading. Even if the script is cacheable, extra HTTP requests will occur when a user reloads the page.

In addition to generating wasteful HTTP requests, time is wasted evaluating the script multiple times. This redundant JavaScript execution happens in both Firefox and Internet Explorer, regardless of whether the script is cacheable.

One way to avoid accidentally including the same script twice is to implement a script management module in your templating system. The typical way to include a script is to use the `<script>` tag in your HTML page.

Configure ETags

An ETag (Entity Tag) is a string that uniquely identifies a specific version of a resource or component, such as an image, stylesheet, or script. ETags are a mechanism that web servers and browsers use to determine whether the component in the browser's cache matches the one on the origin server.

ETags were added to provide a mechanism for validating entities that is more flexible and robust than the last-modified date, which provides only a weak form of validation (browsers apply heuristics to determine whether or not to fetch a resource from the server, and each browser applies the heuristics differently).

Here's what the ETag response header looks like:

```
HTTP/1.1 200 OK
Last-Modified: Tue, 29 May 2012 00:00:00 GMT
```

```
ETag: "8e12af-3bd-632a2d18"
Content-Length: 14625
```

To validate the resource at a later stage, the browser uses the `If-None-Match` header to pass the ETag back to the origin server. A server returns a 304 status code if the ETags match (in this case, reducing the size of the response by 14,625 bytes):

```
GET /images/logo.png HTTP/1.1
Host: yourhostname.com
If-Modified-Since: Tue, 29 May 2012 00:00:00 GMT
If-None-Match: "8e12af-3bd-632a2d18"
HTTP/1.1 304 Not Modified
```

If your application uses a web farm or cluster of web servers, it is important that each server assign the same unique ETag—otherwise, the browser will treat them as different versions and download the full resource when served by different servers, defeating the purpose of providing an ETag.

Unfortunately, both Apache and IIS include data in the ETag that make it practically impossible to generate the same ETag across servers in a web farm. This greatly reduces their chance of passing a validity test on the browser in a web farm scenario. In such cases, it might be easier to just use the `Last-Modified` header to perform this validation. If you take this route, you should remove the `ETag` header from the response altogether, which will reduce the size of the HTTP request and response. This Microsoft Support article (*http://support.microsoft.com/?id=922733*) describes how to remove ETags from IIS: *http://support.microsoft.com/?id=922733*.

Note that you only need to set `Last-Modified` or an ETag. Setting them both is redundant.

Measuring Client-Side Performance

In order to "optimize" something, you first need to be able to "measure" or "quantify" it. Without profiling or instrumenting, you cannot identify bottlenecks, much less substantiate the improvements.

There are many tools available for this purpose, but probably the easiest and simplest to use is YSlow (*http://yslow.org*). YSlow is available for many browsers, and while the rest of this section will focus on Firefox, you can choose the one you like because the core concepts and techniques remain the same. YSlow uses all 23 of the 35 rules that Yahoo!'s performance team outlined as quantifiable or testable.

To get started, install the YSlow Firefox add-on (*https://addons.mozilla.org/en-US/fire fox/addon/5369*). Once it's installed, you can create a new basic ASP.NET MVC project and see how it grades on YSlow's benchmarks.

To do so, go to File > New Project > ASP.NET MVC 4 Application and choose the Internet Application template, as shown in Figure 13-10.

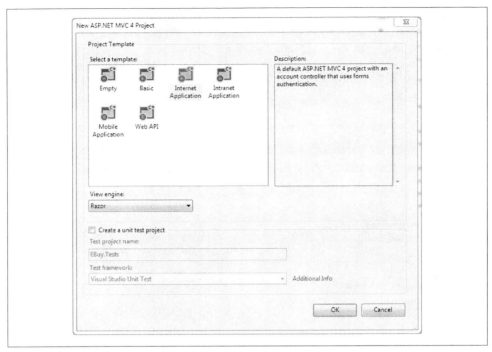

Figure 13-10. Creating a basic ASP.NET MVC 4 application

Without touching a single line of code, build and run the application. If your default browser is not Firefox, open up Firefox and navigate to the new application. Bring up Firebug, navigate to the YSlow tab (shown in Figure 13-11) and hit Run Test.

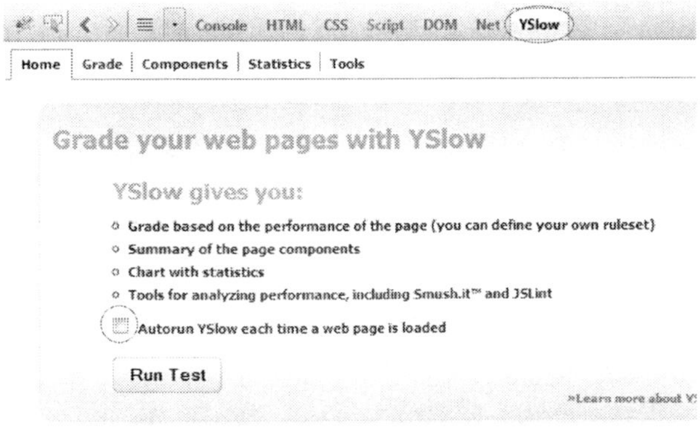

Figure 13-11. The YSlow tab in Firebug

Using the default rule set (YSlow V2), the results are impressive. The starter template already follows many of the best practices and scores an *A* grade in almost all sections, as you can see in Figure 13-12. Overall, the page gets a *B* grade.

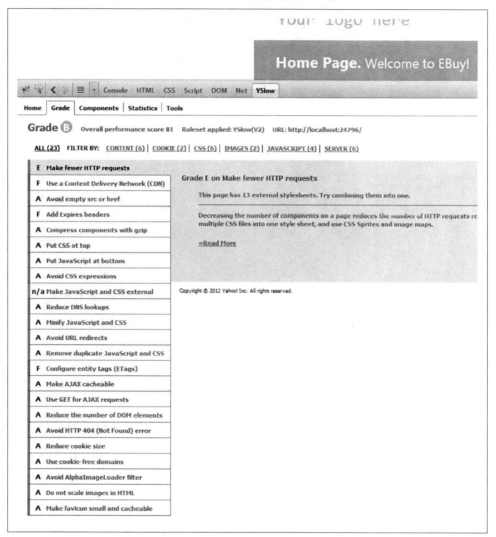

Figure 13-12. The starter template scores pretty well on its own!

The first bad score is on rule# 1, "Make fewer HTTP requests." The Grade tab suggests an immediate way to improve this—combining 13 stylesheet files. If you check the Components tab (Figure 13-13), you'll see how many components of different types the page requests. Note that only two JavaScript (JS) files are being used in the starter template, but as your application grows, you'll have more JavaScript files that you will need to bundle together.

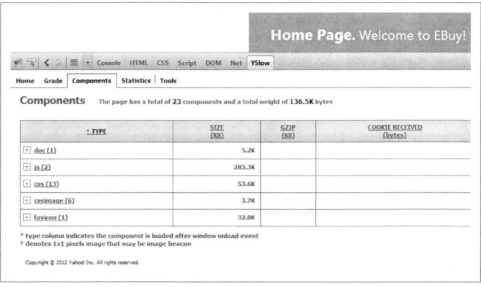

Figure 13-13. YSlow's Components tab shows how many components this page requests

Let's see how we can use ASP.NET MVC 4's built-in bundling feature to reduce the number of HTTP requests on this page.

Putting ASP.NET MVC to Work

ASP.NET MVC 4 and .NET Framework 4.5 provide a new `System.Web.Optimization` library that offers bundling and minification support out of the box. It provides basic features for bundling different resources according to custom rules (we'll see *how* in coming sections), as well as a built-in JavaScript minifier and stylesheets. It also includes automatic cache busting—i.e., invalidating the browser cache when any content changes. Another important feature that it offers is the ability to duplicate stylesheets and script files automatically (as long as they are not in different paths).

For most scenarios, this will suffice. However, you can always choose to implement third-party solutions if your application's needs demand more.

Bundling and Minification

If you inspect the head of *Layout.cshtml*, you'll notice two new helpers provided by the `System.Web.Optimization` library, `@Styles` and `@Scripts`:

```
@Styles.Render("~/Content/themes/base/css", "~/Content/css")
@Scripts.Render("~/bundles/modernizr")
```

As their names suggest, they bundle and minify stylesheets and JavaScript files or resources, respectively.

The `Render()` method takes a list of virtual paths to render. These paths are translated to regular HTML tags at runtime, like so:

```
<link href="/Content/site.css" rel="stylesheet" type="text/css" />
<script src="/Scripts/modernizr-2.0.6.js" type="text/javascript"></script>
```

You have full control over defining these bundles, as you'll see in the next section. For instance, as the above example illustrates, you can create multiple bundles and render them in a single call. Here, two style bundles are rendered in one call—one for the base theme and one for the site's default stylesheet.

Looking further, you'll find that just above the closing body tag, you have the remaining JavaScript `Render()` call:

```
@Scripts.Render("~/bundles/jquery")
```

The starter template therefore automatically adheres to our "stylesheets at the top" and "JavaScript at the bottom" rules.

 The only exception is *modernizr.js*, which is being rendered in the document head. The role of the Modernizr JavaScript library is to detect the features (such as video, audio, SVG, newer HTML 5 features, etc.) that are supported by the target browser and to attach stylesheet class names to the `<head>` tag. Using these classes, you can style and script your page to degrade gracefully in the absence of a particular feature on which the page depends. Moving Modernizr to the bottom will defer this detection until page load, and thus your styles will not work initially, creating a glitch as the page loads (certain elements will appear broken or not styled at first, and then, as the page loads, they will appear correctly).

Defining bundles

You define a bundle by calling `BundleCollection.Add()` (in `System.Web.Optimization`) and passing in an instance of a `ScriptBundle` or a `StyleBundle`. To create a `ScriptBundle`, you instantiate it by giving it a virtual path (that will be used in views) and including one or more scripts, like this:

```
// wildcard inclusion - include all scripts that start with "jquery-1"
var jQueryBundle = new ScriptBundle("~/bundles/jquery").Include(
                    "~/Scripts/jquery-1.*");

// explicit script file inclusion
var jQueryValBundle = new ScriptBundle("~/bundles/jqueryval").Include(
                    "~/Scripts/jquery.unobtrusive-ajax.js",
                    "~/Scripts/jquery.validate.js",
                    "~/Scripts/jquery.validate.unobtrusive.js")
```

You can create a StyleBundle in a similar fashion:

```
var siteBundle = new StyleBundle("~/Content/css").Include("~/Content/site.css")
```

The starter template does this automatically for you for the included resources—head over to *App_Start\BundleConfig.cs*. This file is thoughtfully placed under the *App_Start* folder to highlight the fact that this code needs to run only once, at application startup. However, you can define bundles anywhere in the project, as long as you don't forget to register them during the application's startup phase:

```
public class MvcApplication : System.Web.HttpApplication
{
    protected void Application_Start()
    {
        AreaRegistration.RegisterAllAreas();

        FilterConfig.RegisterGlobalFilters(GlobalFilters.Filters);
        RouteConfig.RegisterRoutes(RouteTable.Routes);

        // Registers bundles
        BundleConfig.RegisterBundles(BundleTable.Bundles);
    }
}
```

Enabling bundles

If you remember, on our first test, YSlow complained about too many HTTP requests —which brings us to the question, with all this plumbing code already there, why didn't bundling combine them into fewer requests?

The answer is that the bundling and other optimizations are automatically disabled in Debug mode, to make it more convenient to develop and debug your code. You can force the optimizations in Debug mode by setting BundleTable.EnableOptimizations to true.

To see it in action, let's compile our application under Release mode and rerun the YSlow test. The overall grade is still B (due to other factors), but you can see that YSlow is happy about the reduced number of HTTP requests on the page (Figure 13-14). The Components tab (Figure 13-15) reflects the bundling in action and shows only two stylesheet files now: */Content/themes/base/css* and */Content/css*, just as we defined earlier.

Doing a "view source" on the stylesheet URLs also confirms the minification!

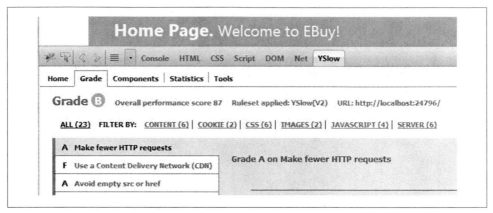

Figure 13-14. Using bundles to reduce the number of HTTP requests

Figure 13-15. The stylesheet files are now bundled into two files

Cache busting

Remember that browsers cache resources based on URLs. Whenever a page requests a resource, the browser first checks in its cache to see if it has a resource with a matching URL. If yes, then it simply uses the cached copy instead of fetching a new one from the server. So, in order to be able to leverage the browser cache, the URL must not change between visits.

This, however, presents a dilemma to you as the web developer. When you change the content in JavaScript files or stylesheet files, you'd like the browser to get the updated copy instead of the old cached copy. However, keeping the same URL is not going to help, because the browser will continue to use the old cached copy. A common solution is to append the version number to the URL, as in:

```
<link type="text/css" rel="stylesheet" href="/Content/site.css?v=1.0">
```

Now when you change the content, you can simply bump up the version and the browser will download the new copy instead. This method of manually editing the version numbers is tedious and error prone, however. Bundles automatically take care of this by adding a hashcode of the bundle as a query parameter to the URL, like this:

```
<link type="text/css" rel="stylesheet"
      href="/Content/themes/base/css?v=UM624qf1uFt8dYtiIV9PCmYhsyeewBIwY4ObOi8OdW81">
```

Now anytime you change the file's content, a new hash will get generated and will be rendered to the page automatically. The browser, seeing a different URL, will fetch the newer copy instead of using the cached version.

Summary

This chapter showed you basic rules for making your pages run faster. You saw how to implement some of the rules it outlined using IIS and leveraging ASP.NET MVC's built-in features, such as bundling, minification, and cache busting. The tips shown here are simple enough to implement and will give you a head start in optimizing the performance of your pages.

Advanced Routing

The first chapter of this book gave you a brief introduction to the fundamentals of ASP.NET MVC routing. That chapter shows the default route that Visual Studio generates for you when you create a new ASP.NET MVC project, and it talks about how the routing framework uses that route to determine which controller and action should be used to execute each request.

For the most part, you will not need to worry about anything more advanced than the default route that Visual Studio initially generates. The default route follows the standard ASP.NET MVC convention and allows you to create new controllers and actions without having to worry much about how the routing engine will locate them. Only if your application moves beyond these common scenarios will you have to gain a better understanding of ASP.NET MVC's powerful routing framework in order to operate outside of the default URL pattern and the default values.

In this chapter, we will go beyond ASP.NET MVC's conventional route and take a deeper look at the powerful routing engine that drives ASP.NET MVC applications. We'll start with a discussion about why URLs are so important to a web application's user experience and how your application's URLs can affect how your site ranks in search engine results. Then we'll dive into creating more advanced routes by exploring different URL patterns. We'll also consider defining constraints on those routes and look at a useful tool, called *Glimps*, for helping to debug routing failures. Finally, we will look at ways that you can extend the basic routing framework to help improve your development experience, then see how you can leverage the routing engine's extensibility to create your own custom routing logic.

Wayfinding

The term *wayfinding* refers to all of the ways that people orient themselves in a space and navigate from place to place. In the context of browsing the World Wide Web, one of the most natural mechanisms for wayfinding is URLs. In fact, that's how most people initially orient themselves on the Web: by opening a browser and entering a URL.

For example, everyone knows Yahoo's URL:

```
www.yahoo.com
```

URLs are a simple and intuitive way for users to get to where they want to go and, more importantly, to get to the information they are seeking. URLs are easy to remember and also easy to communicate to others.

In the early days of the Web, URLs' simplicity extended from the domain name through the entire URL, as you'll see in the following URL for a specific page from a 1996 version of Yahoo!:

```
http://www.yahoo.com/Computers_and_Internet/Software/Data_Formats/HTML/HTML_2_0/
```

In this example URL, the directory structure is fairly logical and very readable. It's also what some would call "hackable," meaning users can easily experiment by changing parts of the URL to navigate up to higher levels in the site hierarchy, as well as making fairly well-educated guesses as to what other categories in the URL might be.

Simple URLs are an important—if often overlooked—aspect of the experience that a website gives its users. In fact, over a decade ago noted usability expert Jacob Nielsen recognized that a good URL structure contributes to the overall usability of a website, and as recently as 2007, separate eye-tracking studies performed by Nielsen's team and by Edward Cutrell and Zhiwei Guan from Microsoft Research showed that users spend 24% of their gaze time looking at the URLs.

As dynamic web page frameworks became more popular, developers saw that they could use URLs not just as a means to let users access resources on their sites, but also as a place to store information about a user's activity and the application's state. As developers applied this technique more and more, URLs became increasingly oriented toward the machines running a website rather than the humans using it, full of cryptic codes and database IDs such as:

```
http://demo.com/store.aspx?v=c&p=56&id=1232123&s=12321-12321321312-12312&s=0&f=red
```

These kinds of URLs are certainly not very readable or memorable. Try telling someone that URL over the phone!

Thankfully, those same web developers have subsequently started to recognize what Nielson and others have long known: the structure of a URL is important, and URLs play an important role in the usability of a website. To address the problems that have arisen and bring some sanity back to URLs, newer web frameworks often introduce the concept of *routing* as a layer of indirection between URLs and the application functionality to which they refer.

Routing allows you to place the facade of a URL over the logic of the application. For example, applying routing to the previous URL allows you to hide the *store.aspx* endpoint and all of its query string values and instead map friendly URL segments into the parameters that the page needs in order to function.

In other words, you can turn that ugly URL into something more meaningful, like:

```
http://example.com/store/toys/RadioFlyer/ClassicRedWagon/12321-12321321312-12312/red
```

While it conveys much of the same information as the previous URL, this URL does so in a far more user-friendly way. You can easily tell that we are in the store, shopping for a "Radio Flyer Classic Red Wagon" in the "toys" category. A user can even remove the bulk of the URL to experiment with navigating to other pages on the site.

In the world of ASP.NET MVC, rather than acting as a facade over *.aspx* endpoints, the routing engine acts as a facade over the application's controllers and actions. So, as you write your ASP.NET MVC application, it's helpful to take a step back and think about the URLs that your application will expose to the world.

URLs and SEO

In addition to general website usability, creating friendlier URLs can offer your site yet another very important benefit: improved search engine rankings. URLs that are more human-friendly also happen to be more search-engine friendly. URL optimization is part of a larger technique for improving search engine ranking called *Search Engine Optimization* (SEO).

The goal of SEO is to optimize a site in such a way that it increases how high the site's pages rank in search engine results. If search ranking is an important consideration for your website, there are a number of tips for SEO that may influence how you design your application's URLs. Keep in mind, however, that SEO remains a bit of a black art and that each search engine uses its own proprietary—and usually secret—algorithms for ranking web pages, so there are no clear-cut rules.

In general, though, here are a few good tips to consider when optimizing your site:

Short URLs are better.
> Google has stated that its algorithms give less weight to words occurring after the first five in a URL, so longer URLs are not really an advantage. Additionally, shorter URLs help to increase usability and readability.

Separate multiple words using dashes instead of underscores.
> Google will interpret the dashes as a word delimiter and index each of those words separately.

Stick to lowercase.
> Be conscious of capitalization in your URLs and try to stick to all lowercase if possible. Most search engines follow the HTTP standard, which states that URLs are case-sensitive; therefore, a search engine recognizes *Page1.htm* and *page1.htm* as two different pages. This can cause the content to be indexed twice, which may result in a penalty to the ranking for those pages.

For more information about optimizing URLs, check out the SEO Cheat Sheet (*http://www.seomoz.org/blog/seo-cheat-sheet-anatomy-of-a-url*) created by the folks at SEOmoz.org.

Building Routes

Hopefully, by now we have thoroughly convinced you of how important URLs are to your site's overall user experience. With that in mind, let's look at how you can use the ASP.NET MVC routing framework to control which URLs users will use to access your site.

We'll start by taking a deeper look at the different ways you can define a URL pattern in a route. We will use the URL defined in the default route that is created when you create a new ASP.NET MVC project as a point of reference:

```
routes.MapRoute(
        "Default", // Route name
        "{controller}/{action}/{id}", // URL with parameters
        new { controller = "Home", action = "Index", id = UrlParameter.Optional }
        );
```

The URL in a route is formed by combining a series of one or more "segments." Segments can be constants or placeholders and are delimited by the forward slash character.

Because routes are always relative to the application root, they cannot start with a forward slash (/) or a tilde (~). The routing engine will throw an exception if it comes across routes that break this rule.

You can tell each of these segments is a placeholder because they are each wrapped in curly braces:

```
{controller}
```

In this case, each placeholder is also a single segment, delimited by a forward slash. It's possible to create segments that contain multiple placeholders by separating each placeholder with a string constant, as in:

```
{param1}-{param2}-{param3}
```

When the routing engine parses a URL, it extracts the values at each placeholder position and uses them to populate an instance of the `RouteData` class. This class maintains a dictionary of all the important values contained in the route and is used by the ASP.NET MVC Framework itself. It's also important to know that the values added to the dictionary are converted to strings by default.

In the case of the default route shown earlier, this means that if the actual requested URL were:

http://demo.com/Home/Index/1234

the routing engine would parse the three key/value pairs listed in Table 14-1 into the RouteData class.

Table 14-1. Key/value pairs passed to the RouteData class

Parameter	Value
{controller}	Home
{action}	Index
{id}	1234

Default and Optional Route Parameters

As shown in Chapter 1, the routing system uses the {controller} and {action} values to determine which controller to instantiate and which action to execute. But if you recall, the URL that is loaded in the browser does not contain any values for the URL placeholders. This is where the third parameter of the MapRoute() method comes into play, allowing you to set default values for any of the placeholders.

If we go back and look at the default route, you'll see that in the call to MapRoute() an anonymous type—which is a special object type that the compiler generates on the fly —is created that sets the default values for each of the three defined placeholders:

```
routes.MapRoute(
    "Default", // Route name
    "{controller}/{action}/{id}", // URL with parameters
    new { controller = "Home", action = "Index", id = UrlParameter.Optional }
);
```

Ah ha, we've now solved the mystery of how an application knows to load the Home Controller by default! Even though the request URL does not contain values for the controller or action, the route has default values defined, which the routing system uses to locate the default controller and action. As the routing engine evaluates a URL, the default values are inserted into the RouteData dictionary, and if a placeholder value is found during the parsing of the URL, it simply overwrites the default value.

Let's take a look at some other examples of route URLs. In the following example, a constant segment has been prepended to the beginning of the URL. That means that the request URL must contain that segment in order to match this route:

```
routes.MapRoute(
    "Default",
    "Admin/{controller}/{action}/{id}",
    new { controller = "Home", action = "Index", id = UrlParameter.Optional }
);
```

Here are some examples of URLs that would match this route:

- *http://demo.com/Admin*
- *http://demo.com/Admin/Home*
- *http://demo.com/Admin/Home/Index*
- *http://demo.com/Admin/Home/Index/1234*

```
routes.MapRoute(
    "Default",
    "{site}/{controller}/{action}/{id}",
    new { controller = "Home", action = "Index", id = UrlParameter.Optional }
);
```

Here are some examples of URLs that satisfy this route:

- *http://demo.com/Admin*
- *http://demo.com/Store/Home*
- *http://demo.com/Store/Home/Index*
- *http://demo.com/Store/Home/Index/1234*

The following route definition contains a single placeholder for an ID, relying on the default values set for the controller and action:

```
routes.MapRoute(
    "Default",
    "{id}",
    new { controller = "Home", action = "Index", id = UrlParameter.Optional }
);
```

This route matches URLs such as:

- *http://demo.com/*
- *http://demo.com/1234*

This next route combines the constant segment with a single placeholder value, again relying on the default values for the controller and action:

```
routes.MapRoute(
    "Default",
    "users/{id}",
    new { controller = "Home", action = "Index", id = UrlParameter.Optional }
);
```

Examples of URLs that would match this route are:

- *http://demo.com/users*
- *http://demo.com/users/1234*

```
routes.MapRoute(
    "Default",
    "category/{id}/export{type}.{format}/",
```

```
            new { controller = "Category", action = "Export" }
        );
```

An example of a URL that would match this route is:

- *http://demo.com/category/123abc/exportEvents.json*

Routing Order and Priority

As your application becomes more complex, you are likely to want to register multiple routes. When you do this, it is important that you consider the order in which you register them. When the routing engine attempts to locate a matching route, it simply enumerates the collection of routes, and it stops enumerating as soon as it finds a match.

This behavior can cause plenty of problems if you're not expecting it. Consider the following snippet, which registers two routes:

```
routes.MapRoute(
    "generic",
    "{site}",
    new { controller = "SiteBuilder", action = "Index" }
);

routes.MapRoute(
    "admin",
    "Admin",
    new { controller = "Admin", action = "Index" }
);
```

The first route contains a single placeholder segment and sets the default value of the controller parameter to SiteBuilder. The second route contains a single constant segment and sets the default value of the controller parameter to Admin.

Both of these routes are completely valid, but the order in which they are mapped may cause unexpected problems because the first route matches just about any value entered. That means it will be the first to match *http://demo.com/Admin*, and since the routing engine stops after finding the first match, the second route will never get used.

Be sure to keep this scenario in mind, and consider the order in which you define custom routes.

Routing to Existing Files

The ASP.NET MVC routing engine gives preference to physical files located on the server over "virtual" routes defined in the route table. Thus, a request made for a physical file will short-circuit the routing process, and the engine will simply return that file rather than trying to parse the URL and locate a matching route. In certain cases, it can be useful to override this behavior, forcing ASP.NET MVC to attempt to route all requests. You can do this by setting the RouteCollections. RouteExistingFiles property to false.

Ignoring Routes

In addition to defining routes that map to controllers and actions, ASP.NET MVC also allows you to define routes with URL patterns that it should simply ignore. The same `RoutesTable` object that exposes the `MapRoute()` method also exposes an `Ignore Route()` method, which adds a special route that tells the routing engine to ignore requests for any URL that matches a given pattern.

Consider the following snippet from the default routing logic that Visual Studio generates, which instructs ASP.NET MVC to ignore routes that contain *.axd*, the file extension used for common ASP.NET handlers such as *Trace.axd* and *WebResource.axd*:

```
routes.IgnoreRoute("{resource}.axd/{*pathInfo}");
```

With this call to `IgnoreRoute()` in place, requests for these URLs are handled as normal requests to ASP.NET instead of being handled by the routing engine.

You can use the `IgnoreRoute()` method to ignore other requests as well. For instance, consider a scenario in which a section of your website contains code written in another framework or language that should not be handled by the ASP.NET MVC runtime. In this case you might use something like the following snippet to tell ASP.NET MVC to ignore URLs that start with *php-app*:

```
routes.IgnoreRoute("php-app/{*pathInfo}");
```

Note that if you are going to use the `IgnoreRoute()` method in your application, it's important to place calls to this method *before* adding standard routes via the `Map Route()` method.

Catch-All Routes

Another feature of the URL parsing engine in ASP.NET MVC is the ability to specify a "catch-all placeholder." Catch-all placeholders are created by placing an asterisk (*) character at the beginning of the placeholder and can only be included as the last segment of a route.

In fact, you saw an example of the catch-all placeholder in action in the previous *php-app* example:

```
routes.IgnoreRoute("php-app/{*pathInfo}");
```

Catch-all placeholders can also be used in normal mapped routes. For example, you can use a catch-all placeholder in a search scenario to gather raw search terms:

```
routes.MapRoute(
    "Default",
    "{controller}/{action}/{*queryValues}",
    new { controller = "Store", action = "Search" }
);
```

In this route we've used the normal controller and action placeholders, but added a catch-all placeholder to capture everything that follows the controller and action portions of the URL. So, if the requested URL were *http://demo.com/store/search/wagon/RadioFlyer*, the routing engine would parse it as shown in Table 14-2.

Thus, if the user types in a URL such as *http://demo.com/store/search/wagon/RadioFlyer*, the routing engine parses the *\{controller\}* and *\{action\}* placeholders, then assigns any other content after the *\{action\}* placeholder to a single key in the RouteData dictionary named queryValues:

Table 14-2. Parsing a catch-all route

Parameter	Value
{controller}	store
{action}	search
{queryValues}	wagon/RadioFlyer

You can also use the catch-all parameter to have the routing engine ignore any request that contains a specific file extension. For instance, if you want the routing engine to ignore any request for an ASPX file, you could use a catch-all route like this:

```
routes.IgnoreRoute("{*allaspx}", new {allaspx=@".*\.aspx(/.*)?"});
```

In this case we're using an overload of the IgnoreRoute method that takes both the URL to ignore and a set of expressions that specify values for the URL parameter. The URL is a catch-all URL that basically says evaluate every URL request, while the expression assigned to the URL parameter is a regular expression that evaluates whether or not the request contains a file with the *.aspx* extension.

Route Constraints

So far we've looked at how you can create routes in your application and the different ways that you can construct URLs using placeholders, but one aspect of the routes we've shown so far is that they do not restrict the values that users can enter. This means that even if you intend the URL to contain only an int, for example, the user is free to specify some other type of value, causing model binding to fail for strongly typed action parameters that expect an int.

Thankfully, the routing engine includes a way to let you put some validation around the placeholder values, called *route constraints*.

The MapRoute() method includes a method override that allows you to set constraints in the placeholders in your route. Much like setting default placeholder values, setting constraints is as easy as creating a new anonymous type.

In this example, a simple regular expression is used to restrict the values that can be used as the value of the ID placeholder:

```
routes.MapRoute(
    "Default",
    "{controller}/{action}/{id}",
    new { controller = "Home", action = "Index", id = UrlParameter.Optional },
    new { id = "(|Ford|Toyota|Honda)" }
);
```

while this example restricts the id value to only numeric values:

```
routes.MapRoute(
    "Default",
    "{controller}/{action}/{id}",
    new { controller = "Home", action = "Index", id = UrlParameter.Optional },
    new { id = "\d+" }
);
```

and this one restricts it to only three numeric digits:

```
routes.MapRoute(
    "Default",
    "{controller}/{action}/{id}",
    new { controller = "Home", action = "Index", id = UrlParameter.Optional },
    new { id = "\d{3}" }
);
```

By using regular expressions to define constraints, you have an immense amount of power to control the placeholder values.

If a constraint is not met by a route, the routing engine considers that route not to be a match and continues enumerating the route table looking for a matching route. Knowing this, you can actually use constraints to help you resolve scenarios where you have identical route URLs that you want to resolve to different controllers or actions.

The code below shows two routes that have identical URLs set, but different constraints:

```
routes.MapRoute(
    "noram",
    "{controller}/{action}/{id}",
    new { controller = "noram", action = "Index", id = UrlParameter.Optional },
    new { id = "(us|ca)" }
);

routes.MapRoute(
    "europe",
    "{controller}/{action}/{id}",
    new { controller = "europe", action = "Index", id = UrlParameter.Optional },
    new { id = "(uk|de|es|it|fr|be|nl)" }
);
```

Finally, while the majority of validation use cases can be covered by providing a regular expression constraint, there are times when you need more complex validation routines. In those cases you can use the IRouteConstraint interface to create a custom constraint.

As shown in the following code, the IRouteConstraint interface has a single method, Match(), that must be implemented:

```
public class CustomerConstraint : IRouteConstraint
{
    public bool Match(HttpContextBase httpContext, Route route, string parameterName,
                      RouteValueDictionary values, RouteDirection routeDirection)
    {
        var cdx = new UsersDataContext();

        //Perform a database lookup
        var result = (from u in cdx.Users
                          where u.Username = values["user"]
                          select u).FirstOrDefault();

        return result != null;
    }
}
```

This code shows how you can create a more complex route constraint that performs a query to verify that the provided value exists in a database. The following code shows how you would use this custom constraint when creating a route:

```
routes.MapRoute(
    "Default",
    "{controller}/{action}/{id}",
    new { controller = "Home", action = "Index" },
    new { id = new CustomerConstraint()  }
);
```

Keep in mind that while this is a valid use case for a route constraint, and one that may be fairly common, in a real-world scenario you would want to make sure that you take into consideration the performance implications of needing to look up a value on an application request.

It's also worth mentioning that there are a number of open source projects that offer prebuilt route constraints that provide a level of capability beyond what the simple regular expression provides—which means you don't have to write your own. One of those is the ASP.NET MVC Extensions project (*http://mvcextensions.codeplex.com/*), which includes a number of routing constraints such as Range, Positive Int/Long, Guid, and Enum.

Peering into Routes Using Glimpse

Because routing adds a level of indirection to an application, debugging route problems can be a bit tricky. One really useful tool for letting you see route information at runtime is Glimpse.

Glimpse includes a Routes tab that shows you not only what routes have been registered, but also lots of other information, like which route was matched to load the current page, what the default values and constraints are for defined routes, and what the actual values are for route placeholders. Figure 14-1 shows the Routes tab in Glimpse.

Figure 14-1. The Routes tab in Glimpse

Attribute-Based Routing

Using the `MapRoute()` method is a simple way to register routes for your application, but it does have some drawbacks. Routing registration code is isolated from the actual controllers and actions that they are ultimately mapping to, which in large applications can be a maintenance headache.

One way to work around this issue is to use a technique called *attribute-based routing*. This simple technique builds on top of the base routing engine, combining it with standard .NET attributes, and it allows you to apply specific routes directly to actions by adorning them with custom attributes.

To show how this technique works, let's build a simple route attribute. To do this we're going to need to build two pieces of infrastructure:

- An attribute class
- A class that generates new routes from those attributes

To start, let's build the new `RouteAttribute` class that derives from `System.Attribute`:

```
[AttributeUsage(AttributeTargets.Method, Inherited = true, AllowMultiple = true)]
public class RouteAttribute : Attribute
{
    /// <summary>
```

```
/// JSON object containing route data part constraints
/// </summary>
public string Constraints { get; set; }

/// <summary>
/// JSON object containing route data part defaults
/// </summary>
public string Defaults { get; set; }

/// <summary>
/// URL routing pattern, including route data part placeholders
/// </summary>
public string Pattern { get; set; }

public RouteAttribute(string pattern)
{
    Pattern = pattern;
}
}
```

The RouteAttribute class exposes a few simple properties for defining the route's URL, default placeholder values, and placeholder constraints. That's all there is to it: the attribute portion of our attribute-based routing sample is done.

To use the attribute, you simply decorate an action in your controller like so:

```
[Route("auctions/{key}-{title}/bids")]
public ActionResult Auctions(string key, string title)
{
    // Retrieve and return the Auction
}
```

In this case, the Route attribute is simply defining the routing pattern that should map to this controller action. You could use the other attribute properties to set default placeholder values or placeholder constraints. You can even apply more than one Route attribute in order to map multiple routes to the same action.

Next, we need to create a way for our application to turn the RouteAttribute we've applied into real route registrations. For that, we'll create a new class called RouteGenerator.

The constructor of our RouteGenerator class will require us to pass in a number of parameters, including the RouteCollection instance, the current RequestContext, and a collection of all the controller actions in the application. In the constructor, we're also going to create a new instance of the JavaScriptSerializer object, which will allow us to serialize and deserialize JSON objects:

```
public RouteGenerator(
        RouteCollection routes, RequestContext requestContext,
        ControllerActions controllerActions
    )
{
    _routes = routes;
    _controllerActions = controllerActions;
```

```
    _requestContext = requestContext;

    _javaScriptSerializer = new JavaScriptSerializer();
}
```

Next, we need a method that generates new routes:

```
public virtual IEnumerable<RouteBase> Generate()
{
    IEnumerable<Route> customRoutes =
        from controllerAction in _controllerActions
        from attribute in controllerAction.Attributes.OfType<RouteAttribute>()
        let defaults = GetDefaults(controllerAction, attribute)
        let constraints = GetConstraints(attribute)
        let routeUrl = ResolveRoute(attribute, defaults)
        select new Route(routeUrl, defaults, constraints, new MvcRouteHandler());

    return customRoutes;
}
```

The Generate() method takes the list of controller actions and uses a LINQ query to select all those that have been marked with the RouteAttribute, registering a new route for each of them. In order to accomplish this, the LINQ query applies a number of helper methods whose job it is to retrieve the attribute's properties, URL, default values, and constants, and convert them into values that the new route instance understands.

Example 14-1 shows the RouteGenerator class in its entirety.

Example 14-1. RouteGenerator

```
public class RouteGenerator
{
    private readonly RouteCollection _routes;
    private readonly RequestContext _requestContext;
    private readonly JavaScriptSerializer _javaScriptSerializer;
    private readonly ControllerActions _controllerActions;

    public RouteGenerator(
            RouteCollection routes, RequestContext requestContext,
            ControllerActions controllerActions
        )
    {
        Contract.Requires(routes != null);
        Contract.Requires(requestContext != null);
        Contract.Requires(controllerActions != null);

        _routes = routes;
        _controllerActions = controllerActions;
        _requestContext = requestContext;

        _javaScriptSerializer = new JavaScriptSerializer();
    }


    public virtual IEnumerable<RouteBase> Generate()
```

```
{
    IEnumerable<Route> customRoutes =
        from controllerAction in _controllerActions
        from attribute in controllerAction.Attributes.OfType<RouteAttribute>()
        let defaults = GetDefaults(controllerAction, attribute)
        let constraints = GetConstraints(attribute)
        let routeUrl = ResolveRoute(attribute, defaults)
        select new Route(routeUrl, defaults, constraints, new MvcRouteHandler());

    return customRoutes;
}

private RouteValueDictionary GetDefaults(
        ControllerAction controllerAction,
        RouteAttribute attribute
    )
{
    var routeDefaults = new RouteValueDictionary(new {
        controller = controllerAction.ControllerShortName,
        action = controllerAction.Action.Name,
    });

    if (string.IsNullOrWhiteSpace(attribute.Defaults) == false)
    {
        var attributeDefaults =
            _javaScriptSerializer.Deserialize<IDictionary<string, object>>(
                attribute.Defaults);

        foreach (var key in attributeDefaults.Keys)
        {
            routeDefaults[key] = attributeDefaults[key];
        }
    }

    return routeDefaults;
}

private RouteValueDictionary GetConstraints(RouteAttribute attribute)
{
    var constraints =
        _javaScriptSerializer.Deserialize<IDictionary<string, object>>(
            attribute.Constraints ?? string.Empty);

    return new RouteValueDictionary(constraints ?? new object());
}

private string ResolveRoute(
        RouteAttribute attribute,
        RouteValueDictionary defaults
    )
{
    // An explicit URL trumps everything
    string routeUrl = attribute.Pattern;

    // If one doesn't exist, try to figure it out
```

```
            if (string.IsNullOrEmpty(routeUrl))
                routeUrl = _routes.GetVirtualPath(_requestContext, defaults).VirtualPath;

            if ((routeUrl ?? string.Empty).StartsWith("/"))
                routeUrl = routeUrl.Substring(1);

            return routeUrl;
        }
}
```

Finally, we need to wire up the `RouteGenerator` class so that it is able to run and register all of the routes when the application starts. To do this, we'll create a new instance of `RouteGenerator` in the `RegisterRoutes()` method, tell it to generate all of the routes, and then simply loop through them, inserting each route into the `RouteTable`:

```
var routeGenerator = new RouteGenerator(routes,
    HttpContext.Current.Request.RequestContext,
    ControllerActions.Current);

var actionroutes = routeGenerator.Generate();

foreach (var route in actionroutes)
{
    RouteTable.Routes.Insert(0, route);
}
```

With the `RouteGenerator` in place, we can now register routes simply by decorating our actions with attributes, instead of having them isolated from the actions. Obviously, the `RouteGenerator` shown here is merely one way to accomplish this. There are actually a number of good open source projects available that take attribute-based route registration to the next level, so if you don't feel like writing your own implementation, you can quickly and easily add one of these libraries to your application.

Extending Routing

At this point, you should have a fairly extensive understanding of how to create routes in an ASP.NET MVC application, and it's likely that what you've learned so far will be all you ever need to know. However, there are times when the built-in capabilities of ASP.NET MVC are simply not enough.

Thankfully, the framework was designed in such a way that there are multiple extensibility points throughout, including in the routing engine. In this section, we will look at some of the lower-level details of the routing pipeline and talk about some of the extensibility points it offers.

The Routing Pipeline

We'll start by looking in more detail at the ASP.NET MVC pipeline (Figure 14-2).

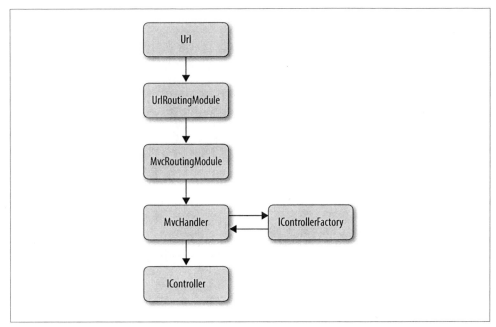

Figure 14-2. The ASP.NET MVC pipeline

First, the incoming request is handled by the UrlRouteModule, which is responsible for matching the requested URL to a route in the application. If the module finds a match, it creates an instance of the IRouteHandler associated with the route. By default in ASP.NET MVC, this is an instance of the MvcRouteHandler class. It's the job of the IRouteHandler to return an instance of the HTTP handler that will actually handle the incoming request.

You can probably guess that in ASP.NET, the default IRouteHandler is the MvcRoute Handler and the default Http hander it creates is the MvcHandler. This HTTP handler uses a controller factory to create a new instance of the correct controller class. The amazing part about this pipeline is there are extensibility points along the entire path. It's entirely possible to derive from the UrlRouteModule to add additional functionality to its route mapping behavior, or to plug in your own implementation of the IRoute Handler or IHttpHandler interfaces.

Let's look at a simple custom route handler class:

```
public class SimpleRouteHandler : IRouteHandler
{
    public IHttpHandler GetHttpHandler(RequestContext requestContext)
    {
        return new SimpleHandler(requestContext);
    }
}
```

As this example shows, the `IRouteHandler` interface has a single method that you must implement called `GetHttpHandler()`. Inside this method, you can control which `IHttpHandler` is instantiated and used to process the route. `MvcRouteHandler` normally creates an instance of the `MvcHandler` class, but with a custom `IRouteHandler`, you can instantiate instances of your own custom handler classes. In this sample, we created a new `SimpleHandler` class, passing in the `requestContent` to its constructor and then returning the handler.

The following code shows how you can register the newly created `SimpleRoute Handler` with your application:

```
routes.Add(new Route("{controller}/{action}/{id}", new SimpleRouteHandler()));
```

As you can see, one of the `Route` class's constructors takes a route handler as a parameter. If this route is chosen by the `UrlRoutingModule`, it will know to create an instance of the `SimpleRouteHandler`, instead of defaulting to the `MvcRouteHandler`.

Now let's take a look at a real-world example of how building your own route handler can be useful. When you work in an organization that has been around for more than a few years, you may occasionally have to deal with legacy Component Object Model (COM) objects that provide functionality on which your site depends. Though the .NET Framework makes it easy to call COM components, this kind of interaction is not quite as simple as interacting with native .NET Framework objects.

For example, in the ASP.NET runtime, each request is handled in its own thread, and when it comes to dealing with COM, each of these threads is its own "multithreaded apartment," or MTA.

However, VB6 COM components are not compatible with ASP.NET's COM MTAs; thus, every time an ASP.NET request interacts with one of these COM objects, COM must execute these requests through a "single-threaded apartment," or STA. This situation can result in a serious bottleneck because, as the name implies, each application can have only one STA, and this becomes the bottleneck that all COM requests must wait in line to execute against.

It's very simple to find out the apartment state of your request by using the `GetApart mentState()` method, as shown by the following code:

```
public string ThreadState()
{
    var thread = System.Threading.Thread.CurrentThread;
    ApartmentState state = thread.GetApartmentState();
    return state.ToString();
}
```

If you run this method in a normal ASP.NET application, you will see that it spits out "MTA" to the browser.

By design, COM doesn't spin up multiple STA threads per request. When the first request comes in, COM creates the STA thread to process it. Then, for each subsequent request, rather than spinning up a new thread, COM queues up the calls with the same thread.

ASP.NET Web Forms offers a simple solution: the AspCompat page directive. If you set the AspCompat directive to true on a Web Forms page, COM gets access to the page's request and response objects, along with creating and using a pool of STA threads. This also lets the COM objects that are registered with ThreadingModel="Apartment" be created in their creators' apartments, provided the creators are running in STAs themselves. The advantage to this is, because the COM object shares the apartment with the creator, multiple requests can now execute in parallel without any bottlenecks.

Unfortunately, ASP.NET MVC doesn't offer anything that works like AspCompat out of the box, so you need to implement your own solution to mimic the behavior of the AspCompat directive. This is a perfect opportunity for you to create your own custom route handler that allows the request thread to be run in an STA instead of an MTA.

Let's take a look at how we can create some custom logic using the extensibility points of ASP.NET MVC to mimic the AspCompat directive in an ASP.NET MVC application. We'll start by creating a new route handler that redirects incoming URL requests to our custom HTTP handler class:

```
public class AspCompatHandler : IRouteHandler
{
    protected IHttpHandler GetHttpHandler(RequestContext requestContext)
    {
        return new AspCompatHandler(requestContext);
    }
}
```

As shown earlier, in the AspCompatHandler class we are using the GetHttpHandler to provide ASP.NET MVC, an instance of the AspCompatHandler, which is what we want to use to route incoming requests.

Next, we can create the AspCompatHandler. To do that, we start by creating a new class derived from the System.Web.UI.Page class. By deriving from the standard Web Forms Page class, we can access ASP.NET's AspCompat directive:

```
public class AspCompatHandler : System.WebForms.UI.Page
{
    public AspCompatHandler(RequestContext requestContext)
    {
        this.RequestContext = requestContext;
    }

    public RequestContext RequestContext { get; set; }

    protected override void OnInit(EventArgs e)
    {
        string requiredString = this.RequestContext.RouteData.GetRequiredString↵
        ("controller");
        var controllerFactory = ControllerBuilder.Current.GetControllerFactory();
        var controller = controllerFactory.CreateController(this.RequestContext, ↵
```

```
        requiredString);
        if (controller == null)
            throw new InvalidOperationException("Could not find controller: " ↵
            + requiredString);
        try
        {
            controller.Execute(this.RequestContext);
        }
        finally
        {
            controllerFactory.ReleaseController(controller);
        }
        this.Context.ApplicationInstance.CompleteRequest();
    }
}
```

In this class, we override the `OnInit()` method to add the code that finds and executes the controller we want to process the request. This mimics the basic behavior of the standard `MvcHandler` class, which is normally used to route requests. We are also going to override the `Page` class's `ProcessRequest()` method and make sure it won't get called accidentally.

Once we have the basic route class created, we need to add an implementation of the `IHttpAsyncHandler` interface to the class. Implementing this interface is what allows ASP.NET MVC to use the `AspCompatHandler` class as a route handler. The `IHttpAsyncHandler` interface has two methods that we need to implement, the `Begin ProcessRequest()` and `EndProcessRequest()` methods, which we will use to tell ASP.NET to process the request using the `AspCompat` directive:

```
public IAsyncResult BeginProcessRequest(HttpContext context, AsyncCallback cb, ↵
object extraData)
{
        return this.AspCompatBeginProcessRequest(context, cb, extraData);
}

public void EndProcessRequest(IAsyncResult result)
{
        this.AspCompatEndProcessRequest(result);
}
```

You can see that using the `IHttpAsyncHandler` methods, we are simply passing the request to the `AspCompatBeginProcessRequest()` method and then receiving the result back from the `AspCompatEndProcessRequest()` method (both of which are exposed by the `Page` class).

Now that we have the route handler written, the final piece to the puzzle is to attach this `RouteHandler` to a route definition:

```
context.MapRoute("AspCompatRoute", "{controller/{action}",
                new { controller = "Home", action = "Index"}
                ).RouteHandler = new AspCompatHandler();
```

If you now run the same code to retrieve the current `ApartmentState`, you'll see that the controller is now executing in STA mode.

And, since requests are running in STA threads, COM doesn't have to create its own STA threads in order to execute calls to COM components. Further, since the COM components live in their creators' STAs, they can all execute independently of each other, allowing for true parallel execution.

Summary

This chapter introduced you to the major concepts of routes and routing in the ASP.NET MVC Framework. We started by explaining why thinking about the URLs of your application is important, both from a usability standpoint and from an SEO standpoint.

We then moved on to demonstrate how to create new routes by using the `RouteTable.MapRoute()` method, which adds routes to the static `RouteTable` dictionary, as well as how to form different structures of route URL.

Next, we looked at how to create and use route constraints to control the values the users can submit to your applications via routes, as well as how to create custom route constraints for your application.

Finally, we looked at an alternative way to create routes using an attribute-based approach, as well as some of the lower-level extensibility points in the ASP.NET MVC routing pipeline. You should now understand routing in the ASP.NET MVC Framework.

Reusable UI Components

So far, you have seen a variety of options for creating reusable components for your ASP.NET MVC application. However, these options allow you to create views or actions that can be reused only within a single project. In other words, they are more "shareable" components than truly "reusable ones," since you cannot use them outside of your project without resorting to "code reuse" (aka "copy/paste").

In this chapter, you'll learn how to create truly reusable components that can be used as a library across different projects.

What ASP.NET MVC Offers out of the Box

Before we take a deep dive into creating cross-project reusable components, let's take a quick look at what ASP.NET MVC offers out of the box.

Partial Views

Partial views allow you to create reusable content. In order to remain truly reusable, partial views should contain little or no functional logic, as they represent a modular unit of layout in a larger view. Partial views are files that have the same *.cshtml* or *.vbhtml* extension but are created under the */Views/Shared/* folder. To render them, you use the syntax `@Html.Partial("_partialViewName")` as shown below:

```
@Html.Partial("_Auction")
```

HtmlHelper Extensions or Custom HtmlHelpers

Custom HTML helpers are extension methods applied to the `HtmlHelper` class that can be used in views to output clean HTML. They follow the same rules as partial views—i.e., having no functional logic and representing a small unit of layout—but are more focused. A common example is an `HTMLHelper` extension that renders a text box along with a matching label, often for accessibility purposes:

```
@Html.TextBoxAccessible("FirstName", @Model.FirstName)
```

And here's the corresponding extension code:

```
public static class HtmlHelperExtensions
{
    public static HtmlString TextBoxAccessible(this HtmlHelper html, string id, ↵
    string text)
    {
        return new HtmlString(html.Label(id)
                + html.TextBox(id, text).ToString());
    }
}
```

Display and Editor Templates

Display and editor templates were introduced in ASP.NET MVC 2 and allow you to create strongly typed views such as:

```
@Html.DisplayFor(model => model.Product)
```

Display and editor templates are partial views located in the *DisplayTemplates* or *EditorTemplates* subfolders under the controller (or under *Views\Shared*). For example, if you create a partial view called *Product.cshtml* in *Views\Shared\DisplayTemplates* or *Views\Product\DisplayTemplates*, with some markup to display a "Product" in a certain way, `@Html.DisplayFor(model ⇒ model.Product)` will use this `DisplayTemplate` to render a `Product`:

```
@model Product

@if (Model != null) {
    <!-- Markup to render a product -->
}
```

If it cannot match a type to a template, it'll fall back to the `.ToString()` representation of the object.

Since they are often tied to a specific model, these templates can contain a certain amount of business logic. Being strongly typed, they also help catch errors during compile time, rather than at runtime.

Html.RenderAction()

The `RenderAction()` helper method executes a controller action and then inserts the HTML output into the parent view. Because of this, `RenderAction()` allows for reuse of functional logic as well as layout. This HTML helper is used when the layout is complex and often when the business logic needs to be reused.

Taking It a Step Further

The previously discussed options work well when it comes to reusing a component within the same application. Multiple controller actions can reference the same view when the shared view lives in the same folder as the other views for that controller or in the website's *Shared* folder, and different views can call custom helpers within themselves to reuse the presentation logic. But how do you share views/components across projects?

In the ASP.NET Web Forms world, you can achieve this by creating user controls or custom controls that can be compiled into standalone assemblies. These assemblies can be distributed across projects, thereby enabling their reuse across projects.

The Web Forms view engine offers the `ViewUserControl` class, which can be leveraged to create such components for the MVC framework. The Razor view engine in ASP.NET MVC, however, does not offer any such method out of the box. In this section, you'll see how you can achieve something similar using the Razor API.

The Razor Single File Generator

Razor views are really just fancy designers that eventually generate .NET code that can be compiled into assemblies, and compiled assemblies are certainly reusable across projects! Thus, what you need is a tool that can take the Razor views that you author in a separate project and run the Razor API directly against them to generate .NET code. Though this chapter gives you all the information you need to build such a tool, the good news is that you don't have to. Some folks in the open source community have already created it for you!

Installing the Razor Single File Generator

Though the complete source code is hosted on CodePlex, the Razor Single File Generator installer is available in the Visual Studio Extensions Gallery, so the easiest way to get started with the Generator is to install it from the Gallery. Open the Visual Studio Extension Manager (Tools→Extension Manager...) and search the Online Gallery for "Razor Generator," as shown in Figure 15-1.

After the Razor Generator is installed (be sure to restart Visual Studio!), create a new project to house the shared views. Aside from the fact that you will be applying a custom tool to your view files, there is nothing special about this new project. Just create a new Class Library project (as shown in Figure 15-2) in the solution that you've been working in and name it *ReusableComponents*.

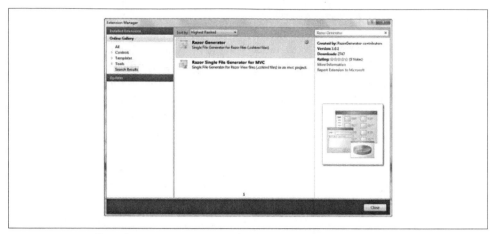

Figure 15-1. Installing the Razor Generator in the Extension Manager

Figure 15-2. Creating the new Class Library project for reusable views

Creating Reusable ASP.NET MVC Views

One of the most widely used scenarios for a view that is shared across projects is a generic error page. So let's create one and see how the Razor Single File Generator handles ASP.NET MVC views.

Creating reusable ASP.NET MVC views with the Razor Single File Generator is almost the same as creating views within an ASP.NET MVC project itself. When you create a folder structure similar to the ~/Views folder convention that ASP.NET MVC expects, the only thing you have to do is associate the views with the Razor Single File Generator by setting each view's *Custom Tool* property to *RazorGenerator*.

Since the new *ReusableComponents* class library is not an ASP.NET MVC project, it will not have the ~/Views folder, so go ahead and create one. The new view you are about to add will be used across multiple controllers, so the class library's folder structure should reflect this: create another folder directly under ~/Views named *Shared*, mirroring the ASP.NET MVC application folder convention. When you're done, the *ReusableComponents* class library should look like Figure 15-3.

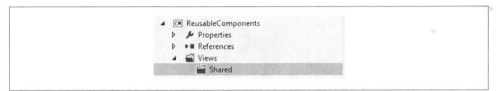

Figure 15-3. The ReusuableComponents project with the ~/Views folder structure

Now that the folder structure is in place, add a new file named *GenericError.cshtml* to the *Shared* folder by right-clicking on it and selecting Add→New Item... from the context menu. Since the project is a Class Library project and not an ASP.NET MVC project, Visual Studio will refuse to show the *MVC 4 View Page (Razor)* item type. That's OK; just choose another plain-content item type such as *Text File* or *HTML Page*. Since your new item (*GenericError.cshtml*) has the *.cshtml* file extension, Visual Studio will know that it is a Razor template.

Though Visual Studio recognizes the new file as a Razor template, you need to tell the Razor Single File Generator to start generating code from that template. To wire up the Generator, open up the properties for the *GenericError.cshtml* file and set its *Custom Tool* property to *RazorGenerator*. Figure 15-4 shows a properly configured Razor Generator.

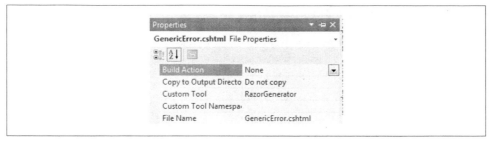

Figure 15-4. Setting the RazorGenerator Custom Tool property

Completely replace any content in the new *GenericError.cshtml* file with the following Razor markup:

```
@{ Layout = null; }
<html>
<head>
    <title>Website Error!</title>
    <style>
        body { text-align: center; background-color: #6CC5C3; }
        .error-details .stack-trace { display: none; }
        .error-details:hover .stack-trace { display: block; }
    </style>
</head>
<body>
    <h2>We're sorry, but our site has encountered an error!</h2>
    <img src="http://bit.ly/pjnXyE" />

@if (ViewData["ErrorMessage"] != null) {
    <div class="error-details">
        <h2>@ViewData["ErrorMessage"]</h2>
        <div class="stack-trace">@ViewData["StackTrace"]</div>
    </div>
}
</body>
</html>
```

Immediately after you specify the *Custom Tool* property, you should see that the Razor Single File Generator has generated the class *GenericError.cs*, grouped underneath *GenericError.cshtml* (Figure 15-5).

Figure 15-5. New file generated by the Razor Generator

If you do not see the generated file, something has gone wrong! Be sure that you have spelled the name of the custom tool correctly (`RazorGenerator`, with no spaces). If it still does not work, try going back and following the steps from the beginning of this section. Make sure that you restart Visual Studio after installing the Razor Generator tool and check all the installation logs to make sure that there were no errors during installation.

Feel free to open this new file and inspect its generated contents. The generated code acts like any other code, compiling into an assembly that you can share with any number of websites.

Including Precompiled views in an ASP.NET MVC web application

After following the steps in this section you are left with a project library filled with precompiled ASP.NET MVC Razor views. So now what? Due to the standard conventions that the ASP.NET MVC Razor view engine uses, the view engine will not be able to locate views outside of its standard search paths (the *Views* folders in the ASP.NET MVC web application), so it has no idea that your precompiled views even exist, let alone how to execute them.

The answer to this problem is to use the `PrecompiledMvcEngine`, a custom view engine built by the developers of the Razor Single File Generator that extends the core Razor view engine to look for precompiled views. The easiest way to begin using the `PrecompiledMvcEngine` is to use the NuGet Package Manager to install the *PrecompiledMvcEngine* package to the class library project that contains your precompiled views. The *PrecompiledMvcEngine* package adds several artifacts to your project:

Several web.config files
> The Razor API and Visual Studio Razor IntelliSense assume that Razor views live within a web application project, and read their configuration information from the project's *web.config* files. Even though your project is a class library project, the *web.config* files that the *PrecompiledMvcEngine* package adds give Visual Studio enough information to enable Razor IntelliSense, even for views that use the Razor Single File Generator.

A sample Razor view
> The *PrecompiledMvcEngine* package adds a sample Razor view named *Test.cshtml* in the project's *~/Views/Home* folder to show how precompiled views should be configured. If everything is working properly, you should see this view generate a code-behind (*Test.cs*) file immediately. The *Test.cshtml* view is just a reference, so you can modify it as you wish, rename it, or even delete it entirely.

~/App_Start/PrecompiledMvcViewEngineStart.cs
> Though its name is not important, the *PrecompiledMvcViewEngineStart.cs* file contains logic (shown below) that tells your ASP.NET MVC application to use the `PrecompiledMvcEngine` for all the precompiled Razor views in this class library

project. The *PrecompiledMvcViewEngineStart.cs* file also includes the `WebActiva tor.PreApplicationStartMethod` attribute, which tells the `WebActivator` library to execute the `PrecompiledMvcViewEngineStart.Start()` method when the web application starts up, registering the `PrecompiledMvcEngine` in the web application's `ViewEngines` collection. The contents of the *PrecompiledMvcViewEngineStart.cs* file look like this:

```
[assembly: WebActivator.PreApplicationStartMethod(
    typeof(ReusableComponents.App_Start.PrecompiledMvcViewEngineStart),
    "Start"
)]

public static class PrecompiledMvcViewEngineStart {
    public static void Start() {
        var currentAssembly = typeof(PrecompiledMvcViewEngineStart).Assembly;
        var engine = new PrecompiledMvcEngine(currentAssembly);
        ViewEngines.Engines.Insert(0, engine);
        VirtualPathFactoryManager.RegisterVirtualPathFactory(engine);
    }
}
```

Once the *PrecompiledMvcViewEngine* NuGet package is installed and you've moved the *~/Views/Home/Index.cshtml* file from the sample blog site to the *ReusableComponents* class library project, you should be able to run the website and see that everything works just as it did before. ASP.NET MVC now executes the precompiled *Index.cshtml* file from the class library, not caring that the file did not exist in its local *~/Views* folder. But how did the `PrecompiledMvcViewEngine` know which view to render?

We've seen that the `PrecompiledMvcViewEngine` knows how to render precompiled Razor views in an ASP.NET MVC application and that `PrecompiledMvcViewEngineStart` takes care of registering the `PrecompiledMvcViewEngine` with the web application, so there is only one missing piece in the puzzle: locating the precompiled view. Though it may be surprising, the `PrecompiledMvcViewEngine` still relies on the ASP.NET MVC *Views* folder convention, using relative file paths to locate the views. However, this is slightly misleading. The `PrecompiledMvcViewEngine` doesn't look at physical files—it looks for the `System.Web.WebPages.PageVirtualPathAttribute` that the Razor Single File Generator adds to every view that it generates, which includes the view's relative file path.

The following shows the first few lines of the sample view, *Test.cshtml*, which includes that `PageVirtualPathAttribute`:

```
[System.Web.WebPages.PageVirtualPathAttribute("~/Views/Home/Test.cshtml")]
public class Test : System.Web.Mvc.WebViewPage<dynamic>
```

Since the virtual path name is relative, regardless of whether the *~/Views/Home/Test.cshtml* view resides in the ASP.NET MVC application or in the class library project, its virtual path is the same. Thus, when the ASP.NET MVC application requests the *Test* view in the `Home` Controller, the `PrecompiledMvcViewEngine` knows to use the precompiled *Test.cshtml* view registered with the virtual path *~/Views/Home/Test.cshtml*.

Be sure to add the *PrecompiledMvcEngine* package to the class library project that contains your precompiled views, *not* your ASP.NET MVC web application project. Your web application will need the *PrecompiledMvcEngine* assembly at runtime, but the artifacts that the NuGet package installs to your package are only meant for class library projects that contain precompiled Razor views.

Creating Reusable ASP.NET MVC Helpers

You can also apply the Razor Single File Generator to Razor templates that include Razor helpers to produce a similar result as if the templates resided in an ASP.NET MVC application's *App_Code* folder.

The Razor Single File Generator expects Razor helper templates to live in the *~/Views/ Helpers* folder, so before you can create any helpers you'll need to create this folder. After you create the *Helpers* folder, follow the same steps you followed earlier to add a Razor template file to the new *Helpers* folder. Name the file *TwitterHelpers.cshtml*. Then set the *Custom Tool* property to *RazorGenerator*, just as you did for the ASP.NET MVC view template.

Immediately after setting the property, you should see the autogenerated file *TwitterHelpers.cs*. Open the file and take a look: the Razor Generator has successfully parsed the empty Razor template and generated a C# class for you, ready to hold some helper functions.

An empty class doesn't do you any good, however, so let's create a helper function using the standard Razor syntax:

```
@helper TweetButton(string url, string text) {
    <script src="http://platform.twitter.com/widgets.js" type="text/javascript">
    </script>
    <div>
        <a href="http://twitter.com/share" class="twitter-share-button"
            data-url="@url" data-text="'@text'">Tweet</a>
    </div>
}
```

Saving the file and switching back to the generated *TwitterHelpers.cs* file shows that it's been updated again in real time. This time the static helper class contains the code for our custom TweetButton helper. Example 15-1 contains the complete autogenerated code (the comments and some whitespace have been removed for better readability).

Example 15-1. Auto-generated MvcHelper code

```
namespace ReusableComponents.Views.Helpers
{
    using System;
    using System.Collections.Generic;
    using System.IO;
    using System.Linq;
    using System.Net;
```

```
using System.Text;
using System.Web;
using System.Web.Helpers;
using System.Web.Mvc;
using System.Web.Mvc.Ajax;
using System.Web.Mvc.Html;
using System.Web.Routing;
using System.Web.Security;
using System.Web.UI;
using System.Web.WebPages;

[System.CodeDom.Compiler.GeneratedCodeAttribute("RazorGenerator", "1.1.0.0")]
public static class TwitterHelpers
{
    public static System.Web.WebPages.HelperResult
                       TweetButton(string url, string text) {
        return new System.Web.WebPages.HelperResult(__razor_helper_writer => {
            WebViewPage.WriteLiteralTo(@__razor_helper_writer,
                "<script src=\"http://platform.twitter.com/widgets.js\" "+
                "type=\"text/javascript\">" +
                "</script>\r\n");

            WebViewPage.WriteLiteralTo(@__razor_helper_writer,
                "<div>\r\n" +
                "<a href=\"http://twitter.com/share\" "+
                "class=\"twitter-share-button data-url=\""
            );

            WebViewPage.WriteTo(@__razor_helper_writer, url);

            WebViewPage.WriteLiteralTo(@__razor_helper_writer, "\" data-text=\"\'");

            WebViewPage.WriteTo(@__razor_helper_writer, text);

            WebViewPage.WriteLiteralTo(@__razor_helper_writer,
                "\'\">Tweet</a>\r\n" +
                "</div>\r\n"
            );
        });
    }
}
```

With the autogenerated class in place, ASP.NET MVC websites that reference the *ReusableComponents* assembly will be able to use the TweetButton helper just like any other helper method defined in the website's *App_Code* folder.

For example:

```
@using ReusableComponents.Views.Helpers
<div>
    @TwitterHelpers.TweetButton(url, message)
</div>
```

Unit Testing Razor Views

Many best practices advocate keeping the logic in your views as limited and simple as possible. However, the ability to execute unit tests against Razor-based MVC views can still be beneficial in some scenarios.

Take a look at the code snippet below for an example of an ASP.NET MVC Razor view:

```
<p>
    Order ID:
    <span id='order-id'>@Model.OrderID</span>
</p>
<p>
    Customer:
    @(Html.ActionLink(
        @Model.CustomerName,
        "Details", "Customer",
        new { id = @Model.CustomerID },
        null))
</p>
```

The default ASP.NET MVC Razor view class exposes properties such as `Model`, `Html`, etc., that this view relies on. Thus, in order to compile and execute the view outside of the ASP.NET MVC runtime, you must create a custom template base class that implements these properties as well. This next example contains a snippet from the `OrderInfoTemplateBase` class, modified to include the `Model` and `Html` properties so that it may be used to compile the previous view:

```
public abstract class OrderInfoTemplateBase
{
    public CustomerOrder Model { get; set; }
    public HtmlHelper Html { get; set; }
}
```

The `OrderInfoTemplateBase` class now fulfills the template's dependencies on the ASP.NET MVC base classes, causing it to act as a stand-in for the ASP.NET MVC base classes. Introducing custom base classes such as `OrderInfoTemplateBase` provides you with complete control over the properties and functionality provided to the template. Custom base classes also alleviate the need to execute ASP.NET MVC views within the ASP.NET MVC runtime.

Example 15-2 shows the power of swapping production components with mock objects.

Example 15-2. Unit test executing a Razor template instance using mock objects

```
public void ShouldRenderLinkToCustomerDetails()
{
    var mockHtmlHelper = new Mock<HtmlHelper>();
    var order = new CustomerOrder()
        {
            OrderID = 1234,
            CustomerName = "Homer Simpson",
```

```
    };

    // Create the instance and set the properties
    var template = (OrderInfoTemplateBase)Activator.CreateInstance(/*...*/);

    template.Html = mockHtmlHelper.Object;
    template.Model = customerOrder;

    template.Execute();

    // Verify that the link was generated
    mockHtmlHelper.Verify(htmlHelper =>
        htmlHelper.ActionLink(
            order.CustomerName,
            "Details", "Customer",
            It.IsAny<object>()
        )
    );
}
```

By replacing the production `HtmlHelper` class with a mock implementation, the unit test can easily make assertions against—and therefore confirm the validity of—code in the view without relying on the ASP.NET MVC runtime.

 If you are using the Razor Single File Generator to create reusable views, you do not need to use reflection-based approaches such as `Activator.CreateInstance()`.

Since the Razor Single File Generator generates actual classes, all you need to do is create a new instance of the class (e.g., `var template = new CustomerOrderTemplate();`) and run tests against the new instance.

The ability to inject mock and stub objects to take the place of production types is a great boon for unit tests. Without this ability, most sites must resort to running all UI tests through slow and unreliable browser-based testing. In stark contrast, injecting mock and stub objects allows developers to create unit tests that execute in mere milliseconds.

Summary

ASP.NET MVC offers many ways to create reusable components. Partial views, display and editor templates, HTML helpers/functions, and `RenderAction()` offer easy ways to reuse components within a single project. Using the Razor API, it is also possible to create reusable components that can be shared across projects. This chapter walked you through installing and using the Razor Single File Generator to create reusable views. Finally, you learned how to unit test the views, using mock objects.

Quality Control

Logging

Software bugs are a fact of life—no matter how much thought you put into your application's architecture or how well you write your code, sooner or later you will experience issues.

In order to minimize the impact that these errors can have on your site, you need to treat error handling and logging just like you would treat any other important feature: by planning to put it into your project and your application design as early as possible.

In this chapter, we'll take a look at the error handling, logging, and monitoring tools that you can use to help increase your application's performance, and we'll track down issues when they arise.

Error Handling in ASP.NET MVC

There are plenty of things that can go wrong when your application is busy processing an HTTP request. Fortunately, ASP.NET MVC makes it relatively easy to handle all of these situations with ease.

Since ASP.NET MVC applications run on top of the core ASP.NET Framework, they have access to the same core framework capabilities as Web Forms applications, including the ability to set up a custom error page to handle specific status codes when they occur.

Let's see how to deal with errors in your ASP.NET MVC web application by deliberately introducing an exception to the Ebuy reference application. To introduce the exception, open up the HomeController and add code to throw a new exception into the About controller action:

```
public ActionResult About()
{
    ViewBag.Message = "Your quintessential app description page.";

    throw new Exception("Something went wrong!");
}
```

To trigger this exception, simply run your site and navigate to the */home/about* URL, which should greet you with the standard ASP.NET error page (Figure 16-1).

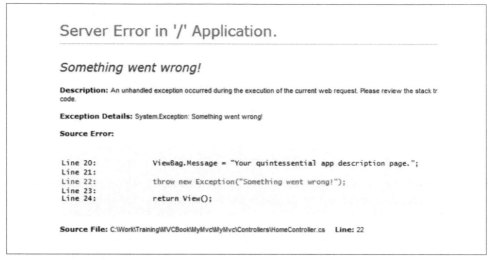

Figure 16-1. Standard ASP.NET error page

Now that the site is producing an exception, let's add the proper error handling to deal with it!

Enabling Custom Errors

The first step to handling errors in an ASP.NET MVC application is the same as in any ASP.NET application: enabling ASP.NET's *custom errors* feature.

This feature offers three modes:

On
> Enables custom error handling, displaying the custom error pages when different errors occur.

Off
> Disables custom error handling, displaying the default diagnostic error page whenever an error occurs.

RemoteOnly
> Enables custom error handling, but only for requests that originate from a remote machine. If you access your application from the server it's hosted on, you will see the default diagnostic error page to help debug issues with your application. Your users, however, will continue to see the custom error pages.

To enable custom errors, simply change the `mode` attribute of the `system.web > customErrors` configuration setting in the application's *web.config* file to either `On` or `RemoteOnly`:

```
<customErrors mode="On" defaultRedirect="GenericErrorPage.htm">
    <error statusCode="404" redirect="~/error/notfound"></error>
</customErrors>
```

With this configuration in place, the next step is to enhance the default ASP.NET MVC error handling experience.

Handling Errors in Controller Actions

While enabling custom error handling gives you the ability to display a custom error page whenever an error occurs in your site, there may be times when a custom error page simply isn't enough.

For these cases, ASP.NET MVC offers the `HandleErrorAttribute`, which provides you with much more fine-grained control over what happens when errors occur in your controller actions.

The `HandleErrorAttribute` exposes two properties:

`ExceptionType`
> The type of exception to handle

`View`
> The name of the view to display when the given exception type is encountered

Just apply this attribute to any controller action to tell it how to react when a given exception occurs.

For instance, whenever a database exception (`System.Data.DataException`) occurs during the execution of the `Auction` action in the following example, ASP.NET MVC will display the *DatabaseError* view:

```
[HandleError(ExceptionType = typeof(System.Data.DataException),
View = "DatabaseError")]]
public ActionResult Auction(long id)
{
    var db = new EbuyDataContext();
    return View("Auction", db.Auctions.Single(x => x.Id == id));
}
```

Like most other controller action attributes, the `HandleErrorAttribute` may also be placed at the controller level so that it applies to all the actions in the controller:

```
[HandleError(ExceptionType = typeof(System.Data.DataException),
View = "DatabaseError")]]
public class AuctionsController : Controller
{
    /* Controller actions with HandleError applied to them */
}
```

Defining Global Error Handlers

If you'd like to go even higher in the hierarchy than the controller level, you can also apply the HandleErrorAttribute to the entire site by registering it as a global error handler.

To register a global error handler, open the */App_Start/FilterConfig.cs* file and find the RegisterGlobalFilters() method. Here you can see that the ASP.NET MVC template has already registered a global HandleErrorAttribute to the GlobalFilterCollection for you.

To register your own custom logic, simply add your custom filter to the global filter collection:

```
public static void RegisterGlobalFilters(GlobalFilterCollection filters)
{
    filters.Add(new HandleErrorAttribute
    {
        ExceptionType = typeof(System.Data.DataException),
        View = "DatabaseError"
    });

    filters.Add(new HandleErrorAttribute());
}
```

Keep in mind that, by default, global filters are executed in the order that they are registered, so be sure to register error filters for specific exception types before any other, more generic error filters (as shown above).

Alternatively, you may provide a second parameter to the filters.Add() method to specify the order of execution for the filters, like so:

```
public static void RegisterGlobalFilters(GlobalFilterCollection filters)
{
    filters.Add(new HandleErrorAttribute
    {
        ExceptionType = typeof(System.Data.DataException),
        View = "DatabaseError"
    }, 1);

    filters.Add(new HandleErrorAttribute(), 2);
}
```

Here you can see the ordinal values 1 and 2 applied when each filter is registered. This will guarantee that our custom DatabaseError filter will always execute before the more generic error handler.

Customizing the error page

When custom errors are enabled, the global HandleError filter you added intercepts the error and redirects to the error page (see Figure 16-2).

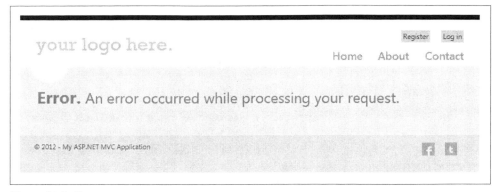

Figure 16-2. Custom error page

 The HandleErrorAttribute only handles 500 errors (exceptions) raised by the ASP.NET MVC pipeline; you will need to define custom error rules for the other types of HTTP errors, such as 404.

If custom errors are enabled and you are using the HandleErrorAttribute, the ASP.NET MVC runtime looks for the *Error.chtml* file in the current requests folder or in the shared views folder. In this setup, the defaultRedirect (to *GenericErrorPage.htm*) and status code redirect URI are ignored.

If custom errors are enabled and you are *not* using the HandleErrorAttribute, the application will redirect the user to the defaultRedirect attribute in *web.config*. To demonstrate this behavior, comment out the call to FilterConfig.RegisterGlobalFilters(GlobalFilters.Filters); in *Global.asax.cs* .

The ASP.NET MVC project templates include a default error page (*~/Views/Shared/Error.cshtml*) that you can customize for your application. The HTML for the default error page looks like this:

```
@model System.Web.ASP.NET MVC.HandleErrorInfo

@{
    ViewBag.Title = "Error";
}

<hgroup class="title">
    <h1 class="error">Error.</h1>
    <h2 class="error">An error occurred while processing your request.</h2>
</hgroup>
```

The default error page is very basic, so you're going to want to spruce it up a bit with your own custom content. For example, you may want to provide information on how users can contact your customer support services to help resolve the problem.

The default error page is also a strongly typed view that references the `HandleError Info` model class. This class exposes properties with information about the exception that triggered the error page, as well as the controller action where the error occurred.

Logging and Tracing

When an issue occurs in your application, you need as much information as possible to track down and fix whatever caused it. And while displaying error pages is a great way to inform users that an application exception has occurred, it doesn't do anything to let *you*, the developer, know about the problem.

In order for you to find out about any issues that occur on your site, you must add logic to your application to enable it to keep a record of what it does and any problems it may experience. This record keeping is referred to as *logging*, and it is perhaps the most important tool in your debugging arsenal.

Logging Errors

When it comes to logging exceptions in your ASP.NET MVC web application, you have plenty of options.

A Simple Logging Helper

The following examples refer to a custom logging helper called `Logger`, shown below. This class logs exceptions to the local machine event log, and if you are trying this code on your machine, you will first need to create an event source for your application.

```
public class Logger
{
    public static void LogException(Exception ex)
    {
        EventLog log = new EventLog();
        log.Source = "Ebuy";
        log.WriteEntry(ex.Message);
    }
}
```

The easiest way to do this is to use *regedit.exe* to add a new key called *Ebuy* to the registry hive at `HKEY_LOCAL_MACHINE\SYSTEM\CurrentControlSet\Services\Eventlog \Application`.

Simple try/catch handler

Your first option is to place a `try/catch` block inside each of your controller's controller actions, as shown below:

```
public ActionResult About()
{
    try
```

```
    {
        ViewBag.Message = "Your quintessential app description page.";
        throw new Exception("Something went wrong!");
    }
    catch (Exception ex)
    {
        LogException(ex);
    }

    return View();
}
```

However, this approach requires you to add a lot of code to each controller method, and it should be avoided unless there is a specific type of exception you want to handle directly or you have some special requirement for logging.

Overriding Controller.OnException()

Rather than adding **try/catch** blocks to each controller method, you can instead override the OnException() method of your controller, like so:

```
protected override void OnException(ExceptionContext filterContext)
{
    if (filterContext == null)
        base.OnException(filterContext);

    LogException(filterContext.Exception);

    if (filterContext.HttpContext.IsCustomErrorEnabled)
    {
        // If the global handle error filter is enabled, this is not needed
        filterContext.ExceptionHandled = true;
        this.View("Error").ExecuteResult(this.ControllerContext);
    }
}
```

An even better option would be to create a base controller so you only have the logging code in one place. When you override the method, you should make sure the context passed in is not null and mark the exception as handled. If you don't mark the exception as handled, it will continue to propagate up the ASP.NET MVC pipeline.

> If you are using the HandleError global filter shown earlier, you should remove the code for marking the exception handled and for displaying the error view, since the global filter will have already handled the error.

Custom error filters

Yet another option for handling errors in an ASP.NET MVC application is to create a custom error filter. Custom error filters allow you to define error handling logic in one place and apply it throughout your site, limiting the amount of duplicate code that you have to maintain. Custom error filters also allow controllers to stay focused on the logic of processing requests, rather than worrying about what to do when exceptions occur.

To create a custom error filter, inherit from the `HandleErrorAttribute` class and override the `OnException()` method. After you log the exception, you should check to see if custom errors are enabled:

```
public class CustomHandleError : HandleErrorAttribute
{
    public override void OnException(ExceptionContext filterContext)
    {
        if (filterContext == null)
            base.OnException(filterContext);

        LogException(filterContext.Exception);

        if (filterContext.HttpContext.IsCustomErrorEnabled)
        {
            filterContext.ExceptionHandled = true;
            base.OnException(filterContext);
        }
    }

    private void LogException(Exception ex)
    {
        EventLog log = new EventLog();
        log.Source = "Ebuy";
        log.WriteEntry(ex.Message);
    }
}
```

ASP.NET Health Monitoring

While logging to the event log is a good first step in monitoring your application, an even better option is to enable *ASP.NET health monitoring*. ASP.NET health monitoring goes beyond logging exceptions to include monitoring events that occur during an application and a request's lifetime.

The ASP.NET health monitoring system monitors the following events:

- Application lifetime events, including when an application starts or stops.
- Security events, such as failed login attempts and URL authorization requests.
- Application errors, including unhandled exceptions, request validation exceptions, compilation errors, etc.

ASP.NET health monitoring is configured through the `healthMonitoring` section of your application's *web.config* file, which contains three main subsections:

eventMappings
    Defines the types of events you want to monitor

providers
    Defines the list of available providers

rules
    Defines the mapping between events and the providers used for logging an event

You configure ASP.NET health monitoring as follows:

```
<healthMonitoring enabled="true">
  <eventMappings>
    <clear />
    <!-- Log ALL error events -->
    <add name="All Errors"
        type="System.Web.Management.WebBaseErrorEvent"
        startEventCode="0"
        endEventCode="2147483647" />
    <!-- Log application startup/shutdown events -->
    <add name="Application Events"
        type="System.Web.Management.WebApplicationLifetimeEvent"
        startEventCode="0"
        endEventCode="2147483647" />
  </eventMappings>
  <providers>
    <clear />
    <add connectionStringName="DefaultConnection"
        maxEventDetailsLength="1073741823"
        buffer="false"
        name="SqlWebEventProvider"
        type="System.Web.Management.SqlWebEventProvider" />
  </providers>
  <rules>
    <clear />
    <add name="All Errors Default"
        eventName="All Errors"
        provider="SqlWebEventProvider"
        profile="Default"
        minInstances="1"
        maxLimit="Infinite"
        minInterval="00:00:00" />
    <add name="Application Events Default"
        eventName="Application Events"
        provider="SqlWebEventProvider"
        profile="Default"
        minInstances="1"
        maxLimit="Infinite"
        minInterval="00:00:00" />
  </rules>
</healthMonitoring>
```

Out of the box, ASP.NET health monitoring includes providers for logging to a Microsoft SQL Server database, logging to the local event log, as well as notifying administrators via email. It also allows you to create your own health monitoring providers that enable you to log to additional data sources.

 To use the SQL database health monitoring provider, you need to add the necessary tables to your web application database using the aspnet_regsql.exe command located in your .NET Framework directory.

Now that you have health monitoring enabled, you need to update the custom error filter you previously created so it logs exceptions to the health monitoring providers you just set up.

Since the health monitoring system's System.Web.Management.WebRequestErrorEvent class does not have any public constructors, you must first create a custom web request error event class:

```
public class CustomWebRequestErrorEvent : WebRequestErrorEvent
{
        public CustomWebRequestErrorEvent(
            string message, object eventSource,
            int eventCode, Exception exception)
          : base(message, eventSource, eventCode, exception)
    {
    }

        public CustomWebRequestErrorEvent(
            string message, object eventSource, int eventCode,
            int eventDetailCode, Exception exception)
          : base( message, eventSource, eventCode,
                eventDetailCode, exception)
    {
    }
}
```

After you create the class, update CustomHandleError to call the custom web request error class:

```
public class CustomHandleError : HandleErrorAttribute
{
    public override void OnException(ExceptionContext filterContext)
    {
        if (filterContext.HttpContext.IsCustomErrorEnabled)
        {
            base.OnException(filterContext);
            new CustomWebRequestErrorEvent(
                "An unhandled exception has occurred.",
                this, 103005, filterContext.Exception)
                .Raise();
        }
    }
}
```

With this class in place—and registered as a global error filter—all of your site's exceptions will now be routed to the ASP.NET health monitoring system.

Summary

When designing and building a web application, it's important to consider how you will handle errors, log and monitor events that occur while your application is running, and tune your application to increase performance.

In this chapter, you learned about the powerful built-in features of ASP.NET for error handling, logging, and health monitoring. You can leverage all of these techniques to build a rock-solid web application using the ASP.NET MVC Framework.

Automated Testing

Throughout this book , we've promoted architectural patterns and application development practices such as the Model-View-Controller pattern, separation of concerns, SOLID, and others, stating that they make the components in your application more reusable and maintainable, resulting in a higher-quality application. The problem with these techniques is that they focus on long-term benefits whose value is not always apparent in the short term. For instance, why does it matter that a component is extensible, if it never gets extended in the first iteration of an application?

The true value of these techniques really starts to become clear in the later stages of an application's life, when it has been released and developers must be able to fix outstanding issues and add new features while reducing the risk of introducing new breaking changes to the working, released application.

However, these techniques can also provide value in the short term. Luckily, there is one way to take advantage of that value *and* help guarantee the ongoing quality of your application at the same time: by testing your components with automated testing techniques.

This chapter discusses what it takes to test your application, using various tools and techniques to write and exercise your code effectively and verify that it does what it was designed to do. We'll also explore how to apply these concepts to your entire codebase, with an emphasis on testing ASP.NET MVC applications all the way from server-side controllers and services to the client-side code running within the browser.

The Semantics of Testing

Software development focuses on the task of creating software applications that solve problems by performing any number of specific behaviors that we developers call "requirements." But before we put our applications into widespread use (a.k.a. "production"), we must first somehow verify that those behaviors are properly implemented. That is, we must validate that we have written high-quality code that performs in the intended manner and is reliable.

Manual Testing

The easiest way to verify that a feature has been implemented is also the most literal: run the application and attempt to trigger the behavior just like any normal user would do. For the purposes of this chapter, we'll refer to this approach—and any other approach that involves human verification—as *manual testing*, and it has plenty of negatives associated with it.

Humans are error prone

First and foremost, manual testing is based on human judgment, and humans are notoriously error prone.

While a human will eventually need to make the final judgment call to say whether a feature has been implemented correctly or not, most human judgment up to that point is subjective, sometimes to the extent that it becomes impossible for a human to tell whether something works or not.

For instance, even when you are awake, alert, and ready to spot even the smallest bug, will you ever be able to tell the difference between the `string` value 1 and the `int` value 1 just by looking at it on the screen? As any developer who's done any kind of bug fixing knows, these kinds of issues may sound innocuous, but they can end up meaning the difference between an application that works and one that fails miserably.

Computers are more efficient

Next comes the matter of efficiency. When a human user tests an application, he is not instantiating classes and calling methods; he is interacting with the application through some kind of UI.

The user must use the application as it was intended, since changing the application to allow for easier testing may jeopardize the results of the test, or those changes may even introduce bugs themselves.

This often means that a single test to reproduce a particular scenario can involve many steps that must be followed correctly and in a specific order, making manual testing quite tedious and laborious, and making the chances of human error even greater. Computers are much more efficient at performing such procedures.

Manual testing takes time

And then there is the biggest issue: manual testing takes time—human time that could be better spent doing something else.

Consider, for instance, a developer implementing a feature and having to stop after each small change she makes to (correctly) execute a series of potentially complex steps in order to verify that change. Now consider what happens if that small change doesn't work and another change needs to be made. And another, and another...

Now think about how that same developer is supposed to test an *exceptional* condition —a condition that, by its very nature, is very difficult to reproduce!

Clearly, computers are much better suited to performing these types of tasks. The answer to all the problems inherent in manual testing, then, is to automate these tests so that the computer can run them for you.

Automated Testing

Automated testing refers to the idea of writing software that tests other software and, in doing so, helps address the shortcomings of manual testing methods by asking the computer to do what it does best: automating our testing tasks. Using automated testing approaches, humans are still able to define the tests that they'd like to execute— and make assertions against the results of those tests—just as they have always done. The biggest difference is that after an automated test is first created, it can easily be run as many times as needed in order to verify that the test continues to pass. Not only is it easier to run automated tests than it is to execute manual tests, but computers can perform the same tasks exponentially quicker than humans can, drastically reducing the time it takes to achieve the same results!

Clearly, automated testing is the way to go. In the remainder of this chapter, we'll look at the different levels of automated testing, learn how to create an automated test project, and explore some best practices for testing an ASP.NET MVC application.

Levels of Automated Testing

In addition to reducing the time it takes to run tests, automated tests are better able to target specific components, such as the *unit under test* (sometimes referred to as the *system under test*, or SUT), a term that refers to the component whose quality, performance, or reliability is being tested.

In the context of software development, the "unit under test" may refer to any level of software architecture, such as methods, classes, entire applications, or even multiple applications working together. Likewise, it is a good idea to create multiple sets of automated tests, with each set of tests targeting a particular level of the software architecture.

Depending on which architectural layer they target, each set of tests may be classified as *unit tests*, *integration tests*, or *acceptance tests*, and as you'll see in the following sections, each of these categories has a pretty specific meaning.

Unit Tests

Unit tests aim to validate the lowest levels of an application through a very narrow focus. In a unit test, the unit under test is a very specific, low-level component, such as a class or even a single method in a class. In fact, since they are testing such specific, low-level functionality, it often takes a number of unit tests to validate just one unit under test.

The goal of unit tests is to verify the actual logic of the unit under test. In short, failed unit tests should indicate a legitimate bug in the code and nothing else.

In order to accomplish this level of reliability, unit tests must be *atomic*, *repeatable*, *isolated*, and *fast*. Tests that do not meet these four fundamental requirements cannot be considered true "unit tests."

The following sections explain what each concept means in the context of automated testing.

Atomic

A unit test should focus on validating one small piece of functionality. Generally, this will be a single behavior or business case that a class exhibits. Quite often, this focus may be as narrow as a single method in a class (sometimes even a specific condition in a single method). In practice, this equates to short tests with only a couple of deliberate and meaningful assertions (`Assert.That([...])`).

Common pitfalls and code smells include:

- Dozens of lines of code in one test
- More than two or three assertions, especially when they're against multiple objects

Repeatable

A unit test should produce exactly the same result at any time in any environment, given that the environment fulfills a known set of dependencies (e.g., the .NET Framework). Tests cannot rely on anything in the external environment that isn't under your direct control. For instance, you should never have to worry about having network/ Internet connectivity, access to a database, filesystem permissions, or even the time of day (think `DateTime.Now`).

Common pitfalls and code smells include:

- Tests pass on the first execution, yet some or all fail on subsequent executions (or vice versa). For example, you might see a comment like this: "NOTE: The XYZTest must be run prior to this or it will fail!"

Isolated/Independent

As an extension of the first two qualities, a unit test should be completely isolated from any other system or test. That is to say, a unit test should not assume that any other test has been run, or depend on any external system (e.g., database) having a specific state or producing some specific result. Additionally, a unit test should not create or leave behind any artifacts that may trip up other tests. This is certainly not to say that unit tests cannot share methods or even whole classes between one other—in fact, that is encouraged. What this really means is that a unit test should not assume that some other test has run previously or will run subsequently. These dependencies should instead be represented as explicit function calls or be contained in your test fixture's setup and tear-down methods that run prior to and immediately following every single test.

Common pitfalls and code smells include:

- Database access
- Tests fail when your network or VPN connection is disabled
- Tests fail when you have not run some kind of external script (other than perhaps a build script to execute)
- Tests fail when configuration settings change or are not correct
- Tests must be executed under specific permissions

Fast

Assuming all of the above conditions are met, all tests will be fast (i.e., complete in fractions of a second). Regardless, it is still beneficial to explicitly state that all unit tests should execute almost instantaneously. After all, one of the main benefits of an automated test suite is the ability to get near-instant feedback about the current quality of your code. As the time required to run the test suite increases, the frequency with which you execute it decreases. This directly translates into a larger amount of time between when bugs are introduced and when they are actually discovered.

Common pitfalls and code smells include:

- Individual tests take longer than a fraction of a second to run

 Clever readers might notice that the above list could be arranged into a cute little acronym like FAIR. While this can be helpful for remembering the four key characteristics of unit tests, the order used here is deliberate—it represents their rough order of importance.

To help demonstrate these guidelines, here is an example unit test that follows all of them:

```
[TestMethod]
public void CalculatorShouldAddTwoNumbers()
{
    var sum = new Calculator().Add(1, 2);
    Assert.AreEqual(1+2, sum);
}
```

This test is quite simple and straightforward. To begin, it creates a new instance of the Calculator class and calls its Add() method, passing in the two numbers that should be added together. Next, the test uses the `Assert.AreEqual()` method to make the assertion that ensures the `Add()` method did what it was supposed to: add the two numbers.

Not only is this test easy to read and understand, but it also adheres to all of the guidelines above that make for a good unit test:

- First, it is *atomic*: it focuses on validating the behavior of the `Calculator.Add()` method (the unit under test) and nothing more. What's more, it does so in a simple and direct way.

- Second, it is *repeatable*: this test will produce the same result at any time of day, on any developer's machine, no matter how many times it's executed.

- Next, it is *isolated*. The test does not have any preconditions that must be met, nor does it change the state of the testing environment when it's done. It executes independently of any other test.

- Finally, it is *fast*. It's conceivable that buried within that `Add()` method might be a horrible algorithm that takes over an hour to add two numbers, but fortunately that is not the case. This test produces a reliable result within milliseconds.

Integration Tests

As opposed to unit tests—whose sole purpose is to validate the logic or functionality of a specific class or method—*integration tests* exist to validate the interaction (or "integration") between two or more components. In other words, integration tests give the system a good workout to make sure that all of the individual parts work together to achieve the desired result: a working application.

Integration tests do have their drawbacks, however. Since they focus on verifying that multiple components work well together, it becomes increasingly difficult to isolate those components from the outside world while trying to test them. This opens the door to a whole slew of problems, starting with the fact that you usually have to break most—if not all—of the rules outlined above that apply to unit tests.

The slow speed and fragility of integration tests can be major drawbacks. Not only does this mean that they will get executed less frequently than unit tests, but the rate of *false negatives* (test failures that do not correspond to broken application logic) tends to be much higher.

When a unit test fails, it is a sure indication of a bug in the code. In contrast, when an integration test fails, it may mean there is a bug in the code, but the problem could also have been caused by other issues in the testing environment, such as a lost database connection or unexpected test data. These *false positives*—though a useful indicator that something is wrong in the developer's environment—usually just serve to slow down the development process by taking the developer's focus away from writing working code.

Despite this somewhat negative description, integration tests are just as valuable as unit tests—if not more so.

Assuming you strive to avoid potential distractions whenever possible, you should also strive to rely on extensive test coverage via a solid unit test suite, then supplement that coverage with an integration test suite (and not vice versa).

Acceptance Tests

The final type of test is the *acceptance test*, which has one goal: to ensure that the system that has been built meets the requirements that were requested. In short, acceptance tests make sure that the system does everything the users expect it to do.

Since acceptance tests are—by their very definition—usually pretty subjective, they are often difficult to automate. That said, there are several different techniques that allow developers to automate the execution of their applications in order to validate that they behave as they should. By applying these techniques, developers are able to avoid tedious manual testing of their applications while still maintaining a high level of confidence that the applications will function in a way that makes their users happy.

User acceptance testing

How do you know when your users are happy with your application? Ask them!

Though this chapter concentrates on developers exercising their own applications in order to verify that they work properly, a subset of acceptance testing named *user acceptance testing* (UAT) brings the user directly into the development process by getting the software into their hands and having them test it. Even if it is generally not wise to expose all of your users to a product that is, perhaps, not final-release quality, user acceptance testing embraces the fact that an application's users are the only ones who can truly call a product "done."

What's more, involving application users in the development process by allowing them to use even a partially working implementation of an application can help expose both technical and communication issues. And the earlier in the process that users are able to provide feedback, the easier and cheaper it is to fix those issues. So, while user acceptance testing may not be easy to automate into your default solution, performing testing early and often can reap great benefits.

 Though anyone may write any of these three types of tests, the first few levels—unit and integration tests—are generally very technical and implementation-specific, so they are usually written by the development team in order to validate that the technical requirements have been met before passing the application on to other groups of testers (e.g., the Quality Assurance, or QA, team) to verify that the business requirements have been met.

What Is an Automated Test Project?

In order to create and execute the kinds of automated tests discussed in this chapter, you will need to create a test project to contain them.

In the Visual Studio world, a *test project* is a relatively normal class library project comprising a group of *test classes* (often referred to as *test fixtures*), each of which is a normal .NET class that contains a set of tests represented as methods of that class. Each of these test methods creates the unit under test, then executes that component to validate its behavior by using the test API to make assertions about the component (such as whether the value of a property is equal to an expected value).

This approach—in which components are created, executed, and validated in that order—is known as the "Arrange-Act-Assert" pattern.

In order to execute automated tests in a test project, the project is compiled and passed to a *test runner*, an application that locates all of the tests within that assembly and executes them, keeping track of the outcome for each test. As the test runner executes each test, it also keeps track of everything that happens during the course of the test, including any console or debug output that the test produces.

As each test succeeds or fails, the test runner displays the results of the test in a summary that allows users to easily see at a glance how many of their tests pass and how many fail.

The following examples use the tools and APIs included by default in all non-Express versions of Visual Studio, but if you are using an Express version of Visual Studio—or if you find yourself at all unhappy with the automated testing tools built into Visual Studio and the .NET Framework—you'll be happy to know that there are several other automated testing tools and frameworks available to choose from, and many of them are open source software. Though they may or may not provide the same level of integration as the Visual Studio tools, they all tend to follow this same basic workflow, so everything you learn in this book should translate quite easily.

It is a good idea to evaluate all of the tools available to you to determine which is the best fit for you and your team. An Internet search for the term ".NET unit testing" should get you started.

Creating a Visual Studio Test Project

There are several ways to create a new Visual Studio unit test project.

The first way is to check the "Create a unit test project" checkbox in the New ASP.NET MVC 4 Project dialog (Figure 17-1), which will automatically create the unit test project and add it to your ASP.NET MVC website solution.

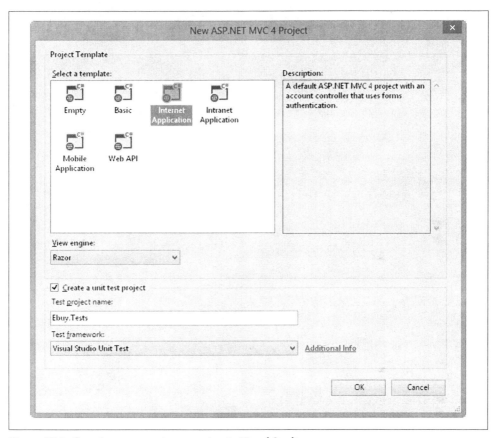

Figure 17-1. Creating a new unit test project in Visual Studio

Alternatively, you can add a new unit test project to an existing solution at any time by selecting File> Add > New Project..., then selecting the Unit Test Project type in the Test category for your favorite language (see Figure 17-2).

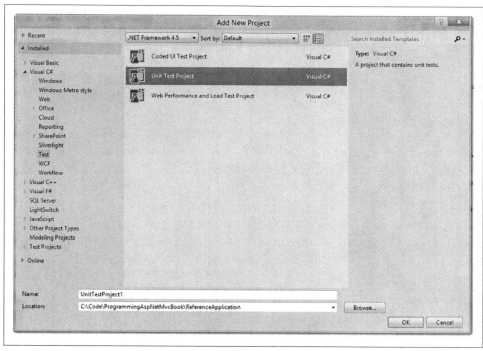

Figure 17-2. Adding a unit test project to an existing application

Either one of these approaches will add a new unit test project to your solution, ready for you to begin adding unit tests.

Creating and Executing a Unit Test

To verify that everything works, try to add a new unit test by right-clicking on a folder in the unit test project and choosing Add > Unit Test... from the context menu. Add your test logic in the method that is created for you, and make use of the testing API's helper functions to help make assertions about your code.

For example, try typing in the following code so that your test class looks like this:

```
using Microsoft.VisualStudio.TestTools.UnitTesting;

namespace Ebuy.Tests
{
    [TestClass]
    public class UnitTestExample
    {
        [TestMethod]
        public void CanAddTwoNumbersTogether()
        {
            var sum = 1 + 2;
            Assert.AreEqual(3, sum);
```

```
        }
      }
    }
```

When you're finished, you can right-click anywhere in the code editor and choose "Run Unit Tests..." (or use the Ctrl-R, T shortcut if you have the default Visual Studio key-bindings) to run the test. This will compile the unit test project (if it needs to be compiled) and bring up the Unit Test Explorer window (Figure 17-3) to show you the status of your running tests. When the test completes, you will see a green checkmark next to it to indicate that the test has passed.

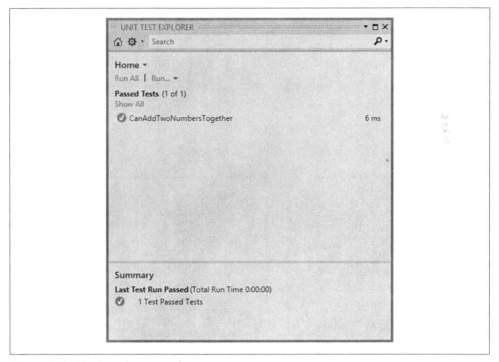

Figure 17-3. Checking the status of your running tests

If the test fails—say, if you somehow break the logic that the test is validating (such as changing var sum = 1 + 2; to var sum = 1 + 3;)—the Unit Test Explorer will display a red cross next to the failed test, as shown in Figure 17-4. Plus, if you click on the failed test in the Unit Test Explorer, you will be able to see the details of why the test failed.

Figure 17-4. The Unit Test Explorer will show you when a test fails, and why

Notice in this example the message `Message: Assert.AreEqual failed. Expected: <3>.`
`Actual: <4>.`, indicating that we told the `Assert.AreEqual()` helper call that the value
should be 3, but the test failed because the actual value at runtime was 4.

Now that you know your way around the Visual Studio unit test project, it's time to
put that knowledge to good use and test your ASP.NET MVC application!

Testing an ASP.NET MVC Application

In order to effectively test your ASP.NET MVC application and ensure that it works
properly at every level, you'll need a suite of automated tests that includes a generous
mix of unit, integration, and acceptance tests.

Though there are plenty of different approaches to accomplish this kind of coverage,
one approach that works very well is to take advantage of ASP.NET MVC's separation
of concerns and test each architectural layer in isolation. As the following sections
show, testing each architectural layer by itself is also a good idea because some testing
techniques work better on some layers than others. However, if you take care to thoroughly test each layer in isolation, you can be much more confident that the layers will
experience few problems when it comes time to test them all together.

Testing the Model

Since the model is arguably the most important part of your application, it is the most logical place to focus most of your testing efforts. As you will see when we test the other layers, the model is also the easiest layer to test, because it is typically the most straightforward and has the fewest external dependencies. In other words, models usually consist of plain old .NET classes that are easy to instantiate and execute in isolation.

To demonstrate, let's write some unit tests that validate the logic in the `Auction.PostBid()` method:

```
public class Auction
{
    public long Id { get; internal set; }
    public decimal CurrentPrice { get; private set; }
    public ICollection<Bid> Bids { get; private set; }

    // ...

    public Bid PostBid(User user, decimal bidAmount)
    {
        if(bidAmount <= CurrentPrice)
            throw new InvalidBidAmountException(bidAmount, CurrentPrice);

        var bid = new Bid(user, bidAmount);

        Bids.Add(bid);

        CurrentPrice = bidAmount;

        return bid;
    }
}
```

Focus on the positive

Before testing any component, you first need to take a moment to define in simple terms what, exactly, the component does. Only then can you write unit tests to validate that behavior! With this information in mind, consider what tests need to be written in order to validate those behaviors, starting with the positive outcomes that you expect to occur in the best-case scenario(s).

In the case of Auction.PostBid(), the method is responsible for adding a winning bid to the auction's bid history and updating the auction's current bid price accordingly. In other words, when the winning bid amount exceeds the current bid amount, the following should happen:

- A new bid should be added to the auction's bid history (`Bids`), containing the user who submitted the bid (`user`) and the bid amount (`bidAmount`).
- The auction's current price (`CurrentPrice`) should be updated with the winning bid amount (`bidAmount`).

Here are those expectations translated into unit tests:

```csharp
using System.Linq;
using Microsoft.VisualStudio.TestTools.UnitTesting;

namespace Ebuy.Tests
{
    [TestClass]
    public class AuctionTests
    {
        [TestMethod]
        public void ShouldAddWinningBidToBidHistory()
        {
            var user = new User();
            var auction = new Auction { CurrentPrice = 1.00m };

            var bid = auction.PostBid(user, 2.00m);

            CollectionAssert.Contains(auction.Bids.ToArray(), bid);
        }

        [TestMethod]
        public void ShouldUpdateCurrentPriceWithWinningBidAmount()
        {
            var user = new User();
            var auction = new Auction { CurrentPrice = 1.00m };

            var bid = auction.PostBid(user, 2.00m);

            Assert.AreEqual(auction.CurrentPrice, 2.00m);
        }
    }
}
```

When you compile and run these tests using the Visual Studio test runner you should see them both pass, indicating that the `Auction.PostBid()` method does what it's supposed to do (see Figure 17-5).

Protect against the negative

Now that we've validated that the `Auction.PostBid()` method does what it's *supposed* to do, let's make sure that it *doesn't* do what it's *not* supposed to do. In other words, let's try to break it!

We'll start by flipping the expected condition around. The previous tests validated what the correct behavior was when the winning bid amount exceeds the current bid amount, so we will now validate what is supposed to happen when the attempted bid amount is *less* than the current bid amount:

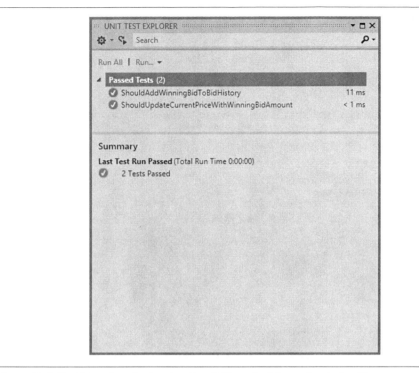

Figure 17-5. Verifying that the Auction.PostBid() method does what it should

```
[TestMethod]
[ExpectedException(typeof(InvalidBidAmountException))]
public void ShouldThrowExceptionWhenBidAmountIsLessThanCurrentBidAmount()
{
    var user = new User();
    var auction = new Auction { CurrentPrice = 1.00m };

    auction.PostBid(user, 0.50m);

    // No assertions because the previous line threw an exception!
}
```

This test tries to post a bid (0.50m) that is less than the current winning bid amount (1.00m) and uses the ExpectedExceptionAttribute to indicate that the logic within the test should throw an exception of type InvalidBidAmountException. If the test finishes executing without throwing the exception, the test is considered a failure.

What might happen when we pass in a null user? The Auction.PostBid() method doesn't currently check for a null user, but it should. Here, we see that it's possible to discover an issue with the code simply by applying the *process* of unit testing, rather than writing a unit test for it.

Test-Driven Development

Instead of correcting the `Auction.PostBid()` code immediately, let's take this opportunity to try a style of automated test authoring called *test-driven development* (also known as *TDD*, or sometimes *test-first development*).

Test-driven development follows the mantra "Red-Green-Refactor," which means that you start with a failing ("red light") test, then write the bare minimum (and perhaps messiest and shameful) code possible in order to get that test to pass ("green light"). Finally, when you've got a passing test in place to guarantee that your code works, circle back and refactor the code you just wrote in order to clean it up and bring it in line with your project's standards.

To apply the TDD approach to the `Auction.PostBid()` method, we must define our goal —to guard against `null` user values—and start in the "red" state with a failing test:

```
[TestMethod]
[ExpectedException(typeof(ArgumentNullException))]
public void ShouldThrowAnExceptionWhenUserIsNull()
{
    var auction = new Auction { CurrentPrice = 1.00m };

    auction.PostBid(null, auction.CurrentPrice + 1);

    // No assertions because the previous line threw an exception!
}
```

This test creates a new auction and attempts to pass a `null` value as the `user` parameter to the `PostBid()` method. This test also uses the `ExpectedExceptionAttribute` to assert that the code within the test triggers the exception that we expect, just as in the previous example.

The difference between what we did in the previous example and what we're doing now is that when we run this test with the current implementation of the `Auction.Post Bid()` method, the test will fail because the method does not yet check to make sure the `user` parameter is not `null`.

Now that we are in the "red" state with a broken test, let's make the test pass.

To do this, simply add a condition that checks to see if the `user` value is `null`:

```
public Bid PostBid(User user, decimal bidAmount)
{
    if(user == null)
        throw new ArgumentNullException("user");

    if(bidAmount <= CurrentPrice)
        throw new InvalidBidAmountException(bidAmount, CurrentPrice);

    var bid = new Bid(user, bidAmount);

    Bids.Add(bid);
```

```
        CurrentPrice = bidAmount;

        return bid;
    }
```

With the null user check in place, our new unit test will pass: we're now in the "green" state.

Typically, after you reach the "green" state with all of your tests passing, you can take some time to circle back and review the code you just wrote to make sure that there are no optimizations that can make it cleaner, faster, or otherwise better.

Writing Clean Automated Tests

Though they are written for an entirely different purpose than "production" code, automated tests are still code, so most of the standard coding practices apply.

Duplicate code

For starters, duplicate code is discouraged just as much in automated tests as it is in production code.

Take the tests that we just wrote, for example. Almost all of them start with the same two lines:

```
var user = new User();
var auction = new Auction { CurrentPrice = 1.00m };
```

Though these two lines create objects that are crucial to executing our tests, they are not particularly relevant to the *logic* that we are testing. For instance, the tests we've written so far don't care what the exact value of the auction's CurrentPrice property is, only that it has one.

Luckily, just about all unit test frameworks provide a way to execute setup code right before every test is executed. The Visual Studio test API supports this by allowing you to use the TestInitializeAttribute to specify a method in the test class that contains the test setup code.

Example 17-1 shows what the example unit test class looks like after applying the TestInitializeAttribute to centralize all of that duplicate code.

Example 17-1. AuctionTests.cs

```
using System;
using System.Linq;
using Microsoft.VisualStudio.TestTools.UnitTesting;

namespace Ebuy.Tests
{
    [TestClass]
    public class AuctionTests
    {
```

```
            private User _user;
            private Auction _auction;

            [TestInitialize]
            public void TestInitialize()
            {
                _user = new User();
                _auction = new Auction { CurrentPrice = 1.00m };
            }

            [TestMethod]
            public void ShouldAddWinningBidToBidHistory()
            {
                var bid = _auction.PostBid(_user, _auction.CurrentPrice + 1);

                CollectionAssert.Contains(_auction.Bids.ToArray(), bid);
            }

            [TestMethod]
            public void ShouldUpdateCurrentPriceWithWinningBidAmount()
            {
                var winningBidAmount = _auction.CurrentPrice + 1;

                _auction.PostBid(_user, winningBidAmount);

                Assert.AreEqual(_auction.CurrentPrice, winningBidAmount);
            }

            [TestMethod]
            [ExpectedException(typeof(InvalidBidAmountException))]
            public void ShouldThrowExceptionWhenBidAmountIsLessThanCurrentBidAmount()
            {
                _auction.PostBid(_user, 0.50m);
            }

            [TestMethod]
            [ExpectedException(typeof(ArgumentNullException))]
            public void ShouldThrowAnExceptionWhenUserIsNull()
            {
                _auction.PostBid(null, _auction.CurrentPrice + 1);
            }
        }
    }
```

As you can see, moving the duplicate initialization logic to the `TestInitialize()` method makes each individual test much simpler and more to the point.

Naming

Since automated test code will never be consumed by an application (other than the test runner), there are a few notable exceptions to standard coding rules. Naming is one area where such exceptions arise. Class and method names are incredibly important in production code because they inform developers how the class or method participates in the application—what a method does or what a class is responsible for.

Naming is equally important in the context of automated testing, with one fundamental difference: test classes always serve the single purpose of acting as containers for test methods, and test methods always serve the single purpose of testing a particular unit. Therefore, test classes should be named for the units that their test methods target, and test methods should describe the behavior that they validate.

Go back and take a look at the class and method names that we've applied to the tests we've shown in this chapter. So far, we've only tested a single target class, so we only have one test class: it is named `AuctionTests`, indicating that all of the methods in the class target the `Auction` class in our model.

The test method names are far more interesting. Notice how the test methods have names that are not only very descriptive, but they almost read like an actual sentence. For example, the `ShouldAddWinningBidToBidHistory` test validates that the `Auction` class should add a winning bid to its bid history. Test method names can be as long as the language will allow (e.g., `ShouldThrowExceptionWhenBidAmountIsLessThanCurrentBidAmount`).

We can feel free to take these liberties with our naming scheme because of the role that test classes and methods serve: they exist to validate our code and alert us to potential issues. So, whenever a test fails, it helps that the name itself is as descriptive as possible. That way, it's very easy to determine which part of the application's logic failed.

Testing Controllers

The great thing about the ASP.NET MVC Framework is that it is written with testability in mind. That means that it's very easy to create an instance of just about any class in the framework and execute it within a unit test, just as we are able to do with our models.

ASP.NET MVC controllers are no exception to this rule—in fact, they are nothing but simple classes, and controller actions are nothing but simple methods!

Take the default `HomeController`, for instance:

```
using System.Web.Mvc;

namespace Ebuy.Website.Controllers
{
    public class HomeController : Controller
    {
        public ActionResult Index()
        {
            ViewBag.Message = "Your app description page.";

            return View();
        }
```

```
        public ActionResult About()
        {
            ViewBag.Message = "Your quintessential app description page.";

            return View();
        }

        public ActionResult Contact()
        {
            ViewBag.Message = "Your quintessential contact page.";

            return View();
        }
    }
}
```

In order to test the HomeController controller actions, all we need to do is create a new instance using the default constructor and call the action. To demonstrate, let's perform a simple test that validates that the Index action returns a view:

```
[TestClass]
public class HomeControllerTests
{
    [TestMethod]
    public void ShouldReturnView()
    {
        var controller = new HomeController();

        var result = controller.Index();

        Assert.IsInstanceOfType(result, typeof(ViewResult));
    }
}
```

Notice how the unit test is able to create an instance of the HomeController and call its action entirely outside of the ASP.NET MVC pipeline. Here is where you start to see the power of the ASP.NET MVC Framework's loose coupling and why controller actions return ActionResult objects rather than executing the rest of the request themselves. Not only does it provide great power and flexibility during the execution of requests; it also allows unit tests to validate the behavior of each part of the request individually.

Testing data access logic

With the HomeController Index action example out of the way, let's move on to an example that involves data access. Take a look at the Auction action of the original AuctionsController implementation from early on in the book, before we refactored it in Chapter 8 to use the more testable repository pattern:

```
public ActionResult Auction(long id)
{
    var db = new EbuyDataContext();
```

```
        var auction = db.Auctions.Find(id);

        return View(auction);
    }
```

Just as with the tests that we wrote previously, we'll start the testing process by defining exactly what this controller action is supposed to do, using normal language. It retrieves the auction with the given Id from the database and displays it in a view. Simple, right?

But when it comes time to write the unit test, some complications arise, such as:

- Do any auctions even exist in the database for the test to retrieve?
- If auctions exist, which Id should the test use to retrieve them?
- And, assuming that auctions exist and we know their Id, how can the test verify that it has retrieved the correct auction? (For example, if the test requests auction 5, how can it test to make sure that it didn't receive auction 8?)

The simple answer to all of these questions is to have the test create an auction in the database so it's guaranteed to have an auction to retrieve every time it runs.

So, let's try that out and see how it works:

```
using Ebuy.Website.Controllers;
using Microsoft.VisualStudio.TestTools.UnitTesting;

namespace Ebuy.Tests.Website.Controllers
{
    [TestClass]
    public class AuctionsControllerTests
    {
        private Auction _auction;

        [TestInitialize]
        public void TestInitialize()
        {
            using(var db = new EbuyDataContext())
            {
                _auction = new Auction { Title = "Test Auction" };
                db.Auctions.Add(_auction);
                db.SaveChanges();
            }
        }

        [TestMethod]
        public void ShouldRetrieveAuctionById()
        {
            var controller = new AuctionsController();

            dynamic result = controller.Auction(_auction.Id);

            Assert.AreEqual(_auction.Id, result.Model.Id);
            Assert.AreEqual(_auction.Title, result.Model.Title);
        }
```

```
        }
    }
```

Notice how this test class leverages the `TestInitialize()` method to add the test auction to the database prior to executing the test logic. The test can then reference the test auction's `Id` value to retrieve the auction from the database. Finally, in order to confirm that the controller action retrieved the correct auction, we ensure that the `Id` and `Title` properties are the same.

Note that before you can run this test successfully, you must first configure the Entity Framework connection string in the test project's configuration. To configure the connection string (if you have not already done so), add the following section to the *App.config* file:

```
<connectionStrings>
<add name="DefaultConnection"
    connectionString="Data Source=(LocalDb)\v11.0;Initial Catalog=EBuy.Tests;↵
    Integrated Security=true"
    providerName="System.Data.SqlClient" />
</connectionStrings>
```

When everything is configured and ready to go, run the test to see that it passes and that your controller works as it should. You have now used automated testing to validate your controller logic!

Refactoring to Unit Tests

Though the tests in the previous example may validate the logic in the `AuctionsController`, they also inadvertently test the data access logic at the same time. While this approach is valuable in that it does a good job of mimicking the integration that will occur in a production environment, it also suffers from all of the unfortunate side effects that integration tests bring to the table, which make these kinds of tests slow and unreliable. The biggest issue with testing two components at the same time comes when the tests fail. How do you easily determine which component is to blame?

The best way to pinpoint issues when they arise is to focus on validating each component's logic with targeted unit tests individually, and *then* put multiple components together to see how well they integrate. As you test each component in your application, stop to consider what, exactly, that component's job is, and be sure that your tests target only that component's behavior and do not accidentally expand to a wider scope.

When writing automated tests—particularly unit tests—it is much easier to focus on the unit under test if you assume that all other components that the unit under test interacts with work as they should.

In fact, when you write tests for all of your components in this way, what you end up with is a comprehensive suite of very focused tests! With this kind of focused automated test suite in place, it is generally much easier to pinpoint problem components when something goes wrong, because the tests that focus on that component will be the ones to break, rather than a bunch of tests for other, unrelated components.

For example, when you write tests for a controller action that retrieves data from a repository and performs some action on that data, what you are really testing is the logic within the controller action, *not* the data access layer that retrieves the data. The problem is, the tests that we just wrote test both layers. In the next section, we'll look at a way to work around this issue.

Mocking Dependencies

When you run into problems like the one just described, techniques such as the *repository pattern* described in Chapter 8 really start to show their value. Patterns like this one introduce a layer of abstraction that lets you easily replace production components with fake components so you can control the data that is provided to the unit under test (the controller action, in this case).

The act of replacing components with their fake counterparts for the purpose of testing is called *mocking*, and the replacement components are called *test doubles*. They are also commonly referred to by any number of other names, such as *dummies*, *fakes*, *stubs*, and (most commonly) *mocks*.

Once you are able to ensure that the behavior of the dependency will never change by using these techniques, you can begin turning your integration tests into unit tests by removing the external dependency and focusing only on the controller's logic. To demonstrate how to perform this transformation, let's take a look at how we can apply the mocking technique to the AuctionsController, as refactored to the repository pattern in Chapter 8:

```
using System.Web.Mvc;

namespace Ebuy.Website.Controllers
{
    public class AuctionsController : Controller
    {
        private readonly IRepository _repository;

        public AuctionsController()
            : this(new DataContextRepository(new EbuyDataContext()))
        {
```

```
        }

        public AuctionsController(IRepository repository)
        {
            _repository = repository;
        }

        public ActionResult Index()
        {
            var auctions = _repository.Query<Auction>();

            return View(auctions);
        }

        public ActionResult Auction(long id)
        {
            var auction = _repository.Single<Auction>(id);

            return View(auction);
        }
    }
}
```

Notice that there are two constructors: one that accepts an IRepository that the controller uses for all of its data access, and another that creates the default implementation of the IRepository that will be used in production.

This way, when the controller is created using the default constructor (i.e., the constructor that the ASP.NET MVC Framework uses), it will use the production IRepository implementation (DataContextRepository). However, the constructor that accepts the IRepository provides a seam into which unit tests may inject a mock object to control the data provided to the controller.

Manually creating mock objects

Before we can take advantage of the fact that the AuctionsController is able to accept a mock IRepository, we must first create one. Perhaps the most straightforward way to create a mock IRepository is to write one ourselves—that is, create a class that implements the IRepository interface and exists for the sole purpose of aiding automated tests.

The following code snippet shows an example of a very basic implementation of IRepository that enables us to control what the Single<TModel>() method returns:

```
public class MockAuctionRepository : IRepository
{
    private readonly Auction _auction;

    public MockAuctionRepository(Auction auction)
    {
        _auction = auction;
    }
```

```
    public TModel Single<TModel>(object id) where TModel : class
    {
        return _auction as TModel;
    }

    public IQueryable<TModel> Query<TModel>() where TModel : class
    {
        throw new System.NotImplementedException();
    }
}
```

The MockAuctionRepository class has several important distinctions:

- First—and most importantly—the class exposes methods that behave the same way every time they are called, which makes other components' interaction with class very predictable.

- Second, the mock class allows tests to control the data that the Single<TModel>() method returns. It does this by returning the Auction object that is passed via the constructor every time the Single<TModel>() method is executed.

- Finally, the MockAuctionRepository implements the bare minimum of the IReposi tory contract necessary to be useful in our automated tests. In other words, the MockAuctionRepository targets a specific test scenario and is not designed to be a general-purpose repository. This is evident in the fact that the Query<TModel>() class throws a NotImplementedException, and it does so on purpose—since we know that the unit under test (the AuctionsController.Auction() method) is only supposed to call the IRepository.Single<TModel>() method. If Query<TModel>() ever executes in the course of our tests, this exception will be thrown and that test will (correctly) fail.

Now let's rewrite our earlier integration test (shown in "Testing data access logic" on page 362) to make use of this new mock repository class:

```
[TestClass]
public class AuctionsControllerTests
{
    [TestMethod]
    public void ShouldRetrieveAuctionById()
    {
        var auction = new Auction { Id = 123 };
        var mockRepository = new MockAuctionRepository(expectedAuction);

        var controller = new AuctionsController(mockRepository);
        dynamic result = controller.Auction(expectedAuction.Id);

        Assert.AreSame(expectedAuction, result.Model);
    }
}
```

Here you can see how the test makes use of the repository-based AuctionsController by creating and passing an instance of our new MockAuctionRepository class to take the place of the default database-based IRepository implementation. The test can then call the `controller.Auction()` method with the expectation that it will call the `MockAuction Repository.Single<Auction>()` method. The test then makes any assertions against the `result.Model` object that it needs to make in order to prove that it is the same `Auction` instance (`expectedAuction`) that the test provided to the mock repository.

 Notice how this test sets the value of the `Auction.Id` property even though the setter for this property is marked with the `internal` access modifier and the test class is located in a different assembly than the `Auction` class (i.e., it's not in the same `internal` scope). This is possible by applying the following `InternalsVisibleTo` assembly-level attribute to the *Ebuy.Core* project (where the `Auction` class is defined), which exposes all of the internals of *Ebuy.Core* to the *Ebuy.Tests* test project:

```
[assembly: InternalsVisibleTo("Ebuy.Tests")]
```

This approach offers yet another bonus: since the test replaces the database-based `IRepository` implementation with our new mock `IRepository`, it no longer needs to make sure that an `Auction` with the specific `Id` exists in the database (the test creates this `Auction` itself).

And just like that, we are able to replace an external dependency on a database with a mock object and turn an integration test into a unit test!

Using a mock framework

Though manually creating mock classes such as `MockAuctionRepository` is a great way to replace production components during testing, it has its share of problems.

To begin with, despite the fact that mock classes are only used during testing, they are still real implementations of application interfaces, which means that not only do developers need to write more code in order to write effective unit tests, they must continue to maintain that code as the codebase matures. This issue is compounded by the fact that it is common for developers to write multiple mock implementations of a single interface to target various usages of that interface, just as the `MockAuctionRepository` example only implemented the `Single<Auction>()` method and nothing more. Consider the effect of changing the underlying interface when there are dozens or more mock implementations of that interface!

Luckily, there is an alternative to manually creating mock classes: use a *mock framework* to do it for you.

A mock framework is a framework that provides developers with an API to dynamically create mock classes on the fly and easily configure those classes to suit a particular situation. In short, mock frameworks give you all the benefits of manually created mock classes with a fraction of the work, during both the initial test development and the ongoing maintenance of the unit test suite.

Though there are a wide variety of mock frameworks available to .NET developers, they all perform essentially the same task: creating mock objects on the fly. Since their major differences tend to be in the form of the syntax they use to create those mock objects, the choice of which mock framework to use generally comes down to developer preference.

In this book, we've chosen to show examples of the excellent open source Moq framework (*http://code.google.com/p/moq/*), but you are free to use any mock framework that you like. For instance, you may want to look into some of the other open source mock frameworks, such as Rhino Mocks (*http://hibernatingrhinos.com/open-source/rhino-mocks*), EasyMock.NET (*http://sourceforge.net/projects/easymocknet/*), NMock (*http://www.nmock.org/*), or FakeItEasy (*https://github.com/FakeItEasy/FakeItEasy*), or even one of the several commercial frameworks that are available.

For example, take a look at the following snippet, which replaces the manual MockAuctionRepository from the previous example with a mock IRepository object generated by the Moq framework:

```
[TestClass]
public class AuctionsControllerTests
{
    [TestMethod]
    public void ShouldRetrieveAuctionById()
    {
        var expectedAuction = new Auction { Id = 123 };

        var mockRepository = new Moq.Mock<IRepository>();
        mockRepository
            .Setup(repo => repo.Single<Auction>(expectedAuction.Id))
            .Returns(expectedAuction);

        var controller = new AuctionsController(mockRepository.Object);
        dynamic result = controller.Auction(expectedAuction.Id);

        Assert.AreSame(expectedAuction, result.Model);
    }
}
```

Here you can see that the mock framework is able to stand in for the IRepository interface with just a few lines of code. First, the test dynamically creates a new mock IRepository instance via the Moq.Mock<T> object: new Moq.Mock<IRepository>(). Next, the test tells the mock object how it should behave, using the Moq framework's Setup() method to specify the exact call the mock object should expect (repo.Single<Auction>(expectedAuction.Id)) and the Returns() method to indicate the value that should be returned in response to the expected call.

The net result of this example is that we are able to replace the manually created MockAuctionRepository class with a dynamic mock IRepository implementation that provides all the benefits of a mock class, but requires a lot less code and ongoing maintenance. And since the mock framework drastically reduces the amount of effort it takes to effectively mock out dependencies, this approach helps developers write more effective test suites that consist of far more unit tests than integration tests.

Testing Views

With the model and controller layers successfully under test, it's time to move on to testing views. There is some bad news, though: you've got your work cut out for you.

To see why it's going to be so much work, ask yourself the same question we've been asking throughout this chapter before we begin testing something: what, exactly, am I trying to test here? Consider the interaction that a user has with an ASP.NET MVC application. The ASP.NET MVC Framework is strictly worried about rendering HTML to the user's browser, but as far as the user's browser is concerned that's just the beginning!

As Chapter 4 discusses, there is far more to a modern web page than just rendering HTML and CSS in a browser. Advanced JavaScript and AJAX techniques have evolved the modern Web from a simple content-delivery mechanism to an immersive experience that can turn the browser into a full-fledged application development platform in itself—and this platform may have very little to do with ASP.NET MVC!

What this all boils down to is that testing your application's view layer is a lot more involved than simply instantiating an object and writing a few lines of code to validate its behavior. In fact, the "view layer" can actually be divided into several different layers itself: the rendered HTML that contains the initial content and structure of the page, the JavaScript that contains the application logic, and the CSS rules that style it all. All three of these aspects of a page need to be perfect in order to achieve the desired experience—and all of them require very different testing approaches and techniques.

Testing application logic in the browser

While the above examples show that text-based automated testing of your website is certainly possible, the benefits of a text-based approach can be rather limited, because the content that the browser receives and the way that it chooses to render that content can be two very different things. And it gets even worse when you consider just how differently the various browsers can render the same HTML markup. In order to truly test how your site will interact with actual users, you'll inevitably need to load it into a browser and see the site like your users will see it.

This approach is called *browser testing*, because it involves opening up an actual browser and using virtual mouse clicks and keystrokes to mimic actions that the users of your site will carry out. Clearly, the easiest way to perform browser testing is to manually open a browser and begin interacting with it as you expect a normal user would. However, this chapter is about automated testing, so we'll focus instead on the various ways that you can have the computer perform those tasks for you; in other words, *automated browser testing*.

There are a number of tools that let you perform browser testing from within an automated test suite, but the one we're going to look at in this chapter is a tool called WatiN (*http://watin.org/*).

To begin using WatiN in your solution, all you need to do is use the NuGet Package Manager to add the *WatiN* package to your test project's list of references. After the reference is added, create a normal test class and a normal test method—just as we did in the previous sections—and import the WatiN.Core namespace. Then, use an instance of the WatiN.Core.IE class to open up an instance of Internet Explorer and begin interacting with the browser in your tests.

For example, the following test uses Internet Explorer to navigate around the EBuy website:

```
using Microsoft.VisualStudio.TestTools.UnitTesting;
using WatiN.Core;

namespace Ebuy.Tests.Website.Browser
{
    [TestClass]
    public class AuctionTests
    {
        [TestMethod]
        public void ShouldNavigateToAnAuctionListingFromTheAuctionsList()
        {
            const string baseUrl = "http://localhost:65193";
            using (var browser = new IE(baseUrl + "/auctions", true))
            {
                var auctionDiv = browser.Div(Find.ByClass("auction"));
                var auctionTitle = auctionDiv.Element(Find.ByClass("title")).Text;

                auctionDiv.Links.First().Click();

                Assert.IsFalse(string.IsNullOrWhiteSpace(auctionTitle));
                Assert.AreEqual(
                    auctionTitle,
                    browser.Element(Find.BySelector("h2.title")).Text);
            }
        }
    }
}
```

This test instructs Internet Explorer to navigate to *http://localhost:65193/auctions*, the URL to display the list of auctions running on the local development web server on port 65193. Once the page loads, the test locates the first Auction element (<div class="auction">), then snoops further in the Auction element to discover the title of the auction (<span class="title">), which it saves to confirm that the correct page is loaded later in the test.

After all of this discovery is complete, it's time to execute the test. The test finds the first link in the Auction element and triggers a click using the link's .Click() method, which redirects the browser to the details page for the selected auction.

Finally, the test validates that everything worked as expected by asserting that the auction's title (which it retrieved from the auction list page) matches the text in the <h2 class="title"> element on the details page. If everything went as planned, there should be no problem locating the <h2> element and it should contain the proper auction title.

 If you attempt to execute the unit test and receive a message indicating that the test runner could not load the assembly *Interop.SHDocVw*, this means that the COM interop object is not being properly located.

In order to fix this issue, find the *Interop.SHDocVw* assembly in your test project's References list and change the value of the Embed Interop Types property to false and the Copy Local value to true.

This should allow the test runner to communicate with Internet Explorer and execute the tests successfully.

This example, while simple, is a powerful demonstration of the capabilities of automated browser testing. Notice the various ways in which the test is able to interact with the browser through WatiN's extensive API. For instance, the IE class provides a representation of the browser that tests can order around, while the various helper methods available on the Find class offer many different ways to quickly and effectively search through the DOM to find elements. And not only can you locate and analyze browser elements, but various methods available off of the element objects—such as the .Click() method—give tests a way to mimic user interaction with the browser.

Code Coverage

Code coverage is a code analysis technique that judges how well an automated test suite tests an application based on how many lines of code are executed over the course of executing the test suite. Code coverage is generally stated in terms of percentages; e.g., if a component contains 100 lines of code and a test suite executes 75 of those lines, that component is said to have 75% code coverage.

In order to evaluate a project's code coverage, you must use a code coverage tool. This tool executes a suite of automated tests within a profiler process and keeps track of every line of code that gets executed over the course of each unit test run. When the test run is complete, the code coverage tool typically creates a report to show you how well the tests covered the various parts of your application.

If you are running a non-Express version of Visual Studio, you are in luck, because it ships with a code coverage tool built right into the IDE. To use the Visual Studio Code

Coverage tool, expand the Unit Test > Analyze Code Coverage menu and choose one of the "Selected Tests" or "All Tests" options.

This will cause the tool to execute your unit tests, analyze the code coverage results, and display them in the Code Coverage Results window in your IDE (as shown in Figure 17-6).

Hierarchy	Not Covered (Blocks)	Not Covered (% Blocks)	Covered (Blocks)	Covered (% Blocks)
⊿ 🖳 ebuy.core.dll	26	36.62 %	45	63.38%
⊿ { } Ebuy	26	36.62 %	45	63.38%
⊿ ⚙ Auction	0	0.00 %	24	100.00 %
⚙ Auction()	0	0.00 %	9	100.00 %
⚙ PostBid(Ebuy.User, decimal)	0	0.00 %	15	100.00 %
⊿ ⚙ Bid	0	0.00 %	6	100.00 %
⚙ Bid(Ebuy.User, decimal)	0	0.00 %	6	100.00 %
⊿ ⚙ DataContextRepository	3	33.33 %	6	66.67 %
⚙ DataContextRepository(System.Data.Entity.DbContext)	0	0.00 %	2	100.00 %
⚙ Query<T>()	3	100.00 %	0	0.00 %
⚙ Single<T>(object)	0	0.00 %	4	100.00 %
⊿ ⚙ EbuyDataContext	0	0.00 %	4	100.00 %
⚙ EbuyDataContext()	0	0.00 %	4	100.00 %
⊿ ⚙ EbuyDataContext.Initializer	23	100.00 %	0	0.00 %
⚙ Seed(Ebuy.EbuyDataContext)	23	100.00 %	0	0.00 %
⊿ ⚙ InvalidBidAmountException	0	0.00 %	5	100.00 %
⚙ InvalidBidAmountException(decimal, decimal)	0	0.00 %	5	100.00 %

Figure 17-6. Visual Studio code coverage results

As this image shows, Visual Studio can show you—right down to the method level—exactly how much of your code is "covered" or "not covered" through your automated test suite.

In this case, you can see that 63.38% of the entire *ebuy.core.dll* assembly is getting covered. If you assume that this project has an extensive automated test suite in place, this number may come as a surprise, since you may have expected something much closer to 100%.

To see what is keeping us from 100% code coverage, first try to find where the holes in the coverage are. A quick glance down the list of methods shows that two methods are not covered: `DataContextRepository.Query<T>()` and `EbuyDataContext.Initial izer.Seed()`.

These methods have one thing in common: they both interact with the database. Furthermore, `EbuyDataContext.Initializer.Seed()` only gets executed when the database is first created and never again after that.

This information has several implications, but one of the more important things that it points out is that our tests always execute against an existing database and never create a new database. This may be by design, in which case the lack of code coverage on this method may be acceptable. Or, it may expose that we've made a very important mistake and that our tests should be creating a new database for every test run!

The fact that the `DataContextRepository.Query<T>()` method was never executed is interesting as well. This information may also indicate that we need to write some more tests that target this method, or perhaps that the method may not even be needed at all.

Ultimately, these are all judgment calls that you must make. Depending on the situation, you may have very valid reasons for leaving parts of your code uncovered by automated tests and not obtaining "100% code coverage"—and that's OK!

The Myth of 100% Code Coverage

Evaluating your test suite's code coverage is an excellent way to make sure that you are exercising as much of your application as possible, and you should strive to test as many lines of code as you are realistically able to.

However, while it's sensible to try to test every single line of code in your application, there are two problems with the quest for 100% code coverage:

1. *It's practically impossible.* Even though there are plenty of ways to develop code so that it is very easy to test (as the next section shows), there are many situations that are very difficult to cover with automated tests. One of the best examples of this is any component that interacts directly with an `HttpRequest`, a framework component that takes quite a bit of work to instantiate. The simplest and most effective way to test these components is to run them within the ASP.NET pipeline, which breaks most of the unit test guidelines mentioned earlier in this chapter.

2. *It gives a false sense of security.* Consider the sample unit test we created earlier. Assume that this test provides 100% code coverage of the `Calculate.Add()` method —that is, it executes every single line of code in that method without failing. Does that mean that the `Calculate.Add()` method can never fail? We only tested it with the values 1 and 2; does that mean that it will properly support any value it's given? (Hint: try `Calculate.Add(double.MaxValue, double.MaxValue)`.)

This is not to say that it is not a noble cause to shoot for as high a code coverage percentage as you can achieve. Just be sure to keep these concepts in mind as you do, and don't consider your test suite a failure if you're not able to reach the mythical 100% code coverage!

Developing Testable Code

If effective software testing focuses on verifying that a component or an application will work as expected in a production environment, then anything that stands in the way of running that code as closely to how it will run in a production environment can be said to make that code more difficult to verify and thus less "testable."

For instance, think of the most recent component you've worked with and ask yourself a few questions:

- How much setup or configuration does it take to prepare the component for testing?
- How many other components (which may demand their own additional configuration) does that component interact with?
- Does the component depend on any third-party libraries, databases, external web services, or even the local filesystem?
- How reliable and consistent are these dependencies? For example, do you have a test web service that always returns the same results?

All of these things can affect the "testability" of a software component.

Take, for example, the two methods shown below. Though both methods contain only one line of code, the first method is far more testable than the second method, which represents one of the most difficult scenarios to test reliably. First up is GetVersion Number():

```
public static int GetVersionNumber()
{
    return 1;
}
```

What makes GetVersionNumber() so testable is the fact that it will always return the same result (the int value 1) regardless of how many times it's called. Perhaps even more important is how accessible this method is. Since it is exposed with a public access level, any component may execute the method and evaluate its response. Its static modifier also means that consumers don't need to create an instance of the containing class in order to execute the method—it's just a simple method call.

The CallRemoteWebService() method, on the other hand, is an entirely different story:

```
private ServiceResult CallRemoteWebService()
{
    return new WebService("http://thirdparty.com/service")
    .GetServiceResult("some special value");
}
```

For starters, this method is closed off from the world via its private access level. This means that in order to even execute the method, a test must first call another method in the same class, introducing unrelated logic into the mix that we'd rather avoid. It also means that the test will have to create an instance of the class before being able to call any of its methods, which, depending on the class's dependencies, may not be a trivial task.

The next thing that CallRemoteWebService() has going against it is that it accesses an external dependency (a remote web service), which introduces a whole slew of issues that can occur when attempting to execute this method. Is the web service active? Might we run into networking issues attempting to access it? Is it returning the correct data? If it's a third-party service, have we paid our bill lately?

The final, most notable issue that makes `CallRemoteWebService()` difficult to test is *how* it accesses the external web service dependency. Notice that the method creates a new instance of the `WebService` class and uses a hardcoded URL to reference the external service. Because of this, there is no way to test this method without making the actual call to the external production web service, which means that there is no way to control the behavior of the web service dependency.

Be wary of the `new` keyword—it's usually an indication that there is an opportunity to use dependency injection to help create a looser coupling between components.

When a component receives an instance of the other object via dependency injection, it makes it much easier to replace that behavior with a test object during testing. But when that component creates an instance itself, replacing that logic is nearly impossible.

Therefore, any test that executes this method is effectively a test of the integration with the external web service. While this is not a bad thing, it means that this method can never be *unit* tested, since it breaks all of the aforementioned guidelines for a true unit test.

When you consider the downstream effects of this situation, it gets much worse. Not only can this method not be unit tested, but no other method that *calls* this method can be unit tested either. If you get enough of these methods in your application, pretty soon it becomes impossible to unit test the entire application!

Summary

Automated testing is a great way to ensure the ongoing quality and functionality of your entire application. Traditionally, it's been somewhat difficult to apply automated testing techniques to ASP.NET web applications. However, the loosely coupled architecture that the ASP.NET MVC Framework provides makes automated testing of ASP.NET MVC applications a cinch.

Couple the ASP.NET MVC Framework with the helpful patterns, practices, and tools introduced here, and pretty soon you'll be able to bask in the confidence that a full suite of automated tests brings.

Build Automation

In order to move from raw source code to a fully functioning application, many things need to happen. For instance, applications written using a static language such as C# must be compiled and, perhaps, copied to a special folder (such as the *bin* folder in the case of an ASP.NET web application). An application may also require a number of other artifacts to function properly, such as images, script files, or even entire database schemas. The act of preparing these artifacts—as well as anything else that an application requires in order to function—is often referred to as "the build."

Previous chapters explored the idea that, while humans are notoriously bad at performing repetitive tasks with accuracy, computers handle these types of tasks with ease and precision. Chapter 17 demonstrated a great example of this by taking advantage of the computer's talents to perform automated testing of an application.

This chapter expands on the theme of automating the various aspects of software development by applying automation techniques to the act of building and deploying your application. Along the way, we'll explore how to use automation to improve the interaction between members of your development team and the other groups involved in creating, validating, and delivering your software.

Though the examples in this chapter demonstrate common automated build and deployment scenarios using Microsoft's MSBuild and Team Foundation Server tools, there are numerous commercial and open source alternatives to MSBuild and Team Foundation Server, and each has its own way of creating and executing build scripts.

Despite their differences, however, almost all build and deployment frameworks are driven by the same fundamental concepts and techniques. So, as you follow the examples in this chapter, keep in mind that it's the *concepts* of automated build and deployment that are important, not which tools you use to implement them.

Creating Build Scripts

Before you can begin automating a build, you must first define what it is that you'd like the computer to do for you. You do this through the use of *build scripts*—files that contain a set of tasks you need the computer to perform.

The actual format and syntax of the build scripts will vary depending on the tool that you use, but regardless of how they are written, build scripts can contain logic that extends far beyond simple code compilation to include tasks such as executing the application's unit test suite, evaluating the application's source code quality, generating and executing database scripts—just about any task you can imagine.

Development environments such as Visual Studio often set the groundwork for build automation via concepts such as "solutions" and "projects" that make it very easy to define which artifacts the application requires, and what to do with those artifacts in order to produce a working application. For example, a Visual Studio C# Project (*.csproj*) file may include a collection of C# source code files as well as the logic to call the C# compiler (*csc.exe*) to compile those source code files into a .NET assembly or executable. Regardless of how useful they might be within the Visual Studio IDE, projects and solutions only begin to scratch the surface of what is possible in the world of automated builds.

Visual Studio Projects Are Build Scripts!

While there are numerous scripting tools available to help you create automated tasks, you may be surprised to find that you already have a very powerful scripting tool installed as part of Visual Studio: the *Microsoft Build Engine* (or, as it's more commonly known, *MSBuild*). MSBuild relies on scripts defined using a custom XML schema to execute various tasks. In fact, all of Visual Studio's project and solution files are just MSBuild files with special file extensions, and—every time you hit F5—Visual Studio hands these files to MSBuild in order to compile your application!

Adding a Simple Build Task

To prove it, open up Windows Explorer, navigate to the *EBuy.Website* folder inside of the Ebuy solution folder, and open the *EBuy.Website.csproj* file in a text editor by right-clicking on it and selecting "Open With," then choosing your favorite text editor. Inside the project file, you'll find a `<Project>` XML node with various children such as `<Import>`, `<PropertyGroup>`, and `<ItemGroup>` elements—these elements all work together to tell MSBuild how to build the project.

Scroll to the end of the project file and look for the following commented-out lines:

```
<!-- To modify your build process, add your task inside one of the targets below and
     uncomment it. Other similar extension points exist, see Microsoft.Common.targets.
<Target Name="BeforeBuild">
</Target>
<Target Name="AfterBuild">
</Target> -->
```

As their names imply, these two targets—`BeforeBuild` and `AfterBuild`—allow you to execute tasks before and after the rest of the build tasks execute.

To see how easy it is to modify a build file, let's change the file so it displays a message after the build completes. To do this, we'll uncomment the `AfterBuild` target and add a call to the MSBuild `<Message>` task within it, like so:

```
<!-- To modify your build process, add your task inside one of the targets below and
     uncomment it. Other similar extension points exist, see Microsoft.Common.targets.
<Target Name="BeforeBuild">
</Target>
 -->
<Target Name="AfterBuild">
  <Message Importance="High" Text="**** The build has completed! ****" />
</Target>
```

Executing the Build

Now that this change is in place, it's time to execute the build to see it in action. You have two options here: build within Visual Studio or execute MSBuild directly from the command line.

Building in Visual Studio

Executing MSBuild from within Visual Studio is trivial—in fact, it's exactly what you've been doing for as long as you've been using Visual Studio to develop and execute .NET applications! Open the solution that contains your project and hit one of the many Visual Studio shortcuts (such as Ctrl-B) that trigger a build.

Once the build completes, you will see your custom message displayed in Visual Studio's Output window. For example:

```
3>---- Rebuild All started: Project: Ebuy.Website, Configuration: Debug Any CPU ----
3>  Ebuy.Website -> C:\Code\EBuy\trunk\Website\bin\Ebuy.Website.dll
3>  **** The build has completed! ****
========== Rebuild All: 3 succeeded, 0 failed, 0 skipped ==========
```

Building from the command line

One of the nice things about Visual Studio projects and solutions is that you don't actually have to open them in Visual Studio in order to build them. Instead, you can skip Visual Studio all together and execute your project file's "build script" by invoking MSBuild directly from the command line.

To do this, find and execute the Visual Studio Command Prompt shortcut in your Start menu. This will open a Windows command prompt (*cmd.exe*) and automatically configure its environment so the .NET tools—including MSBuild—are available.

Then, you can execute the `msbuild` command and pass the solution or project file name as an argument to execute the build:

```
msbuild Ebuy.sln
```

This command executes the MSBuild toolchain against the solution and produces a much more verbose version of the text in Visual Studio's Output window. Somewhere within this verbose output you should be able to locate your custom `AfterBuild` message:

```
[...]
AfterBuild:
  The build has completed!
Done Building Project "C:\Code\EBuy\Website\Ebuy.Website.csproj" (default targets).
[...]
```

The Possibilities Are Endless!

Though adding a custom message to Visual Studio's build output may seem underwhelming, keep in mind that this is a simple example. What this example really demonstrates is the ability to insert your own custom logic into the build process, allowing you to execute literally any logic that you can call from .NET code or script via the command line.

Automating the Build

While it's nice to be able to execute a build script by triggering it with a keystroke within Visual Studio or executing a command-line tool, these approaches are less than ideal because they require manual, human intervention. *Build automation*, where the computer is able to execute build scripts without human involvement, exposes the true value in creating build scripts.

Once you've created build scripts that detail what you'd like to happen during the course of an automated build, the next step in removing human involvement from the mix is to hand the script off to the *build automation service*, more commonly known as the *build server*. A build server is a service that is always running, waiting for the opportunity to execute the build scripts it's been given.

One build server product favored by .NET development teams is Microsoft's Team Foundation Server (TFS). The Team Foundation Server product is a popular choice because it integrates a number of important concepts of the application development lifecycle, such as source control, work item tracking, reporting, and automated build and deployment.

 Since this chapter is only concerned with demonstrating the concepts of automated builds, we are going to assume that you have already installed and configured Team Foundation Server and are using it as your source control system. If you would like to follow along with the following examples but do not have access to a Team Foundation Server installation, you may be eligible for free or low-cost access to Microsoft's Team Foundation Server hosting (*http://tfspreview.com*), which provides all of the features that we cover in this chapter. If you choose to use one of the many other popular build automation servers, it is up to you to apply the concepts shown in this chapter to your specific tool.

Types of Automated Builds

Because build scripts may execute just about any logic you can imagine, it's important to define a scope for each build that determines what, exactly, the build expects to accomplish.

For example, the following list includes several common types of automated builds:

Continuous builds
> Continuous builds are triggered whenever any team member commits a change to the codebase and their primary purpose is to provide near-immediate feedback about the quality of the change that was committed. In order to validate quality, the tasks that a continuous build executes are usually restricted to compiling the application and running a suite of unit tests that provide a baseline verification that the code works. These unit tests complete in a short amount of time. Because of the frequency with which continuous builds are triggered, it is crucial that these types of builds finish as quickly as possible in order to both tighten the feedback loop and avoid multiple builds stacking up on one another.

Rolling builds
> Rolling builds are just like continuous builds, except they impose limits as to how many builds may execute within a certain timeframe. For instance, you may configure a rolling build to execute only once every five minutes, rather than every time someone commits a change. As developers commit changes within that five-minute period, those changes accumulate until the five minutes elapse and the next build executes.

Gated check-in builds

Gated check-in builds are also like continuous builds, but rather than raising a red flag when someone commits a breaking change, gated check-ins serve to disallow the breaking commit from even reaching the codebase. Gated check-ins may execute once per commit (like continuous builds), or you may impose a limit on how many times they can run in a given timespan (as with rolling builds).

Scheduled builds

Scheduled builds execute on a specific schedule and are not explicitly tied to commit activity. The most popular example of a scheduled build approach is known as a *nightly build*, because it is scheduled to run at the same time every night, after the development team is done working for the day. Since these types of builds are not directly tied to commit activity, it is generally more acceptable for them to be somewhat out-of-date and to not reflect the most up-to-date code in the codebase. Scheduled builds are also able to take more time to execute, perhaps executing more in-depth automated tests or creating artifacts such as installation packages that should only be produced in limited quantities.

The primary theme among the various types of automated builds is how often they execute and how long each build execution takes to finish. The work each type of build performs is an extension of this. As builds become less frequent, they have more time to accomplish their tasks and thus can perform a larger number of increasingly complex and time-consuming tasks.

For instance, continuous builds focus on performing the minimum amount of work in order to verify the ongoing quality of the codebase, while at the other end of the spectrum, nightly or weekly builds may take hours or even days to perform massive tasks, such as executing an extensive suite of in-depth automated tests, compiling large amounts of documentation, or packaging a product suite for release.

 The best approach to build automation typically includes a few different types of builds operating at the same time, each with different priorities.

For instance, you might consider implementing three different builds for the same application:

1. A continuous build to validate the quality of every check-in
2. A rolling build that occurs no more than once every hour and executes more detailed automated tests, but takes a while to do so
3. A nightly build that publishes the day's changes to a test website so users or a QA team can track progress and report bugs as early as possible

Creating the Automated Build

After you've determined what type of build you'd like to create, it's time to define it. There are a few things that the build server requires in order to do its job: first, the build script that contains the tasks that the build server must execute; and second, the source code (and other artifacts) that the build script will be executed against.

To define a build using Team Foundation Server, select the Builds option from within the Team Explorer tab, then click "New Build Definition." This will bring up the New Build Definition Wizard, allowing you to configure your new build.

For this example, we'll be creating a continuous build, so enter *Continuous* in the "Build definition name" field on the General tab (Figure 18-1), and leave the rest of the defaults alone.

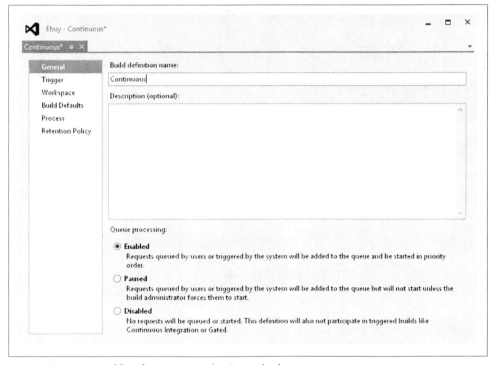

Figure 18-1. New Build Definition Wizard—General tab

Next, choose the "Continuous Integration" option from the Trigger tab (Figure 18-2).

You can skip the Workspace and Build Defaults tabs because their default values are fine. Instead, click on the Process tab and look for the *Items to Build* configuration property (Figure 18-3).

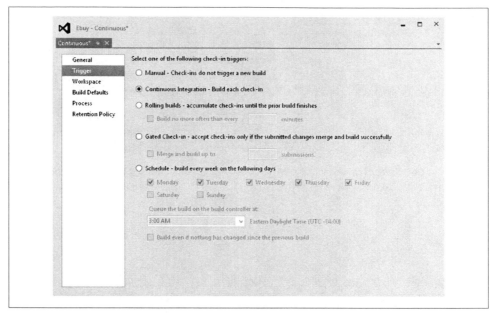

Figure 18-2. *New Build Definition Wizard—Trigger tab*

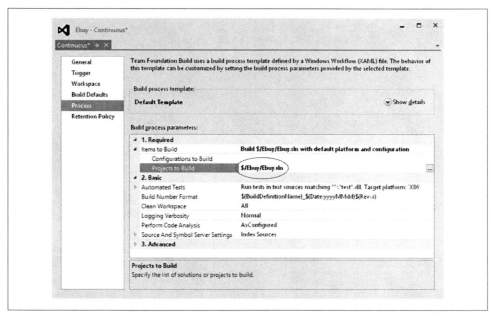

Figure 18-3. *New Build Definition Wizard—Process tab*

The *Items to Build* configuration property contains the list of MSBuild project files that the build will execute. Visual Studio automatically selects the current solution, assuming that you want to at least compile everything. Use this configuration property to select any additional MSBuild project files you've created to provide additional build logic. When you supply multiple project files, MSBuild will execute them in the order that you provide, stopping on any failures that may occur.

Also notice the *Automated Tests* configuration property, whose default behavior is to execute all automated tests that it can discover in any assemblies whose name matches the expression **test*.dll*. This default value means that if you've created any automated test projects with the word "test" somewhere in their name, Team Foundation Server will automatically execute them without any further configuration.

When you're finished configuring the new build definition, save the definition just like you would any other file (e.g., Ctrl-S). It should then appear under the "All Build Definitions" section in the Team Explorer tab (Figure 18-4).

Figure 18-4. New Build Definition Wizard—Team Explorer tab

To see if it works, try to commit a changeset into source control, or right-click the new build, select the "Queue New Build..." menu option, then click Queue in the dialog. Team Foundation Server will then start the build, retrieving the solution's source code from version control and executing the build scripts you specified.

With any luck, the build should succeed, indicating that you've done everything correctly. If the build fails, correct any build errors that you find in the detailed logs. The next time you check in, a new build will automatically be triggered.

Congratulations—you've created your first working build!

Continuous Integration

Though it may have seemed innocuous among the list of automated build types above, continuous integration is actually much more than a type of automated build that executes every time someone commits code.

In fact, *continuous integration* (or *CI*) also describes a process of ensuring the quality of an application by implementing small, focused sets of functionality and integrating that functionality into the larger application on a regular basis. This practice not only tightens the feedback loop so that new features are introduced as quickly as possible; it also serves a much more important role in discovering—and fixing—issues with the codebase as soon as they are introduced.

Under continuous integration, all members of the team are encouraged to check their changes into a centralized source control repository early and often, *integrating* their work with that of the other team members frequently. This helps avoid the alternative, where individual developers modify their local copies of the application but don't commit the changes to the centralized repository. As time goes by, the differences between the central version of the application and each developer's local copy become so unwieldy that it takes hours to reconcile the differences. Had the developers merged early and often, the integration time would have been spread out in small doses across several check-ins, drastically reducing the impact.

Discovering Issues

Consider the "software development lifecycle" that is so common: requirements are gathered, the software is built, and then the completed software is tested to make sure that it was built correctly. These steps are repeated until the product is released. The fundamental problem with this approach is that there is often a good deal of time in between the development phase, when a bug is introduced, and the testing phase, when it is discovered—which makes the bug exponentially more costly to fix.

There is a simple reason for this: when you've just finished writing code to implement a feature, that code is fresh in your mind, which generally makes it easy to locate and fix the issue quickly. On the other hand, if a considerable amount of time elapses between when you wrote that code and when the bug is found, not only might you have become unfamiliar with the code, but it may have gone through several more iterations that serve to compound the issue. Thus, it makes sense to raise issues as early as possible.

The Principles of Continuous Integration

Below is a list of the 10 core principles that are crucial to effectively implementing continuous integration. You may not need to implement all of them in order to benefit from continuous integration, but the benefit you gain is usually proportional to the number of principles that you are able to incorporate.

 These principles are generally attributed to Martin Fowler, one of the originators of the Agile software development movement. For more information about continuous integration (and much more), feel free to peruse the extensive set of articles on his website (*http://martinfowler .com/articles/continuousIntegration.html*).

Maintain a single source repository

Source control systems provide a centralized repository that enables members of a team to share source code and other artifacts effectively. Centralized source control systems also represent "the truth"—the centralized repository is the one place that contains that latest, working version of the application.

Automate the build

You should be able to build the entire application on any given machine in two steps:

1. Retrieve the source from the source control repository.
2. Execute a single command.

In order for this to work, you must make sure that the source control repository contains everything that the build needs, outside of core, system-level dependencies (such as the operating system features, database services, or the .NET Framework). Nothing more should need to be installed in order to build and execute the application. When additional installations are unavoidable, they should be included as part of the automation process that occurs when that single command is executed.

This rule particularly includes databases. Whenever possible, local builds should not rely on existing, remote databases; instead, the automated build should include the database schema and seed data required to create the database from scratch. Preferably, this is accomplished without having to install anything on the local machine (for example, using an embedded version of Microsoft's LocalDb rather than a native installation of Microsoft SQL Server or SQL Server Express).

Make your build self-testing

This is the point where many of the patterns and practices that you've learned throughout this book all come together. The SOLID practices and loosely coupled architecture pave the way for fast and effective unit tests, which makes it possible to exercise your code very frequently.

The continuous integration process can then leverage these tests by executing the automated test suite against every source code check-in to discover issues as soon as they are introduced. When a unit test fails during the course of a continuous integration build, the tight scope of the failed test coupled with the relatively low number of changes to the source code make locating and fixing the issue very easy.

A continuous integration build that does not know how to verify the quality of its output is not very valuable at all.

Have everyone commit to the mainline frequently

In order to do their work, developers must get a local copy of the source code. Over time, the number of changes that the developers make to their local copies increases, as does the disconnect between their local copies and the main source control repository (the "truth"). If this pattern is allowed to continue, these differences can become so overwhelming that it takes considerable effort to reintegrate the two sources.

Thus, it's important that all members of the team avoid their local repositories becoming out of sync with the main repository by committing to the main repository as frequently as possible—no less than once a day, and preferably multiple times a day. This way, everyone on the team can remain in sync and the main source control repository is always an accurate representation of the current state of the project.

Every commit should build the mainline on an integration machine

The claim "It works on my machine!" is commonly heard throughout development teams everywhere. This phrase refers to the fact that, when one developer configures everything just right on his individual workstation, the application works perfectly. On the one hand, this is a great sign that a feature has been implemented or a bug has been fixed; on the other hand, the phrase is a very bad omen, indicating that the feature or bug fix may not work at all on any other machine.

To address this problem, continuous integration dictates that you set up a machine (or set of machines)—known as the *integration machine(s)*—that compiles and executes every commit to the mainline branch of the codebase. The integration machine must try to mirror the production environment as closely as possible, such that the assumption can be made that if the application compiles and executes on the integration machine, there is an excellent chance that it should do the same in the production environment.

With the integration machine in place validating every commit, the fact that the application runs on a given developer's machine is irrelevant—the application *must* run on the integration machine, and if it doesn't, the build (and the application) should be considered "broken" and be fixed immediately.

Keep the build fast

Since discovering issues as close as possible to the time that they are introduced is perhaps the most crucial aspect of continuous integration, it is imperative that continuous integration builds complete quickly, reporting any issues that arise as quickly as possible.

Time is money: the longer it takes between the time the issue is introduced and the time it's discovered, the more that issue costs to fix.

Test in a clone of the production environment

When an application is tested in an environment that does not match the environment it will be expected to work in upon release, it becomes less likely that errors associated with the release environment will be identified.

Make it easy for anyone to get the latest executable

Continuous integration encourages a tighter feedback loop that allows customers to take an active role in the development of their application.

Being able to access the actual assemblies from the latest build is usually quite beneficial, but in the case of web applications, it is sometimes even better for the application to be deployed to a centralized test server so that anyone is able to test the application and provide feedback.

Everyone can see what's happening

Perhaps you've heard the age-old philosophical question, "If a tree falls in the woods and no one is around, does it make a sound?" The software development equivalent to this question is: "If a build fails and no one knows (or cares), does it offer any value?"

The status of the continuous build has a direct correlation to the overall health of the codebase and, perhaps, to the entire project. This extends far beyond the obvious metric —whether the build is passing or failing—into other metrics such as the time it takes for a build to complete and the amount of code coverage that occurs during the build. Therefore, it is crucial for everyone involved in the project to have access to all the details of the automated builds, and to pay close attention to how they perform.

People have come up with many creative ways to keep their teams in the loop on the status of the build. These ideas range from notifications by system tray applications all the way to large televisions mounted on the wall for everyone to see.

What's important is that everyone is aware of the builds, not necessarily the way that they get the information. So, pick a way that works for you and make sure you pay attention to it.

The most important concept to understand about continuous integration is this: when a build breaks, it means that *your application is broken in some way,* and nothing is more important than getting it fixed. When a build breaks, the team needs to drop whatever they're doing and make fixing the build—fixing the application—their top priority.

 A broken build should always be a show-stopper. If you consistently experience broken builds that are not the result of your application being broken (e.g., they may be caused by network connectivity issues, errors accessing third-party APIs, etc.), you need to strongly reconsider how you can rearrange your builds or refactor your tests to avoid these false positives.

In such circumstances, your continuous build is no longer an accurate reflection of the health of your codebase, and its value decreases dramatically. You may start to become inured to broken builds, and stop paying attention to them.

A broken build should always indicate a problem with the codebase, and never become such a common occurrence that it's considered acceptable to ignore it.

Automate deployment

The final continuous integration principle focuses on making it easy for people to use your application. Just as it's wise to test in a clone of the production environment, successful continuous integration builds should always include an automated deployment of the application to an environment that mimics the production environment as closely as possible.

Automated deployment has two primary benefits. First, it offers the obvious benefit of being able to see and use the latest version of the application at all times, making it much easier to test for bugs and verify when bugs have been fixed.

Second, carrying out automated deployments of your application to a production-like environment as often as possible extends the value of continuous integration well past validating that your application works and into validating that your application *deployment* works. Much as automated tests can help to expose bugs as soon as they are introduced into the codebase, automated deployments can uncover deployment issues (such as missing dependencies or security permissions issues) as soon as they are introduced.

While you won't ever be able to avoid deployment issues, you'll at least experience them outside of the production environment, well before it's time for the final release. This means that you will know exactly what needs to happen to get your application into the production environment because you will have already encountered and addressed the deployment issues that would have delayed your production release. Now, instead of being exceptions, they are simply another step in the (automated) deployment process.

 See Chapter 19 for more detail about how to automate your deployments.

Summary

This chapter showed how you can leverage the patterns and practices that you've learned throughout this book to reduce the amount of human effort that goes into your software development lifecycle by automating as much of that lifecycle as possible. Once you've invested in things such as SOLID development practices and a suite of automated tests that validate your application, it's incredibly easy to leverage that effort to ensure the continued quality of your application.

Going Live

Deployment

You can spend plenty of time using ASP.NET MVC to build the best website in the world, but it's not going to do anyone any good until it gets hosted on a web server so that users can actually access it. The act of copying your website to a web server and exposing the site to users is called *deployment*, and it is certainly not a concept that is unique to ASP.NET MVC websites.

In this chapter, we'll cover a handful of the most popular techniques that you can choose from to get your website onto the Internet—everything from simple file copying to working with "cloud" hosting providers for the ultimate in scalability and uptime.

As you read this chapter, keep in mind that many web applications have unique deployment needs, and the techniques that we show in this chapter may not directly apply to your exact situation. Instead of seeing this chapter as a "how-to" guide with detailed steps, try to think of it as an overview of the various deployment tools at your disposal and be on the lookout for the tools and techniques that apply to your situation.

What Needs to Be Deployed

Before we start creating websites and copying files, let's take a step back to discuss what it is that we're going to be doing. At a high level, there are three kinds of dependencies that most web applications have: the .NET assemblies and various files that contain the logic for the site, any custom content (such as CSS or JavaScript files) that the site relies on, and any kind of external runtime dependencies that the website requires (such as a database or external services).

Core Website Files

At a minimum, every ASP.NET web application must include a */bin* folder that contains the assemblies with the application's compiled code and other .NET assemblies that the application depends on. As such, the */bin* folder is a crucial part of any ASP.NET web application deployment strategy.

So too, however, are the various other "special" files that are not necessarily required for the site to function properly, but often contain crucial information such as the site's configuration. These files—files such as *web.config* and *Global.asax*—almost always must be included, in addition to the assemblies in the */bin* folder.

If you're already an ASP.NET Web Forms developer, none of this will come as a surprise to you, since what we have described up to this point is how to deploy a plain old ASP.NET web application.

However, ASP.NET MVC web application deployments begin to diverge from those of traditional ASP.NET Web Forms applications when it comes to the views. In addition to the application assemblies in the */bin* folder and any "special" ASP.NET-related files, ASP.NET MVC web applications must also include local copies of all of their views (i.e., the */Views* folder), along with the rest of the deployed content. This is because ASP.NET MVC views follow the same Just-In-Time (JIT) compilation, deployment, and maintenance procedures as Web Forms *.aspx* views; in fact, the two are practically synonymous.

"bin-deploying" ASP.NET MVC libraries

It probably goes without saying, but in order for your ASP.NET MVC website to work, the deployed application will need access to the ASP.NET MVC Framework assemblies. You can go about this in two ways: you can install the ASP.NET MVC Framework directly on the web server, or you can include the ASP.NET MVC libraries along with the rest of the assemblies in the application's */bin* folder.

The steps to install the ASP.NET MVC Framework on the server are exactly the same as those covered in the first chapter of this book—simply run the Web Platform Installer (*http://www.microsoft.com/web/downloads/platform.aspx*) directly on the server and choose to install the ASP.NET MVC Framework package.

It's often a good idea to avoid installing anything at all on the web server, so you may prefer to treat the ASP.NET MVC assemblies just like any other application dependency and copy them into the */bin* folder along with everything else. This technique is often referred to as "bin-deploying," and it is usually the approach that is the simplest, most stable, and easiest to maintain.

Thankfully, Visual Studio makes bin-deployment very easy by including a menu option that automatically adds a folder containing the ASP.NET MVC dependencies to your application: simply right-click on the ASP.NET MVC project in Visual Studio and choose the "Add Deployable Dependencies..." option, as shown in Figure 19-1.

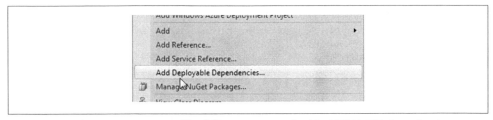

Figure 19-1. The menu option to add a folder containing the ASP.NET MVC dependencies to your application

When you choose this option Visual Studio will let you select which dependencies you want to include in your project. Choose the ASP.NET MVC option, as shown in Figure 19-2, and click OK.

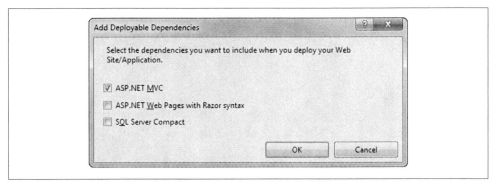

Figure 19-2. Select ASP.NET MVC

Visual Studio will then create a new folder called /_bin_deployableAssemblies that contains the framework assemblies to include in the deployment (Figure 19-3).

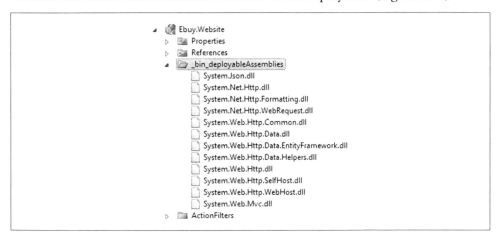

Figure 19-3. The new _bin_deployableAssemblies folder

Now when you publish the website, Visual Studio will deploy the assemblies in this new folder along with the rest of your application.

Static Content

Static content can refer to any type of file, but the majority of these files will almost always be the JavaScript files, CSS stylesheets, and images that provide your application's client-side logic and styling. Although these files can technically live anywhere in your site's folder structure, the default ASP.NET MVC project templates create the */Scripts*, */Images*, and */Content* folders for you to place all of your JavaScript files and other content in. Therefore, if you use this out-of-the-box convention, these three folders will contain all of your site's static content.

 Be sure to set the *Build Action* property on each static content file in your Visual Studio project to *Content* so that Visual Studio is aware that it is static content that should be deployed along with your site.

What Not to Deploy

If you're following the conventions defined in the default ASP.NET MVC project templates, just about every ASP.NET MVC website deployment will look similar to the directory hierarchy shown in Figure 19-4.

Figure 19-4. Conventional ASP.NET MVC deployment hierarchy

Note that this directory structure is very different from the set of files that you work with in the application's Visual Studio project (for example, the project shown in Figure 19-5).

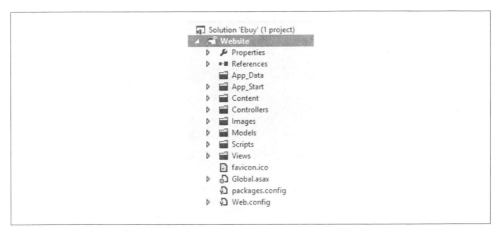

Figure 19-5. Default ASP.NET MVC project structure

More specifically, the deployed application will not include any of the source code files that define the application's logic. Since the project is compiled before it is deployed, these source code files are already "included" in the deployment in the form of the application's compiled assemblies in the */bin* directory. With this in mind, you're free to create any folder structure that you please to store and organize your source code files, since these folders will not become part of the deployed application.

Databases and Other External Dependencies

Though almost every ASP.NET MVC application deployment will include a directory structure similar to the one shown in Figure 19-5, this is where the similarities between ASP.NET MVC application deployments usually end and the unique deployment needs begin.

Most web applications will also depend on things other than the physical files that get deployed to the server, such as the ability to store data in and retrieve it from a database, or to interact with a web service. These dependencies only increase as applications become less tightly coupled and distributed or service-oriented architectures grow more common.

While exploring the details of how to coordinate the deployment of your website with these systems is well beyond the scope of this book, the high-level discussion of how to plan for these kinds of deployments is not. Below is a list of questions you can ask to help discover the dependencies and tasks that your application deployment requires:

1. What system-level applications and APIs does the application require (e.g., OS version, IIS version, .NET Framework version)?
   • Does any software need to be installed on the server?
2. What system-level folders or files does the application require?

- Does the application require a specific folder path to anything? (This is usually something that you should avoid.)

3. Does the application require a database?
   - If so, have there been any updates to the database schema since the last release?
   - Does the application use a particular database user? If so, is that user's database access properly configured?

4. What other servers or services does the application interact with?
   - Are any networking changes required to access them (e.g., firewall rules, user or role security)?

5. Do I have all of the appropriate licenses purchased and available?

Note that this list certainly does not include everything that you'll need to consider in order to have a successful release. These questions should, however, help address the most common situations and get you thinking about any additional requirements that your particular application may have.

What the EBuy Application Requires

To give an example of the thinking that goes into website deployment, let's take stock of what dependencies and configurations might be involved in deploying the EBuy reference application:

- **System-level APIs and services**. The EBuy application is a pretty basic application that doesn't depend on any system-level APIs other than the .NET 4.5 Framework. It provides all its other API dependencies—including ASP.NET MVC 4—in its /bin folder (which, of course, must be deployed).

- **Views, scripts, stylesheets, and images**. In addition to the assembly dependencies, such as the .NET Framework and the assembly that includes the application's logic, these artifacts are the most obvious dependencies that the application requires in order to function. We'll need to be sure these files get copied along with everything else

- **A database**. The EBuy website is a data-driven website, backed by an Entity Framework Code First data model that requires a database to persist the application's data.

- **A place to store uploaded images**. When users create a new auction listing, they have the option to upload images of the item to display in the listing, and the application must store these images somewhere. The actual location and method of storing the image files may vary, depending on whether the application is hosted on a single server, a server farm, or with a cloud hosting service such as Azure. Regardless of where they are stored, the application must be sure to have both "physical" access (i.e., network or filesystem access) to the location, and the appropriate security permissions to read and write the images.

Once we have answered all of these questions and made sure that we know everything that must be deployed in order for our application to function properly, it's time to begin deploying!

Deploying to Internet Information Server

Perhaps the most common ASP.NET MVC application hosting scenario involves creating and configuring a website using Internet Information Server (IIS). The good news is that ASP.NET MVC applications are—for the most part—just like any other ASP.NET application, so if you are already familiar with deploying an ASP.NET web application to IIS, you do not have much to learn, and none of the steps should come as a surprise to you. If this is your first time working with IIS websites or ASP.NET applications, fear not—the following sections will walk you through everything you need to know in order to get started.

Prerequisites

Before we can create and deploy our website, we first need to ensure that the target web server has all of the prerequisites necessary to host an ASP.NET MVC application. In the early days of the .NET Framework, it took quite a few steps to get an ASP.NET application and all of its prerequisites deployed to a web server.

Luckily, things have progressed to the point where the only prerequisite that needs to be installed on the web server—other than IIS itself—is the .NET Framework (version 4.0 or greater).

Deploying the ASP.NET MVC Framework assemblies

The ASP.NET MVC 4 assemblies themselves also need to be available, but you have two options for deploying those. You can either:

1. Run the ASP.NET MVC 4 installer as described in Chapter 1.
2. Include the ASP.NET MVC Framework assemblies in your application's */bin* folder using the bin-deploying method mentioned earlier in this chapter.

If you plan to run many ASP.NET MVC 4 websites on a single server, it may make sense to choose the first option: install ASP.NET MVC 4 once and not worry about it again. However, there is no compelling reason to go this route other than saving the disk space that the ASP.NET MVC Framework assemblies would occupy in each application.

In almost every scenario, it is advisable to choose the second option and deploy the ASP.NET MVC Framework assemblies in your application's */bin* folder, just as you would any other assembly that your application depends on. Deploying the assemblies with the application makes it very easy to manage, maintain, and even upgrade each individual website in isolation, without worrying about the effect that a server-wide change might have on other sites.

Creating and Configuring an IIS Website

Creating a new IIS website is a very straight-forward process.

To begin, create the directory that your website will be hosted from; for example, *C: \inetpub\wwwroot\Ebuy*. Then, open the IIS management application (Internet Information Services (IIS) Manager), right-click on "Default Web Site," and choose the "Add Application..." menu option, as shown in Figure 19-6, to display the Add Application dialog.

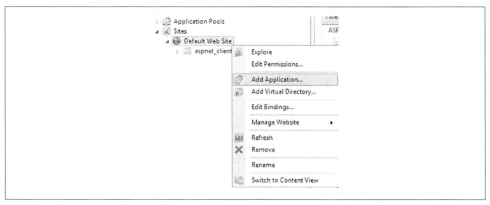

Figure 19-6. Creating a new IIS website

In this dialog (Figure 19-7), enter the name of your website (e.g., *Ebuy*) and the path to the directory that you created in the first step (e.g., *C:\inetpub\wwwroot\Ebuy*).

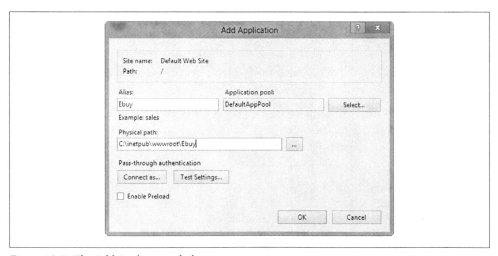

Figure 19-7. The Add Application dialog

You can feel free to leave the rest of the defaults in this dialog alone, but—just for good measure—click the Select... button next to the "Application pool" field to pop up the Select Application Pool dialog and verify that the default application pool uses version 4.0 of the .NET Framework (as shown in Figure 19-8).

If the default application pool is not configured to use version 4.0 of the .NET Framework, create a new application pool that does use .NET 4.0.

If you do not see version 4.0 in the list of available .NET Frameworks, it may mean that the .NET Framework was not properly installed. Try reinstalling the .NET Framework and, if necessary, running the `%FrameworkDir%\%FrameworkVersion%\aspnet_regiis.exe` command to properly configure the .NET Framework inside IIS.

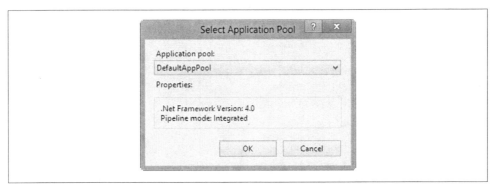

Figure 19-8. The default application pool configured to use .NET Framework version 4.0

Finally, click OK to have IIS create your website. Now you have a website that you can deploy your site to!

 Previous versions of ASP.NET MVC hosted in IIS 6 required special configuration steps to allow for ASP.NET MVC's extension-less URL routing. This is no longer an issue, however, because ASP.NET 4 configures IIS to route anything without an extension directly to ASP.NET.

Note that if you are running IIS 7 or IIS 7.5 on Windows Vista SP2, Windows Server 2008, Windows Server 2008 R2 SP2, or Windows 7, you will need to apply a patch (*http://support.microsoft.com/kb/980368*) to your system.

Publishing from Within Visual Studio

Once you have your application created and configured in IIS, you have several deployment techniques at your disposal.

The most accessible deployment technique is Visual Studio's built-in publishing mechanism. To use it, right-click on the ASP.NET MVC project and choose the "Publish" option from the context menu, as shown in Figure 19-9, to open the Publish Web wizard.

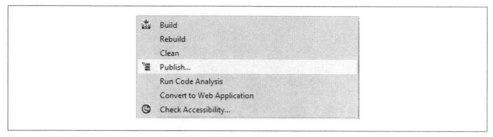

Figure 19-9. Opening the Visual Studio Publish Web wizard

To create a new publishing profile that will allow you to deploy your website, select the "<New...>" option from the drop-down list in the Profile tab and give the new profile a name (e.g., "Local IIS Website"). Then, since we are deploying to the local filesystem, select the "File System" option from the list of available publish methods, as shown in Figure 19-10.

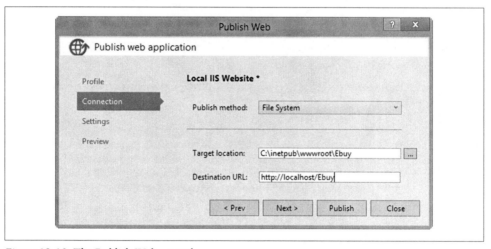

Figure 19-10. The Publish Web wizard

 The "File System" publishing option is only suitable if you are deploying to a web server that you have direct filesystem access to via your network. If you are using a web hosting service, this is probably not the case, so you will have to choose the FTP publishing approach to deploy your website via the universal FTP protocol that all major web hosts support.

Once you choose a publish method, the dialog will change to allow you to fill in the rest of the configuration information needed for Visual Studio to publish using the selected method. You can even save multiple publish configurations by choosing a profile name from the publish profile list and then clicking the Save button.

When you've configured all of the required publish method options, click the Publish button and Visual Studio will deploy your site to the location you specified. After it has successfully deployed the website, Visual Studio will automatically open your browser and navigate to the newly deployed site.

If you've been following along and trying this out on your machine, however, the deployment has probably failed—this was deliberate, in order to show you how to diagnose deployment issues! As it deploys your site, Visual Studio logs everything it's doing to the Output window. If it comes across any issues during deployment, they should be displayed here.

For example, the deployment you just tried to execute may have failed due to the fact that you do not have access to the *C:\inetpub\wwwroot\Ebuy* folder. If this is the case, you should see the "ACCESS DENIED" message in the Output window. To fix this error, update the security options on the target folder to include write access for the current user and try to publish the site again. This time the publish should succeed and a browser window should now open displaying your deployed site.

Copying files with MSBuild

As Chapter 18 showed, it's a good idea to automate as much of your application development process as possible—and nowhere else is this more true than when it comes to deployment. Though Visual Studio's publishing mechanism is quite convenient, having to open Visual Studio every time you need to deploy your site can become pretty tedious. So, let's see how we can reproduce what Visual Studio's Publish Web wizard does with an automated MSBuild script.

The following example shows an MSBuild script that first builds the solution using the `MSBuild` build task, then copies the web application files to the destination website directory using the `Copy` task:

```xml
<?xml version="1.0" encoding="utf-8"?>
<Project ToolsVersion="4.0" DefaultTargets="Deploy"
         xmlns="http://schemas.microsoft.com/developer/msbuild/2003">

  <PropertyGroup>
    <BuildDir>$(MSBuildProjectDirectory)\build\</BuildDir>
  </PropertyGroup>

  <Target Name="Deploy">
    <MSBuild Projects="EBuy.sln" Properties="OutDir=$(BuildDir)" />

    <ItemGroup>
      <WebsiteFiles Include="$(BuildDir)\_PublishedWebsites\Ebuy.Website\**" />
```

```
    </ItemGroup>

    <Copy SourceFiles="@(WebsiteFiles)"
          DestinationFiles="@(WebsiteFiles->'$(DeploymentDir)\%(RecursiveDir)%↵
          (Filename)%(Extension)')"
          SkipUnchangedFiles="true"
    />
  </Target>
</Project>
```

In order to execute this script, open the Visual Studio Command Prompt, navigate to the Ebuy solution folder, then execute the following command:

```
msbuild.exe deploy.proj /p:DeploymentDir="_[Path to Destination]_"
```

This will build the application and direct the output to a temporary build directory (*build* in the current directory), then copy the contents of the *_PublishedWebsites* folder that MSBuild creates for web applications to the destination folder of your choosing.

Executing database scripts with MSBuild

Both the Visual Studio File System Publish and the MSBuild deployment mechanisms are great for deploying files, but what happens when your application depends on a database that can't be deployed with a simple file copy?

One of the great features of Entity Framework Code First is its ability to automatically manage database versions for you—you can tell the framework to upgrade the database automatically during the startup phase of your site whenever it sees that there has been a model change that necessitates a database schema change. If, however, you are not using this Entity Framework Code First feature, it is up to you to track and deploy any database schema changes that may arise during the course of development.

When it comes to deploying database changes, you typically have two choices:

1. Recreate the entire database every time.
2. Keep each database upgrade in its own script file, and execute these files in order to bring the target database up-to-date with the latest schema.

Naturally, Option 1 is the easiest solution during development—it is always less complex to build a database from scratch than to worry about upgrading an existing database. Unless you are developing toward your first production release, however, this approach does not match your final production deployment and therefore does not fulfill the spirit of continuous integration: testing the production deployment as often as possible to discover issues as early as possible.

If you take Option 1 off the table, Option 2—multiple script files with incremental database schema changes—becomes your de facto choice.

Luckily, deploying either of these approaches is pretty simple using MSBuild and SQL Server's *SQLCMD* utility. To add SQL script execution to your build, add the following lines to your MSBuild file:

```
<Target Name="DeployDatabase">
    <ItemGroup>
        <ScriptFiles Include="$(ScriptsDir)\*.sql" />
    </ItemGroup>

    <Exec Command="sqlcmd -E -S $(SqlServer) -i &quot;%(ScriptFiles.FullPath)&quot;" />
</Target>
```

These few lines will locate the SQL scripts in the path that you've provided (*$(Scripts-Dir)*.sql*), then execute the SQLCMD utility for each *.sql* file it finds against the SQL Server instance configured in the `$(SqlServer)` property. Note that these scripts will execute in the order in which MSBuild discovers them. This will be the order in which they appear on the filesystem—by filename—so it often helps to apply a naming convention such as a number prefix on each of the script filenames.

Then you can execute the following command (all on one line) to have MSBuild execute the SQL scripts and build your database automatically:

```
msbuild.exe deploy.proj /t:DeployDatabase /p:ScriptsDir=Scripts /p:SqlServer=.\SQLEXPRESS
```

The SQLCMD utility is installed as part of the standard Microsoft SQL Server installation, but you do not need to have Microsoft SQL Server installed in order to use SQLCMD.

As an alternative to installing Microsoft SQL Server, you can install the free Microsoft SQL Server Feature Pack. You can download and install the latest version of the Microsoft SQL Server Feature Pack by using your favorite search engine to find it by name, or you can use the following link for the Microsoft SQL Server 2008 R2 SP1 Feature Pack: *http://www.microsoft.com/en-us/download/details.aspx?id=26728*.

Deploying to Windows Azure

If you'd like to avoid hosting your own website and take advantage of the increasing amount of "cloud capacity" available to you, one other deployment and hosting option is Microsoft's cloud hosting platform, Windows Azure. With Windows Azure, you can concentrate on your application and let Microsoft worry about the infrastructure required to host it on the Internet.

The rest of this section will walk you through the simple steps for deploying your application to the cloud using Windows Azure. When you're finished, you will have a public website hosted in the cloud.

Creating a Windows Azure Account

Before you can deploy your website to the cloud using Windows Azure, you must first register for a Windows Azure account. To do so, visit the Windows Azure website (*http://www.windowsazure.com*), find and click the link that says "Free trial" or "Register," and create your new account.

Once your account is created, you'll be taken to the Windows Azure Management Portal, the online portal for managing your cloud hosting services.

Creating a New Windows Azure Website

To create a new website using the Windows Azure portal, click the New menu at the bottom-left of the page and choose the "Web Site" option, then click "Create with Database" to open the New Web Site wizard (Figure 19-11). Fill out the information for your new site, such as the DNS name of the site and the region (i.e., data center) in which the site should be hosted. Since the EBuy application requires a database to store its information, choose the "Create new SQL database" option from the Database drop-down list.

Figure 19-11. The Windows Azure New Web Site wizard

The next few steps will help you configure your new database; the default values are generally fine for most small websites. When you're done providing all the information for your new site and its database, click "Create Web Site" to create your new site.

After providing Windows Azure with plenty of time to create and provision your new web application, click on the web application from the list of applications to begin managing it.

Publishing a Windows Azure Website via Source Control

By far the easiest way to deploy your application to a Windows Azure website is to leverage the built-in support for source control publishing via the Team Foundation Server (TFS) or Git source control systems.

Since Chapter 18 already introduced TFS, we'll continue to use it in this example. However, keep in mind that the overall process you're about to see is the same process that's used with the Git source control publishing method.

To begin using TFS source control publishing, click the "Set up TFS publishing" link from your Azure website dashboard (Figure 19-12) to bring up the TFS source control configuration wizard. Then, enter the username that you used to create your TFS Preview account in the previous chapter (or click on the link to create a new TFS Preview account if you have not already done so) and click on the "Authorize now" link to authorize Windows Azure to access your TFS Preview account.

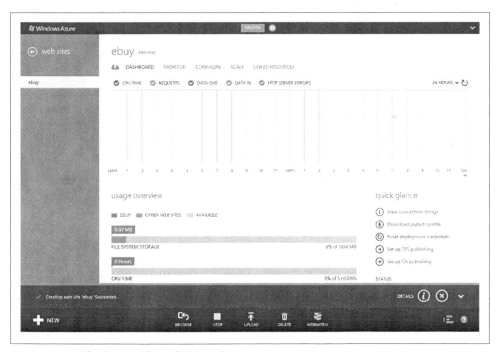

Figure 19-12. The Azure website dashboard

After you've successfully authorized Windows Azure, go to the next dialog and select the source control project that you'd like to link with this website, then click the checkmark to complete. After a few seconds, Windows Azure will link your website to the TFS project that you specified.

With this link in place, every checkin that you perform on your TFS project will trigger a new build of your project in TFS. Upon each successful build, the newly built website will be deployed to Windows Azure and your new changes will be live, without any additional effort on your part.

Continuous Deployment

One of the primary benefits of automated deployments is that it becomes incredibly easy—and often relatively quick—to deploy the application to any environment. Once you have an automated deployment in place, the next logical step is to execute that deployment as often as possible—perhaps even with every checkin. This process of deploying the application very frequently is referred to as *continuous deployment*.

Continuous deployment is a great way to increase the transparency of a project by providing an easy way for anyone to see *exactly* what condition the application is in at the current moment. This allows users to try out new features the moment they are checked in and begin providing feedback on them very early in their development. Consider this the manual, human-driven variation of the continuous integration concept of catching issues as soon as possible.

If you're using TFS deployment with Windows Azure as shown in the previous section, you're already performing continuous deployments. But if you're not using Windows Azure with TFS, that doesn't mean that you can't still take advantage of continuous deployment—it just means that you're going to have to do a little more work to get it set up.

To add a similar sort of continuous deployment mechanism to your project, take some time to determine which of the concepts from this chapter and Chapter 18 apply to your project and combine them together to automate all the steps that it takes to deploy your application.

Done properly, continuous deployment can be a great way to keep an application moving forward by getting changes to the application into users' hands as quickly as possible, and gaining valuable feedback in the process.

Summary

The final task in developing any kind of software is getting it into the hands of your end users. In the case of an ASP.NET MVC website, this may include several tasks, but the most important of them all is copying the files that run the application to a properly configured IIS-powered website, whether it's on your local network or hosted somewhere in the cloud.

There are plenty of ways to deploy an ASP.NET MVC application—from Visual Studio's built-in publishing mechanism to a custom automated deployment using MSBuild—and no one way is appropriate for every application, so it's important to find the approach that works for your project.

Once you've found your ideal publishing mechanism, try to automate it to make your life—and the lives of anyone else who needs to deploy your application in the future—much easier.

Appendixes

ASP.NET MVC and Web Forms Integration

The ASP.NET MVC Framework was not Microsoft's first foray into the web development ecosystem. Far from it, in fact. ASP.NET MVC's predecessor, dubbed ASP.NET Web Forms (simply referred to as "ASP.NET" before the introduction of ASP.NET MVC), was introduced with the first version of the .NET Framework in early 2002. Over the next decade, adoption of the ASP.NET Web Forms Framework steadily grew to achieve a critical mass, powering a good deal of the websites on the Internet. Likewise, a significant number of developers built a strong skill set around creating and maintaining ASP.NET Web Forms websites. Then, a few years later, ASP.NET MVC was released.

Existing websites and skill sets don't cease to exist or immediately get thrown to one side simply because a new technology gets released. Quite the opposite, in fact—many of these sites represent a significant investment and deliver real, ongoing business value. This appendix takes a look at various concepts and strategies that can help you introduce the ASP.NET MVC Framework into existing ASP.NET Web Forms applications. You'll also see several pitfalls to avoid to help make your transition much smoother.

The following sections will show a variety of techniques to achieve increasing levels of integration and cohabitation between ASP.NET MVC and Web Forms applications. Feel free to pick and choose which techniques work for you and your team.

Choosing Between ASP.NET MVC and ASP.NET Web Forms

In many ways, despite sharing a common platform, ASP.NET MVC and ASP.NET Web Forms represent two competing frameworks. Both frameworks help ASP.NET developers quickly and efficiently deliver web-based solutions, but they each do so in their own unique ways.

Web Forms applications don't generally encourage the SOLID design practices detailed in Chapter 2. This means that many developers who prefer a SOLID approach have begrudgingly used ASP.NET Web Forms to deliver .NET-based web applications, yet yearned for a framework that better suited their needs. When these developers encountered ASP.NET MVC, they immediately saw how it met their needs as developers by allowing them to better leverage the SOLID principles, and they were instantly sold on the framework.

If you and your team do not fit into this group of developers—if the concepts and techniques described in this book have not gotten you *excited* about using the new framework—then perhaps ASP.NET MVC is not the right framework for your project. If this is the case, there is absolutely nothing wrong with continuing to use the Web Forms Framework rather than switching to ASP.NET MVC. The Web Forms Framework is certainly not going anywhere; in fact, it continues to get more and better functionality with each release of the .NET Framework.

 Before deciding to migrate to the new framework, be sure that you and your team understand and agree with the fundamental concepts that drive ASP.NET MVC—those described in Chapter 2—such as SOLID architecture.

Transitioning applications or teams from Web Forms to ASP.NET MVC without this solid understanding, just for the sake of using the "latest, greatest framework," can have disastrous effects. Because the two frameworks are so closely related and share the same underlying platform, it is very easy to write a "Web Forms application" by applying Web Forms principles to the ASP.NET MVC Framework. This is exactly why it's often beneficial for developers to have no previous Web Forms experience: so that their prior training doesn't interfere with applying MVC concepts.

Keep this in mind if you or members of your team are seasoned Web Forms developers, and continually evaluate the code you write to ensure that you are following the MVC pattern and not "falling back to the Web Forms ways."

Transitioning a Web Forms Site to ASP.NET MVC

For new "greenfield" applications, it is generally advisable to pick one framework and use it exclusively. However, if you have an existing Web Forms application that you would like to port to ASP.NET MVC, it is not necessarily an either/or decision. The reason that the previous section describes the two frameworks as competing with each other is also the reason that makes it quite possible to integrate the two in a single application: they are both built on the ASP.NET platform.

Consider how requests are processed in a Web Forms application: IIS receives the request, finds that it maps to a physical file (an *.aspx* page) in the site's folder structure, then executes the Web Forms HTTP handler to execute the page. Then consider ASP.NET MVC request handling. IIS receives the request but does not find a corresponding physical file, so it queries the route table, which states that the request should be handled by the MVC HTTP handler, and then executes that handler. Now consider this: the route table is a core ASP.NET feature that works just as well in Web Forms applications as it does in ASP.NET MVC applications!

It's quite easy to grasp the notion of ASP.NET MVC and Web Forms concepts coexisting in the same application when you take a step back to see that you are not creating "an ASP.NET MVC application" (based on controllers and views) or "a Web Forms application" (based on *.aspx* pages), but rather *an ASP.NET application* based on `HttpModules` and `HttpHandlers`. When you consider your application in these terms, getting the two frameworks to work together is simply a matter of file placement and configuration!

The following sections describe several techniques that you can leverage to make the transition from Web Forms to ASP.NET MVC much less painful, allowing you to get the most out of your existing Web Forms investment. However, all of these techniques rely on one fundamental concept: IIS needs to be able to figure out whether a given request is an ASP.NET MVC or a Web Forms request. Once it determines that, IIS can send the request to the appropriate handler and the application behaves as you'd expect.

Adding ASP.NET MVC to an Existing Web Forms Application

If you are very risk-averse and would like to change as little of your application as possible, you might consider augmenting your existing Web Forms application with ASP.NET MVC functionality. In other words, you are not letting ASP.NET MVC "take over" your application; you're letting it handle certain very specific requests. Using this approach, you will define which requests ASP.NET MVC will handle by registering specific routing rules.

In order to have your existing application start routing requests to ASP.NET MVC, you will first need to perform a few configuration steps:

1. Add the *System.Web.Mvc* and *System.Web.Razor* assemblies to your application's assembly references.
2. Add the following entries to the `system.web > compilation > assemblies` collection in your root *web.config*:

    ```
    System.Web.Mvc,Version=4.0.0.0,Culture=neutral,PublicKeyToken=31BF3856AD364E35
    System.Web.WebPages,Version=2.0.0.0,Culture=neutral,PublicKeyToken=31BF3856AD364E35
    ```
3. Create a */Views* folder in the root of your application. The location of this folder within your application is important because the ViewFactory will attempt to look in the same physical file paths as in a regular ASP.NET MVC application.

- As you would do in a standard ASP.NET MVC application, create a */Views/Shared* folder to hold any common views.
- Copy the */Views/web.config* file from an existing ASP.NET MVC website, or use the file shown in Example A-1. This configuration file is important because it registers the Razor file type handler and tells IIS that the files underneath this folder are for internal application use only and should not be accessible to the public (if they are requested, IIS should return a "404 Not Found" error).

4. Optionally, create a *Controllers* folder to hold your ASP.NET MVC controllers. Unlike with the */Views* folder, the location of ASP.NET MVC controllers does not matter, so you can feel free to put this folder wherever you like. Technically speaking, you can even put your controllers in a completely different project.

5. Finally, you'll need to add the routing configuration in the class that defines your HttpApplication (generally in your *Global.asax.cs* file), just as in a standard ASP.NET MVC application. From a technical standpoint you'll use the same API to register which routes the ASP.NET MVC portion of your site will handle. The fundamental difference in this scenario is that you have two frameworks competing for the same URLs, so you'll need to consider this when creating your routes.

Example A-1 shows the sample */Views/web.config* file mentioned above.

Example A-1. /Views/web.config configuration file

```xml
<?xml version="1.0"?>

<configuration>
  <configSections>
    <sectionGroup name="system.web.webPages.razor"
        type="System.Web.WebPages.Razor.Configuration.RazorWebSectionGroup,System.Web.↵
        WebPages.Razor,Version=2.0.0.0,Culture=neutral,PublicKeyToken=31BF3856AD364E35">
      <section name="host"
        type="System.Web.WebPages.Razor.Configuration.HostSection,System.Web.WebPages.Razor,↵
        Version=2.0.0.0,Culture=neutral,PublicKeyToken=31BF3856AD364E35"
        requirePermission="false" />
      <section name="pages"
        type="System.Web.WebPages.Razor.Configuration.RazorPagesSection,System.Web.WebPages.↵
        Razor,Version=2.0.0.0,Culture=neutral,PublicKeyToken=31BF3856AD364E35"
        requirePermission="false" />
    </sectionGroup>
  </configSections>

  <system.web.webPages.razor>
    <host factoryType="System.Web.Mvc.MvcWebRazorHostFactory,System.Web.Mvc,Version=4.0.0.0,↵
    Culture=neutral,PublicKeyToken=31BF3856AD364E35" />
    <pages pageBaseType="System.Web.Mvc.WebViewPage">
      <namespaces>
        <add namespace="System.Web.Mvc" />
        <add namespace="System.Web.Mvc.Ajax" />
        <add namespace="System.Web.Mvc.Html" />
        <add namespace="System.Web.Routing" />
      </namespaces>
```

```
      </pages>
  </system.web.webPages.razor>

  <appSettings>
    <add key="webpages:Enabled" value="false" />
  </appSettings>

  <system.web>
    <httpHandlers>
      <add path="*" verb="*" type="System.Web.HttpNotFoundHandler"/>
    </httpHandlers>

    <pages
        validateRequest="false"
        pageParserFilterType="System.Web.Mvc.ViewTypeParserFilter, System.Web.Mvc, ↵
        Version=4.0.0.0, Culture=neutral, PublicKeyToken=31BF3856AD364E35"
        pageBaseType="System.Web.Mvc.ViewPage, System.Web.Mvc, Version=4.0.0.0, ↵
        Culture=neutral, PublicKeyToken=31BF3856AD364E35"
        userControlBaseType="System.Web.Mvc.ViewUserControl, System.Web.Mvc, ↵
        Version=4.0.0.0, Culture=neutral, PublicKeyToken=31BF3856AD364E35">
      <controls>
        <add assembly="System.Web.Mvc, Version=4.0.0.0, Culture=neutral, ↵
        PublicKeyToken=31BF3856AD364E35" namespace="System.Web.Mvc" tagPrefix="mvc" />
      </controls>
    </pages>
  </system.web>

  <system.webServer>
    <validation validateIntegratedModeConfiguration="false" />

    <handlers>
      <remove name="BlockViewHandler"/>
      <add  name="BlockViewHandler" path="*" verb="*"
          preCondition="integratedMode" type="System.Web.HttpNotFoundHandler" />
    </handlers>
  </system.webServer>
</configuration>
```

Keep in mind that physical files (e.g., Web Forms *.aspx* pages) will always take precedence over any routes you define, which means that the Web Forms portions of your application will be chosen over any ASP.NET MVC controller logic. With this exception aside, you are free to follow the rest of the techniques in this book to build your Web Forms/MVC hybrid application just like a "pure" ASP.NET MVC application.

Copying Web Forms Functionality to an ASP.NET MVC Application

As the previous section shows, the bulk of the work in getting ASP.NET MVC and Web Forms to play well together in the same application is in configuring the ASP.NET MVC side of things. Thus, it makes sense—depending on your current Web Forms application—to create a new ASP.NET MVC application to start with, and port your existing Web Forms pages over to this new application.

Although this new application will be configured with ASP.NET MVC in mind, the fact still remains that physical Web Forms *.aspx* pages will take precedence over any ASP.NET MVC routing logic. Regardless of how you get there, both approaches achieve the same result: Web Forms and ASP.NET MVC functionality coexisting in the same site.

Integrating Web Forms and ASP.NET MVC Functionality

The previous few sections described techniques that allowed the ASP.NET MVC and Web Forms Frameworks to coexist in the same application. However, since these two frameworks are built on top of the ASP.NET platform, they both share core functionality that allows them to go beyond simply "coexisting" with each other to actually sharing data and functionality—in other words, *integrating*—with each other.

User Management

Perhaps the most important—or at least the most frequently used—bit of shared functionality is user management based on ASP.NET's *Forms Authentication*, *Windows Authentication*, *Role*, *Membership*, and *Profile* providers. Not only will these providers continue to work perfectly well with your ASP.NET MVC application, but you may even be able to retain any Web Forms code (such as login pages, user profile or administration pages, etc.) that leverage the providers.

For example, when a Web Forms page uses the Forms Authentication provider to validate and authenticate a user, the token that is generated for that user is an ASP.NET session token that is used by the core ASP.NET API to authenticate the user for each request. This means that a user can authenticate herself via a Web Forms page, then be redirected to an ASP.NET MVC controller and still show up as authenticated.

Cache Management

Yet another widely used integration point is ASP.NET's caching functionality. Web Forms developers have been leveraging the application-scoped `System.Web.Caching.Cache` class (typically accessed via the `HttpContext.Cache` property) and the user-scoped `System.Web.HttpSessionState+class` (available via the `+HttpContext.Session` property) to manage cached data since .NET Framework version 1.1, and there's no reason to stop now!

Just like the previously mentioned user management providers, these two classes are part of the core ASP.NET API and are accessible to both Web Forms and ASP.NET MVC developers alike. When Web Forms and ASP.NET MVC coexist in the same website, they also share the application processes, which means data written via the `Cache` and `HttpSessionState` APIs by one framework will be available during subsequent requests to the other framework.

Many, Many More!

There are plenty more APIs that play well with both ASP.NET MVC and Web Forms. To find them, check the API documentation and your existing code—just about any namespace that doesn't start with `System.Web.UI` is probably a candidate for cross-framework integration.

 Though many parts of the ASP.NET Framework are accessible by both Web Forms and ASP.NET MVC, one significant piece of the Web Forms Framework that is *not* supported in ASP.NET MVC is `ViewState`. Most often, `ViewState` is used for a Web Forms page to communicate with itself, so the chances of running into `ViewState` issues when cross-posting between Web Forms pages and ASP.NET MVC controllers are slim.

However, when transitioning your Web Forms application to ASP.NET MVC, be on the lookout for any code in your Web Forms application that expects `ViewState`—the `ViewState` data will not exist during the course of an ASP.NET MVC request, so code that depends on it will likely break!

Summary

This appendix analyzed how the "new" ASP.NET MVC Framework fits into existing "legacy" ASP.NET Web Forms applications. As it turns out, the ASP.NET API that they both share provides an impressive upgrade path to port existing Web Forms code to ASP.NET MVC. When existing code can't be easily upgraded or replaced, the underlying ASP.NET platform also supports a largely seamless cohosting environment where the two frameworks can not only live side-by-side, but even integrate with each other.

Leveraging NuGet as a Platform

Chapter 1 introduced the NuGet package management tool, which helps you install, configure, and maintain your application's various dependencies, and other chapters throughout the book showed a handful of examples of consuming packages published and maintained by Microsoft and the community at large. However, you don't have to limit yourself to packages that other people have published.

This appendix will provide a brief introduction to creating your own packages and an overview of what, exactly, a NuGet package really is. Once you have the basics down, you'll find some NuGet tips and tricks that may help make development more enjoyable for you and your team.

 The goal of this appendix is not to teach you everything there is to know about NuGet—NuGet's own documentation is far too good to compete with! Instead, this appendix briefly shows the fundamentals of using NuGet as a *tool*, then quickly moves on to showing how you and your team can leverage NuGet as a *platform*.

Installing the NuGet Command-Line Tool

Though the ASP.NET MVC installation package installs the NuGet Package Manager to consume NuGet packages in your projects, in order to create and distribute your own packages you'll first need to download the *NuGet command-line tool* from the NuGet CodePlex site (*http://nuget.codeplex.com/releases*).

Look for the download called "NuGet Command Line Bootstrapper" in the Downloads section of the NuGet CodePlex site, then download and execute it. This initial download is actually just a bootstrapper—the first time it executes it will retrieve the latest version of the *actual* NuGet command-line tool and replace itself with this updated version.

After you've downloaded and executed the bootstrapper to upgrade to the latest version of the NuGet command-line tool, move the executable to a folder that is available from your Visual Studio command prompt (e.g., the .NET Framework directory).

Then it's time to create packages!

Creating NuGet Packages

The easiest way to create a NuGet package is to execute the `nuget pack` command against an existing Visual Studio project. For example:

```
nuget pack MyApplication.csproj
```

This command will create a NuGet package using the assembly version, project name, and other metadata that it retrieves from your project's *AssemblyInfo.cs* file.

The NuSpec File

A NuSpec file is an XML configuration file that specifies a package's contents and metadata (e.g., package ID, version, name, dependencies, etc.). NuGet requires this file for every package it creates, because the metadata contains crucial information that NuGet uses to determine which packages—and which versions of those packages—it needs to download in order to satisfy a dependency.

This is true even when generating a NuGet package from a Visual Studio project file, as in the previous example. Even though you never saw it, NuGet actually generated a temporary NuSpec file that it used to generate the final NuGet package.

The problem with allowing NuGet to automatically generate this crucial file is that you give up a lot of control over the generated package. What's more, you probably have a much better idea about what your assemblies depend on than what NuGet can determine from looking at your project file.

Therefore, it is a good idea to generate and customize your own NuSpec file rather than letting NuGet generate it for you. The following sections show several methods that you can use to create and customize NuSpec files.

Using the NuGet command-line tool

The first method of creating a NuSpec file is a variation of a previously used command: `nuget spec`. The `nuget spec` command is very much like the `nuget pack` command, except that the `nuget spec` command saves the generated NuSpec file to disk so that you can continue modifying it prior to using it to generate the final package.

For example, you could execute the following statement in the Visual Studio command prompt to generate the NuSpec file for the aforementioned *MyApplication.csproj*:

```
nuget spec MyApplication.csproj
```

Alternatively, you can execute the same command against a prebuilt assembly:

```
nuget spec -a MyApplication.dll
```

These commands will both create a file named *MyApplication.nuspec* that looks like this:

```xml
<?xml version="1.0"?>
<package >
  <metadata>
    <id>$id$</id>
    <version>$version$</version>
    <title>$title$</title>
    <authors>$author$</authors>
    <owners>$author$</owners>
    <licenseUrl>http://LICENSE_URL_HERE_OR_DELETE_THIS_LINE</licenseUrl>
    <projectUrl>http://PROJECT_URL_HERE_OR_DELETE_THIS_LINE</projectUrl>
    <iconUrl>http://ICON_URL_HERE_OR_DELETE_THIS_LINE</iconUrl>
    <requireLicenseAcceptance>false</requireLicenseAcceptance>
    <description>$description$</description>
    <releaseNotes>Summary of changes made in this release of the package.</releaseNotes>
    <copyright>Copyright 2012</copyright>
    <tags>Tag1 Tag2</tags>
  </metadata>
</package>
```

In its initial state, the fields in the generated NuSpec file are all populated with tokens following the pattern $[name]$, which NuGet replaces with actual values during execution of the nuget pack command.

Clearly, this template doesn't have very specific information. It merely defines a starting point that you can customize to define the details related to your project.

At this point, you'll need to open the NuSpec file in your favorite XML editor (such as Visual Studio's built-in XML editor) and modify the file by hand to define how you'd like your package to be configured.

Using the NuGet Package Explorer

As an alternative to manually editing NuSpec XML files, you can revisit the NuGet download page (*http://nuget.codeplex.com/releases*) and download the *NuGet Package Explorer*.

Along with other package management functionality, the NuGet Package Explorer provides an excellent GUI that can help you build your NuSpec files.

The NuGet Package Explorer makes it somewhat easier to create a NuSpec file:

1. First, select the Create New Package (Ctrl-N) option from the application's home screen.
2. Then choose the Edit > Edit Package Metadata... menu option to create a new project that you can begin editing.

3. At this point, the Package Explorer is in edit mode (Figure B-1), and you can use the GUI to specify the various aspects of your packages.

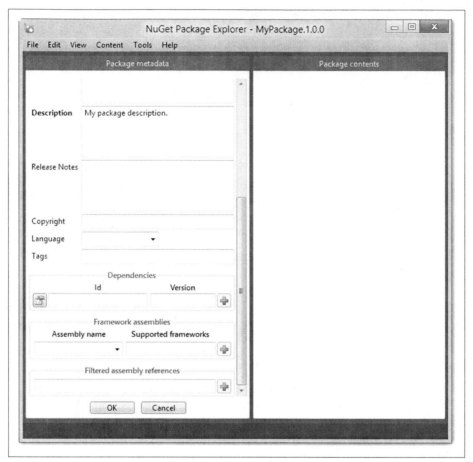

Figure B-1. Editing a package with the NuGet Package Explorer

4. Once you've finished customizing your package, you can use the File > Save menu option (or hit Ctrl-S) to generate and save the NuGet package to disk, and/or choose File > Save Metadata As... to save the NuSpec file to disk.

Generating the NuGet Package from a NuSpec File

Once you have a NuSpec file that defines the contents of your package, you can then use the nuget pack command to generate the NuGet package.

For example, in order to generate a NuGet package from the *MyApplication.nuspec* file created in the previous example, you'd execute the following command:

```
nuget pack MyApplication.nuspec
```

With any luck, this command will generate a new NuGet package named *MyApplication.1.0.0.nupkg* containing all of the content and assemblies specified in the NuSpec file.

You can then deploy this NuGet package to a NuGet package repository to begin using it in your applications!

Specifying token values

When your NuSpec file contains tokens such as those in the default generated template, the `nuget pack` command will likely complain that it does not know how to handle them. When this is the case, you can specify the values for these tokens by using the `-Properties` switch and providing a semicolon-delimited list of key/value pairs.

For example, the following command (which should all be typed on a single line!) will substitute any references to the `$description$` token with the phrase "My custom package description":

```
nuget pack MyApplication.nuspec -Properties description="My custom package description"
```

Setting the version

Likewise, the `nuget pack` command exposes a `-Version` switch that enables you to specify the version of the package you'd like to generate. The `-Version` switch can be applied to any NuSpec file, regardless of whether it specifies a token value for its Version field.

For example, the following command will generate version 1.7.0 of the "MyApplication" package, regardless of the value of the `version` property that may or may not be specified in the NuSpec file:

```
nuget pack MyApplication.nuspec -Version 1.7.0
```

The Anatomy of a NuGet Package

Now that you've seen how to create your own NuGet packages, let's take a step back and analyze what a NuGet package really *is*.

When it comes down to it, NuGet packages are just fancy ZIP files that contain custom metadata (in the form of *.nuspec* files) and some or all of the following: assemblies (a.k.a. "libs"), content, and tools.

For example, if you open a NuGet package using your favorite archiving program, you might see a folder structure that resembles Example B-1.

Example B-1. Example NuGet folder structure

```
\Content
        \App_Start
                ConfigureMyApplication.cs.pp
        web.config.transform
```

```
                [Other content files and folders]
        \libs
                \net40
                        MyApplication.dll
                \sl4
                        MyApplication.dll
                [Folders for other supported frameworks]
        \tools
                init.ps1
                install.ps1
                uninstall.ps1
        MyApplication.nuspec
```

Content

The *Content* folder represents the root folder of the target application. Anything that is placed in this folder—images, text files, class templates, or even subfolders—will be copied directly into the target application.

In addition to normal file-copying behavior, the *Content* folder may also include *configuration file and source code transformation templates*. These make it easy to selectively modify certain parts of the target project.

For instance, Example B-1 shows the *web.config.transform* configuration file transform. This file may include the following:

```xml
<configuration>
    <system.webServer>
        <handlers>
            <add name="MyHandler" path="MyHandler.axd" verb="GET,POST"
                type="MyApplication.MyHandler, MyApplication" preCondition=↵
                "integratedMode" />
        </handlers>
    </system.webServer>
</configuration>
```

When NuGet adds the package containing this *web.config.transform* to a project, NuGet will update that project's *web.config* and add the "MyHandler" HTTP handler configuration.

Example B-1 also contains the *App_Start\ConfigureMyApplication.cs.pp* source code transformation template, which may resemble the following:

```csharp
[assembly: WebActivator.PreApplicationStartMethod(
                    typeof($rootnamespace$.MyHandlerInitializer), "Initialize")]

namespace $rootnamespace$
{
        public class MyHandlerInitializer
        {
                public static void Initialize()
                {
                        // Configure MyHandler settings at runtime
                }
```

```
        }
    }
```

As with the *web.config* transform, when NuGet installs this package, it will copy *ConfigureMyApplication.cs.pp* into the project's *App_Start* folder, run the transformation, then remove the *.pp* extension, creating a fully functional class that the project can use immediately.

Assemblies

After the *Content* folder is the *libs* folder. This folder is pretty straightforward: any assembly contained within it is added to the target project's *References* collection.

Assemblies may be placed in the root of the folder or—even better—placed within a framework-specific folder, such as *net40*, to indicate which framework and version those assemblies target. By splitting assemblies into several different folders, you can effectively target multiple frameworks and multiple versions of those frameworks with a single package.

As of this writing, NuGet recognizes three different frameworks, listed in Table B-1.

Table B-1. Frameworks recognized by NuGet

Framework	Abbreviation
.NET Framework	*net*
Silverlight	*sl*
.NET Micro Framework	*netmf*

Example B-1 shows this functionality in action by including two versions of the *MyApplication.dll* assembly: one that targets .NET Framework version 4.0 ("net40"), and a second that targets version 4 of the Silverlight framework ("sl4").

Tools

Finally, there is the *tools* folder. This folder contains any scripts, executables, or other content that developers may be interested in consuming, but not interested in including in their project, as content or referenced assemblies.

The *tools* folder can also contain one or more of the following "special" PowerShell scripts, which NuGet looks for and executes as it processes each package:

init.ps1
> Runs the first time a package is installed in a solution

install.ps1
> Runs each time a package is installed

uninstall.ps1
> runs every time a package is uninstalled

NuGet executes these scripts within the context of Visual Studio, providing them with full access to Visual Studio's DTE API. This enables you to use these scripts to query and manipulate just about anything within Visual Studio any time a package is initialized, installed, or uninstalled.

In addition to executing the special scripts noted above, NuGet will add any *tools* folder to the path available in the Package Management Console whenever it installs a package in a solution. This makes it very easy to distribute scripts and executables that support active development but won't be deployed with the final application.

For example, the *MvcScaffolding* package contains a handful of PowerShell scripts that help developers generate models, views, and controllers in their ASP.NET MVC applications. These PowerShell scripts are incredibly valuable time-savers and productivity boosters, but they are meant to aid in the development process and are not intended to actually ship along with the final product.

Types of NuGet Packages

Now that you've seen what a NuGet package can contain, let's take a look at how you can use NuGet packages to your advantage.

From a high level, NuGet packages tend to fall into a few categories: *assembly packages*, *tool packages*, and *meta packages*. Though they are all created using the same specification and managed via NuGet, packages from each category are used for very different reasons.

Assembly Packages

Assembly packages are packages whose purpose is to add one or more assemblies to a project, as well as any auxiliary content or configuration that those assemblies require or expect. Assembly packages are the most common, since they are the primary reason that NuGet was created in the first place.

Tool Packages

Tool packages introduce tools into the development environment for use during development. In this context, "tools" are meant to help aid development and testing and are generally not part of the final released application. Tools can be anything from PowerShell scripts to full-blown applications.

Meta Packages

Meta packages are packages that reference other packages. The primary purpose for meta packages is to help get a project up and running quickly by automatically downloading and configuring a number of dependencies with the installation of one package.

For example, we might create the theoretical "EF Code First + ELMAH + Glimpse + Ninject" package, which includes all of the packages you need to write the sample application in this book. Then, to follow all of the examples in the book, all you'd need to do is go to File > New Application… > ASP.NET MVC 4 Web Application and use NuGet to install this meta package, and you'd have all the references you need.

Sharing Your NuGet Packages

Once you've created a NuGet package, you'll need to add it to a *package repository* in order to distribute it to other developers so they can consume it in their applications.

When it comes to distributing packages you've built, you essentially have two options to choose from: publish your package to the public NuGet.org package repository, or host your own package repository.

Publishing to the Public NuGet.org Package Repository

During installation, the NuGet installer preconfigures a single repository for you—the public NuGet package repository hosted on NuGet.org. Because it comes preconfigured, the public NuGet.org package repository is the most convenient way to share packages with other developers, and if the package you've created contains functionality that you'd like to share with the world, uploading the package to the public NuGet.org repository is generally a great idea.

Before you can publish a package to the public NuGet.org repository, you'll first need to create an account on the NuGet.org website by visiting *http://nuget.org* and choosing the Register option in the main menu.

Using the NuGet.org package upload wizard

Once you've created your account, you can begin using the public repository to distribute your packages. The easiest way to get a package onto the public repository is to use the online package upload wizard, which walks you through all the steps required to upload your package.

You can begin the online package upload wizard by choosing the Upload Package menu option on the NuGet.org website.

Using the NuGet command-line tool

Alternatively, you can utilize the publishing functionality built into the NuGet command-line tool to deploy your packages. This method is often preferred over using the NuGet.org website directly, because if you used the command-line tool to generate your packages, it's easy to execute the tool one more time to publish those packages as well.

The command is pretty straightforward: `nuget push [package name]`.

For instance, the command to publish the *MyApplication* package created earlier would be:

```
nuget push MyApplication
```

The first time you attempt to execute this command, you'll most likely encounter an error indicating that you have not specified an API key for the package source that you're attempting to publish to (the public NuGet.org repository). API keys are unique and secret tokens created by the repository so that it can control access to the repository. While the public NuGet.org repository allows anyone with an account to publish packages, you must at least have an account in order to do so. Luckily, NuGet.org automatically generates an API key for you when you create your account. In order to retrieve the key, simply log in to the site and visit your profile page. On this page there is an "API Key" section that contains a link that says "click to show." Click this link and copy your API key.

Once you've copied your API key, you'll need to tell NuGet about it. To do this, execute the command `nuget setApiKey [API key]`. For example:

```
nuget setApiKey ae19257f-9f0c-4dcf-b46a-60792fd5ff2d
```

With your API key in place, you should now be able to execute the `nuget push` command to publish your packages to the public NuGet.org package repository.

Host Your Own Package Repository

You don't have to put packages on the public NuGet.org repository to consume them in your projects. In fact, you don't even need to leave your local machine!

NuGet offers two primary ways to host and consume your own packages: setting up a file system repository, and hosting your own instance of the NuGet web server.

Using a filesystem repository

A filesystem repository is exactly what it sounds like—a collection of packages stored on a filesystem that you have access to. What's more, it's very easy to get up and running.

To see the filesystem repository in action, follow these few short steps:

1. Begin by creating a new folder named *C:\NuGetPackages* on your local hard drive.

2. Then, open up NuGet's settings dialog (Tools > Library Package Manager > Package Manager Settings in Visual Studio), and switch to the Package Sources section to add the new package source.

3. Next, add a new package source by specifying a name for the new source in the Name field and entering the path to the package source in the Source field (in this case, *C:\NuGetPackages*), as shown in Figure B-2.

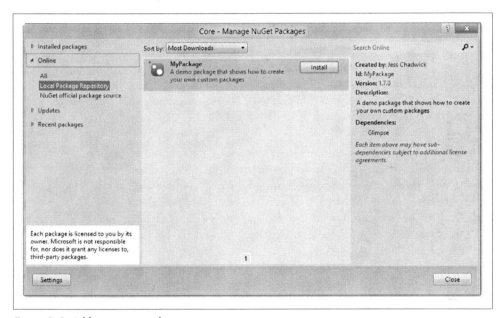

Figure B-2. Adding a new package source

4. Finally, click the Add button to add the repository to the list of sources.

The next time you use the Package Manager, you'll see your new source listed, and any packages you add to the source (i.e., your *C:\NuGetPackages* folder) should show up in the Package Manager's list of packages for installation into your project (see Figure B-3).

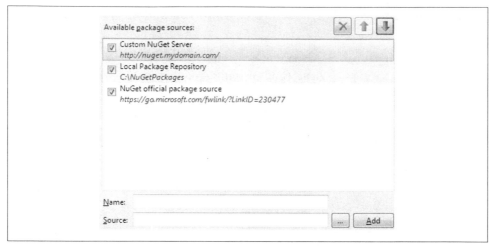

Figure B-3. Your new source should now show up in the Package Manager's list

At this point you might be thinking that cultivating a package repository on your local hard drive seems kind of silly—and you're probably right. However, keep in mind that the file path doesn't have to be on your local hard drive. The "filesystem" that hosts your packages can be any share that you can access via the Windows File Explorer—including network file shares! In fact, hosting your team's custom NuGet package on a centralized file share is an easy and efficient way to ensure that everyone has access to the same packages.

Hosting a NuGet Server repository

The NuGet Server is a website that hosts a set of OData web services that contain NuGet package information—it's the same website that powers the public NuGet.org package repository. While hosting a filesystem package repository is an easy way to get up and running quickly, hosting your own NuGet Server instance is almost as easy but provides you with much more power and flexibility.

Here's how to host your own NuGet Server instance:

1. To begin, open Visual Studio and create a new web application project using the ASP.NET Empty Web Application template.

2. Use the NuGet Package Manager to find and install the *NuGet.Server* NuGet package, which will download and configure everything you need to run a NuGet Server.

3. By default, the *NuGet.Server* package also creates a *Packages* folder to act as the default location for hosting your NuGet package files. If you would like to store your NuGet packages somewhere else, enter the path to the new *Packages* folder in the `appSettings` > `packagesPath` setting in the project's *web.config* file.

---

4. Once you have everything up and running, you can deploy the website just as you would any other site. Keep in mind that the site does need to be able to access files in the *Packages* directory, wherever that may be.

After you've deployed your site and determined that everything is working, it's time to add the new site as another package source via the NuGet settings dialog (Tools > Library Package Manager > Package Manager Settings in Visual Studio).

This step is just like adding the filesystem repository in the previous example, except this time the value of the Source field will be the URL to your NuGet Server instance. Your list of available package sources should now look like Figure B-4.

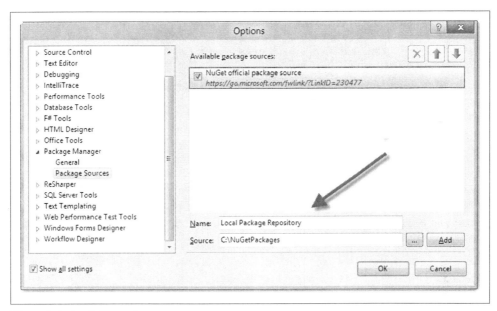

Figure B-4. Available package sources

Once again, the next time you use the Package Manager, you'll see your new source listed, and any packages you add to the source should show up in the Package Manager's list of packages for installation into your project.

Tips, Tricks, and Pitfalls

From a technical standpoint, it is very easy to use NuGet to download, install, and configure assembly dependencies, and even add content to your application. It's also very easy to create and distribute your own custom NuGet packages. There are, however, a few scenarios in which NuGet can introduce some friction, particularly when dealing with large applications with many projects and/or multiple development teams.

The following list contains some pitfalls to watch out for when working with NuGet, as well as some tips and tricks to help you get the most out of NuGet in your projects.

Pitfall: NuGet Does Not Solve "DLL Hell"

The phrase "DLL hell" (or the more general "dependency hell") refers to the difficulties that arise when applications have dependencies such as assemblies or other libraries that are dynamically referenced at runtime. While it's true that one of NuGet's main goals is to ensure that your assemblies are both up-to-date and do not conflict with one another—and it generally does a great job of this—it's not always possible to deliver on this promise.

The most common conflict occurs when two packages expect very different versions of a third package. For example, both Ninject and Glimpse share a dependency on NLog; however, Ninject depends on a *maximum* NLog version of 2.0 and Glimpse depends on a *minimum* NLog version of 2.5. Clearly, the two packages can't be included in the same project! Luckily, this conflict arises very early and NuGet makes it easy to discover (NuGet will display an error and fail to add the packages), so its effects can be minimized.

An even worse conflict can arise when two packages depend on different versions of a third package—as in the first conflict—but their NuSpec metadata does not provide enough information to let NuGet know that the two packages conflict with each other. In other words, the logic that NuGet uses to determine which assembly versions belong in your application is only as good as the information provided in the specification files it reads, so when packages fail to accurately and fully describe their dependencies, they open the door to unintended conflicts.

Consider the previous example, in which Ninject depends on NLog v2.0 and Glimpse depends on NLog v2.5. Let's assume in this case that the specifications for the Ninject package fail to mention that it only works with NLog v2.0 and earlier and does not support NLog v2.5. Without this information, NuGet will happily install the incompatible NLog v2.5—and the Ninject assemblies will fail at runtime.

These are just a few examples of classic assembly versioning conflicts that continue to be a problem, even when using tools such as NuGet. With proper version and dependency information, NuGet is very effective at helping you avoid potential dependency problems, but nothing is foolproof—you still need to be cautious when mixing and matching various assemblies!

Tip: Use Install-Package -Version to Install a Specific Package Version

There may be times when you need to install or upgrade a package, but would like to avoid the most recent version of that package.

For example, suppose your application is currently using Ninject v2.1.0 and you'd like to upgrade to a later version (e.g., v2.2.5) that has some new features that you want to take advantage of. The problem is, you've also discovered that the *latest* Ninject release (e.g., v2.4.0) has a known bug that will break your application.

In this scenario, if you request the Ninject package using the Manage NuGet Packages GUI or the `Install-Package` command-line prompt, NuGet will see that version v2.4.0 is the latest version and assume that it is the version you'd like to have installed. Of course, you know otherwise.

Luckily, NuGet offers the `-Version` flag: a mechanism that allows you, the developer, to override NuGet's versioning intelligence and specify the exact version of a package that you'd like to install (although this option is not exposed in the UI). In order to use this option, simply tack it on to the end of an `Install-Package` command in the Package Manager Console.

For example, you could use the following command to install the specific Ninject package version 2.2.5 and avoid upgrading to version 2.4.0:

```
Install-Package Ninject -Version 2.2.5
```

This command will download and install Ninject v 2.2.5, regardless of what NuGet calculates the most recent version of the Ninject package to be.

Tip: Use Semantic Versioning

Regardless of whether you actually care about an assembly's version number, all assemblies must have one. What's more, in order to create and distribute NuGet packages, you must give them unique version numbers that not only distinguish them from other releases of the same package, but also indicate their order of release. By default, Visual Studio generates these version numbers for you, but when you start creating custom NuGet packages version numbers become much more meaningful, and you'll likely want to take a more active role in defining and managing them.

By their very nature, product and assembly versions are relative at best—and arbitrary at worst. For instance, "version 1.0" of one product usually doesn't have anything to do with "version 1.0" of another product. For that matter, what does "version 1.0" mean, anyway? How does it differ from versions "0.1", "1.5", or "2.0" of the same product?

Since package versioning is arguably the most important aspect of dependency management, NuGet employs a popular versioning scheme called Semantic Versioning (*http://semver.org*). While the Semantic Versioning specification lays out a number of detailed rules that define the various parts of version numbers, semantic versions really boil down to the pattern `[Major].[Minor].[Patch]`. Each part in the semantic version is a non-negative integer that starts at 0 and is incremented by 1 each time there is a change to the codebase that is significant enough to warrant a change in version.

What, then, is "a change to the codebase that is significant enough to warrant a change in version"? Generally speaking, semantic version parts are incremented in the following instances:

Major

Any time backward-incompatible changes are introduced

Minor

Any time new backward-compatible changes are introduced

Patch

Any time backward-compatible changes to existing behavior are introduced

You are free to apply any kind of versioning scheme you like to the NuGet packages that you distribute, but NuGet will apply the above rules to any version numbers in order to determine when updates are appropriate.

Tip: Mark "Beta" Packages with Prerelease Version Markers

What happens when you'd like to distribute a "test" package to certain users that is not quite ready to be released to the general population? In most cases, when you release this package to a repository, NuGet will automatically download and install it for all users, which is clearly not what you want to happen! Luckily, NuGet supports the concept of *prerelease packages*—packages that live side-by-side in the same repository with normal "release" packages, yet are hidden to users unless they specifically ask to see them.

In order to mark a package as a prerelease package, convert the package's version number to a Semantic Versioning prerelease version number by adding a dash ("-") after the primary version number, then any alphanumeric prerelease version number. For instance, the version number "1.0-beta" indicates that the package is a prerelease package for "version 1.0," which will come sometime in the future.

Then, deploy the prerelease package to the same repository as your normal packages, where they will be available to NuGet but not visible to users performing normal package-management actions. In order to consume prerelease packages, add the `-Prerelease` flag to any NuGet queries or installation commands. For example, if a version of the *MyApplication* package is released with the prerelease version number "1.0-beta", the `Get-Packages` command without the `-Prerelease` flag will fail to find any available packages:

```
PM> Get-Packages MyApplication
```

However, adding the `-Prerelease` flag shows the beta package in the same repository:

```
PM>  Get-Package -ListAvailable -Filter -Prerelease MyApplication
Id                              Version         Description/Release Notes
--                              -------         -------------------------
MyApplication                   1.0-beta           My awesome package.
```

The prerelease package can then be installed with the standard `Install-Package` command by applying the same -Prerelease flag:

```
PM> Install-Package -Prerelease MyApplication
```

Finally, when testing is complete and the package is ready to be released, the "-beta" suffix can be dropped; the package version "1.0" will be visible to everyone and from that point on, it will be included as a possible installation candidate in all of NuGet's package operations.

 Prerelease versioning is defined as part of the Semantic Versioning schema, so this tip is, in fact, just an extension to the previous Semantic Versioning tip.

One more reason to apply Semantic Versioning to your packages!

Pitfall: Avoid Specifying "Strict" Version Dependencies in Your NuSpec Files

NuSpec configuration files allow packages to specify other packages—and versions of those packages—that they depend on. The dependencies section of a NuSpec file should be as extensive and detailed as possible so that NuGet has as much information as possible in order to make the correct decision about which packages may conflict with one another and which package versions it can safely install.

As the earlier "DLL hell" section pointed out, it is a hard fact of software development that sometimes versions of various assemblies simply don't mix. The effects can cripple an application. Thus, when a package that you are distributing has known issues with the latest versions of a library that it depends on, it is generally a good idea to specify that conflict very clearly in your package's NuSpec configuration file.

For example, the Ninject package in the "DLL hell" example was only compatible with NLog versions up to v2.0, and has known issues with NLog v2.5. Its NuSpec file may contain the following line, indicating that it expects at *maximum* v2.0 of NLog, and that NuGet should not install any NLog package version higher than this:

```
<dependency id="NLog" version="2.0" />
```

Though specific version specifications such as this may be necessary to avoid runtime conflicts, keep in mind that they indirectly affect all of the packages in your project and the restrictions they impose can produce numerous conflicts, making it very difficult to manage packages. In fact, the worst part is that these conflicts often apply when upgrading to later versions of the same package in which the specific version dependency has been resolved.

Having to depend on a specific version of an assembly is indeed unavoidable sometimes, but be very hesitant before introducing such a restriction, because this decision is very time-consuming to undo later on.

If you ever do come across the situation of trying to upgrade from a specific version of a package to a higher, non-specific version of that package, you will need to drop to the Package Management Console and use the -IgnoreDependencies switch of the Install-Packages command to override any conflicts that NuGet reports. For example:

```
Install-Package -IgnoreDependencies Ninject
```

This will inform NuGet that it should install the latest version of the package and ignore any dependency conflicts that it may discover.

 Keep in mind that when you use the -IgnoreDependencies flag you are circumventing all of NuGet's safeguards, and it is now your responsibility to ensure that all package dependencies are correct!

Tip: Use Custom Repositories to Control Package Versions

NuGet comes preconfigured with a single repository: the public repository hosted on NuGet.org. For most developers this is a good thing, given that the public NuGet.org repository is likely all they will ever want to use. The downside of using the public NuGet repository is that you and your organization have no control over the packages hosted on that repository.

While a steady package release cycle with constant updates and increasing versions is generally hailed as a good thing, some teams might be uncomfortable with the frequent change and lack of control that come with it. For example, if you are using the public NuGet repository as your primary package source and the Ninject team releases a new version that is incompatible with your application, NuGet will attempt to get you to upgrade to the latest Ninject package, even if you are aware of the incompatibilities with your application.

Though it's easy to ignore NuGet's update recommendations, the situation gets a bit more complicated when other packages that your application uses release updates that list a dependency on this later version of Ninject, and NuGet refuses to update these packages without getting the latest version of Ninject as well.

One way to avoid these "forced" updates is to regain control over package updates by removing the default public NuGet repository and replacing it with your own custom repository. Then, you can fill your custom repository with only the packages that you and your team deem "acceptable."

These packages can come from anywhere. Some of them may be custom packages that you've created, but most of them will likely be packages that you've cherry-picked right from the public NuGet repository. Replacing the default NuGet repository with your own repository provides you with the best of both worlds. It allows you to continue to use NuGet's powerful dependency management features while still retaining full control over the packages available for installation.

It's true that many developers may not be interested in choosing specific packages that NuGet has access to, but in some scenarios—particularly when multiple teams are involved—establishing a stable, cultivated repository helps create a controlled environment to minimize the effects of DLL hell.

Tip: Configure Your Continuous Integration Builds to Generate NuGet Packages

Continuous integration builds and NuGet are a match made in heaven!

Though the specifics will be different for different continuous integration platforms, the general process of producing NuGet packages from a continuous integration build is the same:

1. Create NuSpec files for all of the NuGet packages you'd like to generate, and be sure to check them into source control.
2. Configure your builds to execute the NuGet command-line tool at the end of each successful build.
3. Be sure to pass along a unique package version each time you generate a new set of packages. In fact, most continuous integration systems include a unique build number for each build that you may be able to use.
4. Finally, have the build server move the generated packages to a central repository.

See "Host Your Own Package Repository" on page 432 for more information on how to set up a custom NuGet repository.

Generating NuGet packages as part of a continuous integration build can be an incredibly valuable addition to your continuous integration and deployment process.

Summary

Though the act of managing assembly references can still be difficult at times, NuGet is a powerful dependency management system that helps take a lot of the pain out of doing so. NuGet packages are incredibly easy to consume and almost as easy to create and distribute. When used wisely, NuGet can be the next most powerful tool in your development toolbox after Visual Studio itself.

Best Practices

This book covers a multitude of topics in varying degrees of detail and offers a lot of advice. However, it is sometimes difficult to judge just how important any given piece of information is in the context of a long, technical description.

This appendix consolidates many of the best practices noted throughout the book into a single list, so you can tell at a glance whether you are following the popular and recommended patterns and practices set forth in this book.

Use the NuGet Package Manager to Manage Dependencies

The NuGet package manager is a great boon to developers and teams alike. Instead of spending loads of time checking to see if the projects that your application depends on have released new versions, let NuGet handle all of that for you!

If your organization has several teams that share common libraries, consider creating custom NuGet packages for those shared libraries and hosting a custom NuGet repository to provide more effective distribution and versioning.

Depend on Abstractions

Abstractions encourage loosely coupled systems with a healthy separation of contracts and implementations. Abstractions are easily interchanged, which not only provides easier maintenance but is also crucial to unit testing.

Avoid the New Keyword

Any time you employ the new keyword to create a new instance of a concrete type, you are—by definition—not depending on an abstraction. Though this is often not a problem at all (e.g., new StringBuilder(), new List<string>(), etc.), take a moment any time you use the new keyword to consider whether the object you are creating might be better expressed as a dependency to be injected. Whenever possible, let another component create it!

Avoid Referring to HttpContext Directly (Use HttpContextBase)

ASP.NET MVC (and later, .NET 4) introduced `System.Web.Abstractions`, a set of abstractions over many of the core parts of the ASP.NET Framework. The "depend on abstractions" advice given earlier extends to these classes as well. In particular, one of the most often referenced objects in ASP.NET development is `HttpContext`—prefer using the `HttpContextBase` abstraction instead.

Avoid "Magic Strings"

"Magic strings"—crucial, yet arbitrary string values—may be convenient and in many situations, required; however, they have many issues. Some of the biggest issues with magic strings are that they:

- Don't have any intrinsic meaning (e.g., it's difficult to tell how or if one "ID" relates to another "ID")
- Are easily broken with misspellings or incorrect case
- Don't react well to refactoring
- Promote rampant, pervasive duplication

Here are two examples, the first using magic strings to access data in a `ViewData` dictionary, and the second a refactored example with that same data in a strongly typed model:

```html
<p>
    <label for="FirstName">First Name:</label>
    <span id="FirstName">@ViewData["FirstName"]</span>
</p>

<p>
    <label for="FirstName">First Name:</label>
    <span id="FirstName">@Model.FirstName</span>
</p>
```

Magic strings carry the allure of being very simple to use when you introduce them, but that ease of use often comes back to bite you later when it comes time to maintain them.

Prefer Models over ViewData

As the preceding example suggested, the `ViewData` dictionary is one of the most tempting places to leverage magic strings in an ASP.NET MVC application. However, these are best avoided. Strongly typed models can be a handy tool to avoid assigning and retrieving data directly to and from the `ViewData` dictionary.

Do Not Write HTML in "Backend" Code

Follow the practice of separation of concerns: it is not the responsibility of controllers and other "backend code" to render HTML. The exceptions here, of course, are UI helper methods and classes whose only job is to help the views render code. These classes should be considered part of the view, not "backend" classes.

Do Not Perform Business Logic in Views

The inverse of the previous best practice is true as well: views should not contain any business logic. In fact, views should contain as little logic as possible! Views should concentrate on how to display the data that they have been provided and should not take action on that data.

Consolidate Commonly Used View Snippets with Helper Methods

The notions of "user controls," "server controls," and "controls" in general are very widespread—and for good reason. These concepts help consolidate commonly used code and logic in a central location to make it easier to reuse and maintain. ASP.NET MVC is not control-driven, however—instead, it relies on the "helper method" paradigm in which methods do the work that controls once did. This can pertain to an entire section of HTML (what we're used to calling a "control"), or to something as simple as strongly typed access to a commonly referred URL. For example, you may notice many of the same references to the Membership page (*~/membership*), like so:

```
@Html.ActionLink("Membership", "Index", "Membership", [...])
```

You can consolidate this call (and eliminate the magic strings!) by turning it into a helper method instead:

```
@Html.MembershipLink()
```

Prefer Presentation Models over Direct Usage of Business Objects

In general, try to avoid allowing changes to the business model to directly affect the view. Presentation models help with this.

Encapsulate if Statements with HTML Helpers in Views

Integrating code and markup is quite powerful; however, it can get quite messy. Consider the following (relatively simple) if/else statement:

```
@if(Model.IsAnonymousUser) {
    <img src="@Url.Content("~/content/images/anonymous.jpg")" />
} else if(Model.IsAdministrator) {
    <img src="@Url.Content("~/content/images/administrator.jpg")" />
} else if(Model.Membership == Membership.Standard) {
    <img src="@Url.Content("~/content/images/member.jpg")" />
} else if(Model.Membership == Membership.Preferred) {
    <img src="@Url.Content("~/content/images/preferred_member.jpg")" />
}
```

That's quite obscure code for rendering out essentially the same markup with the exception of one part (the URL). Consider this approach instead:

```
public static string UserAvatar(this HtmlHelper<User> helper)
{
    var user = helper.ViewData.Model;

    string avatarFilename = "anonymous.jpg";

    if (user.IsAnonymousUser)
    {
        avatarFilename = "anonymous.jpg";
    }
    else if (user.IsAdministrator)
    {
        avatarFilename = "administrator.jpg";
    }
    else if (user.Membership == Membership.Standard)
    {
        avatarFilename = "member.jpg";
    }
    else if (user.Membership == Membership.Preferred)
    {
        avatarFilename = "preferred_member.jpg";
    }

    var urlHelper = new UrlHelper(helper.ViewContext.RequestContext);
    var contentPath = string.Format("~/content/images/{0}", avatarFilename);
    string imageUrl = urlHelper.Content(contentPath);

    return string.Format("<img src='{0}' />", imageUrl);
}
```

You can now simply call this helper method everywhere you need the user's avatar:

```
@Html.UserAvatar()
```

Not only is this cleaner, it's also more declarative and moves this logic into a central location so that it can be maintained more easily. For instance, if the requirements change and the site needs to support custom avatars, the `Html.UserAvatar()` helper method can be modified in one place.

Prefer Explicit View Names

A majority of ASP.NET MVC controller action code samples call the `View()` method without specifying a view name. This is suitable for simple demo code, but when tests or other actions begin calling each other, the detriments to this approach become clear. When no view name is specified, the ASP.NET MVC Framework defaults to the name of the action that was originally called. Thus, calling the `Index` action in the following example will cause the framework to attempt to locate a view named *Index.cshtml*—a view that probably doesn't exist (but *List.cshtml* certainly does!):

```
public ActionResult Index()
{
    return List();
}

public ActionResult List()
{
    var employees = Employee.GetAll();
    return View(employees);
}
```

If the `List` action is modified to call the `View()` method with a specific view name (as shown below), everything works fine:

```
public ActionResult List()
{
    var employees = Employee.GetAll();
    return View("List", employees);
}
```

Prefer Parameter Objects over Long Lists of Parameters

This advice is not specific to ASP.NET MVC—long parameter lists are commonly considered a "code smell" and should be avoided whenever possible. Additionally, ASP.NET MVC's powerful model binders make following this advice incredibly easy. Consider the following two contrasting snippets, the first using a long parameter list:

```
public ActionResult Create(
        string firstName, string lastName, DateTime? birthday,
        string addressLine1, string addressLine2,
        string city, string region, string regionCode, string country
        [... and many, many more]
    )
{
    var employee = new Employee( [Long list of parameters...] )
    cmployee.Save();
```

```
        return View("Details", employee);
    }
```

and the second a parameter object:

```
    public ActionResult Create(Employee employee)
    {
        employee.Save();
        return View("Details", employee);
    }
```

The parameter object example is much more straightforward, and it leverages the ASP.NET MVC Framework's powerful model binders and model validation, making this code much safer and easier to maintain.

Encapsulate Shared/Common Functionality, Logic, and Data with Action Filters or Child Actions (Html.RenderAction)

Every website of any significant complexity will have common elements that appear on multiple (or perhaps all) pages in the application. A global website navigation menu—the kind that appears on every page in the site—is a canonical example of this type of globally applied logic and content. The data for these common elements needs to come from somewhere, yet explicitly retrieving the data in every controller action would create a maintenance nightmare. Action filters and/or child actions (executed via the Html.RenderAction() method) provide a central location to hold this kind of logic.

Consider the following layout snippet (cut from the larger layout page), which renders navigation items in a list:

```
    <ul id="global-menu">
        @foreach (var menuItem in ViewData.SingleOrDefault<NavigationMenu>()) {
            <li class="@(menuItem.IsSelected ? "selected" : null)">
                @Html.RouteLink(menuItem.DisplayName, menuItem.RouteData)
            </li>
        }
    </ul>
```

The NavigationMenu ViewData object needs to come from somewhere. Since they can be configured to execute prior to every controller request, action filters make an excellent candidate to populate ViewData with globally required data like this. Here is the action filter that populates the navigation menu data required in the previous example:

```
    public class NavigationMenuPopulationFilter : ActionFilterAttribute
    {
        private readonly INavigationDataSource _dataSource;

        public NavigationMenuPopulationFilter(INavigationDataSource dataSource)
        {
            _dataSource = dataSource;
        }
```

```
public override void OnActionExecuting(ActionExecutingContext filterContext)
{
    NavigationMenu mainMenu = _dataSource.GetNavigationMenu("main-menu");
    filterContext.Controller.ViewData["MainNavigationMenu"] = mainMenu;
}
}
```

This filter is pretty straightforward—it gets the correct navigation menu data model from some data source and adds it to the ViewData collection prior to executing the requested action. From this point on, any component that requires it can retrieve the navigation menu from ViewData.

Prefer Grouping Actions into Controllers Based on How They Relate to Business Concepts

For example, consider creating a CustomersController to hold the actions related to dealing with customers.

Avoid Grouping Actions into Controllers Based on Technical Relation

For example, avoid creating an AjaxController to contain all of the AJAX actions that your site exposes. Instead, group these actions together with their related concepts (e.g., the AJAX actions that provide customer data or partial views should be in the CustomersController with all of the other customer-related actions).

Prefer Placing Action Filters at the Highest Appropriate Level

Most action filter attributes can be applied at either the method (action) or class (controller) level. When an attribute applies to all actions in a controller, prefer placing that attribute on the controller itself rather than on each individual class. Also consider whether or not the attribute may be appropriate further up the controller's dependency chain (i.e., on one of its base classes) instead.

Prefer Multiple Views (and/or Partial Views) over Complex If-Then-Else Logic That Shows and Hides Sections

The Web Forms Page Controller pattern encourages posting back to the same page, possibly showing or hiding certain sections of the page, depending on the request. Due to ASP.NET MVC's separation of concerns, this can often be avoided by creating separate views for each of these situations, lowering or eliminating entirely the need for complex view logic. Consider the following example, *Wizard.cshtml*:

```
@if(Model.WizardStep == WizardStep.First) {
    <!-- The first step of the wizard -->
} else if(Model.WizardStep == WizardStep.Second) {
    <!-- The second step of the wizard -->
} else if(Model.WizardStep == WizardStep.Third) {
    <!-- The third step of the wizard -->
}
```

Here the view is deciding which step of the wizard to display, which is dangerously close to business logic! Let's move this logic to the controller (*WizardController.cs*), where it belongs:

```
public ActionResult Step(WizardStep currentStep)
{
    // This is simple logic, but it could be MUCH more complex!
    string view = currentStep.ToString();

    return View(view);
}
```

and split the original view into multiple views, e.g., *First.cshtml*:

```
<!-- The first step of the wizard -->
```

Second.cshtml:

```
<!-- The second step of the wizard -->
```

and *Third.cshtml*:

```
<!-- The third step of the wizard -->
```

Prefer the Post-Redirect-Get Pattern When Posting Form Data

The Post-Redirect-Get (PRG) pattern is a common design pattern used by web developers to help avoid certain duplicate form submissions and allow user agents to behave more intuitively with bookmarks and the Refresh button. Because the Web Forms Page Controller pattern typically requires developers to post back to the same page for all actions in a particular context (e.g., displaying employee data so it can be edited and resubmitted), the PRG pattern is not used as much in Web Forms environments. However, because ASP.NET MVC separates actions into separate URLs, it is easy to run into trouble with update scenarios. Consider the following `EmployeeController` implementation:

```
public class EmployeeController : Controller
{
    public ActionResult Edit(int id)
    {
        var employee = Employee.Get(id);

        return View("Edit ", employee);
    }

    [AcceptVerbs(HttpVerbs.Post)]
```

```
public ActionResult Update(int id)
{
    var employee = Employee.Get(id);

    UpdateModel(employee);

    return View("Edit", id);
}
```

In this example, when a user posts to the Update action, even though the user will be looking at the *Edit* view as desired, the resulting URL in the browser will be */employees/update/1*. If the user refreshes the page, bookmarks a link to that URL, etc., subsequent visits will update the employee information again, or possibly not even work at all. What we really want the Update action to do is update the employee information and then redirect the user back to the Edit page so he is back at the original "Edit" location. In this scenario, the PRG pattern may be applied thusly (the first part of the file has been omitted, we're showing only the changed Update section):

```
[AcceptVerbs(HttpVerbs.Post)]
public ActionResult Update(int id)
{
    var employee = Employee.Get(id);

    UpdateModel(employee);

    return RedirectToAction("Edit", new { id });
}
```

Though it's a subtle change, switching from the View() method to the RedirectToAction() method will produce a client-side redirect (as opposed to a server-side redirect in the original example) after the Update() method has finished updating the employee information, landing the user on the proper URL: */employees/edit/1*.

Prefer Startup Tasks over Logic Placed in Application_Start (Global.asax)

Most ASP.NET MVC demos will advise modifying the Application_Start() method in the *Global.asax* file in order to introduce logic that will execute when the application starts. While this is certainly the easiest and most straightforward approach, the WebActivator framework provides the alternative concept of startup tasks. These tasks are easy to implement and are automatically discovered and executed during application startup. They help provide cleaner code and encourage proper adherence to the Single Responsibility Principle mentioned in Chapter 5.

Prefer Authorize Attribute over Imperative Security Checks

Traditionally, authorization control resembles the following:

```
public ActionResult Details(int id)
{
    if (!User.IsInRole("EmployeeViewer"))
        return new HttpUnauthorizedResult();

    // Action logic
}
```

This is an imperative approach, and it makes it difficult to implement application-wide changes. The ASP.NET MVC `AuthorizeAttribute` provides a simple and declarative way to authorize access to actions. This same code may be rewritten as:

```
[Authorize(Roles = "EmployeeViewer")]
public ActionResult Details(int id)
{
    // Action logic
}
```

Prefer Using the Route Attribute over More Generic Global Routes

Of course, the most specific route is one that maps directly to one action and one action only.

Consider Using an Antiforgery Token to Avoid CSRF Attacks

For form posts where security is a concern, ASP.NET MVC provides measures to help deter certain kinds of common attacks. One of these measures is the antiforgery token. The token has both server- and client-side components. This code will insert a user-specific token in a hidden field on your form:

```
@using(Html.Form("Update", "Employee")) {
    @Html.AntiForgeryToken()
    <!-- rest of form goes here -->
}
```

and this code will validate that token on the server side prior to executing any further processing of the data being posted:

```
[ValidateAntiForgeryToken]
[AcceptVerbs(HttpVerbs.Post | HttpVerbs.Put)]
public ActionResult Update(int id)
{
    // Process validated form post
}
```

Consider Using the AcceptVerbs Attribute to Restrict How Actions May Be Called

Many actions rest on a number of assumptions about how and when they will be called in the context of an application. For instance, one assumption might be that an `Employee.Update` action will be called from some kind of Employee Edit page containing a form with the employee properties to post to the `Employee.Update` action in order to update an employee record. If this action is called in an unexpected way (e.g., via a `GET` request with no form posts), the action will probably not work, and in fact may produce unforeseen problems.

The ASP.NET MVC Framework offers the `AcceptVerbs` attribute to help restrict action calls to specific HTTP methods. Thus, the answer to the aforementioned `Employee.Update` scenario would be:

```
[AcceptVerbs(HttpVerbs.Post | HttpVerbs.Put)]
public ActionResult Update(int id)
```

Applying the `AcceptVerbs` attribute in this way will restrict requests to this action to those made specifying the `POST` or `PUT` HTTP methods. All others (e.g., `GET` requests) will be ignored.

Consider Output Caching

Output caching is one of the easiest ways to get additional performance from a web application. Caching the rendered HTML is a great way to speed up response times when little or no content has changed since the previous request. The ASP.NET MVC Framework offers the `OutputCacheAttribute` to accomplish this. This attribute mirrors the Web Forms output caching functionality and accepts many of the same properties.

Consider Removing Unused View Engines

ASP.NET MVC registers both the Web Forms and Razor view engines by default, which means that the view locator will search the view locations for both Web Forms and Razor views. This makes it possible to use either or both types of views in your application.

However, for consistency's sake, most teams choose one type of view and use that type exclusively throughout the application, making it a bit wasteful for the ASP.NET MVC view locator to look for views of the type that aren't being used. For example, if you choose to use only Razor views in your application, the view locator will continue to search for Web Forms views even though you know that it will never find one.

Luckily, you can avoid this unnecessary overhead and slightly optimize your application by unregistering the view engine that you are not using.

The following example shows how to unregister the Web Forms view engine (leaving only the Razor view engine):

```
var viewEngines = System.Web.Mvc.ViewEngines.Engines;

var webFormsEngine = viewEngines.OfType<WebFormViewEngine>().FirstOrDefault();

if (webFormsEngine != null)
    viewEngines.Remove(webFormsEngine);
```

Just execute this snippet during the application's startup phase, and the view locator will no longer waste time looking for views that aren't there!

Consider Custom ActionResults for Unique Scenarios

The ASP.NET MVC request pipeline has a deliberate separation of concerns in which each step in the process completes its task and no more. Each step does just enough to provide the subsequent tasks with enough information to do what they need to do. For instance, a controller action that decides a view should be rendered to the client does not load up a view engine and order it to execute the view. It merely returns a ViewResult object with the information that the framework needs to take the next steps (most likely loading a view engine and executing the view!).

When it comes to the results of controller actions, declarative is the name of the game. For instance, the ASP.NET MVC Framework provides an HttpStatusCodeResult class with a StatusCode property, but it also goes one step further, defining a custom HttpStatusCodeResult named HttpUnauthorizedResult. Though the following two lines are effectively the same, the latter provides a more declarative and strongly typed expression of the controller's intent:

```
return new HttpStatusCodeResult(HttpStatusCode.Unauthorized);

return new HttpUnauthorizedResult();
```

When your actions produce results that don't fit the "normal" results, take a moment to consider whether returning a custom action result may be more appropriate. Some common examples include things like RSS feeds, Word documents, Excel spreadsheets, etc.

Consider Asynchronous Controllers for Controller Tasks That Can Happen in Parallel

Parallel execution of multiple tasks can offer significant opportunities to enhance the performance of your site. To this end, ASP.NET MVC offers the AsyncController base class to help make processing multithreaded requests easier. When creating an action with processor-intensive logic, consider whether that action has any elements that may safely be run in parallel. See Chapter 11 for more information.

Cross-Reference: Targeted Topics, Features, and Scenarios

The following are lists of the concepts that we've targeted, cross-referenced with where they appear throughout the book.

Topic	Chapter(s)
Features new in ASP.NET MVC 4	**Features new in ASP.NET MVC 4**
Mobile templates	Chapter 10
JavaScript bundling and minification	Chapter 13
ASP.NET Web API	Chapter 7
Asynchronous controllers	Chapter 11
AllowAnonymousAttribute	Chapter 9
ASP.NET MVC features	**ASP.NET MVC features**
Controller actions	Chapter 1
Action filters	Chapter 1
Routing	Chapter 1, Chapter 14
Razor markup	Chapter 1
HTML helpers	Chapter 1, Chapter 3
URL helpers	Chapter 1
Form helpers	Chapter 3
Client validation	Chapter 3, Chapter 8
Areas	Chapter 1
JSON result	Chapter 6
Partial views	Chapter 1, Chapter 6Chapter 15,
Razor @Helper	Chapter 15
Model binding	Chapter 6

Topic	Chapter(s)
Validation	Chapter 3
Error handling	Chapter 16
View engines	Chapter 1
Child actions	Chapter 12
Output caching	Chapter 12
`bin_DeployableAssemblies`	Chapter 19
Custom item templates	Chapter 15
ASP.NET MVC project types	**ASP.NET MVC project types**
Empty	Chapter 1
Internet Application	Chapter 1
Intranet Application	Chapter 9
Mobile Application	Chapter 10
Web API	Chapter 6
Patterns and practices	**Patterns and practices**
Model-View-Controller pattern	Chapter 5
N-Tier model	Chapter 5
SOLID	Chapter 5
Model binding & validation	Chapter 6
Object-Relational Mapping (ORM)	Chapter 8
Logging and health monitoring	Chapter 16
Unit testing	Chapter 17
Automated browser testing	Chapter 17
SEO	Chapter 14
Graceful degradation	Chapter 13
Progressive enhancement	Chapter 10
Client-side templates	Chapter 4
Mobile development	Chapter 10
Cross-site scripting attacks (XSS)	Chapter 9
Cross-site request forgery (CSRF)	Chapter 9
SQL injection attacks	Chapter 9
Web services and REST	Chapter 7
Repository pattern	Chapter 8
Continuous integration	Chapter 18
Continuous deployment	Chapter 18

Topic	Chapter(s)
Cloud/farm deployment	Chapter 19
Server-side caching	Chapter 12
Client-side caching	Chapter 12
Tools, Frameworks, and Technologies	**Tools, Frameworks, and Technologies**
jQuery	Chapter 4
Client validation	Chapter 3
Authentication/authorization	Chapter 9
Bundling and minification	Chapter 13
ASP.NET Web API	Chapter 7
Entity Framework	Chapter 3, Chapter 8
jQuery Mobile	Chapter 10
Web Sockets	Chapter 11
SignalR	Chapter 11
Windows Azure	Chapter 19
Browser: local storage	Chapter 12

Index

Symbols
\# symbol, 73
\$() function, 71, 73
: (semicolon), 27
<% %> code syntax, 54
> symbol, 74
@ symbol, 27, 54

A
absolute expiration, 251
abstractions
    best practices, 443
    repository pattern and, 365
Accept header (HTTP), 150
acceptance tests, 349
AcceptVerbsAttribute class, 143, 453
ActionFilterAttribute class
    about, 23, 90
    OnActionExecuted() method, 126
ActionResult class, 19, 24, 454
actions (see controller actions)
Active Server Pages (ASP), 3
adaptive rendering
    about, 217
    browser-specific views, 221–222
    CSS media queries, 220
    mobile feature detection, 218–220
    viewport tag, 217
Add Application dialog box, 403
Add Controller dialog box, 36
Add View wizard, 39
ADO.NET Entity Framework (see Entity Framework)
aggregate root, 155

AggregateCacheDependency class, 252
AJAX (Asynchronous JavaScript and XML)
    client-side development and, 77–79
    cross-domain, 133–138
    Forms Authentication and, 190
    JavaScript rendering, 117–123
    partial rendering and, 111–117
    responding to requests from, 124
    reusing logic across requests, 123–127
    sending data to the server, 128–133
AllowAnonymousAttribute class, 186, 188, 191
AntiXssEncoder class
    about, 198
    CssEncode() method, 199
    HtmlAttributeEncode() method, 199
    HtmlEncode() method, 199
    HtmlFormUrlEncode() method, 199
    UrlEncode() method, 199
    UrlPathEncode() method, 199
    XmlAttributeEncode() method, 199
    XmlEncode() method, 199
App Cache, 265–267
application development (see web applications)
application service account, 178
application-scoped caching, 250
ASP (Active Server Pages), 3
ASP.NET health monitoring, 338–341
ASP.NET MVC Framework
    about, 3, 4, 317–318
    adding to existing Web Forms, 417–419
    associated namespace, 17, 45
    authentication, 41–43
    authoring using Web Forms syntax, 54
    choosing between Web Forms and, 415

We'd like to hear your suggestions for improving our indexes. Send email to *index@oreilly.com*.

creating applications, 9–15, 35–40
deployment and runtime, 47
differences from Web Forms, 47–54
EBuy project, 8
HTTP handlers and modules, 46
installing, 9
integrating with Web Forms functionality,
          420–421
IoC and, 108
logical design in, 90–92
MVC pattern and, 4–6
new features, 6–7
open source availability, 8
project folder structure, 13
rendering HTML, 50–54
routing traffic, 15–18
state management, 46, 49
tools, languages, APIs, 46
transitioning from Web Forms, 416–420
web development platforms, 3–4
ASP.NET platform
    about, 45
    routing and, 49
ASP.NET session state, 249
ASP.NET Web API
    about, 7, 139
    building data service, 139–145
    exception handling, 147–149
    media formatters, 149–152
    paging and querying data, 146
asp:Hyperlink tag, 53
asp:Repeater tag, 52
AspCompat page directive, 313
aspnet_regsql.exe command, 340
.aspx pages, 48
ASPX view engine, 55
assemblies
    dependencies and, 436
    naming, 93
    semantic versioning, 437
assembly packages, 430
AsyncController class, 234, 454
asynchronous controllers
    about, 6, 233
    creating, 234–236
    usage considerations, 236
Asynchronous JavaScript and XML (see AJAX)
AsyncManager.OutstandingOperations
          property, 235

attribute-based routing, 306–310
authentication
    about, 41–43, 177
    Forms Authentication, 183–191
    Single Sign On Authentication, 90
    user, 186–187
    Windows Authentication, 178–181
authorization
    defined, 177
    user, 191
AuthorizeAttribute class
    action filters and, 23
    best practices, 452
    controller actions and, 42, 177
    usage considerations, 182–183
    user authorization and, 191
Autofac site, 107
automated testing
    defined, 345
    levels of, 345–349
    test projects for, 350–354
    writing clean tests, 359–361
.axd file extension, 302

B
"backend code", 445
Basic template, 11
BindAttribute class, 176
blacklist-based approach, 196
browsers, 271
    (see also web pages)
    cache management, 264, 292
    HTTP polling and, 238, 239
    server-sent events, 240
    specific views for, 221–222
    testing application logic in, 370
    WebSocket API, 241
BufferedMediaTypeFormatter class, 150
build automation
    about, 377, 380
    continuous integration and, 386, 441
    creating, 383–385
    creating build scripts, 378–380
    executing the build, 379
    types of, 381
build scripts, 378–380
bundling concept, 7, 289–293
business rules, specifying with Data
          Annotations API, 63–65

C

Cache class
  about, 251–252
  adding items to, 262
cache management
  about, 420
  best practices, 276–278, 292, 453
  cache dependencies, 252
  client-side, 248, 264–269, 277
  scavenging process and, 252
  server-side, 248–264
Cache-Control header, 264, 276–278
CacheDependency class, 252
CacheItemPriority enumeration, 252
CacheItemRemovedCallback delegate, 252
Castle Windsor site, 107
CDN (content delivery network), 274
CI (continuous integration), 386–391, 441
client-side caching
  about, 248
  App Cache, 265–267
  browser cache, 264
  LocalStorage mechanism, 268
  setting up, 277
client-side development
  AJAX technique and, 77–79
  DOM manipulation, 76–77
  JavaScript and, 69–71
  responding to events, 74–76
  selectors in, 71–74
  validating data, 79–83
client-side optimization
  about, 271
  anatomy of web pages, 271–273
  ASP.NET MVC support, 289
  avoiding redirects, 283–285
  cache expiration, 276–278
  configuring ETags, 285
  content delivery networks and, 274
  externalizing scripts and styles, 281
  GZip compression, 278
  HTTP requests and, 274
  measuring client-side performance, 286
  minifying JavaScript and CSS, 282
  reducing DNS lookups, 282
  removing duplicate scripts, 285
  script placement on web pages, 279
  stylesheets and, 279
client-side templates, 120–123

code blocks, 27
code coverage in testing, 372–374
Code First approach
  about, 159
  annotation attributes, 162
  convention over configuration, 60
  usage considerations, 161
  working with data context, 167–168
code nuggets, 27
comma-separated values (CSV) format, 150
concurrency conflicts (databases), 160
configuring
  ETags, 285
  IIS, 178
  real-time communication, 245–246
  routes, 16–18
#container element, 112
containers, IoC, 107–109
content delivery network (CDN), 274
Content folder, 428
continuous builds, 381
continuous deployment, 410
continuous integration (CI), 386–391, 441
controller actions
  about, 19
  action filters, 23, 449
  action parameters, 21–23
  asynchronous, 233–236
  AuthorizeAttribute class and, 42
  best practices, 447, 449
  building HTML forms, 57–59
  error handling and, 333
  implementation example, 35–37
  JSONP support, 136
  logging errors, 336
  names corresponding to HTTP actions,
      142
  properties for, 16
  repositories and, 155
  returning results, 19
  reusing logic across requests, 123–127
  testing, 361–364
Controller class
  about, 35
  Content() method, 20
  File() method, 20
  HttpNotFound() method, 20
  JavaScript() method, 20
  Json() method, 20, 118

OnException() method, 337
PartialView() method, 20, 112, 114, 124
Redirect() method, 20
RedirectToAction() method, 20
RedirectToRoute() method, 20
View() method, 20, 112
Controller component (MVC pattern)
about, 6, 18
component interaction and, 88–90
Controllers folder, 14, 35
convention over configuration concept
about, 13, 17
Code First approach and, 60
usage considerations, 141–143
CORS (Cross-Origin Resource Sharing), 133,
137
Cross-Site Request Forgery (CSRF), 133, 199–
201, 452
cross-site scripting (XSS) attacks, 133, 198
CRUD operations, 142, 143, 155
.cshtml file extension, 317
CSRF (Cross-Site Request Forgery), 133, 199–
201, 452
CSS
media queries, 220
minifying, 282
CSV (comma-separated values) format, 150
CustomModelBinderAttribute class, 131
CustomValidationAttribute class, 64
Cutrell, Edward, 296

D

data access layer
about, 161
Code First approach, 161–163
EBuy business model and, 163–166
working with data context, 167–168
data access patterns
about, 153
choosing approach, 159
object relational mappers, 156–158
POCO classes, 153
repository pattern, 154–156
Data Annotations API
client-side validation and, 80
Error Message property, 64
specifying business rules with, 63–65
data manipulation
building data access layer, 161–168

building forms, 57–59
data access patterns, 153–158
Entity Framework and, 158–161
filtering data, 168–174
handling form posts, 59
paging data, 146, 168–174
querying data, 146, 168–174
saving data to databases, 59–61
sorting data, 168–174
validating data, 61–67
data services
building, 139–145
exception handling, 147–149
media formatters, 149–152
paging data, 146
querying data, 146
data transfer objects (DTOs), 133
data:URL scheme, 274
Database class
ExecuteSqlCommand() method, 159
SqlQuery() method, 159
Database First model, 159
databases
concurrency conflicts, 160
deployment considerations, 399
many-to-many relationships, 168, 192
object relational impedance mismatch, 156–
158
saving data to, 59–61
DbContext class
about, 61, 167
OnModelCreating() method, 168
DbSet class, 61
DefaultModelBinder class, 129, 131
DELETE method (HTTP), 142
dependencies
best practices, 443
cache, 252
deployment considerations, 399
IoC principle and, 102
mocking, 365–370
version, 439
dependency injection (DI) pattern, 102, 104,
156
Dependency Inversion Principle (DIP), 101
dependency management, 13
DependencyResolver class, 109
deployment
ASP.NET MVC, 47

automating, 390

considerations for, 395–401

continuous, 410

to Internet Information Server, 401–407

web application options, 94

Web Forms, 47

to Windows Azure, 407–410

desktop views

avoiding in mobile site, 216

switching between mobile and, 212

development, application (see web applications)

DI (dependency injection) pattern, 102, 104, 156

DIP (Dependency Inversion Principle), 101

display modes feature, 7, 204

display templates, 318

distributed caching, 259–264

"DLL hell", 436

DNS lookup, 272, 282

document object

DocumentElement property, 70

getElementById() method, 71

write() method, 280

DOM (Document Object Model)

manipulating, 76–77

referencing elements, 71–74

donut caching, 255–257

donut hole caching, 257–258

DRY (Don't Repeat Yourself) principle, 110

DTOs (data transfer objects), 133

E

EBuy project

about, 8

business domain model, 163–166

creating, 9

deployment considerations, 400

editor templates, 318

.edmx file extension, 159

Empty template, 10

Entity class, 164

Entity Framework

about, 60, 158

Code First approach, 60, 159, 161–163, 167–168

database concurrency, 160

Database First model, 159

Model First approach, 159, 161

Entity Tag (ETag), 285

EntityObject class, 161

error and exception handling

about, 331

ASP.NET Web API, 147–149

concurrency conflicts, 160

controller actions and, 333

Data Annotation API, 64

data validation and, 65–67

defining global error handlers, 334–336

enabling custom errors, 332

logging errors, 336–338

ETag (Entity Tag), 285

events

monitoring, 338–341

responding to, 74–76

server-sent, 239

exception handling (see error and exception handling)

ExceptionFilterAttribute.OnException() method, 148

ExpectedExceptionAttribute class, 357

expiration, cache, 251, 276–278

Expires header, 264, 276–278

extension methods, 53

F

filesystem repositories, 432

filtering

controller actions, 23, 449

data, 168–174

errors, 337

foreach loop, managing complexity with, 116

formatters, media, 149–152

forms (see HTML forms; Web Forms)

Forms Authentication, 183–191

FormsAuthentication.SetAuthCookie() method, 187, 188

Fowler, Martin, 387

Franklin, Benjamin, 175

front controller pattern, 89

G

gated check-in builds, 382

GET method (HTTP), 119, 128, 142

Get-Packages command, 438

Git source control systems, 409

Glimpse tool, 305

Global.asax file, 107, 451
GlobalFilterCollection class, 334
Google's best practices rules, 274
Grant-CacheAllowedClientAccount cmdlet,
    261
Guan, Zhiwei, 296
GZip compression, 278

H

HandleErrorAttribute class, 149, 333–336,
    338
health monitoring, 338–341
HTML
    building forms, 57–59
    handling form posts, 59
    rendering, 50–54, 58
HTML helpers, 52, 317, 446
HtmlHelper class
    about, 33, 317
    ActionLink() method, 53
    EditorFor method, 57
    extending, 53
    HiddenField method, 57
    LabelFor method, 57
    Partial() method, 117
    Password method, 57
    RenderAction() method, 318
    TextBox method, 57
    ValidationMessage() method, 66
    ValidationSummary() method, 66
HTTP handlers, 46
HTTP headers, 150
HTTP Long Polling technique, 238
HTTP methods
    best practices, 274, 285
    CRUD operations and, 142
    JSON hijacking and, 119
    sending data to servers, 128
HTTP modules, 46
HTTP polling, 237–239
HttpActionExecutedContext class, 148
HttpApplicationState class, 250, 251
HttpBrowserCapabilities class, 214, 224
HttpContext class
    Application property, 250
    best practices, 444
    Cache property, 251, 420
    Items property, 47, 249
    Session property, 249, 420

HttpGetAttribute class, 143
HttpPostAttribute class, 142, 143
HttpRequest class
    anatomy of request, 272
    Browser property, 214, 224
    Unvalidated() method, 198
HttpResponse.WriteSubstitution() method,
    256
HttpResponseException class, 147
HttpSessionState class, 251, 420
HttpStatusCodeResult class, 454
HttpUnauthorizedResult class, 454
Hub class, 243
hubs, connections and, 243–244

I

ICollection<T> interface, 166
IComparable interface, 64
IConfigurationManager interface, 245
IController interface, 17
IDependencyResolver interface, 109
IDictionary interface, 249
IDisposable interface, 100
IEntity interface, 163
IEnumerable<T> interface, 174
IEquatable interface, 163
IExceptionFilter interface, 148
If-Modified-Since header, 265
If-None-Match header, 286
if/else statement
    best practices, 446
    Web Forms example, 26
IHttpAsyncHandler interface, 314
IHttpHandler interface, 311
IIS (Internet Information Server)
    asynchronous controllers and, 6
    client caching and, 277
    configuring, 178–181
    deploying to, 401–407
IIS Express dialog box, 179
IKernel interface, 109
inheritance concept, 157, 242
Install-Package command, 13, 437, 440
installing
    ASP.NET MVC Framework, 9
    NuGet Package Manager, 423
    packages from PackageManager Console
        window, 13
    Razor Single File Generator, 319

Velocity, 260
integration machines, 388
integration tests, 348
Interface Segregation Principle (ISP), 100
Internet Application template, 11, 42, 184
Internet Information Server (IIS)
    asynchronous controllers and, 6
    client caching and, 277
    configuring, 178–181
    deploying to, 401–407
Intranet Application template, 11, 178
intranet applications, securing, 178–183
Inversion of Control design principle (see IoC
    design principle)
IoC (Inversion of Control) design principle
    about, 102
    dependencies and, 102
    dependency injection pattern, 104
    picking containers, 106–109
    service location and, 104
IQueryable<T> interface, 146
IRepository interface, 143, 168, 366
IRouteConstraint interface, 304
IRouteHandler interface, 311
ISerializable interface, 100
ISP (Interface Segregation Principle), 100

J

JavaScript language
    client-side development and, 69–71
    minifying, 282
    referencing DOM elements, 71–74
    rendering and, 117–123
    responding to events, 74
JavaScript Object Notation (see JSON)
JavaScriptSerializer class, 307
jQuery library
    $() function, 71, 73
    about, 69–71
    .after() method, 77
    .ajax() method, 79, 135
    .before() method, 77
    .click() method, 75
    client-side validation, 79–83
    .contains() method, 74
    .css() method, 73
    .done() method, 79
    .error() method, 79, 136
    .fail() method, 79

.getJSON() method, 142
.height() method, 71
.html() method, 77, 120, 123
JSON data and, 132
.load() method, 112
manipulating elements, 76
.post() method, 128
.prepend() method, 77
referencing DOM elements, 71–74
responding to events, 75
.success() method, 79, 136
.text() method, 73
.val() method, 120
.width() method, 71
jQuery Mobile Framework
    about, 204
    adaptive rendering, 217–222
    creating mobile applications from scratch,
        224–228
    data-filter attribute, 211
    data-role attribute, 210, 228
    enhancing views with, 209–215
    getting started with, 207–209
    improving mobile experience, 216
    Mobile Application template and, 12, 203
    paradigm shift, 224
    "listview" component, 210
jQuery.Mobile.MVC package, 207, 213
JSON (JavaScript Object Notation)
    posting complex objects, 129
    rendering data, 118–119
    requesting data, 119
    responding to requests, 125
    sending and receiving data effectively, 132
JSON hijacking, 119
JSONP (JSON with Padding)
    about, 133–135
    controller actions and, 136
    making requests, 135
JsonRequestBehavior enumeration, 137

L

Language Integrated Query (LINQ), 168–174,
    308
Last-Modified header, 265, 286
layout template, 28
layouts
    loading for mobile views, 207
    master pages versus, 54

web applications and, 28
lazy loading technique, 280
least privilege, principle of, 176
Library Package Manager Console, 13
libs folder, 429
LINQ (Language Integrated Query), 168–174, 308
LINQ to Entities injection attacks, 197
Liskov Substitution Principle (LSP), 98
"listview" component (jQuery Mobile), 210
LocalStorage mechanism, 268
Logger class, 336
logging errors, 336–338
logical design in web applications, 90–93
LSP (Liskov Substitution Principle), 98

M

magic strings, 444
.manifest file extension, 266–267
manual testing, 344
many-to-many relationships, 168, 192
MapRoute() extension method
    about, 17
    method override and, 303
    parameters and, 299
    registering routes for applications, 306
master pages, layouts versus, 54
media formatters, 149–152
media queries, 220
MediaTypeFormatter class
    about, 150
    CanReadType() method, 150
    CanWriteType() method, 150
MEF site, 107
Membership class
    CreateUser() method, 188
    GetUser() method, 189
    ValidateUser() method, 187
MembershipUser class, 189
meta packages, 431
MIME types, 149, 267
minification concept, 7, 282, 289–293
Mobile Application template
    about, 12, 203
    usage considerations, 226–228
    ViewSwitcher widget and, 212
mobile feature detection, 218–220
Mobile template, 224
mobile views

browser-specific, 221–222
creating, 205
enhancing with jQuery Mobile, 209–215
loading layouts for, 207
overriding regular views with, 204
switching between desktop and, 212
mobile web development
    adaptive rendering, 217–222
    creating applications from scratch, 224–228
    features supporting, 203–205
    improving mobile experience, 216
    usability considerations, 205–216
mocking dependencies, 365–370
model binding
    about, 21–23
    data annotations and, 63
    JSON and, 128, 130
    registering binders, 132
    specifying, 131–132
Model component (MVC pattern)
    about, 5, 34
    component interaction and, 88–90
Model First approach, 159, 161
@model keyword, 33
Model-View-Controller pattern (see MVC pattern)
ModelBinderDictionary.GetBinder() method, 131
ModelBinders class, 131
Models folder, 13
ModelState class
    about, 62
    AddModelError() method, 62
monitoring system health, 338–341
MSBuild tool, 380, 405–407
Mustache template syntax, 120
mustache.js library, 120
MVC (Model-View-Controller) pattern
    about, 4–6, 87
    component interaction and, 88–90
    Controller component, 6, 88–90
    Model component, 5, 34, 88–90
    reusing logic across requests, 123–127
    separation of concerns principle, 87, 154
    View component, 6, 88–90
MvcDonutCaching NuGet package, 257
MvcRouteHandler class, 311

N

namespaces
    ASP.NET-related, 45
    naming, 93
navigating data, 158
New ASP.NET MVC Project dialog box, 12
new keyword, 443
Ninject IoC containers, 107, 144
nuget pack command
    about, 424
    -Properties switch, 427
    -Version switch, 427
NuGet Package Explorer, 425
NuGet package management tool
    anatomy of NuGet packages, 427–430
    creating NuGet packages, 424–427
    hosting package repositories, 432–435
    installing, 423
    sharing NuGet packages, 431–435
    SignalR signaling library and, 241
    tips, tricks, and pitfalls, 435–441
    types of NuGet packages, 430
    usage considerations, 424
NuGet Package Manager
    about, 12
    accessing, 13
    best practices, 443
    installing, 423
NuGet packages
    anatomy of, 427–430
    controlling versions, 440
    creating, 424–427
    generating from NuSpec files, 426
    sharing, 431–435
    types of, 430
    version control, 436–441
nuget push command, 432
NuGet Server repository, 434
nuget setApiKey command, 432
nuget spec command, 424
NuGet.org repository
    NuGet package upload wizard, 431
    publishing to, 431
NuSpec files
    about, 424–426
    generating NuGet packages from, 426
    version dependencies, 439

O

obfuscation technique, 283
object relational impedance mismatch, 156–158
object relational mappers (ORMs), 154, 156–158
observer pattern, 88
OCP (Open/Closed Principle), 97
OData (Open Data Protocol), 146
onClick event, 74–76
onsubmit event, 83
Open Data Protocol (OData), 146
Open/Closed Principle (OCP), 97
optimistic concurrency approach, 160
OptimisticConcurrencyException class, 160
optimization techniques (see client-side optimization)
ORMs (object relational mappers), 154, 156–158
output caching, 252–255, 453
OutputCache class, 253, 256
OutputCacheAttribute class
    about, 253
    best practices, 453
    donut hole caching and, 258
    parameters supported, 253–255

P

Page class, 313
paging data, 146, 168–174
partial rendering, 111–117
partial views
    about, 29, 317
    rendering, 112–117
    user controls versus, 54
password management, 188
persistence ignorance (PI), 153
persistent connections, 242
PersistentConnection class, 242, 243
pessimistic concurrency approach, 160
physical design in web applications, 93, 94–96
PI (persistence ignorance), 153
pipeline, routing, 310–315
Plain Old CLR Objects (POCOs), 60, 153
PluralizingTableNameConvention class, 163
POCOs (Plain Old CLR Objects), 60, 153
POST method (HTTP), 128, 142
Post/Redirect/Get (PRG) pattern, 450

precompiled views, 323–324
PrecompiledMvcEngine package, 323
prerelease packages, 438
prerelease versioning, 439
principle of least privilege, 176
project templates, 10–12
projects, naming, 93
properties, controller actions, 16
publishing
    from within Visual Studio, 403–407
    to NuGet.org repository, 431
    Windows Azure website via source control,
        409
PUT method (HTTP), 142

Q

quality control
    automated testing and, 343–376
    build automation and, 377–391
    logging and, 331–341
querying data, 146, 168–174

R

RangeAttribute class, 64
Razor Single File Generator
    creating reusable helpers, 325–326
    creating reusable views, 321–324
    installing, 319
    unit testing Razor views, 327–328
Razor syntax
    @ symbol, 27, 54
    about, 12, 26–27
    differentiating code and markup, 27
    layouts and, 28
    rendering web pages, 51
Razor view engine, 256, 323
real-time data operations
    about, 236
    comparing application models, 237
    configuring and tuning, 245–246
    empowering communication, 241–244
    HTTP Long Polling technique, 238
    HTTP polling, 237
    server-sent events, 239
    WebSocket API, 240
redirects, avoiding, 283–285
Remote Procedure Call (RPC) framework, 243
rendering

adaptive, 217–222
HTML, 50–54, 58
JavaScript, 117–123
JSON data, 118–119
partial, 111–117
partial views, 112–117
web pages, 271–273, 280
repository pattern, 154–156, 365
request-scoped caching, 248
Request.IsAjaxRequest() method, 124, 125
RequiredAttribute class, 63
rolling builds, 381
RouteData class, 298
RouteGenerator class, 308–310
RouteValue dictionary, 214
routing
    about, 15
    ASP.NET approach, 49
    attribute-based, 306–310
    best practices, 452
    building routes, 298–303
    catch-all routes, 302
    configuring routes, 16–18
    determining pattern for, 35
    extending, 310–315
    ignoring routes, 302
    registering Web API routes, 141
    route constraints, 303–306
    URLs and SEO, 297
    wayfinding, 295–297
RPC (Remote Procedure Cal) framework, 243
runtime considerations
    ASP.NET MVC, 47
    Web Forms, 47

S

scavenging process, 252
scheduled builds, 382
scripts
    build, 378–380
    deferring execution of, 280
    executing with MSBuild, 406–407
    externalizing, 281
    lazy loading technique, 280
    placement on web pages, 279–281
    removing duplicate, 285
@Scripts annotation, 289
Search Engine Optimization (SEO), 297
Search view, 170

securing web applications
    about, 177
    defense in depth, 175
    disabling unnecessary features, 177
    distrusting input, 176
    Forms Authentication, 183–191
    guarding against attacks, 192–201
    insecurity of external systems, 176
    intranet applications, 178–183
    principle of least privilege, 176
    reducing surface area, 176
selectors in client-side development, 71–74
Semantic Versioning scheme, 437, 439
semicolon (;), 27
SEO (Search Engine Optimization), 297
separation of concerns principle, 87, 154
server controls, 52
server-sent events, 239
server-side caching
    about, 248
    application-scoped caching, 250
    distributed caching, 259–264
    donut caching, 255–257
    donut hole caching, 257–258
    output caching, 252–255
    request-scoped caching, 248
    user-scoped caching, 249
service locator pattern, 102, 104
session states, 249
SignalR signaling library, 241, 243, 245
Single Responsibility Principle (SRP), 96
Single Sign On Authentication, 90
sliding expiration, 251
SOLID design principles, 96–101, 163
sorting data, 168–174
SQL injection attack, 192–197
SQLCMD utility, 407
SRP (Single Responsibility Principle), 96
SSL encryption, 183
StandardKernel class, 109
Start-CacheCluster cmdlet, 261
state management, 46, 49
static content, 398
stored procedures, 158, 159
storing session data, 250
StringLengthAttribute class, 63
StructureMap site, 107
@Styles annotation, 289
stylesheets, best practices, 279

Substitution control, 256
SUT (system under test), 345
synchronous communication, 78
system under test (SUT), 345
System.Data.Entity namespace, 60
System.Web namespace, 45
System.Web.Mvc namespace, 17, 45
System.Web.Optimization namespace, 289
System.Web.Security.AntiXss namespace, 198
System.Web.UI namespace, 45
System.Xml namespace, 46

T

TDD (test-driven development), 358
Team Foundation Server tool, 381, 383–385,
    409
TempData dictionary, 31
templates
    authentication and, 178, 184
    client-side, 120–123
    controller, 36
    display, 318
    editor, 318
    layout, 28
    mobile application, 12, 203, 212, 226–228
    project, 10–12
test classes, 350
test doubles, 365
test fixtures, 350
test projects
    creating, 350
    defined, 350
test-driven development (TDD), 358
testing
    applications, 354–372
    automated, 345–349, 359–361
    builds, 387
    code coverage in, 372–374
    controllers, 361–364
    developing testable code, 374–376
    manual, 344
    mocking dependencies, 365–370
    models, 355–357
    refactoring to unit tests, 364
    TDD and, 358
    test projects and, 350–354
    views, 370–372
TestInitializeAttribute class, 359
timestamps, 135, 160

tool packages, 430
tools folder, 429
try/catch block, 161, 336
tuning real-time communication, 245–246

U

UAT (user acceptance testing), 349
unit testing
  about, 345–348
  creating and executing, 352
  Razor views, 327–328
  refactoring to, 364
Unity site, 107
UrlHelper class, 33, 116
UrlRoutingModule class, 311
URLs
  ASP.NET MVC approach, 48
  SEOs and, 297
  wayfinding and, 295–297
  Web Forms approach, 48
user acceptance testing (UAT), 349
User class, 164, 191
user controls, partial views versus, 54
user management
  about, 420
  authenticating users, 186–187
  authorization process, 191
  changing passwords, 188
  registering new users, 187
user-scoped caching, 249

V

ValidateAntiForgeryTokenAttribute class, 200
validating data
  about, 61
  best practices, 92
  client-side development and, 79–83
  displaying errors, 65–67
  specifying business rules, 63–65
.vbhtml file extension, 317
Velocity distributed caching solution, 259
View component (MVC pattern)
  about, 6
  component interaction and, 88–90
view engines
  about, 12
  ASPX, 55
  best practices, 453

Razor, 256, 323
  Web Forms, 319
View State mechanism
  about, 46, 50
  usage considerations, 54, 55, 421
View Switcher component, 208
ViewBag object, 32
ViewData dictionary, 31, 65, 444
viewport tag, 217
ViewResult class, 19, 24, 454
views, 204
  (see also mobile views)
  about, 24
  best practices, 445
  creating reusable, 321–324
  differentiating code and markup, 27
  display modes feature and, 204
  displaying data, 31–33
  HTML and URL helpers, 33
  implementation example, 38–40
  layouts and, 28
  locating, 24
  overriding regular with mobile, 204
  partial, 29, 54, 112–117, 317
  precompiled, 323–324
  Razor, 26–27, 319, 327–328
  Search, 170
  separation of application and view logic,
    48
  testing, 370–372
  Web Forms syntax and, 54
Views folder, 14
ViewSwitcher widget, 213–215
ViewUserControl class, 319
Visual Studio, publishing from within, 403–
    407

W

WatiN tool, 371
wayfinding, 295–297
Web API (see ASP.NET Web API)
Web API template, 12
web applications, 69
  (see also client-side development; mobile
    web development; securing web
    applications)
  architecting, 90–96
  authentication and, 41–43

convention over configuration, 13, 17, 60, 141–143
creating, 9, 35–40
deployment options, 94
development techniques, 49
differentiating code and markup, 27
DRY principle, 110
IoC design principle, 102–109
layouts and, 28
logical design in, 90–93
Microsoft development platforms, 3–4
MVC pattern, 4–6, 87–90
naming considerations, 93
physical design in, 93, 94–96
project templates, 10–12
Razor syntax and, 26–27
running, 15
separation of application and view logic, 48
SOLID design principles, 96–101, 163
testing, 354–372
web browsers, 271
(see also web pages)
cache management, 264, 292
HTTP polling and, 238, 239
mobile feature detection, 218–220, 218–220
server-sent events, 240
specific views for, 221–222
testing application logic in, 370
WebSocket API, 241
Web Forms
about, 4
adding ASP.NET MVC to existing applications, 417
AspCompat page directive, 313
associated namespace, 45
authoring ASP.NET MVC views using, 54
choosing between ASP.NET MVC and, 415
deployment and runtime, 47
differences from ASP.NET MVC, 47–54
HTTP handlers and modules, 46
if/else statement example, 26
integrating with ASP.NET MVC functionality, 420–421
rendering HTML, 50–54
state management, 46, 49
tools, languages, APIs, 46

transitioning to ASP.Net MVC, 416–420
ViewUserControl class and, 319
Web Forms Page Controller pattern, 449
web pages
anatomy of, 271–273
avoiding redirects, 283–285
cache expiration, 276–278
configuring ETags, 285
content delivery networks and, 274
externalizing scripts and styles, 281
GZIP compression, 278
HTTP requests and, 274
minifying JavaScript and CSS, 282
reducing DNS lookups, 282
removing duplicate scripts, 285
script placement on, 279–281
stylesheets and, 279
web.config file
authentication-mode element, 178
client-side validation settings, 80
data access class names in, 168
distributed caching settings, 262
membership and role providers, 185
output caching section, 255
packagesPath setting, 434
WebRequestErrorEvent class, 340
WebSocket API, 240
whitelist-based approach, 197
window object
about, 71
onload event, 75
Windows Authentication, 178–181
Windows Azure, 407–410

X

XmlHttpRequest object
about, 77
open() method, 78
send() method, 78
status attribute, 78
XSS (cross-site scripting) attacks, 133, 198

Y

Yahoo!'s Exceptional Performance team, 273
YSlow tool, 286
YUI Compressor, 282

About the Authors

Jess Chadwick is an independent software consultant specializing in web technologies. He has more than a decade of development experience, ranging from embedded devices in start-ups to enterprise-scale web farms at Fortune 500s. He is an ASPInsider, Microsoft MVP in ASP.NET, and is an avid community member, frequently delivering technical presentations as well as leading the NJDOTNET Central New Jersey .NET user group. Jess lives in the Philadelphia, PA, area with his wonderful wife, baby daughter, and black lab.

Also contributing to this book are:

Todd Snyder: Principle Consultant, Infragistics

Hrusikesh Panda: Architect and RIA Specialist

Colophon

The animal on the cover of *Programming ASP.NET MVC 4* is the silver scabbardfish (*Lepidopus caudatus*). Fish of this family are long, slender, and generally steely blue or silver in color, giving rise to their name. They have reduced or absent pelvic and caudal fins, giving them an eel-like appearance, and large fang-like teeth. They grow to over 2 meters in length and reach 9 kg in weight. Their scaleless bodies are compressed and ribbon-like, and leave a silvery tint on anything with which they come into contact. They have long sharp teeth along both jaws, and the lower jaw is very prominent. The female lives longer than the male and is also bigger.

The silver scabbardfish forms schools and is a mesopelagic predator that primarily feeds on crustaceans (especially krill and decapods), small mollusks, and ray-finned fish such as lanternfish, boarfish, and herring. Its major predators are sharks, hake, and squid.

This species is found as far down as 1,000 meters in both cold and warm waters around the Atlantic, Mediterranean, and Pacific. They are so widespread in the Straits of Messina that they have given rise to a profession: the *spadularu*, or silver scabbardfish fisherman. Their tastiness has earned them the name of "young lady of the seas" in the Messina dialect. They are readily consumed (despite their ugly appearance) because of their soft, delicately flavored white meat and lack of scales.

The cover image is from *Johnson's Natural History*. The cover font is Adobe ITC Garamond. The text font is Linotype Birka; the heading font is Adobe Myriad Condensed; and the code font is LucasFont's TheSansMonoCondensed.

Have it your way.

CPSIA information can be obtained at www.ICGtesting.com
Printed in the USA
BVOW040157200912

300907BV00001B/7/P

9 781449 320317